QUEEN BEES & WANNABES

HELPING YOUR DAUGHTER SURVIVE
CLIQUES, GOSSIP, BOYS, AND
THE NEW REALITIES OF GIRL WORLD

THIRD EDITION

ROSALIND WISEMAN

HARMONY
BOOKS • NEW YORK

Library of Congress Cataloging-in-Publication Data
Names: Wiseman, Rosalind, 1969– author.
Title: Queen bees and wannabes : helping your daughter survive cliques,
    gossip, boys, and the new realities of girl world / Rosalind Wiseman.
Other titles: Queen bees & wannabes
Description: 3rd Edition. | New York : Harmony, 2016. | Revised edition of
    the author's Queen bees & wannabes, 2009. | Includes bibliographical
    references and index.
Identifiers: LCCN 2015045803 (print) | LCCN 2016013704 (ebook) |
    ISBN 9781101903056 (paperback) | ISBN 9781101903063 ()
Subjects: LCSH: Teenage girls. | Teenage girls—Psychology. | Parent
    and teenager. | BISAC: FAMILY & RELATIONSHIPS / Parenting /
    General. | FAMILY & RELATIONSHIPS / Life Stages / Adolescence. |
    FAMILY & RELATIONSHIPS / General.
Classification: LCC HQ798 .W544 2016 (print) | LCC HQ798 (ebook) |
    DDC 305.235/2—dc23
LC record available at http://lccn.loc.gov/2015045803

ISBN 978-1-101-90305-6
eBook ISBN 978-1-101-90306-3

Printed in the United States of America

Cover design by Jessie Sayward Bright
Cover photograph: Tetra Images/Getty Images

10 9 8 7 6 5 4 3 2

Third Revised Edition

*To my students and all the young people
who have contacted me over the years.
You inspire me to do my best work.*

Contents

Queen Bees & Wannabes

Introduction

In middle school our group got really close, but we had one friend who was really bad. She would pick one of us to be her BFF. Even in third grade it was a big deal. She needed someone to be with her all the time. She'd force the picked girl to have matching backpacks and shoes. We didn't handle the situation well. We took out our anger and said mean things about her. She doesn't go to school with us now because she left. I asked myself why she was my friend when she made me so miserable. The moments we had were so great but I knew it was so destructive.

—Holly, fourteen

I just went through my daughter's texts and want to throw up. I couldn't believe the language she was using about herself and the other kids in her class.

—Todd

My parents are ridiculously controlling. They investigate the background of every friend. I feel like I'm trapped, and when I talk to them they don't listen. I'm fourteen but mature for my age. I'm really responsible and always get good grades. How can I talk to them? Everything feels like a power struggle.

They're dictator parents, combined with helicopter parents, and they're super judgmental. HELP! I can't talk about any of my problems with them.

—Faith, sixteen

Here we go again. It's time for me to update this book for the second time. I always said I'd have to update *Queen Bees & Wannabes* every five years. What I didn't realize is how fast that time would pass. The baby I rocked to sleep so I could write *Queen Bees* the first time is now six foot three, and his younger brother is taller than I am. But in spite of all of these changes in my life, one thing has been a constant—helping girls, parents, and any adults who care about girls navigate the messy terrain of "Girl World."

If you're parenting or working with girls today, chances are you know about this Queen Bee/Mean Girl stuff already. "Queen Bees" and "Mean Girls" are a part of our language. You can buy "Queen Bee" and "Mean Girl" T-shirts, backpacks, and pencil cases, as if being one is something girls should aspire to.

But "girl" issues, of course, have been around forever. You may have had a few of your own when you were young, or you could be dealing with them now as an adult. So why do I need to keep updating this book? Because even though it's true that some things never change—best friends will grow apart, people will be jealous, and betrayals will happen—we need to put these evergreen feelings and experiences in the context of what girls are going through right now. And having said that, each girl is different. Some girls tell at least one parent everything, and some vow that they will never tell a parent or any other adult anything—and they don't think they need to anyway because they have everything under control. Some girls are obsessed with horses, others with popularity and friendship drama, and others really don't care. Some girls fit into the common idea we have of what girls look like, and some don't. Some girls are boy crazy, some are attracted to girls, some question who they are attracted to, and some are questioning if they're attracted to people at all.

Girls are awesome, brilliant, funny, and inspiring. They are also frustrating, stubborn, messy, and sometimes scary. They will,

just like all of us, get into situations that are overwhelming and not know whom to turn to for help. They will get into conflicts with one another. They will experience people refusing to tell them why they're mad, and they'll do it, too. They will feel frustrated and confused when someone dismisses them with "Just kidding!" or "Why are you overreacting?!"

No matter how many parenting books you read or seminars you go to, you can't protect girls from experiencing conflicts and problems with other people. But you can contribute to an environment and a culture for girls that empowers them to articulate their feelings in positive ways. You can educate her about how the culture we live in makes it hard to develop an authentic identity and critical thinking skills but very easy to be a mindless consumer of superficial ideas and desires. You can get a better handle on your own reactions so you can be a thoughtful adult and the source of guidance she needs. You can be a credible, trusted adult. Even if you feel discouraged or disconnected from the girl you are reading this for, or have come to this book as a last resort, always remember it's never too late to help or repair your relationship with your daughter or any girl you care about.

The first time your daughter tells you that her best friend stopped talking to her and got all the other girls to stop talking to her, too, you may be somewhat upset. You may hate that girl. You may feel that you and your daughter just got recruited into a group that you want no part of but can't leave. If you can relate to what I've just written, please know that so many parents have also had this experience. You aren't alone, and neither is your daughter.

But you still need to know what to say and do—beyond wanting to yell at that horrible child. You also need to know what to do when you pick your daughter up the next day at school and she's arm in arm with that evil girl like nothing ever happened. What do you do when your daughter begs you to let this kid come over, ignoring your *"Are you kidding me? I hate this girl and you should, too!"* expression, because the last thing you want to do is let this girl come over to your house so she can be mean to your daughter all over again.

Most people believe a girl's task is to get through it, grow up,

and put those experiences behind her. But your daughter's relationships with other girls have deep and far-reaching implications beyond her teen years. Her experiences and the thought and behavior patterns she develops as a result fundamentally shape her self-identity and relationships. That's why your daughter's friendships are a double-edged sword. These friendships can be the key to surviving adolescence. Many girls develop into amazing women precisely because they have the support and care of a few good friends.

But I wouldn't be writing this book and you wouldn't be reading it if that's all there was to girls' friendships. Girls' friendships are often intense, confusing, frustrating, and humiliating; the joy and security of "best friendships" can be shattered by devastating breakups and betrayals. Beyond the pain in the moment, girls can develop patterns of behavior and expectations for future relationships that stop them from becoming competent and confident women. They can learn to look and say "I'm fine" when they aren't. They can swallow their feelings because they don't want to be accused of being overly dramatic or needing attention. They can apologize when they haven't done anything wrong to placate someone they perceive has more power. They can focus on maintaining impossible standards of beauty and appearance and hate themselves for not being able to keep up—or judge other women in this rigged competition that no one wins.

All of this doesn't mean that girls' friendships are destined to be terrible. It just means they're complicated and need to be taken seriously. My job is to give you my best suggestions for what kind of guidance to give her and how that information should be presented to her. The goal is for her to develop critical thinking skills, manage her emotions, and integrate her feelings with her thoughts . . . and for you to strengthen your relationship with her through the process. I know, that's a huge goal. It's not going to be an overnight process, but it's not an overnight process for anyone.

There's no way I could write this edition of *Queen Bees* without addressing how technology and the media continue to expand their influence on your daughter's social life for better and worse, and how these issues impact younger girls.

On the technology front, I'm not going to waste your time tell-

ing you things you already know. We all get that technology is integrated into every aspect of our lives. Learning about what to do about it is our goal. I'm also going to challenge some of the most common advice girls hear from adults, and help you to get girls to tell you how and why they use the kinds of technology they do. I'll explain what you can learn from your daughter's social media style. I'll also tell you what I've learned about gaming and girls.

However, I'm not going to ask you to stalk your daughter online. I'm not going to tell you to get monitoring software, because I strongly believe that building a solid relationship with your daughter is more effective than any spying device in helping her behave responsibly online. As soon as a child interacts with technology in any way—including the games she plays when she's a little girl—we must explicitly tie her use of this incredibly powerful tool to her development of ethics, an authentic self-identity, and a voice within a powerful public space.

There is a chapter dedicated to the topic of younger Mean Girls, and their issues are integrated throughout. There's never been an age limit on being mean. You can be five or fifty-five or ninety-five. In addition, we have to consider how girls starting puberty earlier may affect their social development and their friendships. I don't know about you, but I now regularly see girls in elementary school who have the bodies of young women.

But we can't freak out about any of this. If we do, we're going to seriously freak out our girls. We are going to educate ourselves, keep an open mind, and deal. I've also seriously revamped the communication chapters of the book. In writing my boys' book *Masterminds and Wingmen*, I got great feedback from boys about why their parents' attempts to talk to them so often backfire and what parents can do and say to communicate effectively. For this edition, I've worked with girls to find out what parents should say and do to open up the lines of communication. Sometimes it's as simple as driving away from the school before asking how her day was.

Before I go any further, let me reassure you that I can help you even if you often feel helpless or as if you are at war with your

daughter. This book will let you into her world. To start, it's perfectly natural if she:

- Repeatedly makes the same mistakes with her relationships.
- Believes that there's no possible way you could understand what she's going through.
- Is absolutely certain that telling you her problems will only make her life worse.
- Convinces herself she's totally in control of her life even when the facts say maybe not.
- Lies and sneaks around behind your back.
- Denies she lied and snuck behind your back—even in the face of undeniable evidence.

On the other hand, it's natural that you:

- Worry that you won't be able to provide the advice she needs when she's been rejected or betrayed . . . or get her to listen to you and actually follow your advice.
- Feel rejected and angry when she rolls her eyes at everything you say.
- Wonder whose child this is anyway, as this person in front of you couldn't possibly be your sweet, wonderful daughter.
- Feel confused and defeated when conversations end in fights.
- Feel misunderstood when she acts like you're intruding and prying when you ask about what's going on in her life.
- Are really worried about the influence of her friends and feel powerless to stop her hanging out with them.
- Worry about how she can grow up surrounded by toxic messages in the media that are constantly trying to mess with her mind and make her feel insecure.

There's another issue that complicates everything. In the words of one mom who wrote me:

When I was a senior in high school, my best friend since third grade dumped me and had our entire clique turn their back

on me. I was devastated. I found more friends, but the experience left me very insecure in my relationships—something that haunts me to this day (I'm thirty-six). The anger and betrayal I felt at the time has never fully left me, despite my fervent desire to leave it behind. In short, she is the person that I would run out of the grocery store to avoid. The most difficult aspect of all this is that I am trying very hard to "check" this baggage as I witness MY daughter's blossoming best friendship . . . and my deeply wired desire to protect her.

—Ellen

If you're a mom reading this, it's important to remember that your experiences as a girl are both your greatest gift and biggest liability as your daughter navigates her own friendships. They're a gift because they enable you to empathize. They're a liability if your past makes you so anxious or reactionary that you can't separate your experiences from hers.

DADS

This book isn't only for moms. Whether you're worried that you won't be able to hang out with your daughter in the same way once she enters puberty, or if you're the dad who emails me knowing all the seventh-grade girl drama in her class, you—like almost all dads—want to be emotionally engaged with your children and do best by your daughter.

If you read only one paragraph in this book, make it this: Never forget or dismiss that your perspective can help your daughter. Just because you were never a girl, don't know what a menstrual cramp feels like, and have never liked talking for hours about other people's lives doesn't mean you're clueless or useless. I know lots of dads feel rejected and pushed aside when their little girl suddenly dismisses them with "You just wouldn't understand." But in reality, this is an opportunity for you to become a genuinely cool dad. I don't mean you let her get away with stuff, side with her against her other parent, or drive her wherever she wants. I'm talking about the dad who patiently waits around until she wants to talk—and then listens without being judgmental, who isn't afraid

to look foolish or show his emotions, who shares the "boy perspective," who holds her accountable when necessary, and who's able to communicate his concerns without coming across as controlling and dogmatic.

Even if you're dying to warn your daughter off every boy who walks through your door, remember that if you come across as the *crazy, control-freak, doesn't-have-a-clue* father, she'll stop talking to you. Your job is to show her that relationships with men (of any degree) should be based on mutual respect and care.

BELIEVE IT OR NOT, YOUR DAUGHTER STILL WANTS YOU IN HER LIFE

Your daughter craves privacy, and your very presence feels like an intrusion. You feel you have so much to offer her. After all, you've been through the changes she's experiencing, and you think your advice will help. Although this privacy war is natural, it creates a big problem. Girls often see you as intrusive and prying, which equals bad; her peers are involved and understanding, which equals good. When I ask girls privately what they need most from their parents, they tell me they want their parents to be proud of them. You may be really worried that she's shutting herself up in her room all day or look at her in the middle of an argument when she's screaming that she hates you and think there's no way you can get through to her, but you can and will if you learn to see the world through her eyes.

> Parents don't realize that their children look up to them. When I know that deep in my mother and father's hearts they really don't agree with what I'm doing, that really hurts.
> —Eve, twelve

> I know I should listen to my parents, even if they're wrong.
> —Abby, sixteen

DEVELOPING YOUR GIRL BRAIN

One of the hardest truths for parents is that as their daughter gets older they have less control over which people she hangs out with. It's terribly stressful knowing that they can't always be there when their daughter faces the difficult decisions that could impact her health and safety. When your daughter was little and got hurt, she'd run to you and you'd kiss the pain away. Now you're lucky if you have a clue what the problem is. Worse, if you sweep in to save the day instead of teaching your daughter how to handle it, she'll either be angry with you for intruding or she won't learn to take care of herself. How can you help her? Start by thinking the way she does.

In this book I will teach you to develop or restart your girl brain. It's like looking at the world through a new pair of glasses. And even though she may be acting as if you aren't an important influence in her life, you are—she just may not want to admit it because either it feels like she's becoming too mature to need your help or she's afraid of what you'll take away from her if she tells you what's really going on. If you can learn how to be her safe harbor when she's in the midst of Girl World conflicts, your voice will be in her head along with your values and ethics.

The first step is to understand what your daughter's world, Girl World, looks like. You need to know who inspires her, who intimidates her, where she feels safe, and where she doesn't. If she has a problem, does she think going to an adult will make the problem better or worse? Who does she go to for advice? What kind of music does she listen to and why? Does she have a signature pose when she takes a selfie? What common things can ruin her day or make her feel on top of the world?

An even harder task is taking a closer look at her social interactions. What is she being teased about? What would make her lie or sneak behind your back? Why are other children mean to her? Or the worst to ask yourself, why would she be cruel to others or say nothing when someone around her is? Get inside her head and then you'll understand where she's coming from and how to help her.

REMEMBERING THE LUNCH TRAY MOMENTS

It helps to remember what it was like to be your daughter's age. Think back to your experiences, the role models (both good and bad), and the lessons you learned from your family, your school, and your community. Suspend the worry, the common sense, and the wisdom you have accumulated over the last years. Think back to what you were like and what was important to you back then. If you're really struggling to remember, like seventh grade is just a black hole in your mind, you may have to do some reconnaissance. That's right, you know what I'm talking about. It's time to take out the yearbooks and read what people wrote you—or, even scarier, open up your diaries. Elementary and middle school diaries are often filled with embarrassing entries and scribbles of crush's names. Sure, it's probably going to make you cringe, but a trip down memory lane will help you regain a perspective on what it is like to be in school and the drama that comes with it. Remember, just like when your daughter writes in her diary now, you probably wrote in your diary only when you felt extreme happiness or misery.

What's also important to remember about being a child or teen is that parents, teachers, and other adults are telling you what to do—and especially what you *can't* do. They're also giving you advice that often seems hopelessly out of date or unrealistic—and perhaps it is. Maybe you have a close group of friends, but for some reason one of your best friends comes up to you between classes and tells you that one of your other friends is spreading rumors about you. Your face feels hot; you can feel everyone looking at you. Thoughts race through your head. What did you do? Why is she mad at you? Are your friends going to back you or side with her? What can you do to fix the problem? All of a sudden, a question drives an icy stake of fear through your heart as you stand there clutching your orange plastic lunch tray in the cafeteria line: Where are you going to sit at lunch?

Can you remember what it was like? It's horrible and awkward—no matter how often we pretend it's not and pull our phones out now to distract us from that feeling. As adults, we can

laugh at how immense and insurmountable problems like those "lunch tray moments" can feel when you're young. But in Girl World they're vital issues, and to dismiss them as trivial is to disrespect your daughter's reality. Within those moments are ethical choices and complex dynamics that are just as challenging as negotiating a peace treaty. Who says something when someone is being excluded and treated cruelly? Who believes that seeking revenge or teaching someone "her place" justifies humiliating someone? What issues are more important than that? If you want your daughter to be a morally courageous person who can make her own decisions, it starts in recognizing these moments. And, frankly, although the core issues remain the same, it's probably harder for her than it was for you at her age. Did you have to deal with telling someone a secret and then having them forward it to everyone in the school? You didn't. I didn't. But your daughter does.

THE GIRL WORLD POLICE

Girls (like all of us) absorb the cultural messages of how they should appear and how they should conduct themselves, and then take that information and develop social hierarchies based on it. At no time in your daughter's life will it probably feel more important to her to fit these elusive girl standards than during adolescence (but, having said that, I know a lot of adults who are just as obsessed about keeping up their image, and sometimes even more so). It's also confusing because these standards or rules are often invisible or unwritten. Girls are just supposed to know what these rules are. But the reality is that girls learn these rules when they break them or see someone else break them and live with the fallout. And who is the prime enforcer of these rules? The movies? Magazines? Websites? Yes and no. What is often overlooked is that it is the girls themselves who are the enforcers of these cultural rules in their day-to-day lives. They police one another, conducting surveillance on who's breaking the laws of appearance and clothing, boys, and personality. Your daughter gets daily lessons about what's "in" from her friends. She isn't watching televi-

sion, movies, or videos, and surfing social media by herself. She processes this information with and through her friends.

I'm not saying "the media" aren't partially responsible for putting powerful images in our daughters' heads, but we aren't blaming the girls if we admit that they contribute to one another's insecurities. Instead, we're being honest about the complexity of this problem so that we can create effective solutions. We also have to point to ourselves (that is, the adults) for not challenging a culture that so often portrays girls and women as hypersexual, unintelligent, and materialistic. For example, celebrities starve themselves, surgically alter their bodies, and relentlessly pursue fame and then are presented as good role models for girls—not just in movies, TV shows, and music videos but also on morning talk shows and in "respectable" magazines. Many journalists are parents, too, yet often they don't ask substantive questions when interviewing people who create girl-degrading content or who play demeaning roles. And most of us buy magazines and watch shows that are obsessed with being mean. Who's fat this week? Who wore that dress better? Who got pregnant and didn't bounce back right away? Who has had the most or worst plastic surgery? Lots of adults rationalize reading these magazines as a guilty pleasure. But, honestly, if you do this, you aren't being the adult that girls need you to be. You're modeling that you are entertained by pitting one woman against another. Never mind the fact that it's impossible to read one of those things and not suck in your stomach and think about those ten pounds you need to lose.

Last, we often don't want to admit how little supervision we really exert over what our children watch. To be fair, it's really hard to do. You can pick out appropriate shows, but then the ads airing during the commercial breaks are horrible. You can put filters on every device in your house and she can see whatever she wants on a friend's phone. We need to sit down with our daughters (and, of course, our sons as well) and walk them through how to think about the relentless messages they're getting. We must also educate ourselves without being afraid to be labeled as uptight. We must, as must our daughters. Girls will reach their full potential only if they're taught to be the agents of their own social change.

As we guide girls through adolescence, we have to acknowledge exploitation, name it, and empower our girls so they can go into that store with the "Queen Bee" backpacks and tell the manager to take them off the shelf.

SO WHY LISTEN TO ME?

During a fifth-grade assembly, a student asked me, "Are you wise at what you do?" I said, "It's really up to you to decide if I am. Listen to what I say and then tell me." I'm saying the same thing to you. Although I'm a mom and have worked with tens of thousands of children and teens over many years, I don't know your individual child. I could be wrong. Girls often think about Girl World in very different ways from one another. The only thing I know for certain is that each person's dignity is not negotiable. Everyone is worthy. Everyone has the right to have her voice heard. Every girl is entitled to her truth.

I'm frequently asked how I got into this line of work. Or, said another way, "Were you a victim of a Queen Bee?" or "Were you a Queen Bee?" Well, here's the short version of why I do this work.

Until fifth grade I grew up in a close community in Washington, D.C., and attended a small public elementary school. I had many friends of different races, nationalities, and economic backgrounds. I was part of a clique, but I was friends with lots of students. The summer after I completed fifth grade, my family moved to Pittsburgh and I attended a well-respected private all-girls school. That's where I had my first really miserable lunch tray moment when some girls wouldn't let me sit at their tables. But there were also girls who saw that happening to me and invited me to sit with them instead (thank you, Madeline McGrady and Melissa McSwiggen).

I returned to Washington the next year and enrolled in another private but co-ed school where I ran into more Mean Girls—but this time they were charismatic and fun and became my friends. One of them in particular was any parent's nightmare. She was stunningly beautiful, brazen, and funny, and had parents who were rarely home, an exciting older sister, and a cute older brother

who was always bringing his even cuter friends over. From my eighth-grade perspective, there was nothing better than going over to her house and just waiting to see what exciting and dangerous things would happen. Her family also presented well—meaning my parents didn't have a clue about what I was seeing and experiencing in that house, and I certainly wasn't going to tell them.

That's when it got confusing. Think of it this way: When girls are mean to you all the time, it's easy to hate them; but it's a world of difference when the Mean Girls can also be really nice, supportive, and exciting. In the grand scheme of things, it seemed like a good trade-off. So what if they would turn on me any second or make fun of me for the things I was the most self-conscious about? I was willing to pay the price, because speaking my mind meant losing their friendships and all the exciting things that went with it.

Then the first day of ninth grade arrived, and I fell in love. Like really, really fell for a guy and I ended up dating him all through high school. And just like that, my friends stopped teasing and humiliating me. It was like I had an insurance policy against how badly my friends could treat me. Why? Because I had the boyfriend "trifecta." He was cute and charming.

Unfortunately, my relationship with him became incredibly serious and then abusive. How did I, someone with no violence in my family and parents who loved each other, get into an abusive relationship at such a young age and stay in that relationship for five years? On paper, I was no one's idea of a likely target for abuse. I would have known exactly what to say on any self-esteem test. I was a competitive athlete. I had a supportive and loving family. I didn't abuse alcohol or drugs. What was going on?

Like so many girls, I was amazingly good at fooling myself. I convinced myself that I was in a mature relationship and I was in control of the situation. But, more important, my boyfriend made me feel like I was the only one who understood him. I was the special one. It was like having the BFF I'd always wanted with all the benefits that go with having a boyfriend. I was in complete denial that I could get into situations that were over my head, even when I had clear evidence to the contrary.

Looking back, I realized I already knew how to be in an abusive relationship by the time I met him—because of what I had learned from my clique. I believed I didn't have the right to complain when people who were supposed to care about me treated me badly. I had already learned that having the relationship was more important than how I was treated within it. When the relationship was at its worst and even I had to admit things were bad, I felt horribly ashamed and powerless to change my situation, and I didn't think I could go to my friends for help.

When I was in college, I started studying karate and it gave me a new sense of purpose and personal strength. After my college graduation, I moved back to Washington, D.C., and began teaching self-defense to high school girls. That's where I started hearing stories remarkably similar to my own. I began to wonder: Where did these girls learn to be silent? Where did they learn to deny the danger staring them in the face? Why didn't girls trust other girls? Why were they so willing to throw away friendships if a better offer came along? And one of the more frustrating questions that's confused girls and women forever: How in the world is a girl supposed to be sexy enough that she gets boys' attention but not so sexy that other girls turn against her?

Clearly, girls are safer and happier when they look out for one another. But, paradoxically, during their period of greatest vulnerability, girls' competition with and judgment of each other weakens their friendships and effectively isolates all of them. This is what the power of the clique is all about, and why it matters so much to your daughter's safety and self-esteem.

As I taught self-defense, schools asked me to develop other classes that would teach girls self-esteem, confidence, and social competence. And that is exactly what I do today—in addition to working with boys, educators, and parents around the world. Although some things have changed since *Queen Bees* was first published, many challenges are still as true today as they were then. Parents often feel overwhelmed parenting a teen, whether they're trying to deal with a cruel text message, helping their daughter survive the morning bus ride, or trying to get her out of an abusive relationship. Whether I'm teaching in the smallest private school

or the largest public school, the girls all bring similar concerns and fears. No matter their income, religion, or ethnicity, they're struggling with the same issues about the pleasures and perils of friendships and how they act as a portal to the larger world.

I love what I do. There's nothing like the adrenaline rush of trying to engage my students. I have had plenty of young people disagree with me or tell me how they want me to think about things in different ways. But having the conversations and learning from them is my reward. As I talk with girls and boys, something is clear: Adults are struggling. Many of us feel overwhelmed by this relentless new culture. Some of us still dismiss girls' experiences as teen drama; others overreact and get so overinvolved that the girls don't learn how to handle these situations for themselves or stop going to any adults for help.

On the other side, some adults won't get involved at all, because they think the "girls should learn to work it out themselves"— though they provide no guidance or ethical standards about how the girls might do that. Some of us also feel helpless or are stuck in the same patterns as the girls themselves. And, of course, parents often see their children's behaviors as a reflection of the success or failure of their parenting, so it's just that much harder to see their children for who they really are.

HOW THE BOOK WORKS

Many parents have told me that one of the things they appreciated the most about the earlier versions of *Queen Bees* is that they could read it in small bites—like when they're waiting for practice to end or a carpool line. The book begins by giving you a topographical map of Girl World. That's where we will look at technology, social media, appearance, cliques, and popularity. I won't give you a lot of advice in these chapters, but occasionally I won't be able to help myself. Then I'll give you a passport to walk around and get to know how to talk to the natives without them running away or deporting you. Then I'll give you specific step-by-step strategies to help you and the girl you are reading this for keep your sanity and your sense of humor.

There are also specific things to look out for. In the "Checking Your Baggage" sections, I'll challenge you to answer a few questions about your experiences and how they impact these situations. With the help of my editors (the girls and boys who reviewed everything I wrote here), I'm going to give you my best analysis and suggestions for what's going on in the lives of most girls. I'm going to ask you to engage with me, your daughter, and the important boys and girls in your life in the process—and then come to your own conclusions.

As usual, I wrote this edition with the help of parents, teachers, and, most important, children and teens. I've shown multiple drafts of every chapter to girls of different ages, races, cultures, communities, and socioeconomic levels. They've helped me fill in missing perspectives, pushed me to delve more deeply into certain issues, and offered their "political commentary," which you'll find throughout the book. They've anonymously shared personal stories, feelings, and opinions—all to help you learn how to reach out to your daughter in the best possible way. And last, I have included specific questions from girls and their parents with my solutions.

My editors have also taught me about the "Land Mines" you'll find throughout the book: things parents and other adults do that are guaranteed eye rollers and that shut the door to effective communication. They usually seem insignificant (for example, you can't roll *your* eyes when your daughter says something that irritates you), but they can be the difference between your daughter listening to you or tuning out completely. You may think that pointing out land mines is a lost cause, since *anything* you do, including breathing or looking in her direction, makes her roll her eyes. But there are different kinds of embarrassment. Some things, such as the way you laugh or sneeze, are just things you and your kid need to deal with. Other things, such as oversharing information about your child's life with the neighbors, are behaviors you need to check.

You will also see a lot of suggested scripts. These are suggestions for what I think is the best thing to say in a specific situation. *However*, I'm not you, and I don't know your daughter or the

girls you know. What you say has to be authentic. It has to be in your own words. I don't want you reading a script I wrote to your daughter word for word because that will be weird and awkward. Read over the scripts and then write down what you think conveys the meaning in the words in a way that makes sense for you and the situation. You don't have to do it perfectly. Make it your own, and the girls in your life will see that.

The one thing you aren't allowed to do while you read this book is beat yourself up for being a bad parent (or a bad teacher, coach, counselor, whatever). If I say don't do "X" and it's something you've done, don't criticize yourself. It's never too late to transform any relationship in your life. And, hey, I could be wrong.

Parenting is really difficult, and the reward is way down the road when she emerges as a cool adult. Allow me to quote my own mother, who said, "When my children were teens, if I liked them for five minutes a day, that was a good day." Now I can say with absolute authority that if I have gotten through a week without screaming at one of my own children, this is a very good and very rare week.

JUST BETWEEN YOU AND ME

There may be parts in this book that are painful to read. If not painful, maybe uncomfortable. I want them to be uncomfortable, because it means something I'm writing about is connected to what's going on in your life. Part of the goal is to challenge you to think about how you're interacting with girls and what in your behavior might be making it harder for you to be a source of support. If I hit a nerve, or you start hating me or want to hide your daughter in a closet, I have one request. Take a moment to reflect. Life is messy. Parenting is really messy. Working with girls is messy. Ask yourself why what you read bothered you so much. Did it call up memories of your own experience as a victim, bystander, or perpetrator? Did it give you a sinking feeling that your daughter is a target or evildoer? Is it hard to face the fact that your daughter is thinking and acting in ways you aren't happy about? Acknowledge the pain you feel, but don't let it stop you from learning all

you can about your daughter's world. Everything in these pages comes from what people have told me over the years, from my teaching experiences, and from girls' comments as they have read drafts of this book. I'm not accusing girls of being bad people, judging parents as incapable, or predicting which daughters will be Queen Bees when they're adults. I'm reaching out to you, as parents, educators, and role models, to show you what I think girls are up against as they struggle to become healthy young women who will make our communities better.

Cliques and Popularity

Hi, I'm Lauren and I'm a thirteen-year-old girl in seventh grade. I read your book Queen Bees & Wannabes and I must admit most everything was true. I mapped out my clique (popular). I found out that I am the Banker/Champion. Even though I feel as though the girls and boys I hang out with are my friends, my self-esteem is lower when I'm with them. And within the clique is an even more exclusive girls' clique which I am very proud to be a member of. That's where I want to belong. BUT, I'm part of EVERY clique. My best friend is in a less popular clique that I am also friends with. Those are the people I feel most comfortable around. They understand I'm part of another clique but they choose to tell me every little piece of gossip they know, which I tell to everyone in my other clique. But anyway after reading Queen Bees & Wannabes I learned which clique I wanna stay with and that being the Banker isn't a good thing. Because I don't like my friends living in fear of me. So thanks.

Truly Yours,
Lauren

Are you horrified at Lauren's unapologetic social climbing and manipulation? Mystified at her simultaneous self-awareness and

off-center moral compass? Or are you counting your blessings that you aren't in seventh grade anymore or, better yet, wondering why these seventh-grade personalities persist in the adults you know in your family, neighborhood, and workplace?

Welcome to Girl World. If you want to understand girls, you have to examine how and what your daughter understands about the nature and dynamics of friendship, cliques, and popularity. On a daily basis, she learns what kind of girl she is "required" to be in order to be accepted by a group, or the consequence of standing her ground. This chapter will help you analyze and understand the nature of friendship groups so you can better understand what your daughter is going through, identify her position in the clique, help her develop healthy boundaries with friends, and, if necessary, guide her toward taking responsibility for cruel behavior.

The common definition of a clique is an exclusive group of girls who are close friends. I see it a little differently. I see them as a platoon of soldiers who have banded together because they think this is the best way to survive Girl World. There's a chain of command, and they operate as one to the outside world, even if there may be dissatisfaction within the ranks. Group cohesion is based on unquestioned loyalty to the leaders and an *"It's us against the world"* mentality.

> Some members may not even like other members within cliques. There are those you hang out with just because certain people seem to come in a set, like markers, but then there are those you actually trust and respect.
>
> —Amelia, fifteen

That feeling—that she has to stay in the cliques no matter the cost—reinforces your daughter's bond with her friends. It can also break apart or weaken the bond between you and her because the clique can convince her that telling anyone outside the group about a problem she's experiencing is disloyal. But the worst thing some girls learn from cliques is that it's more important to *maintain* a relationship at all costs, instead of realizing that how they are treated *within* that relationship should be the basis for whether or not they stay in it.

It's also true that girls learn it's more [about] high-status re-
lationships instead of pursuing and/or keeping healthy, posi-
tive friendships.

                                            —Amelia, fifteen

Many parents believe there's one particular time in a girl's
life that you can predict when cliques will be the worst. Unfortunately, it doesn't work like that. You can't watch your daughter's
eighth-grade graduation and breathe a sigh of relief that all the
girl drama is now over. I've seen shocking examples of cliques in
kindergarten. More important than trying to figure out a precise
time when these issues will start and stop is keeping in mind that
children and teens often operate in groups, and this can produce
intense power struggles. However, there are times when you can
reliably predict when these dynamics will intensify. For example,
problems are likely to increase when your daughter is new to a
school, when her grade is receiving a large number of new students, or when she's in the youngest grade of a school, because the
social hierarchy is challenged and people want to know how any
changes to that hierarchy will shake out.

Before I go any further, I want to make clear that I don't think
there's anything wrong per se with cliques or groups. Girls tend
to have a group of girlfriends with whom they are close, and often
these friendships are great. They can be themselves, share secrets, hang out, act silly, and have confidence that they will be
supported no matter what. Having said that, the way girls group
together can sow the seeds for cruel competition for popularity
and social status, and for undermining a positive sense of self-
worth.

Why is that? Because girls, like all of us, are vulnerable to
being controlled by the power of the group, need validation from
their peers, and can be obsessed with comparing themselves to
one another. This is why what I speak and write about isn't simply addressing the issue of girls being nice or being friends with
one another. I don't care if girls are nice. What I'm talking about
is how we develop and maintain our ethics and moral compass
when we are in a group, and how group dynamics make it difficult
to do so. It's the same whether you're in third grade, sixth grade,

the principal of a school, or the president of a country. How does the group respond when an individual within it believes members within the group are acting unethically? What will the price of speaking out be? What will the price of silence be? Will the person speaking out be seen as disloyal and get kicked out? It is through understanding their relationship to the group and their right to speak out within it that girls develop their ethics, moral courage, ability to think critically, and belief that their actions can affect change. Here's an excellent example of a girl who understands the process.

> I went to a public school until fourth grade, and I was very sure of who I was. When the girls weren't allowed by the boys to play soccer at recess I, quite literally, petitioned for change. Eventually the boys let us play just to shut me up. I had plenty of "lunch tray moments" until it was discovered midyear that I could sing, something that I guess is an attractive trait in a friend. Same old story, I ended up compromising who I was, working my way up the social ladder, tailoring personalities trying to find one that fit. I'd toss off new friends for newer friends until I reached the heights of Middle School Hierarchy. I wasn't that confident fourth grader or that awkward fifth grader; I was way worse, I was nothing. I was anything my friends wanted me to be and because of that, I was nothing without their guidance. I was called weird by my friends for my infatuation with musical theater, pressured to give up extracurriculars, told I was only liked because I was pretty, mocked for being feminist and anti-drinking. I lost myself; I was the sidekick of the same girl who had made me miserable in grade school. She made me miserable in middle school too, but this time I victimized myself. End of eighth grade I ran against her for class president—that was my idea of taking a stand. The cattiness was ridiculous. I refused to succumb, not so much because I was above it, mostly because I knew that acting like the bigger person could buy votes. It's terrible and I don't want you to think I'm heartless, I hate who I was. I won the election but realized it wasn't worth the fight.

I quit. I quit drama and popularity and competition. I've been clean for two years now.

—Allison, sixteen

POPULARITY

For some girls, popularity is magical. Popularity conveys an unmatched sense of power. Some girls think that if they can achieve it, all their problems will disappear. Some become obsessed and measure the popularity barometer daily on their favorite social networking platform, then issue constant weather reports. Others dismiss it, thinking the whole thing is ridiculous. Some are angry and deny they care, although they often actually do. Some feel so out of it they give up.

Imagine you're invisible, and walk with me into a classroom (feel free to imagine any grade from third grade up) where I'm going to discuss cliques and popularity. This is what you'll see: thirty girls grouped together in clumps of usually four or five. They're sitting on chairs, or on each other's laps, doing one another's hair, texting, reading, or sitting by themselves. Some are even studying. I start the class by asking the girls to close their eyes and answer by a show of hands how many of them have had a friend gossip about them, talk behind their back, force them to stop being friends with someone, or be exclusive. All hands immediately shoot up. I ask the girls to keep their hands up and open their eyes. They laugh. Then I have them close their eyes again and ask them to answer by a show of hands how many of them have gossiped, backstabbed, or been exclusive about a friend. Much more slowly, some bending from the elbow instead of extending their hand, all the hands go up. I tell them to keep their hands up and open their eyes. They look around. They laugh again, but nervously.

After five minutes or so, almost without exception, the following occurs: A girl, usually generically pretty and surrounded by four or five girls, will raise her hand defiantly and say, "Ms. Wiseman, maybe this happens at other schools you work at, but at this school we don't have exclusive cliques like that. It's not like we're

all best friends, but we all have our groups and people are fine with it. People just can't be best friends with everyone." As she's speaking, the other girls react in various ways: Some stare at the floor, others have disbelief all over their faces, and some roll their eyes. It can be difficult for me not to outright challenge this girl. But no one speaks up to dispute her declaration. Almost always, three things will be true about this girl: First, she'll always be one of the meanest, most exclusive girls in the room; second, she honestly believes what she's saying; and third, her parents will be in total denial about how mean she is and completely back her up. It's enough to make your head spin. So how do we get the girls to tell the truth? There's only one way: anonymity.

I tell the girls to take out a piece of paper, sit wherever they want around the room except next to their friends, and anonymously tell me if the girl who spoke is correct. As you watch them find a place to write, the power of the social hierarchy is clear. The girls can't wait to write, but most want to hide as they scribble away. Especially if the girls are younger, they sit in closets, under their desks, under the teacher's desk, and even in lockers (if they're small enough).

When they're done, they get to fold the paper in any way they want—and how they do it also tells me a lot about what they think. Some girls condense the paper into a small ball or the smallest square. Others hand me the paper unfolded and defiantly tell me they don't care who knows what they wrote. I put all the answers in a box and take it with me to the front of the room.

Everyone sits in a circle and the air is tense with expectation. Before I begin, I remind the girls to "own up" to their own behavior and not focus on figuring out who wrote what. I tell them to stare at the ground so they can resist trying to telepathically communicate who they think wrote what. I read aloud most of the responses (girls can write "for your eyes only" if they don't want their answer to be read out loud).

Not surprisingly, the girl who initially raised her hand and declared that there are no cliques holds the minority opinion. Here are the responses from a typical sixth-grade class.

From the bottom of the social ladder:

I'm uncool. Let's face it. There are many cliques among the "cool."

—Emily, eleven

In this grade there are cliques and I hate it. Popular people put other people down all the time. I know I'm part of a clique, but my clique was formed of the girls that were excluded and shunned. We like each other for who we are, and not by our hair, looks, clothes, or popularity. These girls are my real friends.

—Michelle, twelve

From the middle:

I guess, for want of a friend, girls are willing to hurt anyone and don't care what stands in their way.

—Kiana, twelve

There are cliques and even exclusive clubs. There are about three or four cliques and some are nice. The rest are exclusive and mean. Sometimes I feel like I have to conform and be boy crazy.

—Kim, twelve

And from the top:

There are cliques in this class and everybody is popular in their own group. The cliques are intertwined. I think the popular people are really nice. There is gossip but no backstabbing.

—Paige, thirteen

I think there are cliques, but we aren't mean to each other mostly. But there are occasional breakouts of trouble.

—Carrie, twelve

Can you picture what Carrie means by "occasional breakouts of trouble"? This is a classic popular-girl understatement, which

usually refers to one girl completely humiliating another. Why were the girls so reluctant to admit the gossiping and exclusivity out loud? What was silencing the girls from telling the truth? The power of the group silences them, because those in positions of power are often blind to their behavior or justify it so they won't have to take responsibility for their actions. Those not in positions of power fear the consequences of speaking out in public. When girls do talk about it, they talk only with their friends and in private places such as school bathrooms, their bedrooms, or in supposedly private places online. Most of the time, the girls who aren't afraid to speak out in public are those who are so out of the social pecking order that they have nothing to lose by saying what they really think.

Popular girls like this are acting like any other group of privileged people. They don't recognize their privilege because they are blind to it. It's all they know, and they haven't had to go through the experience of understanding what it feels like to be on the outside. They know little to nothing about people outside of their group and are reluctant to admit what they do to put other girls down. In contrast, the girls on the outside usually know a lot about what's going on with the popular girls. But what's critically important about this exercise is that it enables the adult to teach a fundamental value: Each person's truth is of equal value. No one gets to speak for anyone else or dismiss an opinion just because it's not shared by the people who have the most power. Once the silence is broken, the truth comes out. Girls want to talk about what's really going on between them. They just have to be in an environment where they can speak their truth.

Land Mine!

Some girls can't stand the word "clique" and will be immediately defensive if you use this word to describe their group of friends. They assume you're accusing them of being exclusive. If you want to ask a girl about her group of friends, just say the word "group" and she'll be less reactive.

GOOD POPULARITY VERSUS MEAN POPULARITY

I'm not saying it's inherently bad to be popular, but girls had to help me realize that I sometimes make it sound as if it is. When I first started teaching, an adorable sixth-grade girl in pigtails politely raised her hand and asked me, "Ms. Wiseman, why do you think all popular people are bad?" She totally caught me off guard. Of course she was right—there are popular girls whom people really like. From then on I defined "the popular girls" in two ways: The good kind is a girl who is genuinely liked. The mean kind is when other girls are grateful if she's nice to them and terrified when she's angry. Both types of popular girls face a lot of social pressure. If the "good" girl takes a stand about something, such as telling another girl she's angry, she can face backlash from the other girls. If the "mean" girl doesn't live up to her reputation, she may lose power and status.

My students usually want to talk about good popularity for about thirty seconds. They are much more interested in knowing why the definition of good popularity doesn't usually describe the popular girls they know. Very quickly, the questions start to fly: Why are popular girls so mean? Why is everyone so afraid of them? No one likes the most popular girl, so why does she have the most friends? They're describing the bad kind of popularity. In the girls' words:

She's the meanest to everyone.
She has all the power and she'll crush you.
She'll influence you to be her friend, and then backstab you, ruining your life.

Who personifies mean popularity? I bet you have a picture in your mind right now.

THE QUEEN BEE AND HER COURT

We need to give girls credit for the sophistication of their social structures. Our best politicians and diplomats can't match a girl

who understands the social intrigue and political landscape that lead to power. Cliques are sophisticated, complex, and multilayered, and every girl has a role within them. However, positions in cliques aren't static. A girl can lose her position to another girl, and she can move up and down the social hierarchy. The reality is that few girls are stuck in one role, and they can often have moments of being something else or a combination. Here are the different roles that your daughter and her friends might play:

Queen Bee
Sidekick
Banker
Messenger
Pleaser/Wannabe
Torn Bystander
Target
Champion

Because girls' social hierarchies are complicated, I'm going to take you through a general breakdown of the different positions in the clique. But putting labels on girls' behavior can be tricky—and counterproductive. No one, girls included, likes other people to label them. I came up with these characterizations as a way for girls and the people who care about them to identify why a girl acts a specific way when she's in a group, and help them understand the possible consequences. Ideally, a label should be something a person decides to pick and associate with herself—even if there are negative things connected to that label. Likewise, a person should be able to take off a label when it no longer feels right to them.

Girls aren't unique. Every one of us has interacted in various kinds of groups since we were children, so we have all learned ways to operate within them. We may not be thinking about it, but we all learn to constantly assess our social power and influence throughout our lives. For girls, think of it this way: Everyone, even the girl with the highest social status, has moments in her life of trying to please someone with more power. But what's important

to notice is that the roles emerge in full force when there's conflict in the group, or when someone in the group is abusing their power. Instantaneously, each person's role emerges. The behavior behind these roles is in the girls' programming.

But girls can change their roles or play different roles in different environments. A girl may act like a Queen Bee at school but be a Pleaser on her soccer or basketball team. A Queen Bee can have a Champion moment. A Champion can get into such a tough situation that she acts more like a Torn Bystander. Also, your daughter doesn't have to be in the "popular" group to play a role within her group of friends. So if and when you talk to your daughter, or any girl, about cliques, encourage her to come up with her own names and create roles she thinks I've missed. If you can answer yes to the majority of items for each role, you've identified a pattern of behavior that could connect to the girl you're reading this for. Now let's break down what those these roles are.

THE QUEEN BEE

Through a combination of charisma, force, money, looks, will, and social intelligence, this girl reigns supreme over the other girls and weakens their friendships with others, thereby strengthening her own power and influence. Never underestimate her power over other girls (and boys as well). She can and will silence her peers with a look and then turn around and be incredibly nice. But the bottom line is you're on her side or else—you are with her or against her.

> She will do anything to have control. She will humiliate you in front of your whole grade, just if you are getting a little attention from boys, even if the boys are just your friends.
> —Kelly, fourteen

Your Daughter Is a Queen Bee If . . .
- Her friends do what she wants them to do.
- She isn't intimidated by other girls in her class.

- She complains about other people copying her, never leaving her alone, or being too sensitive.
- When she's hanging out in a group, she's in the center. When she moves, they follow.
- She can argue or charm anyone down, including friends, peers, teachers, and parents.
- She can make another girl feel "anointed" by declaring her a special friend.
- She's strategically affectionate. For example, she sees two girls in her group, one she's pleased with and one she isn't. When she greets them, she'll throw her arms around one and insist that they sit together and barely say anything to the other.
- She won't (or is reluctant to) take responsibility when she hurts someone's feelings.
- If she thinks she's been wronged, she feels she has the right to seek revenge and will do so.

She thinks she's better than everyone else. She's in control, intimidating, smart, caring, and has the power to make others feel good or bad. She'll make stuff up about people and everyone will believe her.

—Anne, fifteen

If you have a sinking feeling in your stomach because you're recognizing your daughter in what I've written above, that's a good thing—it just doesn't feel like it. If you are thinking, "How can my daughter already be a Queen Bee at the age of seven?" it's absolutely possible. Seeing it now means you have a better chance of addressing it.

What Does She Gain by Being a Queen Bee?
She feels power and control over her environment. She's the center of attention, and people pay homage to her.

What Does She Lose by Being a Queen Bee?
Her friendships are defined by power, not mutual support, trust, or care. She can be cynical about her friendships with both boys

and girls. She may easily feel that she can't admit to anyone when she's in over her head because her reputation dictates that she always has everything and everyone under control.

I want to share with you an experience I had in a middle school. It resonates with me because it's not often that I come across Queen Bees who admit their fall from power. I'd just finished an assembly with the sixth grade when the counselor asked me if I could talk to a couple of girls. I looked over in the corner to see two beautiful girls with stick-straight brown hair, button-down shirts, plaid skirts, and Ugg boots throwing furtive glances in my direction.

"Hi, girls, what's up?" I said.

Both girls scanned the room anxiously. The smaller one pushed her long bangs out of her face. "OK, we were in this clique with four other girls, but they kicked both of us out. They now talk bad about us and have code words for my name. It's really bad . . ." She looked away, obviously trying not to cry. "When I try to talk to any of them, they just walk away and whisper to each other and laugh."

The other girl broke in, "We've tried to talk to them. But they just throw it back in our face. I know we used to be the Queen Bees, but now I cry every night. And I know the school didn't like us in the group because sometimes I guess we were mean to people. Now . . . I guess I know what it feels like. . . . I guess they were never my friends."

For twenty minutes we talked candidly. One admitted that she had "a serious problem wanting to know everyone's business all the time." They knew they'd abused their power, and that their victims weren't sympathetic to their plight. I left them with a plan based on the idea that this could be a life-changing moment for both of them. Could they learn from this and use their dynamic, powerful personalities for good? Would they remember what it felt like to be excluded and betrayed, and speak out when it was happening to someone else?

But my other reason for sharing this experience is that a lot of people love to see Queen Bees brought down. Of course, we need to hold the Queen Bees accountable for wielding their power

unethically, but we also need to be there to catch them when they fall. Remember, they're still girls. What I want you to take away from this is the understanding that even Queen Bees experience the negative effects of cliques.

If you find out that your daughter has been acting like a Queen Bee, you can't let your anger get the best of you. She can see that you're angry. She can see that you're disappointed. She can even see that her behavior contradicts what you stand for, but you need to come across as wanting to know *why* it was so important to her to act this way. And if you've just finished this section and thought, "Well, I'd rather have a Queen Bee than a pushover," check yourself. I don't want your daughter to be a pushover either, but we need girls who are effective leaders who don't want to crush others.

THE SIDEKICK

She's the lieutenant or second in command—the girl who's closest to the Queen Bee and will back her no matter what because her power depends on the confidence she gets from the Queen Bee. Together they appear to other girls as an impenetrable force. They commonly bully and silence other girls to advance their own agenda. The Queen Bee and Sidekick are usually the first to focus on boys. The difference between the two is that if you separate the Sidekick from the Queen Bee, the Sidekick can alter her behavior for the better, while the Queen Bee would be more likely to find another Sidekick and begin again. On the other hand, sometimes a Sidekick can stage a coup against the Queen Bee and take over her position.

Your Daughter Is a Sidekick If . . .
- She's jealous of someone else being friends with the Queen Bee.
- The Queen Bee is your daughter's authority figure, not you.
- She feels like it's just the two of them and everyone else is a Wannabe (see the Pleaser/Wannabe section).
- You think her best friend pushes her around.

She notices everything about the Queen Bee. She will do ev-
erything the Queen Bee says and wants to be her. She lies for
the Queen Bee, but she isn't as pretty as the Queen Bee.

—Madeline, fourteen

What Does She Gain by Being a Sidekick?

A Sidekick has power over other girls that she wouldn't have without the Queen Bee. She has a close friend who makes her feel
popular and included.

What Does She Lose by Being a Sidekick?

If she's with the Queen Bee too long, she may forget she ever had
her own opinion. Her sense of self and identity is entirely formed
around her alliance with another girl.

THE BANKER

Information about other people is currency in Girl World—
whoever has the most information has the most power. I call
that girl the "Banker." She creates chaos by banking information
about girls in her social sphere and dispensing it at strategic in-
tervals. For instance, if a girl has said something negative about
another girl, the Banker will casually mention it to someone in
conversation because she knows it's going to cause a conflict and
strengthen her status as someone in the know. She can get girls to
trust her because when she pumps them for information it doesn't
seem like gossip; instead, she does it in an innocent, *"I'm trying to
be there for you"* kind of way.

Her power lies in getting girls to confide in her. Once they
figure out she can't be trusted, it's too late because she al-
ready has information on them, and in order to keep her from
revealing things, girls will be nice to her.

—Leigh, seventeen

The Banker can be as powerful as the Queen Bee, but it's easy
to mistake her for the Messenger, the next in line in the hierarchy.

The Banker is usually really cute, quiet, and withdrawn in front of adults. This is the girl who sneaks under adult radar all the time because she seems so harmless.

Your Daughter Is a Banker If . . .
- She is extremely secretive.
- She thinks in complex, strategic ways.
- She seems to be friends with everyone; some girls even treat her like a pet.
- She's rarely the subject of fights.
- She's rarely excluded from the group.

She's the switchboard operator for all the gossip.
—Tessa, eighteen

What Does She Gain by Being a Banker?
She gets to create drama. The Banker is confusing to other girls because she seems harmless yet everyone is afraid of her. People come to her for advice and affirmation.

What Does She Lose by Being a Banker?
Once other girls figure out what she's doing, they don't trust her. With her utilitarian mind-set, she can forget to look to other girls as a trusted resource. If girls do organize against her, it can be really hurtful and unsettling because she's never been on that end of it.

The girls can't oust the Banker from the clique because she has information on everyone and could make or break reputations based on the information she knows.
—Charlotte, fifteen

THE MESSENGER

The Messenger also trades personal information and gossip about others; however, she differs from the Banker in that she wants to prove her usefulness to the other girls in the group. She rational-

izes her behavior by saying that she wants to help the girls get along better or reconcile. By doing this, she hopes to gain recognition and social power. Parents can easily misread their daughter if she's the Messenger, because they see her peacemaking efforts as being entirely altruistic.

Your Daughter Is a Messenger If . . .
- She lives for drama, and she's obvious about it.
- She loves to "help" people out when they are in fights, which most parents describe as "just wanting everyone to get along."
- When a conflict arises between girls, it's all she thinks about.
- She gets an adrenaline rush from being in the middle of a conflict (but it looks to unsuspecting adults as if her only motivation is caring too much, wanting everyone to get along, and trying to make peace).
- She feels better about herself when other girls come to her for help.

What Does She Gain by Being a Messenger?
She feels valued, because friendships will be made or broken based on her involvement.

What Does She Lose by Being a Messenger?
Her position is precarious. Others can easily turn on her, especially if she gets information wrong (which she inevitably will because it's too hard to keep all the details right) or if others deny what she's claimed. She can be easily used, manipulated, and then discarded when no longer useful.

THE PLEASER/WANNABE

This person will do almost anything to be in the group or gain favor from the Queen Bee or the Sidekick. She often observes and imitates their behavior, clothes, and interests but never feels completely in the group—that's why she's always proving her loyalty to the more powerful girls. As a result, she can give up what's

important to her and/or what she enjoys. She constantly antici-
pates what people want from her but doesn't ask herself what she
wants in return.

Your Daughter Is a Pleaser/Wannabe If . . .

- Other girls' opinions and wants are more important than her
  own.
- Her opinions on dress, style, friends, and "in" celebrities
  constantly change according to what the Queen Bee does
  and says.
- She has trouble developing personal boundaries and communicating them to others.
- She can't tell the difference between what she wants and
  what the group wants.
- She's desperate to have the "right" look (clothes, hair, and so
  forth).
- She'll stop doing things she likes because she fears the
  clique's disapproval.
- She avoids conflicts. Her common response when asked her
  opinion is, "Whatever you want, doesn't matter to me."

What Does She Gain by Being a Pleaser/Wannabe?

She has the feeling that she belongs.

What Does She Lose by Being a Pleaser/Wannabe?

Frankly, almost all girls and women have moments of being the
Pleaser. Because girls are rewarded for being "nice," pleasing behavior is reinforced because it is socially condoned. Therefore, it's
really hard to see when a girl is sacrificing her personal boundaries. As a result, many pleasers have low self-esteem from sacrificing their needs and judgment. Pleasers often assume that the
more they please, the more liked they will be, or positively recognized for their actions. But, ironically, that's not true. Instead, the
more Pleasers accommodate, the worse people treat them.

*She thinks she belongs, but the Queen Bee and the Sidekick
are just using her; she'll lose all her friends, then the Queen*

*Bee and her Sidekick will destroy her reputation. Don't be a
Pleaser/Wannabe if you can help it.*

—Trinity, sixteen

THE TORN BYSTANDER

She doesn't want to go against the more powerful people in the
group and usually convinces herself not to challenge them. She
wants to help the Target, the next in line, but she is not sure how,
or thinks it won't make a difference. She may rationalize her own
silence or apologize for others' behavior.

Your Daughter Is a Torn Bystander If . . .

- She's always finding herself in situations where she has to
  choose between friends.
- She tries to accommodate everyone.
- She's not good at saying no to her friends.
- She wants everyone "to get along."
- She can't imagine standing up to anyone she has a conflict
  with; she goes along to get along.

She's confused and insecure because her reputation is over
if she doesn't stick with the Queen Bee, but she can be really
cool when she's alone.

—Anne, thirteen

What Does She Gain by Being a Torn Bystander?

Her silence buys her acceptance into the group. In high-social-
status groups, that also means she has increased access to popularity, high social status herself, and boys.

What Does She Lose by Being a Torn Bystander?

Her fear of the Queen Bee or other girls in power can be so terrifying that she never learns to take a stand. She can't imagine
having the personal power to do it. So she's smart enough to know
something's wrong but feels incapable of exerting any influence
over the situation.

THE TARGET

She's the girl who gets set up by the other girls to be humiliated, made fun of, and/or excluded. Targets are assumed to be out of the clique. Although this is sometimes true, it's not always the case. A girl in the clique not only can be targeted by another girl in the group, but it's often a strategy to reinforce the power dynamics between the girls. Often the social hierarchy of the clique is maintained precisely by having someone clearly at the bottom of the social ladder. Girls who are consistently targeted tend to be perceived to be trying too hard, or are targeted because their style of dress, behavior, or personal background is outside the norms acceptable to the clique.

Your Daughter Is a Target If . . .

- She may be very rule oriented and inflexible or anxious.
- She feels helpless to stop the girls' behavior.
- She feels she has no allies. No one will back her up.
- She may struggle to read people's social cues.
- She can mask her hurt by rejecting people first, saying she doesn't like anyone.

This role can be harder to figure out than you would think, and your daughter may be too embarrassed to tell you. She might admit she feels excluded, or she might just withdraw from you and "not want to talk about it." That's why I'll discuss how to talk with your daughter in the next chapter.

> *Targets don't want to tell their parents because they don't want their parents to think they're a loser or a nobody.*
> —Jennifer, sixteen

What Does She Gain by Being a Target?

This may seem like an odd question, but being a Target can have some hidden benefits. There's nothing like being targeted to teach your daughter about empathy and understanding for people who are bullied and/or discriminated against. Being a Target can also

give her objectivity. She can see the costs of fitting in and decide she's better off outside the clique because at least she can be true to herself and/or find good friends who like her for who she is, not for her social standing. Remember the girl who wrote that she was in the loser clique but at least she knew her friends were true friends? A lot of girls don't have that security. But in general, the benefits of having these experiences usually become clear to girls as they get older. In the meantime, being the Target can be excruciating. At the least, it doesn't seem like a very good trade-off for being made fun of now.

What Does She Lose by Being a Target?

She can feel helpless in the face of other girls' cruelty. She feels ashamed of being rejected by the other girls because of who she is. She'll be tempted to change herself in order to fit in. She feels vulnerable and unable to affect the outcome of her situation. She could become so anxious that she can't concentrate on school-work.

> If a girl's stuck in a degrading clique, it's the same as when she's later in a bad relationship. She doesn't expect to be treated any better.
>
> —Ellen, fifteen

THE CHAMPION

> In every girl there is a Champion who wants to get out.
>
> —Joanna, seventeen

In the first edition, I called these people the "Floaters," but I don't think that was a clear enough definition—and way too many people insisted to me that their daughter was one. So now, I'm calling this person the "Champion." But it's not like this person is walking around all the time being the Champion. The main goal of this book is to help your daughter have more Champion moments at every age. She can take criticism, doesn't make people choose friends, and doesn't blow off someone for a better offer.

She has friends in different groups and doesn't treat people differently when groups are together. She can and will stand up to the Queen Bee in a way that treats them both with dignity.

You can usually spot this girl because she doesn't associate with only one clique. She has friends in different groups but can move freely among them (but remember, so did the Banker who wrote to me in the beginning of the chapter).

Your Daughter Is a Champion If . . .
- She doesn't want to exclude people; you aren't always having fights with her about spending time with people she considers "losers."
- Her friends are comfortable around her and don't seem intimidated; she's not "winning" all the conversations.
- She's not exclusively tied to one group of friends.
- She can and is willing to bring another person into a group of friends.

What Does She Gain by Being a Champion?
Her peers like her for who she is as a person. She'll be less likely to sacrifice herself to gain and keep social status.

What Does She Lose by Being a Champion?
Being a Champion is more complicated than it looks. A parent wrote me the following about her own childhood. I bet a lot of Champions can relate to her experiences.

I was widely respected and liked. I could float among the groups with ease, could stick up for anyone at will (and usually did). But I never belonged to anything in particular, and that is true of all floaters. Also, those girls that do stick by their principles and behave admirably during junior high school are respected, but generally shunned. I was particularly prized as a foul-weather friend, because I was kind, practical, and always kept people's secrets; but when things were going well, I was not particularly needed. What the floater learns is that she is, and probably has to be, an island

unto herself. *That she has the backbone to live by her principles, but that this will come at a price. I feel like being a responsible, well-respected floater left me cut adrift and a little
bit old before my time.*

—Elle

Our goal is to have more Champion moments—in all of our
lives, not just those of our daughters. Think of it this way: If your
daughter has a moment of being the Banker, the Messenger,
or even the Queen Bee, and you can face it with integrity and
honesty—that is *your* Champion moment.

TREACHEROUS WATERS

*How do I hang on to me? Sometimes I think I have no real
opinions of my own or even feelings of my own, because I'm
so worried what everyone else thinks and what they feel. I
don't want to be wrong. I don't want to be caught being wrong.
I don't want to get anyone mad at me. I think that this is a bad
way to be, but I can't stop it. It just happens.*

—Zeina, fifteen

We all want to feel a sense of belonging. This isn't a character flaw. It's fundamental to the human experience. Our finest
achievements are possible when people come together to work for
a common cause. School spirit and the rightful pride we feel in
our community, our heritage, our religion, and our families all
come from the value we place on belonging to a group. But it's
also true that our need to belong can be the cause of our greatest
inhumanity. It can be our collective Achilles' heel as it pushes us
to say nothing when faced with injustice, or to join in the abuse of
people the group has identified as different and therefore deserv-
ing of unequal treatment.

Remember: Conflict is inevitable, and people abuse power.
When conflicts and power plays arise, a cascade of decisions are
made by every other individual in the group based on their own

personal characteristics and history. It's critical to realize that these decisions develop both our collective and individual ethical framework, moral courage, authentic voice, and social competence.

For most girls, the goals of being ethical and honorable, while valued, are vague. In the short term, it's the experiences a girl has in a group that will teach her about friendship and what kind of girl is accepted or rejected by the group. Her experiences in groups will influence how hard she tries in school, her self-confidence, how she presents herself, her choices about sexual activity, and how she faces situations such as bullying, drinking, and drugs.

Group dynamics have distinct but unwritten rules. Understanding what those rules are and how they're created is critical to understanding girls' social dynamics. Let's start with defining "culture." The dictionary defines culture as "the attitudes and behavior characteristics of a particular social group." I define it as everything you intuitively know about how a person in your community should think and act in order to be accepted.

Of course, each of us lives in more than one community. The largest, loudest culture we all live in is our national culture, and we get constant messages from the media about what is valued (and not valued) within it. But we also live in smaller communities. Where we live, our ethnicity or religion, our economic class—all have their own cultural guidelines that react to or reinforce the value messages we get from the overall culture. But almost all cultures, no matter how big or small, base some of their greatest expectations for how a person is supposed to act on whether they're male or female. If you're born a boy, you have to act Y way. If you're born a girl, you must act X way. These specific, detailed gender rules are often the invisible puppet strings controlling people's social behavior.

Not every girl reacts to these rules in the same way. Some girls really drink the Kool-Aid. Others openly despise or rebel against the rules. Some girls are in the middle. We are living in a time when some girls, boys, and nonbinary, gender-fluid adolescents rightfully demand that we expand our definition of gender. But one thing is still true: We interact and measure ourselves against

specified gender rules. In order for a girl, or anyone, to come into her own, she must come to grips with how these messages exist inside her head and how they influence what she thinks, says, and does. Her understanding and internalizing of these rules will determine how she behaves in a group.

Imagine you and your daughter are on a cruise ship. The cruise director's job is to make sure your daughter is reasonably happy and entertained. There are scheduled activities, and if by chance she hurts herself, someone will be there to get her back on her feet. She knows most of the people on the ship and everything is familiar. But all of a sudden, girls start telling one another the ship is stupid and boring and it's time to get off. As you watch helplessly, she leaves behind everything that is safe and secure, gets into a life raft with other girls who have little in common with her except age, and drifts away. Listen to a girl who wrote me after she found her mom reading *Queen Bees.*

> If moms are sitting on a cruise ship wondering, why oh why did she ever leave all this, well, see I wasn't allowed to enjoy the cruise ship. I was locked away in the playroom for kids. Kids are not allowed in most of the cruise ship. When you're little the playroom is fun. When you get too old for stuff like that, they still insist you stay there. So we planned a jailbreak and stole a lifeboat.
>
> —Jordan, fifteen

Once in the raft she may ask herself how she got there or why she even left in the first place, but when she looks around, she sees that the ship is impossibly far away, the waves are too big, and there are a limited number of supplies; she quickly realizes that her survival depends on bonding with the other girls in that life raft. But your daughter isn't stupid. This realization is quickly followed by another one: She's trapped.

I know this is a dramatic metaphor to demonstrate girls' fear, but it shows how trapped many girls feel, forced to be a certain way in order to be accepted by their peers. They perceive their only choices as being stuck in the life raft or thrown into the

water. To girls, the life raft of the clique can truly feel like a matter of life and death.

When I'm teaching girls in a class, I get them to talk about these feelings by giving them the following exercise: I ask them to describe what our society expects a girl with high social status to be like. If she has an opinion, everyone listens and agrees. Then I ask them to describe what our society expects a girl with low social status to be like. This is someone who is likely to be teased, ridiculed, and/or dismissed.

Next, we put the characteristics of high social status within a box and place the characteristics of low social status outside the box (off the raft), as demonstrated in the following "Act Like a Woman" box.

Tries too hard	Pretty	Right brands of	Poor
Inexperienced with guys	Popular	clothes	Uptight
Bad skin	Thin but right curves	Cellphones, etc.	Wrong style/brands
Fat	Good hair	In control	of clothes
Too masculine in appearance	Athletic but not bulky	Smart but not too intense about it	Slut
	Confident	Guys think	Disabilities
	Money	you're hot	Passionate about uncool things

The box shows what girls think they need in order to stay in the life raft and what characteristics will get them thrown out. I visualize most of the girls I teach as squeezing into this raft and hanging on for dear life. They'll tolerate almost anything to stay in—and there's always the threat of being cast out.

> *Being on the lifeboat sucks. And being OUTSIDE of the lifeboat REALLY sucks. But neither sucks as much as being "rescued" and locked back in that playroom. I'd rather try to make it out here.*
>
> —Jordan, fifteen

Are there some girls who are comfortable swimming in the waters? Are there girls who would rather drown than be in the raft? Sure, and sometimes these girls are stronger because of

the struggle. But in many ways, every girl has to deal with the life raft, because her society's social pecking order is based on this metaphor. Even if she doesn't care, her peers do, and they're judging her accordingly. No matter where your daughter is—sitting securely, teetering on the rails, bobbing in the waters with a life preserver, swimming strongly, treading water, or drowning—it is imperative to understand and accept the reasons why she bonds so tightly with her friends and why the idea of being cast out can be so frightening and paralyzing. Her fear also makes it more difficult to ask for help. From her perspective, that cruise ship is very far away, and you probably couldn't get her back on board even if you tried.

How do people get thrown out of the life raft? Look at the words outside the box. These are weapons. For example, imagine your daughter is the Pleaser in her group. The Sidekick in the group teases another girl for being overweight. Your daughter may feel bad, but what would happen if she stood up to the Sidekick? Any challenge to the powers that be is seen as an act of disloyalty and, in turn, she might be thrown out. Just the threat of being thrown out is powerful enough to silence most girls.

Cliques are self-reinforcing. As soon as you define your role and group, you perceive others as outsiders. It becomes harder to put yourself in their shoes, and therefore it is easier to be cruel to them or watch and do nothing. It doesn't matter if we're talking about social hierarchies, racism, sexism, homophobia, or any "ism"; this is the way people assert their power, which really translates into discrimination and bigotry. You've probably raised your daughter to stand up to and for people. But you're a long way away on the cruise ship, and heeding your advice—and perhaps her conscience—won't put her back on board with you. She's the one who has to stay on the raft with the girls.

HOW SCHOOL LOOKS TO YOUR DAUGHTER

Some of us remember school only too well. Others might need to jog their memory to recall what the hallways looked like. I asked a few girls to draw maps of their schools. You might ask

your daughter to do the same. No matter what the details of her drawing, you'll discover the lay of the land your daughter traverses every day. And, if your daughter is willing to share her map with you, how does it compare with your school experience?

CHECKING YOUR BAGGAGE

- Were you part of a group in elementary, middle, or high school?
- Why were you friends with them? What was the best thing about your friendships? What was the worst thing about your friendships?
- Did you ever want to leave the clique but felt like you couldn't?
- Were you ever tormented by someone in a clique?

HER CLIQUES AND YOU

Accept the following:

You'll often have to rely on secondhand information. You won't be around when she gets into trouble. Your influence is limited to what you can do before and after. The only people guaranteed to be around her when she does get into trouble are her peers. Think of it this way: Where does your daughter hang out with her friends? How often do you hang out in these places? What exactly is she texting or posting on her favorite social networking site? Girls have access to one another in ways no adult does. This means that she'll have to stand up for herself with your support, but not your physical presence.

You have to get out of denial. Your daughter will make poor choices, behave in cruel and unethical ways, and/or be on the receiving end of both. She may say nothing when someone else is being targeted. She may laugh and look like she is going along with the cruelty. If you want to raise a girl who survives adolescence and develops into a responsible, ethical woman, you have to accept the reality that there will be hurdles along the way and even some seemingly insurmountable mountains to scale.

Remember the life raft. When she's having a problem with friends, when she dreads going to school because she's having a

fight with another girl, remember how terrifying it can be to swim in an ocean with predators all around and no rescue in sight. On the other hand, it could be that she doesn't realize the water is only ankle deep, and she could stand alone if she chose to leave the raft.

SO YOU WANT TO TALK TO HER ABOUT ALL OF THIS...

It can be really hard to talk to your daughter about her role and experiences in the clique. As a general rule, unless she brings it up, don't begin the conversation by asking about her personal experiences. Instead, start the conversation by asking her opinion. Ask her to read this chapter or a few pages and tell you what she thinks. What rings true for her and what doesn't? If she tells you that there's nothing in the chapter that applies to her experience, don't let that be the end of your conversation. Ask her what does. You're looking for a way for her to begin describing what her version of Girl World looks like.

Approach your daughter as an observer of other girls. Then, when she's opened up to you about what she sees, you can ask what she thinks her role is. Most likely she'll start talking about herself as she talks to you about her friends. You can use the definitions I use in this book, but remember to be ready to discard them if she's reactive. Let her define her experience for you. As I said earlier, it's great if she comes up with her own names for roles in the clique. Some good questions to ask are:

- What do people gain and lose from their role?
- Why does she think that person is in that role?
- How does it impact her to watch these things happen with her friends?
- How does she feel when it happens to her?

In the chapters that follow, I'll give you more specific advice on how to help your daughter. For now, I'll describe your key task as a parent based on your daughter's general position in the clique: from a powerful position, in the middle, or as the Target.

Position of Power (Queen Bee, Sidekick, Banker)

If she's operating from a power position, it'll be hard for her to admit when she's in the wrong, and she will be unlikely to show empathy for other girls. Always emphasize taking responsibility for her actions and not blaming others. She may also be focused on revenge. If you try to talk to her, she'll either put up fierce resistance or be as smooth as silk. Don't be fooled by her approach. She's doing that only because she's smart enough to know that placating you will get you off her back faster.

Caught in the Middle (Torn Bystander, Pleaser/Wannabe, Messenger)

Don't create a situation in which she feels that she has to choose between you and the person described above, because that girl is cooler than you are. Tell her you know she's in a difficult position, but encourage her to take responsibility, because her torn feelings look like two-faced behavior to other girls.

Ask her, "Who's making the decisions in your life?" She doesn't like when you make decisions for her, so she shouldn't like it when the Queen Bee makes decisions for her. But remember, no matter how close you are, you can't provide the social validation she gets from her friends, or convince her that she doesn't need it in the first place. The key to success in this conversation is to make your daughter understand that, by following the clique, she's not in control of her life. Other people are making decisions for her. But don't blame her for not being able to stand up for herself. Give her credit for talking about it openly. Practice with her what she wants to communicate to the more powerful girls (and we will get into how in chapter 7).

Target

If you identify your daughter in this role or if she ever has an experience where she's a Target, let her talk about it at her own pace. These situations can be humiliating, so give her space but make sure she knows you are available to talk to anytime. If she tells you she's a Target, don't freak out and threaten to call the school or other parents unless she asks for your help. If she really doesn't

want to talk to you, respect her feelings. In the next chapter, I'll talk more about the importance of finding an ally for your daughter in those cases where she's not comfortable talking to you. In chapter 7, I'll discuss how to help your daughter stand up to those in power in the clique.

WHAT IF YOUR DAUGHTER DESPERATELY WANTS TO BE ONE OF THE COOL KIDS?

If your daughter is obsessed with the popular girls, they're going to notice and probably see her attention as irritating. Worse, sometimes these girls will react by making fun of her. So . . . not good. Your job is to help your child understand her own motivations and then remind yourself a hundred times that your goal is long-term. Ask her to tell you what she thinks these girls lives are like. If she thinks they're "perfect," ask her to specifically describe what that looks like to her. Where is she getting this information? Do they look like and act like people who would make good friends? What if they were friendly one week, cold the next? Would that be OK? Ideally, she'll realize that even if the girls pay attention to her, the relationships might be far from acceptable. What makes this so hard as a parent is that your daughter probably won't see the light right away. She may have to go through the awful experience of being friends with people who aren't nice to her.

WHAT IF YOU HATE HER FRIENDS?

I think one main reason kids don't tell their parents anything when they are fighting with friends is that things so quickly turn around and if my parents don't see every detail of the turnaround, then they have this image of this bad kid that did something so mean to their child. I told my mom about something that happened on my soccer team and now her one image of that person is horrible because she's not actually there. She doesn't see when the girl does nice things. One girl is kind of tagging along evil and there's one girl who is actually legitimately evil. The girl who is tagging along, she's

*really nice when she's alone. I told my mom this one incident
so my mom tells me that they are a bad crowd.*

—Julia, thirteen

If you don't like someone your child is hanging out with, your
child probably knows how you feel. She may even agree with you
about what you don't like about the kid. But it's also true that
there's something about this kid that your child likes. Maybe she's
a loyal friend. Maybe she's fun to be around. Maybe she has a
terrible home life, so your child doesn't excuse her bad behavior
but understands the context for it. Since you don't see it and your
daughter isn't telling you, it can be easy to assume that she's blind
to what's going on and therefore it's your responsibility as her parent to point it out to her. I guarantee that strategy will backfire.
Your daughter will believe you think she's naive, and she knows
your judgments are based on not understanding the situation like
she does.

If you are really concerned about someone she's hanging
out with, how do you broach the topic without it exploding in
your face? First, be honest with yourself about your agenda and
goals. For example, suppose your daughter has a friend you never
liked—in fact, you've never trusted one hair on her head. In the
last year or so your daughter has drifted away from this friend, and
you couldn't be happier. But the last three times you've picked her
up from school she's been hanging out with this kid again. What
follows is what the girls tell me they've experienced with their
parents in similar situations.

YOU: "So . . . how's Hannah?"

YOUR DAUGHTER (*silent for one second*): "Mom, she's fine."

YOU: "She's not treating you badly?"

DAUGHTER: "No! She's a good friend. Everything's fine. We made
up." (*She takes her phone out of her pocket and starts to text
someone.*)

YOU: "I'm just worried about you. I don't really trust her and I don't
want you to have that experience again."

DAUGHTER (*sighing, refusing to look at you, and starting to play*

a game on her phone): "Mom, can you please stop? She's my friend and I know what I'm doing. We talked everything through and I wasn't a pushover."

YOU: "Honey, I'm your mother. My job is to look out for you." (*You notice she isn't paying attention to you in the least.*) "If you say she's a good friend I believe it . . . but . . . just promise me that you won't let her treat you like that again."

DAUGHTER (*very slowly raising her eyes to you, giving you a blank, bored expression*): "Yes, I promise you. Now can we stop talking about this, please."

Pretty much any parent or person who works with girls is going to have at least one conversation with a girl that goes down like this. But you can change the dynamic in the moment, and at the very least you don't have to make a habit of this kind of conversation. You can change the pattern, but only when you realize that any hope for success in this situation starts with you.

First, you have to admit that your goal is not "finding out what's up," but instead communicating your mistrust of the "friend." You may be absolutely right that that person is a bad influence, but if you talk to your daughter like the parent in the conversation above, you'll exacerbate the problem. Your daughter will now be less likely to tell you anything about that person, or anyone else for that matter, because you weren't really trying to connect with her. You were leading the conversation to confirm your own suspicions and force her to agree with you. Girls see through this easily and will shut down. Anyone would.

Instead, let go of your agenda and allow your daughter to take the lead. Here's a suggested script for how this could go down if you've already had the conversation above:

YOU: "Hey, I thought more about what you said about Hannah . . ."
DAUGHTER: "Okaayyy . . . ?"
YOU: "Actually, I need to apologize. I thought about what I said, and I realized I wasn't listening to you. When you went through that stuff with Hannah last time my emotions got the best of me and I have a hard time changing my mind about her. But I

LAND MiNe!

Be really careful about judging, because sometimes your gut can give way to your biases. For example, have you liked a kid in your daughter's social circle because she comes from such a nice family? How do you know that? Because she looks nice? Because her family's life looks nice? Because she fits into the "good girl" box, and her parents fit into their respective good parenting boxes? Countless times, after something bad has happened and it looks like one of those "nice kids" was responsible, parents have said to me, "But she comes from such a nice family." Exactly—and that's why she thought she could get away with it.

also see how much you like her, so I think you must have a good reason for it."

If you're starting from scratch:

YOU: "Do you mind if I talk to you for a second about Hannah?"
DAUGHTER: "Sure, but everything's OK."
YOU: "I was a little worried that you were becoming friends again. I think it's really cool that you can forgive and trust her again. I want you to help me do the same, so can you tell me why it's better?"
DAUGHTER: "I don't know, it's fine."
YOU: "So I shouldn't be worried?"
DAUGHTER: "Everything's totally cool."
YOU: "Great. But just in case anything goes off, I'm here for you."
DAUGHTER: "Mom, I know. Please stop."
YOU: "OK, I'm going to try."

Neither of these strategies feels good in the moment. They don't guarantee that your daughter is going to stop hanging out with Hannah. But you don't have that guarantee anyway. The hard fact is that kids have to develop boundaries with people by going through the process of having those boundaries crossed

until it's so annoying or painful that they can see that the cost of being in the friendship is higher than the cost of severing the tie.

LanD Mine!

Don't read this chapter and immediately ask your daughter what clique she's in! While we're on the subject, there are some parents who have asked me whether their child should read this book. First, I think you need to read the whole book and decide which parts are appropriate. If you do have her read it, under no circumstances should you say something like, "I think you should read this book because . . ." Instead, say (and this goes for anything you see, read, or hear about relating to your children), "I just read this book, and I want to know if you think the writer is realistic, completely wrong, or out of her mind. Will you read it and tell me what you think?"

HERE'S THE GOAL . . .

When I began writing this third edition, I did what I always do. I put out a call to teachers and counselors to connect me with potential girl editors. One counselor put me in touch with Esme, a high school senior, who assured me that she'd had a really tight group of friends since middle school and they'd never had clique problems. At first I was skeptical. Never? Esme in her extremely cool and confident way assured me it was true. So naturally, I had to meet these girls and ask them how they had escaped the pitfalls so many other girls fall into.

A few weeks later, I met Esme, Ella, Mattie, Erin, and Summer for lunch. I got there first so that I could observe how obviously happy they were to see one another. They couldn't have been more different but it was immediately obvious how much the girls loved each other. And I was meeting them at a special time; they had all recently graduated from high school and were about to be separated from one another for the first time since they met in middle school.

What did they credit for their ability to be so close? They all

agreed: They all had separate interests and allowed one another to have other friends. They joked around with each other but knew what each one was sensitive about. If someone was angry at someone else in the group, they didn't sit on it. They told each other how they felt. Some of the girls were more sexually active than others, and yet there was a mutual respect for one another and the decisions they made. As they talked and laughed and reminisced, they were a powerful example of what the reward can be when girls create these strong bonds. You could feel the bonds of loyalty between them. When inevitable painful challenges hit them, I'm certain that they will be by one another's side. This is what girls deserve from each other. This is what we need to remind them is their right: to sit with a group of your friends who have stood by your side in great times and horrible times. Who will be there for you always.

Is It Really Happening So Much Younger?

Second grade is when everything exploded.

—Ana, nine

I was in first grade and my best friend since I was about two years old had been harassing me all day and when I asked her to stop she punched me in the eye. The school, of course, did nothing, but that's a whole other story.

—Faith, fourteen

Your relationship with your child doesn't begin when she is a teen. It begins the moment she's born. Do you remember looking down on your daughter's adorable face? You know what she was doing? Studying you, so she can instantly understand your facial expressions, the way you raise your eyebrows when you're mad, and the tone of your voice that indicates utter exhaustion. By the time she's a toddler, that girl is an expert on you. She knows how to push your buttons; she knows how to make you melt so she can get her way. She knows exactly when you're so exhausted she can ask you for something that you would never say yes to otherwise. (If you're a teacher reading this, you're not off the hook. I think it takes students about five minutes to size us up.)

Then your daughter gets a little older and she's spending time with other kids at daycare and on "playdates." Then some child hits your daughter in the head with a block or tells your daughter she hates her. Or the girls are playing "school" or "family" and you notice that your daughter's friend is always choosing the roles and your daughter is always playing the family dog. Or . . . it's your daughter who has the power and won't let anyone play a game she doesn't approve of.

By the time kids are five years old, they can have super-intense relationships with each other. Archenemies? Sure. BFFs? Of course. All of this means that when your daughter is a little girl there will be countless opportunities to teach her how to navigate friendships—way before she's in middle school.

As her parent, it will be challenging not to hate these other little girls in pigtails who are being mean to your daughter. What's strange is that we collectively seem shocked when little girls are mean to each other. Maybe it's because the girls are cute and they still give us hugs and listen to our advice. Maybe it's because we assume young kids can only be so mean—after all, how can they humiliate someone without using "bad words"? Or maybe we have tricked ourselves into thinking girls get into conflicts with each other only in middle school. But that's not true. When I ask girls when their first conflict with a friend happened, the majority answered that it was usually in first or second grade.

> I was in first grade and I was really close to two friends. One of them was really protective—she didn't like it when I hung out with other people. She went over to another girl and I remember—it was the first time people were talking about me.
>
> —Pilar, fourteen

> My first memory of a conflict with a girl was around first grade. I used to sit with my best friend Christina every day on the bus. One day, she was talking to another girl in my class instead of me and I was angry about it (or at least I think that's what happened). What I know for sure is that I refused

to sit on the bus with her and wanted to be alone, likely out
of my jealousy and damaged seven-year-old ego. Her mom
knocked on my window and sneered, "That's not nice." I got
mad at the mom, too, since she was making judgments on a
situation that she knew nothing about.

—Sophie, thirteen

For parents I think it can be really hard to deal with your young child's first experiences of rejection and social aggression, because somehow you feel it's your fault that you couldn't shield your daughter from these problems at such a young age. Maybe you thought that if you took her to the "right" school or lived in the "right" neighborhood, you could surround your daughter with only nice children and nice, mature parents. Remember, conflict happens. Blocks thrown at heads happens. People apologize when they don't mean it. Best friends won't let you be friends with other people even when you're five years old. Parents can act defensively.

But you can be the adult your daughter needs you to be right from the beginning.

Things to Keep in Mind with Younger Girls

- Because parents are more involved and therefore physically present in every aspect of a younger girl's life, it's more likely that the adult will overhear or see the conflict—or think they do.
- Younger girls are more likely to tell their parents about a conflict than older girls. That doesn't mean they still won't be selective about what they say, but you're more likely to know that something happened.
- By the third grade there will be girls in your daughter's class (or your daughter) who are going through puberty. This will cause anxiety for your daughter, her peers, or both. It may also cause you anxiety.
- Girls who enter puberty earlier than their peers are not always boy crazy.
- There will be girls who are incredibly boy crazy who are not going through puberty.

- Notwithstanding the serious concerns written above, girls can get into intense conflicts over things like "She knows purple is *my* color." Use whatever issue is bothering them to teach them about ethics and healthy friendships.
- Inside jokes, secret languages, and clubs are normal at this age, but they quickly become hurtful weapons precisely because they can be excused as harmless games.

IS IT STARTING EARLIER?

Many parents ask me this question, usually after they've had an experience that would seem to prove that it is. I don't have the definitive answer to this question. But I can tell you what I try to keep in mind when I am working with younger girls.

Every one of us is a unique combination of nature, nurture, and culture. Said another way, none of us is the way we are only because of our biology or because we are the middle child or of a particular race. Our nature is often influenced by how we are nurtured—and vice versa. And culture influences how we are nurtured. It's an ongoing cycle, and it's different for each of us. When we go deeper into nature, nurture, and culture, subcategories are revealed: socioeconomic class, birth order, access to healthy food, adequate health services, education, ethnicity, history/experience of violence and abuse in the home, and the media messages we receive. The list is long and varied. All of us are many things.

I don't think we as a culture are pushing girls to be meaner, but I do think we live in a culture that normalizes pushing our children to be older—meaning more stereotypically adolescent. Parental culture supports things such as dance and cheerleading groups where the girls are wearing super-sexy costumes, and even if a parent doesn't like it, they're often too intimidated to confront the parents or coaches in charge of the costumes. We focus on getting our children on the "right" track at earlier ages, so the things they love to do or show aptitude for ironically become a track for relentless anxiety, egoism, or insecurity.

We also have to acknowledge that some media companies are made up of adults (many of them parents), who depict girls as

fashion obsessed, superficial, catty, and manipulative; and create and market toys and social media that encourage girls to value their appearance and pursue material things above all else.

But none of that is responsible for the fact that young girls all over the country are going through puberty earlier. I'm not a neuroscientist, but I educate myself on the topic of puberty and adolescent brain development in every way I can. So why are girls (and boys) entering puberty earlier? There are amazing resources on this topic, but here's what I think is the most important:

The science is pretty clear that there's no one reason for girls starting puberty earlier (which is not defined as when girls get their periods, but rather when they begin to get pubic hair or breast buds). It's much more likely to be a variety of interrelated factors in an individual girl's life. Those factors appear to be obesity, stress, and endocrine disruptors (chemicals found in pesticides, polychlorinated biphenyls, and bisphenol A, all of which mimic the effects of estrogen in the body).

According to a study from the authors of *The New Puberty*, who tracked more than 1,200 girls in three U.S. cities from 2005 to 2009, "By age 7 more than 10 percent of Caucasian girls had started growing breasts, along with 25% of African American girls and 15% of Hispanic girls. And by age 8, those percentages had spiked by 18, 43, and 31 respectively." Why would African American and Latina girls experience early puberty? It's not because of their genetics, but because they are disproportionately affected by social inequality and environmental degradation. If they don't live near supermarkets with affordable fresh food, don't go to schools that offer physical education, and don't have safe parks to play in, it's going to have consequences, and this is but one.

HOW IS PUBERTY CONNECTED TO GIRLS' SOCIAL DYNAMICS?

Girls who look older tend to get into social situations where they are pressured to act older and socialize with older peers. Within their same-age peers, these girls often become targets of attention— usually for the worse, because when children are uncomfortable

about puberty it's common for them to lash out at the person who is "making" them uncomfortable.

Now think about adults. Do we ever think about talking to our third- and fourth-grade girls about what happens when a friend starts developing breasts? No, we rarely do, even with our middle school girls. Think about this double standard: A boy who goes through puberty earlier—meaning he has a lower voice and is taller than his peers—is usually treated by adults with more respect than his less physically mature peers. Girls who develop earlier may have noticeable cleavage and hips. The way they are treated as a result is, shall we say . . . not the same. Everyone's baggage about young girls and sexuality falls right on her. She makes us nervous.

BRAIN DEVELOPMENT

It's also important to consider new insights into adolescent brain development in relation to girls' social dynamics. During adolescence, the brain goes through a phase of tremendous change. These changes make it uniquely vulnerable to its environment and driven to pursue rewards. One of my favorite books, *Age of Opportunity* by Laurence Steinberg, offers some insights that I found particularly helpful.

According to Steinberg, what distinguishes adolescence from other periods of brain development is where the changes take place: the limbic system, where emotions are generated, and the prefrontal cortex, which is responsible for self-regulation and rationality. In adolescence a young person's brain goes through three overlapping phases of brain development. The goal here is to get these two areas of the brain to communicate with each other. Again, this has been helpful for me to read and reread when I am working or living with someone at this age who appears to have completely lost their mind. Here's how Steinberg describes the three phases:

> Phase One: Starting the Engines. During this time, teenagers become more emotional (experiencing higher highs and lower lows), are more sensitive to the opinions and evalua-

tions of others (especially peers), and are more determined to have exciting and intense experiences.

Phase Two: Developing Brakes. The second phase of brain development is gradual and not complete until age sixteen. Executive functions [in the prefrontal cortex] strengthen, which improves decision making, problem solving, and planning ahead.

Phase Three: Putting a Skilled Driver Behind the Wheel. Although a fine-tuned braking system is in place by the end of the second phase, the teenager can't always use the brakes effectively and consistently. The brain becomes more interconnected and is less easily disrupted by fatigue, stress, and emotional arousal.

OK . . . so what does all of this mean?

A couple of things. First, teens are motivated to seek the reward of social acceptance and approval of their peers. And their brains are wired to be upset when they are socially rejected. This has always been fairly obvious, but now we know why.

With puberty occurring earlier, the period of time when a young person is vulnerable to these highs and lows may be getting longer. It takes years for people's brains to reach full maturity, but if the process is starting earlier, then the length of time when a girl is vulnerable to these extremes will be longer.

So what does all of this mean for you?

It means that as soon as you notice that your daughter and/or her peers are going through puberty, you need to keep in mind that there's a real possibility that her friendships will be affected by the physical changes they are going through. It also means we need to begin teaching girls about puberty when they're in elementary school.

I remember in sixth grade, in my four-person friend group, two of my friends got their periods early. I used to envy them and marvel at how great it must feel to have such a significant milestone under their belts (Ha! Literally). However, this opinion was received only with judgment and pity.

—Tory, fourteen

THE BOOB RACE: WHO IS COMING IN FIRST?

Do you remember the girl who developed breasts first in your circle of friends? Most likely, it was a significant moment for everybody. Were you that girl? Remember the taunting from boys and comments from other girls? Like the first daffodil of spring, this girl signals that puberty has officially begun. Many boys are transfixed by the changes the girl's body is going through, and the other girls can be simultaneously anxious, intrigued, and envious. She's a lightning rod where all the other children direct their preadolescent anxiety and excitement. And if you're a twelve-year-old girl in full bloom, handling this situation well is really, really hard.

This dynamic can be even more confusing if and when the girl notices. All of a sudden, she is gaining popularity because she literally embodies the girl ideal. She can be conflicted between wanting and liking the attention and being uncomfortable with it.

> When I was in fifth grade, one girl developed DD breasts. Her breasts were the topic of everyone's conversation. It got her a lot of attention. Maybe it was a front, but she seemed to like it. Girls were so envious. When I had a birthday party, we all made fun of her by putting towels down our shirts and pretending to flirt with invisible boys.
>
> —Simone, seventeen

> I developed over the summer before I began seventh grade. I wore big sweatshirts all year.
>
> —Haley, fifteen

BODY HAIR

The first time someone teases a girl or a friend about their leg hair, girls realize being hairless is a critical yet invisible Girl World rule. Truly, it is one of the first issues that push little girls into Girl World and the "Act Like a Woman" box, and because girls are entering puberty at earlier ages, the body hair issue is coming at girls at earlier ages as well. A generation ago, the teasing would

start when the girls were between twelve and fourteen. Now it starts around ten or even younger. It also used to be the case that African American and Latina girls didn't get teased—but not anymore. Having body hair is one of the first things our culture tells our daughters is wrong, unacceptable, and shameful about their bodies—something that they must fix to be valued. Where is that coming from? We will go into more detail later, but depictions of hairless women are the norm in the media.

So you have a ten-year-old girl in your house who is begging to shave. When are you supposed to let her?

First of all, understand that this is often a rite of passage for both you and her. I know it's tempting to say "No way! Talk to me when you're fourteen!" or hand her a razor and be done with it, but this is truly an important moment. Here's what I'd do. Remember that your primary job is to be kind and nonjudgmental throughout the conversation. Because she wants your permission for something, this is a prime time to use that leverage to get her to research the topic. She needs to know when all of this shaving stuff started. Why is it such a big deal? Is it the same in all countries? Then, ask her what she thinks are the pros and cons of shaving for herself. If I were her, they are: pro—she doesn't get teased; con—she changes herself to please others. If she still wants to shave after this conversation, I'd let her—otherwise she just may be too much of an open target for other kids' cruelty. Even if you disagree with the choice she ultimately makes, your conversation hasn't gone to waste. You've had an open, thoughtful dialogue about an uncomfortable subject; these are the kinds of precedents you need to establish for later talks when she's fourteen and asks for a Brazilian bikini wax—which is not OK for her to do.

Here's how to bring it up in general:

"I'm not sure if this has happened already, but people your age can start going through puberty—so their bodies start to change. What can be weird is that people do it at different times. Everyone goes on their own pace, but sometimes it can make people feel uncomfortable with all this change going on, and sometimes people get made fun of because their bodies are different than most of the

other kids'. Or sometimes, it can be the opposite. The whole thing can get a little messy at times. So if you ever want to talk about it or have any questions, let me know and we can."

If she says no, let it go by saying:

"OK, but if you change your mind, I'll be here. Or if it's too embarrassing to talk to me about, is there someone else you'd feel more comfortable talking to?"

Don't say:

"It's OK. You'll get through it. It happens to everyone."

"This is so exciting! You are joining the tribe! Let's have a moon ceremony" (unless that's part of your heritage and/or your daughter is into things like that).

Do say:

"I went through it, so I can imagine it feels weird to you. But you're not me, so you could feel different than I did. Can I tell you what it was like for me, and if you want to, you can tell me what it's like for you?"

The ground rules are no one in the family ever teases her about the changes her body is going through and no little comments or revelations in front of your friends or family members! And absolutely no comments about weight. Everyone has an awkward stage!

—Sydney, seventeen

IF KIDS ARE TEASING HER

What happens if the comments begin to target your daughter? This may be something your daughter really doesn't want to tell you. So my guess is you're going to hear about it in an indirect

way. Like she's been horrible to her younger sister or brother or she picks a fight with you and then runs upstairs, slamming the door behind her. Then you ask her something like, "What in the world has gotten into you?" And then she breaks down and tells you that some boy at school is making her life miserable because he told her in front of everyone that she has hair like a gorilla.

"It's really common for people to get nervous and weird when other people are going through puberty and then they take it out on other people. It's not right but it's common. You have every right to be angry at that boy. So first, why don't you tell me all the things you want to tell him? Don't hold back. Then after you get that out of your system, let's think about what you can say in the situations where you think it's likely to come up. If you don't want to talk to me, let's think of someone that you would like to talk to."

If she's really upset about the changes her body is going through, you can say something like:

"I'm really sorry. You will get through this, but I know it's easy for me to say. You know I'm always here to talk if you want to. But I'd totally understand if it was too weird to talk to me, so maybe there's someone else you think would be better? What's most important to me is that you know you have nothing to be ashamed of and you don't have to go through this alone."

Then don't stand around waiting for her to say something. Instead, immediately do something else to lessen her discomfort, such as ask if she wants to watch a movie with you or if she wants something to drink or eat.

IF YOUR DAUGHTER IS BEING TEASED FOR GETTING HER PERIOD

As soon as you notice your daughter getting breasts, buy some pads for her and leave them in the bathroom. She'll see them and she'll know you put them in there, and she will be grateful that

you were subtle. You could even print out a little letter for her that has the basic facts, such as "It's OK but it can be painful. Here's what I've done when my period has bothered me [heating pads, Advil, and so forth]." If she is teased about getting her period, here's what I'd say to her:

> "That must be incredibly annoying. So let me ask you, if you could say exactly what you want to say to them, what would that be? Just go for it—don't worry if it sounds rude. Just get out all of your feelings. After that we can figure out what to say to this really annoying person."

As for what your daughter can plan to say to that annoying person, something like:

> "I can't help that I got my period, and I can't control what you say. So please stop teasing me about it."

You can also use this as an opportunity to share some of your own experiences at this age.

IF PEOPLE ARE TREATING HER DIFFERENTLY BECAUSE SHE LOOKS OLDER

Whether you say it now or in little doses later, here's the message you need to get across:

> "Don't worry, I'm going to keep this short. Sometimes people will pay attention to you and treat you differently because you look older. I am guessing it could be complicated, so I think we should talk about it. No matter what, I want you to be proud of your body. And if you're not feeling that way right now, that's understand-able. The most important thing for me is that just because you look older or people treat you like you are, you need to take care of yourself. That means to me that you are able to leave situations that you think are too old for you. The funny thing about that is it takes a lot of maturity to do that, but the bottom line is you don't

want to be in a situation where you feel pressured to act older than you are."

I'd encourage her to have a sense of humor. Practice responses like "What do I know about middle school?! I'm only in fourth grade!" that will break the tension but also firmly tell the person that she is not as old as they believe.

—Tessa, eighteen

IF SHE'S DEVELOPING LATER THAN HER PEERS

One of the girls in our class obviously stuffed her shirt with tissue paper and it was coming out during class. The girls destroyed her.

—Evan, eleven

In seventh grade, when we knew a girl stuffed her bra, we would sneeze and say to her, "Hey, we need a tissue!" and then everybody would laugh. So bad but so funny.

—Alex, eighteen

What was cute when she was eight becomes too girly when she's twelve—especially if she has friends who are going through puberty and/or are a lot taller. One of the ways I see girls tease others who are developing later is by making comments about how little or tiny they are. So validate her just like you would if she were on the other extreme.

"I can guess that this is really annoying. I know this doesn't magically change things and make it better right now but it'll happen. I could be wrong here, but is it also a problem that your friends are teasing you about it and you don't think you can say anything about it? If that's part of the problem, let's think about what you can say to them."

IF SHE REALLY WANTS YOU TO BUY HER A
BRA, BUT SHE DOESN'T NEED ONE YET

Don't tell her no because you think she doesn't need one. She thinks she does, so that's what you should focus on. There could be a lot of reasons why she wants to buy a bra. Maybe her best friend has one so she wants to share the bra experience with her— what that means is that she doesn't want to feel left behind as her friend matures. So at the least buy her a camisole. If you decide to go to a bra store, ask for help from a sincerely friendly salesperson—someone who can read the situation for what it is. Once you find that person, have your daughter talk to her about what she's looking for; the woman can give her the guidance she needs. You are there for support and budget considerations. And don't hover around the fitting room—mothers have a way of opening the door at the most embarrassing moments.

As for what to do about the social conflicts younger girls can get into (for example, when girls are whispering behind your daughter's back, or are making a club that she's specifically not allowed to join), I have spread advice throughout other chapters in the book, and I have noted when I think the issue is more likely to be specific for younger girls.

3

Passport to Girl World

I didn't understand why I was so unhappy in sixth grade. I couldn't have told my parents that girls were being mean to me.

—Erin, seventeen

Your parents see you in a specific way and when you act or do something differently they will be more curious about your "outside life."

—Cam, fourteen

I last told my parents in second grade about a problem I was having with a friend and then they told all their friends and my family. So then my cousins knew and teased me. Now, I just tell my brother and he just listens.

—Abby, fourteen

You've now taken an initial tour of Girl World. You've looked around, seen some of the important tourist attractions, and gotten a sense of the culture. You can also see some of the problems that are stressful to the native inhabitants. Now you want to talk to the natives fluently (especially the one you may live with), without saying something that leads to a big misunderstanding.

The next three chapters make up your "passport." They are all about you and the other adults in your daughter's life and how you're all coming across to your daughter. You'll find strategies to help you translate what she's saying and why she's saying it. And I'll also show you how to get the information you need to travel through Girl World without reading your daughter's diary or snooping through her text messages or social networking platforms (although you do have the right to do that as a last, last, last resort).

There's one more thing about entering this world to always keep in mind: You aren't the only stranger interacting with the natives. There are other parents, coaches, administrators, teachers, and other adults in your family who communicate with your child and her peers. So in this chapter we will look at both common parenting styles and what the popular phrase "It takes a village to raise a child" really means.

LOOKING IN THE MIRROR

One of the things I always try to keep in mind is that no parent wakes up in the morning wanting to be an enabling, micromanaging, in denial, or irresponsible parent. Neither does any teacher, coach, administrator, or anyone else who works with your child. And it's relatively easy to keep it together when the social waters are calm in your child's life. But the minute you find out that she's caught up in Mean Girls drama or any other common problem for our girls, it gets infinitely harder. The question is, Why are we so challenged?

Here's my short list:

1. We hate the people who are mean to our kids.
2. When we believe an adult is unkind or unsupportive of our child, we can convince ourselves that this person is incompetent, insane, and must be destroyed.
3. We love our children, and we don't like thinking badly of people we love.
4. It's embarrassing when our children are mean, rude, or obnox-

ious. Rather than admit our embarrassment, it's just too tempting to excuse the behavior. From saying she's "overtired" or "oversugared" when she's little, to "She's moody" or "You know, girls are just catty at this age" when she's a teen, we often miss opportunities to see our children's behavior for what it is, and then use those opportunities to demonstrate our values.

WHAT'S YOUR PARENTING STYLE?

In my work with parents I see a variety of parenting styles and philosophies. Most of them are based on love, but as you probably know, there's a lot of anxiety, fear, and denial out there that mixes with that love. Look over the following styles and see which category you fall into most easily, especially in moments of anxiety. Your style is probably a combination of these profiles, based on the context of the problem or what's going on in your life at the time. If you are curious about how your parenting comes across to your daughter, feel free to ask her which style she thinks you belong to. But don't argue with her when she tells you what she thinks. And remember, we're sort of doing that labeling thing here, so just as you may not like something you read here, keep that in mind when you label a girl a "Queen Bee."

If you can stand it, try doing this exercise with your daughter:

Sit across from her and give her sixty seconds to imitate you when you're angry, worried, or however she would define "freaking out." The rule is you can't say anything, you can only observe. When the sixty seconds are over it's your turn: You get sixty seconds to explain the motivation behind your freak-out—and she can't interrupt you. She has to listen. Then each of you takes a turn sharing what you learned.

THE LOCK-HER-IN-A-CLOSET PARENT

This parent believes it's possible to control their daughter's life and choose the people she hangs out with. This parent also believes that telling her to stay away from bad friends, drugs, alcohol, and sex will work. This parent is judgmental of their children's friends—which makes their daughter that much more likely to hide her personal life from them. I can't tell you how many times I've run into these sort of parents only to find out that their daughters are doing all of the preceding—they're just really good at hiding it. Even if you could lock your daughter away until she's eighteen, you're only prolonging the inevitable. When she comes out, she'll want to experience things on her own. If this is your parenting philosophy, you're teaching your daughter to sneak behind your back and get herself into serious trouble, without giving her the skills to get out of trouble or the resources she needs to help herself. Read what Maxine says about her parents growing out of this parenting style.

> I am a junior in high school. My parents used to control every aspect of my life from people I hung out with and where I went to hang out. I was never allowed to sleep over at other girls' houses because my parents were so protective. I was forced to stay friends until recently with a girl that I didn't really like, but my parents liked her because she was really naive and only ever wanted to play kids' games. Since I've been in high school, they don't really ask about my friends except for the ones they've met. I think they realized that it was kind of ridiculous when I told them that I hated all my friends because they picked them and I would start to rebel.
>
> —Maxine, sixteen

THE BEST-FRIEND PARENT

Best friends? Some of you may laugh at this, thinking it's a great day when you and your daughter are on speaking terms, let alone "best friends." Most parents today who fit into this category know better than to say "I'm best friends with my daughter." But how

about "I know my daughter isn't perfect but I'm just really lucky because she tells me everything and we're just really close"? Never assume that your daughter isn't doing something solely because you don't approve of it or because you believe she tells you everything. *Just because she talks to you a lot doesn't mean she isn't selective about what she says.* In any case, your daughter doesn't want you to be her best friend. She wants you to be her mother (or father). Your connection with her is profound and unique.

Sometimes parents really are their daughter's best friend. However, most often this ends abruptly sometime in early adolescence, and the parents can feel terribly rejected. A few parents manage to think of their daughter as their best friend through high school, but I've rarely seen this work out well. The daughter feels torn between resenting the overinvolved parents and feeling guilty about rejecting them. Or she's so dependent on her parents that she never learns to form her own independent relationships. In the first case, the daughter is forced to take extreme measures to separate from the parents. In the second case, she never grows up.

THE HIP PARENT

This parent believes that they are the only ones that really "get it." "Getting it" means being in the know about what their child and their friends are really doing. These parents think strict parents are in denial and therefore bad parents. Hip Parents also desperately want to be liked by their child's friends. In elementary and middle school, this is the parent who has inappropriate theme parties or buys things for their daughter and her friends (inevitably describing these things as "So cute!"). In high school, this is the parent who buys alcohol for parties and even drinks or does drugs with kids—often justifying this behavior (usually after a party has gotten out of hand) by saying that if the kids are going to drink, they may as well do it under their own roof. From their perspective, teens are going to drink, do drugs, and have sex, so it is better to have them in a "safe place." The problem is it's not a safe place. The parent has no boundaries (and couldn't communicate them if they had them), and creates an environment where things can run off the rails.

I've never seen a child who respected the Hip or Best-Friend Parent. Both types are easily manipulated and disrespected by their children, especially in front of others. While it may feel good in the short term, this style doesn't create healthy parent-child relationships. And forget discipline. Once you go down this road, it's impossible to set guidelines and rules that your daughter will take seriously. Your child wants and needs you to be a parent, not a lame adult they can convince to buy alcohol at a random liquor store, which if you don't know is called "shoulder tapping."

> The difference between a Best-Friend Parent and a Hip Parent is that the Best-Friend Parent's goal is to develop a relationship with their child and be close to them. But the Hip Parent's goal is to be close to the child's friends so they think they're cool. They'll put their own children down in order to be seen as cool by their kid's friends.
>
> —Katelyn, eighteen

> I found out that my daughter was skipping school, going over to a friend's house, and getting high—and the mother knew! The girls were doing it right in front of her. When I figured out what was going on I drove over there . . . and she followed me around the house lying to me about what was going on.
>
> —Carolyn

THE BELIEVER PARENT

I get countless emails from parents describing something that happened to their child as if the parent were actually present at whatever went down—like they were at lunch, on the playground, in the gym during practice, or walking down the school hallway when the incident occurred. These are Believer Parents, the ones who automatically believe their child when she complains. For example, she says something about an adult like, "Mr. Edwards is so unfair! He totally yelled at me after he gave us a pop vocab test today! I swear he gave us the words yesterday!" Ask yourself: Have you ever argued with your daughter and heard in response "Mom, Dad, you're totally yelling at me!" And your reaction to

this accusation could be summed up as "You call this yelling? You haven't even seen yelling yet. I should be getting an award right now for how calm and mature I am being." There's a chance that something similar could be going on here. In fact, Mr. Edwards gave out the vocabulary list a week ago and reminded your child when he handed back the test results. But a Believer Parent never takes that into consideration while furiously typing and then sending an aggressive email to Mr. Edwards or marching over to the school to "get to the bottom of this right now."

I'm not saying your child's truth isn't valid. It is. But if you don't consider the possibility of other perspectives, three things happen: (1) you won't find out what's really going on; (2) when you find out that there's another side to the story you may get embarrassed because your child has just made you look like a fool; and (3) your embarrassment turns into massive denial and defensiveness.

Land Mine!

Do not email or call anyone right after your child has told you something that makes you angry! If the phrase "I'm going over there right now and [insert threat of what you're going to do here]" comes to mind, sit down immediately, because you are in danger of being a crazy parent. If your child is safe, then whatever you need to do or say needs to be done when you are calm and sane.

THE "YOU MESS WITH MY KID, YOU MESS WITH ME" PARENT

Just a little more extreme is the "You Mess with My Kid, You Mess with Me" Parent. I know this comes from a natural place of feeling like a mama or papa bear when someone is hurting your child, but these parents can't pick their child's battles. Everything to do with their child is a battle, and they are always ready to wage war. They rush in, without letting their child either advocate for themselves or be held responsible for bad behavior. They can be big fans of bringing other parents into their conflicts by creating petitions, boycotts, alternative dances, and parties when their child

is punished by other adults. These parents often have favorite coaches, administrators, educators, or parent friends, so they can look like a formidable adult clique. Or, they can go after a coach, administrator, or teacher to run them out of town. Other adults are usually reluctant to confront these parents because they're intimidated (which they rationalize by saying there's no use confronting them because they're not going to change). That's how this parent can so easily dictate school and athletic (and whatever else) policies that affect their children.

THE "LET'S LET THEM WORK IT OUT" PARENT

On the face of it, this makes perfect sense. Your daughter needs to learn how to handle difficult social situations, like being teased or bullied. But the big problem with this is: (1) these parents rarely have this attitude when their child is on the receiving end; and (2) they don't get involved at all—which means they provide little moral guidance or structure as their child navigates complex social dynamics. To this parent, "involvement" means micromanaging a child's life, and they're going to leave that to the helicopter parents they love to make fun of. But what all parents need to realize is that sane involvement means being behind the scenes, asking your child the right questions, and knowing enough of the details to hold your child accountable when necessary.

THE PUSHOVER PARENT

The only girls who don't wish they had this kind of parent are the girls who actually do. Daughters of Pushover Parents are primarily left to make their own mistakes, with no guidance or parental consequences. We all know our children, no matter what their age, need consistent rules and boundaries. They may rebel, but deep down they know that rules and boundaries make them feel safe, that there's order to the world, and that someone's looking out for them.

There's another kind of Pushover Parent, though he or she may not look like it on the surface. This is the parent who isn't around

a lot because of their job (they work long hours or travel a lot) or a divorce. These parents can be really aggressive to everyone else in the child's life (the other parent, a teacher, a coach) but will do anything to be on the child's side.

> What's the difference between the two? I would say that the Pushover lets you change the rules whenever you want and the Hip Parent has rules but they are really cool, like "No beer in the bedroom."
>
> —Becca, sixteen

THE BENIGN-NEGLECT PARENT

This parent wants to do the right thing but is simply too exhausted and distracted by work and other obligations to create the structured environment a daughter needs. The biggest problem is inconsistency—the parent initiates rules but then forgets them because they're distracted or just too tired to enforce discipline. When the daughter breaks a rule, she can take advantage of the parent's guilt and insecurity to transition the conversation from the daughter's behavior to the parent's bad parenting.

THE NO-EXCUSES PARENT

This parent has some wonderful qualities, demanding the best from a child and holding her to a high standard of accountability and personal responsibility. Through their words and deeds, No-Excuses Parents show their daughter that she should always get up no matter how many times she's pushed down. These parents usually raise girls who would make any parent proud: girls who get good grades, are respectful to others, and so on. There's only one problem with this kind of parenting: Since the daughter has been taught that she should take care of whatever problem faces her, she can be reluctant to ask for help. If she's in over her head, she can feel ashamed that she isn't strong enough to overcome her problems on her own. Shame is a powerful feeling, and it can make girls feel so bad that they've let the family down that they

internalize their feelings and become self-destructive and/or disconnected from the family.

THE PRIVATE PARENT

Daughters raised in this style get the message that imperfection, fear, feelings of insecurity, depression, and helplessness may be something other people have but not "us." The Private Parent's daughter can grow up afraid to reach out for help, or simply not know how to. Although privacy is important (especially to a teen!), she could get into situations that are over her head, where her health would depend on reaching out.

THE NO-PRIVACY PARENT

On the other end of the spectrum, and more publicly embarrassing, is the No-Privacy parent. This parent believes that anyone, often unsuspecting strangers or unlucky dinner guests, should be included in family disputes, even if—or especially if—they include the revelation of embarrassing and humiliating information about individual family members. Because teens are often sensitive about sharing any personal information beyond their name, most parents could be innocently accused of this parenting style, but there's a difference between giving factual information and telling your new best friend the gory details of the last fight you had with your daughter. Girls with this parent will go to great lengths to create privacy—usually by sneaking behind their parents' backs.

THE DON'T-ASK, DON'T-TELL PARENT

Through an unspoken agreement, the daughter doesn't tell the parent what's going on, and the parent doesn't ask. When parents feel unprepared and/or don't have the support they need, they often feel that ignorance is bliss. This makes for pleasant yet superficial conversations at the dinner table, but in the meantime, the daughter can be floundering.

THE LOVING HARD-ASS PARENT

Of course, this is my favorite parent. The one I aspire to be. Parents with this philosophy know there may be things their daughter hides from them, but they don't take it as a personal insult or an indication that their relationship with their daughter is weak. When they make mistakes, they own up to their behavior and right the wrong, and they encourage their daughter to do the same. They demonstrate that you can learn from mistakes and be better for it. They hold her accountable for decisions and behaviors that go against the family's values and ethics. When they're told that their daughter may have done something wrong, they listen and don't blame other people for their daughter's behavior. At the same time, they never make her feel ashamed of who she is. They also realize, especially as their children get older, that she may want to confide in someone else about a problem. This parent realizes that the most important goal is that their daughter has someone reliable and sane to talk to—even if it's not them.

Here are some things Loving Hard-Ass Parents do:

- If their daughter has done something really wrong, they go with her and apologize.
- They don't gossip about children while waiting in carpool lanes and watching athletic events.
- They laugh at their own mistakes and use them to inform better judgments in the future.
- They aren't quick to judge other parents.
- They are not afraid to admit when they feel overwhelmed or unsure about how to handle a difficult situation with their kids.

Being a Loving Hard-Ass Parent may be impossible to be all the time. I think of it like the Champion for the girls. We are striving to have Champion/Hard-Ass moments. And even the best parents among us can fall toward the too lenient (Pushover, Hip, and so forth) or too hard-ass (Privacy, No-Excuses, and so forth) sides of things once in awhile. But keep striving toward this Champion/

Hard-Ass ideal—one that allows both you and your daughter to make mistakes and to rise up from them.

> I hate to say it, but my parents really are pretty cool! And all the other parents I can think of that are cool are really very similar to mine. They're laid-back, but not oblivious or completely separate from my life. They trust me. They genuinely like me and like spending time with me. They know what goes on in my life, but they can take a hint when it's time for them to leave me alone. Of course there are the occasional fights or disagreements, but in the end, I think they only help make our family life stronger.
>
> —Julie, sixteen

WHAT YOUR DAUGHTERS WANT YOU TO KNOW

Frequently girls will ask me to share things with their parents that are too difficult to tell them themselves. Here are the girls' most common requests to tell you:

I wish my parents . . .
   Dropped me off and picked me up at places on time. This is a very big deal!
   Taught me more about my culture.
   Asked to meet my friends.
   Let go of stereotypes about other races and religions.
   Let me have the freedom to make more choices.
   Stopped worrying about my messy room.
   Were more patient with me.
   Paid more attention to their own lives.
   Understood that I want freedom, but we can still be close. I'm my own person.
   Wouldn't limit my abilities or who I am, and let me follow my intuition and be supportive.
   Knew I really want to make them proud of me.

And what do they really want me to tell you about how to communicate with her?

I wish my parents . . .

Had more real conversations with me.

Told me when they're proud of me.

Talked to me more about what I'm passionate about.

Understood that when I need to be left alone, my bedroom door is shut. This means I really need to be left alone. Your interference will only make me more irritated.

My parents need to know . . .

That sometimes we just want to vent, but that doesn't mean we want you to interfere.

I don't want them to email all the other parents about some problem I am having! It only makes it worse!

I do want to talk to you but not about everything. If it was my fault or I'm superinvolved, I'll probably wait until after it was resolved to tell you.

Sibling loyalty can be stronger than parental loyalty. I might not tell you something my siblings don't want you to know.

What works:

- When I have problems I go to my mom usually because she doesn't give me specific ways to deal with it; she says, "I have some suggestions."
- She always listens and pays attention. And she says, "I love you," even if I do something wrong. And she's read a lot of books.
- I feel more comfortable with my dad because with my dad he's not really "Let's go tell the teachers"; he's more like "Let's talk about this or try this to make it better." Often I go to my dad to complain about stuff because he listens. I can tell my dad anything.
- She gives me steps. She says, "If this doesn't work, then try that," and "What do you think will work better?"
- My dad makes me laugh. It makes me relax.
- Talking to my grandfather. I know he's older but he seems to understand what's going on.
- Talking to my babysitter. She doesn't give me advice. She

just listens to me and lets me figure it out. Plus, my mom's so involved in the school that I just can't.

What doesn't:
- My mom is so intense that I don't tell her much. If I do, it's when I see someone else do something I don't like. If I'm involved deeply, like it was my fault or I really made a mistake, then I don't tell because then she'll really be on my back. I only tell her things when I know she'd be happy that I've done the right thing.
- If I go to my mom, she tells me to stop whining.
- When I give my mom a situation, either she gets crazy or she immediately says we need to talk to your teacher or the principal.

WHERE IS YOUR VILLAGE?

Have you ever heard someone say "It takes a village to raise a child"? I've had the experience a lot, and every time I have to control myself not to roll my eyes.

OK. Yes, it takes a village to raise a child, but what exactly do we mean by that? Obviously we, the parents, are in the village, along with the people who make up our neighborhoods, our schools, our places of worship, our children's teams, and their after-school activities. But we talk about this village as if everyone loves and trusts everyone else within it, and that's just not true. Sometimes we don't like other people in the village and don't think they are a good influence on our children. Sometimes there are people in our village who are not nice people. Sometimes we jump to conclusions and get mad at other people in the village when we really shouldn't—or at least we should give them the benefit of the doubt.

The bottom line for me is that unless we have a specific experience that indicates a "villager" is insane or badly intentioned, we need to assume that people are doing their best and have good intentions . . . and then speak to them with this front and center in our mind when we are communicating with them.

So when you think about who makes up your village, here are three things to keep in mind.

1. Identify the characteristics you value most in your fellow villagers. Mine are: They treat kids with dignity, they are comfortable calling them out when they do something boneheaded, they don't gossip or bad-mouth other children, they support other parents in their time of need, they're warmhearted (they can still be tough on the outside), they're not pushovers, they laugh when kids make "foolish" mistakes, and—most important—they know my children and still like them.

2. With these characteristics in mind, try to identify two people who have the most of these attributes in each of your smaller villages: your child's school, your neighborhood, your friends, your family, adults involved in your children's extracurricular activities (that includes coaches, of course).

3. Make a list of these people. You don't have to go up to each one and tell them they've officially made your villagers list, but write them down so you don't forget them when you need them most.

THE APPLE DOESN'T FALL FAR FROM THE TREE

I am the co-leader of a Girl Scout Troop and our girls are Cadettes (seventh and eighth grade), and have been together since Daisys (kindergarten). New girls have come along almost each year, and most have stayed. The newest girl is being ignored and avoided at best and shunned and dumped on by the Queen Bee daughter of the Queen Bee troop leader. I am horrified. I am angry at myself because I did not/cannot do more to help Irene. I am angry at the other adults for being clueless, or unwilling to see. After an overwhelming desire to resign as a tactic to avoid the discomfort and pain ... I now know that I have to stay and effect change.

—Mary

My eight-year-old daughter had just started at a new school when the mother of a Queen Bee approached me. She wanted

to invite my daughter to her daughter's birthday party, but she told me to keep it quiet because the two other new girls hadn't been invited. For a moment I was elated that my daughter had made the cut, but then I realized both my daughter and I were being co-opted by the clique. I was so torn. I wanted my daughter to be included, but at what price?

—Roger

I know it's really tempting. When you see a horrible Queen Bee girl, it's natural to look at the mother and draw conclusions that she's a Queen Bee, too. It's also true that sometimes these women make it way too easy to make this assumption. However, I think we need to let go of the "After all, the apple doesn't fall far from the tree" assumption. I don't think that's a helpful way to think about it. When we say that, we blame the mom entirely for her daughter's behavior. Not cool. Also, we never say the same things about girls in any other position in the group, so why just a Queen Bee matriarchy?

It's now time to ask yourself some difficult questions. What is your daughter (or the girls you work with) learning from you? Are you talking about other people in a way that you're proud of? When you run up against a Queen Bee parent, how do you react? Do you want your daughter acting the same way? Are there girls you want your daughter to be friends with (or not) because of social status? Are you living according to your values—not just when things are easy and you're getting along with people, but when it's hard? When you're so angry that the last thing you want to do is treat someone with dignity? When you're so intimidated or nervous to confront a situation that you want to run away? If you want to help your daughter navigate her friendships and peer interactions in a way you can be proud of, you have to look at how you navigate your own. And where better than your relationship with her?

YOUR PARENTAL BILL OF RIGHTS

- What do you need in your relationship with your daughter? *I have the right to get the information I need to keep my daughter safe.*

- What are your responsibilities to your daughter? *I'm responsible for helping her become an independent adult through being a good role model and holding her accountable for her actions.*
- Under what circumstances would you ask someone to help you with a problem you're having with your daughter? *When I believe it's too uncomfortable for my daughter to talk to me, or the issues she's tackling are making me so crazy and anxious that my input would only make the problem worse.*
- Does your daughter know your answers to these questions? *I'm not sure, but I should find out.*

Your daughter also needs a Bill of Rights with you. Here are some questions she can answer.

YOUR DAUGHTER'S BILL OF RIGHTS WITH YOU

- What do you need in your relationship with your parent(s)?
- What are your responsibilities to your parent(s)?
- Under what circumstances would you ask someone for help with a problem you are having with your parent(s)?

THE ALLY

Girls can have feelings or experiences that they don't want to share with their mom or dad. It's actually pretty common. The problem is that sometimes it's really helpful and important to tell an adult what's going on. Even if you have a great relationship with your daughter, she may want to turn to someone else sometimes. Please don't take it as a rejection or as a statement that you don't know how to handle your parenting business. I call this person an "ally." He or she can be a trusted relative (perhaps an older sibling, aunt, or uncle), another parent in the neighborhood, a teacher, a member of the clergy, a coach, or a guidance counselor. Basically, this ally is an all-star on the villagers list.

The following is a list of the qualities of a good ally. If your daughter goes to someone with these qualities for advice, then she's going to the right person and showing that she has good

relationships with other adults. You should be proud of her for exhibiting good judgment. A good ally is:

- Opinionated but not judgmental
- Honest and willing to say things that may be hard for your daughter to hear
- Reliable and always ready to set aside time to listen to your daughter

There's nothing wrong with you reaching out to an ally as well. It's probably inevitable that your daughter will face a situation that's guaranteed to trigger your specific anxieties that prevent you from being able to think clearly. If you cannot exert clear judgment about your daughter's situation because of your own investment in the matter, go get an ally to help. Both you and your daughter will be grateful.

Please remember you aren't a bad parent if your child goes to someone for help. The following story demonstrates how allies can bring a parent closer to their child. I received an email from a thirteen-year-old girl who needed advice telling her widowed dad that she had gotten her period and needed extra money to buy tampons. She was too embarrassed to tell him, and he couldn't figure out why their conversations were ending up in fights and crying. As part of my advice, I suggested she tell a woman she was close to what the problem was so they could go to a store and get what she needed. The girl took my advice and talked to her older cousin, who immediately took her to the drugstore and bought her a six-month supply of tampons. But the cousin also told her mom (the sister of the dad), and then I got this letter.

> I feel like a bit of a fool that my own kid had to write to a stranger for help. She was the little girl who began her period. I guess I am what you call old-fashioned. I run a construction company full of men. My daughter has really been one of the guys till now. I forgot she has different issues than her brothers. But over the past few months, there have been tears and attitude and eye-rolling. I was scared she was trying drugs, but her brothers assure me she is not part of that crowd. Last

*year she got me a Homer Simpson T-shirt on my birthday
and I am afraid this is pretty much the level of sensitivity
and intelligence you're dealing with. Thanks for giving her
good advice.*

—Frank

If your daughter doesn't need encouragement to find her ally, great. But for some girls, it might be unclear where to go in a time of crisis. You and your daughter can work together to find her an ally. Sit down together, each of you with a piece of paper and something to write with. Tell your daughter to think of all the adults she is close to in your family, at school, or in your neighborhood and to come up with a list of people she thinks are cool and smart enough that she would want to talk to them about important things going on in her life. While she does that, I want you to write down the list of adults you trust to give you good advice. When you're finished, compare your lists. Ideally there would be someone who is on both of your lists, and that's the person to ask to be your daughter's ally—someone with whom she can talk on a regular basis for big and little stuff and who can help her think through difficult problems. The agreement is that these conversations are going to be kept confidential unless her physical safety is at risk.

An ally is also great when life gets overwhelming for you or your daughter. Sometimes your family can go through a storm of problems like Catherine explains below, but as hard as it was, she looked for an ally and found one:

In eighth grade, my daughter lost her three best friends, I was diagnosed with breast cancer, and her dog died suddenly. Mia started to go downhill with depression and anxiety and I needed to find someone. I thought of her older cousin but a relative wasn't going to work. I thought of a friend of mine that she had known since she was born but that was just too close. Then the answer came. In the mail Mia and I received two gift cards for having our nails done together. It was in October, which was national breast care awareness month and they were from Colleen, who was the mom of a schoolmate. I

called Colleen to thank her for the gift cards and to ask her if she would consider being that go-to person for Mia. She immediately said yes. That was the beginning of an incredible relationship between my daughter and Colleen. Colleen has done things like coming over at seven o'clock in the morning to get Mia up and get her to school. Sometimes it was the only way Mia would go to school because we, her parents, weren't able to get it done. Mia would fight us about going to school but she didn't fight with Colleen. It was like magic. Colleen would go up to her room and down Mia would come dressed and ready to go. Mia loves that she can tell Colleen anything. It's a great supportive relationship. It's hard to put into words what Colleen has done for Mia and for our family. She is Mia's guardian angel and cheerleader who will always be there. Mia can now rely on herself and her own coping skills when things get tough. This wouldn't have happened without Colleen. Now when people tell me that their daughter is struggling I tell them that they need to find "a Colleen."

—Catherine

YOU AREN'T A FAILURE

Many parents I work with tell me they feel like a failure when their daughter struggles so much and so often. Or they hear me say something in a presentation that is different from what they've done. Please let go of all that. The only way you can fail is if you don't try, you disconnect from her and her world, you don't hold her accountable for her behavior, or you don't teach her and model empathy, thoughtfulness, critical thinking, and the belief that everyone deserves to be treated with dignity. Be kind to yourself. Parenting is often overwhelming, and few of us are taught to develop effective coping skills.

It's so hard for us [parents] to be reflective. It's too painful to be aware of our choices—what we've given up and what they've embraced. When I look at my own daughter, I often feel like a failure. I feel responsible and guilty that I can't fix

her pain, I can't fix society overnight, and I can't find her the help she needs.

—Kara

There's so much shame when your daughter has problems. Other parents talk about their kids' activities and school. It's so hard to discuss what's going on because I feel different and that everyone else is perfect. Part of me knows better and part of me wonders.

—Michaela

I went to a couple of parent meetings and talked about the problems my daughter was having with other girls. All I got was stony silence or people being nice in a patronizing way by expressing sympathy at best, but never suggesting that what I or my daughter are going through has ever happened to them or their daughters. Never did I hear "I know what you mean—this happened to my daughter." So I felt like a freak, and didn't trust what other parents would say about her, so I shut my mouth.

—Susan

I went to a parenting class and I was really glad I went. Not just for the strategies I learned but because so many parents were going through the same problems.

—Belle

You are not alone. If you reach out, you will find a community of parents that will support you through the hardest moments. You will find the village you need.

Breaking Through the Wall

My mom told me, "I got through it, you will too." It doesn't feel like that. You're not in it so you don't know.

—Lily, thirteen

The more questions you ask the less likely you'll get an honest answer. Because at that point we just want you to go away.

—Lauren, fourteen

She gets into the car and you can tell she's in a bad mood. Maybe it's the way she slammed the door. So you ask her what any loving parent would: "Is everything OK?"

"It's fine," she spits out, crossing her arms and staring out the window.

"Are you sure?"

"Sure, Mom, everything's great—never been better."

"Do you want to talk about it?" you hesitantly inquire, trying not to flinch.

"It really doesn't matter. I just want to go home."

You sigh. Unfortunately, you can't take her home right now because you promised another parent that you'd cover your younger son's pickup after practice. You sigh again. This situation is going

to get worse because there are about to be three eleven-year-old boys in the car. You look at her and dread what her reaction is going to be.

You know how parents say "Life's not fair" to their kids? Well, let's apply that here. Parenting isn't fair. When your daughter is upset or angry, it can feel like you're given one chance with very limited information to say exactly the right thing. If you don't get it right, her expression says *"This is why I never tell you anything. And now I will never tell you anything again."*

Your chances of getting it right are about on par with winning Powerball. Except it's worse, because the stakes are higher. When you play the lottery, you're only out a couple of dollars, and no one makes you feel stupid for not picking the right numbers. But when you don't get the "numbers" right with your child, not only do you often feel incompetent, but there's a possibility you are shutting her down or pushing her away when she really needs guidance and comfort.

Or . . . maybe your daughter is completely different than I just described. Maybe she tells you every detail of her day, and you'd like her to tell you just a little bit less. There you are trying your hardest to pay attention to the minutia of her conversation with a group of girls after fourth period and it takes all your willpower not to say, *"Please God get to the point!"*

Either way, problems with other girls, cliques, and boys are the most common challenges girls have. But because most girls can be reluctant to admit to their parents when they're struggling, we're going to begin with girls' top reasons for keeping you in the dark:

1. She believes that talking to you may make the situation worse.
2. She doesn't want you to get angry with her or start lecturing her.
3. She doesn't want you to get angry with the person she's having a problem with because then you won't let her hang out with that person anymore, or she'll have to hide from you the fact that she is.
4. She doesn't want you to think she has bad judgment.

5. She doesn't want to hear the reasons you think she has bad judgment.
6. She doesn't want you to worry.
7. She doesn't want you to take over.
8. She doesn't want you to take away her technology.

We have to convince girls that while we don't need to know every detail of their personal lives, it's not an entirely terrible idea to let us in once in a while. In fact, there's a possibility that we can help. But here's the problem. While it's true that we want to emotionally connect with our children, we can sometimes get in our own way. Our worry and concern can stop us from really seeing them or how they're responding to our well-meaning efforts. Without meaning to, we force bonding moments, micromanage, judge, assume, lecture, or try to control. Ironically, as our girls push us away, what they want most is for us to recognize and acknowledge them.

First, let's look at one of the classic dynamics between children and their parents. It's the "You're embarrassing me!" complaint. It's more than fine to "embarrass" your daughter in a good way: As in, you model how to treat people with dignity when it's hard, you respectfully speak out when she'd rather you keep your opinions to yourself, and you show you are comfortable making a fool of yourself.

Examples of "Good" Embarrassment
1. Giving her a hug or kiss in public.
2. Singing along to the radio, even driving carpool.
3. Apologizing on her behalf when she's in the wrong but she's having a hard time seeing it that way.
4. Signing up to be a chaperone at the school dance and then enforcing the rules . . . and maybe even dancing.

But these are not the only ways we embarrass our kids, and this is where it starts getting a lot harder for us. Sometimes we lose sight of how we're coming across. We blow off our children's complaints because they seem to be embarrassed by everything

we do. While it's hard to admit, our kids have the right to be angry if we discuss their personal lives. They don't want to be labeled and dismissed as moody. They want you to respect their privacy, and that means treating them respectfully in public. Here are the ways parents negatively embarrass their kids, and if you see it from their perspective, I think you'll agree . . . they have every reason to be frustrated.

Introducing Your Child by Deficits

Imagine if your kid introduced you by saying, "This is my mother, Rosalind. She's really shy." Yes, she might be shy, but apologizing to strangers for what you see as your child's flaws because you're anxious about it makes her even more self-conscious than she's already feeling. Teach her how to introduce herself and make her own impression.

TEACHING HER GREETINGS

When she's around five to seven, teach her how to shake hands firmly, make eye contact, and say the basics in social situations, such as, "Nice to meet you." "Thank you for inviting me." "Goodbye and thanks for having me." First role-play it with her several times. Then, when you're going somewhere together, explain that you'll introduce yourself first and then she'll follow. If she's feeling shy, that's OK. Any part she does is a success and will make you proud of her. If she falters, don't make excuses for her with the other person. Afterward, praise her for a small thing she did successfully and then role-play three times what she can do better next time. When you congratulate her, she'll be proud of being mature. By the time she's ten, she should be able to do it herself. You may have to remind her a few hundred times, but the building blocks will be there. If you are off to a late start and she is already fourteen and struggles to introduce herself, start now—teach her a handshake, introduction, and eye contact. She doesn't have to be fake or bubbly. You can even have her think of one backup question she can ask the person to minimize the awkwardness.

Oversharing

"It's amazing how early puberty starts these days! I went bra shopping with Katie last weekend and she's in a B cup!"

You shouldn't be talking to people about your child's physical development, the latest fight you got into with her, or her latest accomplishment or failure as if it's a part of her identity. This includes people in the grocery checkout line, people at parties, strangers you strike up a conversation with, or even good friends if your child is around. When you're having a problem that you really want to talk to another adult about, do it privately—away from your child.

If you're guilty of any of the above, go to your child and say, "I've realized that sometimes I talk for you and don't give you the opportunity to speak for yourself. From now on, I'm going to really try to stop myself. But if I don't, I want you to say politely, 'Mom/Dad, it's OK. I've got it.' I promise I'll stop. If I overshare, you can politely tell me to stop, and I will."

I know we all fall back on talking about our kids, but can we try to give it a rest? Do you have any hobbies? Are you doing anything interesting? You have your own life separate from your children, and there's nothing wrong with talking about that. It's actually pretty cool. And it's really good for your child to have interesting parents with their own interests and passions.

"Having a Moment"

Have you ever temporarily lost your mind and succumbed to being an anxious or overinvolved, self-righteous mess of a parent? Honestly, I haven't met a parent who at some point hasn't done this. The key is to recognize when you're "having a moment," and then change it up. Otherwise, you risk setting a bad example for your daughter and making her feel she should be apologizing for *your* behavior.

Examples of "Having a Moment"

1. Yelling obscenities during a game or verbally attacking anyone on the field or in the bleachers.
2. Gossiping about other children.
3. Approaching another parent, coach, teacher, camp counselor, or school administrator and immediately launching into the

problem you need to discuss without saying hello or giving them any kind of introduction to what you need to discuss. (I've done this, only to stop myself mid-rant, pause, and say, "Wait, I'm sorry. Can I start that again? Good morning! Can I talk to you for a minute?")

Even if you have the best of intentions, in my experience your "enthusiasm" results in your child being so overwhelmed by your reaction that they won't go to you again because they're so worried you'll get out of control.

LanD Mine!

Avoid comparing your daughter to other people. It's not motivating and makes her feel like she has to hide information from you. These are some of the most common examples people have shared with me:

"Your friend got an A, and you got a C. How is that possible?"

"How did your friends do?"

"Couldn't you have studied more? Couldn't you have gotten a better grade on that?"

"We never had these problems with your sister/brother."

"If you just applied yourself, you would succeed."

"Your brother may get it quicker, but if you work harder and put in the time, then you'll be just as successful as him."

OK, YOU WANT TO TALK TO HER ... WHY?

In general, there are four common parent communication agendas.

1. Genuine curiosity—we want to know what's going on in their lives.
2. We want them to pay attention when we need them to do something.

3. We're worried that something bad is happening to them and we want them to talk to us.

4. We're worried they are doing or going to do something stupid, wrong, or dangerous. We need to know what's up to minimize the damage and/or hold them accountable.

All of these agendas intertwine to impact our relationship with our girls. Our seemingly inconsequential daily conversations matter. They're the foundation of our relationships. If we can't listen to each other in the small moments, we'll never listen to each other in the big ones. Notice I said "Listen to each other."

I define "listening" as being prepared to be changed by what you hear. A conversation is a two-way road. If you want a good relationship with your daughter, you have to listen to her, not preach, and respect her world. While her overall concerns and challenges are largely the same as when you were her age, she's really living in a different world than you did. You lived in a time when you had the luxury of making common adolescent mistakes in relative privacy. She doesn't. When you were a teen, your most embarrassing and humiliating moments weren't up for public discussion and entertainment. Every picture taken of you wasn't up for debate about how cute or ugly you looked. Take a second and remember a moment from when you were her age that you'd never want anyone to know about. She's living that moment in public. There's no protection. There's no privacy. This is her regular, ever-present reality. Your daughter is growing up with a different definition of what's public and what's private.

Agenda 1: You Just Want to Know What's Up

No matter what the situation, if there's one thing all teens I work with agree on, it's this: When parents barrage their children with a torrent of questions at first sight, kids completely tune out and answer with the most uninformative responses they can think of in the hope that the adults will give up. I've repeatedly explained to girls that parents usually have good intentions. We love our daughters and want to know what's going on in their lives. We also believe that knowing the details of their daily lives will strengthen our relationship. But here's what the girls have explained to me:

As soon as we parents see our daughters, we overwhelm them. Whether it's when we pick them up from school or after practice or when we walk into the house from work, our questions feel like a physical assault.

Here's how I want you to approach the challenge of finding out about your daughter's day: Take a step back. When she's at school, she's part of a complicated social dynamic with many different kinds of people. Even on the best of days, dealing with all of this can be emotionally and physically exhausting. To get through it, your daughter develops her own personal brand of armor and wears it throughout the day.

None of this excuses bad behavior. She doesn't get to be rude to you in response to your well-meaning inquiries. Nor does she get to text constantly all of her friends that she just left, or keep her earbuds or headphones in the whole time, either. But all that said, I just want you to see it from her perspective so you can enjoy each other's company and create an environment where pleasant, even meaningful, conversation is possible.

Your goal is to make the first few minutes stress-free. If you do this, she'll be much more likely to tell you about how her day was on her own. Try asking no questions when you see her. Let her choose the music—within reason, of course. Experiment with what makes her feel at ease, and do your best to match those conditions.

If you have the child who wants to tell you "everything" and you're good with that, then by all means let her go for it. You also may want to guide her a little to pick and choose. Wait for her to take a breath and then ask, "What was the weirdest/most interesting/surprising thing to you about . . . ?" And if she's telling you everything that happened to her and not picking up on your cues that you want her to get to the point, there's a chance she's speaking the same way to other girls—and other girls don't usually like that.

The Most Common and That Usually Go Nowhere Parent Questions

1. *Seeing your daughter right after school:* "How was your day? What did you learn? Anything interesting?"

2. *Picking up/seeing your daughter after practice:* "How was practice? What did you do? Was it hard? Did you score? Did you win? Did you try your best?"

3. *Picking up your daughter at a party (ages five to twelve):* "What did you do? Did you have fun? Did you have a good time? Who else was there?"

4. *Picking up or seeing your daughter after a party (ages thirteen to eighteen):* "Who was there? Were the parents home? Did you talk to them? Did everyone behave?"

5. *Seeing your daughter in general, coming back home at night:* "Where'd you go? What'd you do? Who was there? Was it fun?"

> Being asked too many questions in general just drives me crazy. If I just got back from some sort of event, I'm most likely at least somewhat emotionally drained so asking me a million questions is really annoying, and it's the fastest way to tick me off.
>
> —Callista, fifteen

Creating Non-Cheesy Quality Time (Well, She Still May Think It's Cheesy, but She'll Do It)

If you're looking for ways to connect with your daughter, the general rule is that it can't feel forced. You can ask her what she wants to do. The goal is to do something else while you're having the conversation or be fine hanging out with her without carrying on an intense conversation at all. Girls really do bond with you when you do things together. Whether you're a mom or dad, or a supportive adult, being quiet with a girl by going on a walk or out to coffee, working on something together, playing soccer or basketball, volunteering as a pair, driving and listening to music, or just hanging out in the same room reading can all be meaningful bonding moments without a lot of words exchanged. Don't be afraid of silence. With all the noise we get from TV, phones, and everything else, we can forget how great silence is.

Plus, remember, if your daughter is too young to drive, you're probably her key to accessing the things she loves. Say she's really into soccer or basketball—take her to a game. Is she's really into

graphic novels? Take her to a convention. Maybe she likes making her own clothes and accessories. Offer to take her to one of the local craft fairs. You don't have to have some deep conversation on the way there or back. Just taking her there is appreciated—and you don't need to buy her anything.

Ideally, once in a while, try to take your daughter out to a coffee shop or some other place she likes to go where the two of you can sit down and hang out, away from other siblings and distractions. Take her to school one day and leave early so you can stop for bagels. Avoid going to a place where either one of you may run into someone you know. At any point, but especially in the beginning, refrain from making any comments about what she's wearing, homework she's supposed to be doing, or the room she's supposed to be cleaning. Don't talk about schedules, upcoming events, or things you need to get information about—unless she brings it up. Just as important, watch out for land mine remarks such as "You should wear your hair pulled back like that more often. You're so pretty when you can see your face."

Get your daughter her favorite drink, and don't make faces when she orders something you think is disgusting or unhealthy. (That's another talk.) Sit down at a table she chooses, get comfortable, and start: "Thanks for getting up early today so we could do this. There's really no pressure to do or say anything. We just don't get a lot of time to talk without a million things going on at the same time so I thought we could spend some time together and you can tell me what you feel comfortable with. So what's up with X?"

If she just sits there for a while and it looks like that's the way it'll stay, remind her there's no pressure so it's totally acceptable for the two of you to just sit together and read. But just one rule: She can't use technology. No games on her cellphone or texting her friends.

Mark these get-togethers in your calendar; they're unbreakable dates. You want to establish a pattern that says you're there for her, that you don't get involved only when there's a problem, and that you're capable of having a conversation that doesn't revolve around your role as the enforcer or logistics coordinator. The

younger your daughter is when you start these one-on-one conversations, the more she'll see that you're someone she can turn to when she needs support.

If your daughter doesn't want to hang out with you the way she used to, that can feel like a deeply painful rejection. Try to stay away from using the phrase "spending time together." As in, "I'd just like to spend some time together," or, "We should spend some time together," or, even worse, "I feel like I don't see you enough anymore." Instead, ask, "Do you want to go to lunch?" Lunch has a definite beginning and end. Plus, you're feeding her. If you have an older teen, lunch is good because it's not at night, so there's no chance it'll interfere with her social plans. If you do ask her if she wants to do something at night and she responds with "I don't know, it depends on what's going on," don't take it personally. She's suffering from FOMO: fear of missing out. That's not an acceptable excuse for her to bail on previous obligations, but I just want you to realize her motivation.

Eventually, you'll get answers from her if you set up a comfortable environment and listen respectfully. Even if she complains later to her friends, believe me, she will appreciate your effort. If, however, you've never done something like this before, expect her to say something during this talk that sets your teeth on edge. She's your daughter so she's an expert button pusher. Let's say she reacts to your overture by being obnoxious. Take a deep breath and remember your goal for the conversation: to connect. For example, she might say disdainfully, "Why do you care all of a sudden? Are you feeling guilty because you're never around? Don't think you can be parent for a day and I'll start telling you things . . . because that's not happening." At this moment, you may wonder why you bothered. Instead of shutting down and fighting with her, ask, "Do you really feel that way? Because if you do, I really need to hear why you think that." Then be prepared to listen.

If you take this advice and try several times to "spontaneously" get your daughter to do something and she always says no, then you have to switch your strategy. If she keeps pushing you away, then you're within your rights to sit her down and ask what's up.

Creating Quiet Private Time

In general, a great time to talk to younger girls is when they're in bed, the lights are out, and you can talk for a few minutes before they go to sleep. For older girls, night is also good. Of course, when we have older girls it can be hard to keep our eyes open past ten P.M. and our girls are still doing homework (and talking to friends). But try to manage once every two weeks to stay up and drop by her room. Your goal is connection. That's it. So stand at her door and say, "Just want to check in." If she says, "I'm fine," give her a kiss or a hug and call it a day. If she does want to talk or she starts telling you something really intense, don't freak out. Go to page 108 for advice on what to say when your daughter reveals a problem she's struggling with. For girls of any age, it's better if you can have these conversations with the lights off, because if she's telling you something really intense, seeing your facial expressions can be really stressful.

> Also, letting you see HER facial expressions is more stressful, too.
>
> —Sophie, sixteen

Agenda 2: You Need for Her to Pay Attention

Now let's move on to a scenario where you go from being in a great mood to a highly irritated one—the moment when you walk through the door with two armfuls of groceries and your phone is buzzing in your pocket and you see her sitting on the couch texting her friends. She glances over at you, sees your distress with no sympathy in her eyes, and goes back to texting. I know how irritating it is to come home from a long day of work or to walk in the door weighed down with the shopping to see your daughter's eyes glued to a screen. Seriously, wouldn't any decent person in your daughter's place leap off the couch to help you? What kind of horrible child have you raised? Does she want you to yell at her? Apparently she does, because she doesn't move. You look at the dog who is desperate to be walked, the trash that obviously needs to be taken out, and her backpack and its contents slung across the floor, and it appears as if you don't exist. Of course you get annoyed and think she's a spoiled, ungrateful, lazy brat. So you

start shooting questions at her like "Have you done your home-work?" "How was your test today?" "Did you bring in that form you've forgotten three times already for the field trip next week?" Using the *"I'm so annoyed that I should get a parenting prize for not screaming at you right now"* tone of voice.

As hard as this is (and I admit it's very hard), I'm asking that you think of the situation from her perspective. Imagine coming home from work every day and your child waiting at the door to bombard your vulnerabilities with questions. "What did you get done at work? Do you have more to do? Do you have more emails you need to look at? Were people nice to you at the office? Isn't that big project due tomorrow?" All you want to do is sit down for a few minutes, and the barrage of commentary about your lazi-ness is not appreciated. Well, it's the same for your kids.

Let's take a step back. You don't need to know anything about your daughter's school obligations at the exact moment you walk in the door. You do need her butt off the couch, helping with the grocery bags. You need the poor dog walked. In moments like these, humor and action are essential. You can start by walking over and putting the grocery bags on her lap. Or tell her she can choose between walking the dog or cleaning up the rug after the dog has had an accident on the carpet. What you absolutely shouldn't do is use the martyr strategy. It's passive-aggressive, you'll get resentful, and all she'll think is that you're annoying. Even if it gets her to take in the grocery bags, this strategy hurts you in the long run because your daughter will lose respect for you. Don't get me wrong: Our girls need to pull their weight and develop a sense of responsibility. But we have to ask ourselves if the way we're communicating is effective. If you lose her respect, you can't be a credible authority figure to her. So before you hone in on her, take a few minutes to unwind.

There are plenty of other chores that turn into power struggles. Say you tell your daughter to take out the trash, which is a com-pletely reasonable request. She says that she will do it in a minute, and you blow up at her and give her an even bigger chore. This sort of scenario can really undermine a girl's relationship with her parents. Of course, it's possible that she's told you before that she'd take care of something and then forgot. It's also possible that you

and she have different definitions of what "soon" or "in a minute" mean. Nevertheless, these small conflicts can have a highly
negative impact on your daughter. Many, many girls respond to
these situations with anger, frustration, and ultimately resignation
because all they hear is that they're lazy, ungrateful, and irresponsible. If we want our children to listen to us, we have to really
acknowledge why they don't.

When you get angry with her without acknowledging or understanding her position, you actually come across as disrespectful.
A lot of people would disagree with that, believing that parents
always have the right to demand what they want and say what they
like to their children. Were you raised to respect your elders? If
you're having a hard time with how I'm approaching this situation
or thinking that I'm coddling your daughters, here's another way
of looking at it.

"Respect" in Latin means "to look at someone's conduct and
admire them." When people say to kids "Respect your elders,"
they're really saying "Obey your elders." But the amazing thing is
that kids inherently know the real meaning of respect, and far too
often they see adults who don't merit it—not only public figures,
such as hypocritical politicians and athletes, but the adults they
interact with on a daily basis. It also could be a school administrator, a school resource officer, a teacher, a coach, or a clergyperson.
For some girls it could be one of their parents. Our children know
that they can't depend on adults to do the right thing just because
they're adults. All of these experiences contribute to this powerful
feeling among young people that there aren't many adults who
they can truly respect.

Still not convinced? Think of the worst boss you've ever had.
You know the one—that jerk who was just awful to work for. How
did she treat you? Did she treat you with respect? Or did she assume that because she was in a position of authority, she could
be as disrespectful as she wanted to be to those under her? I'm
guessing she didn't treat you with respect, and I'm also guessing
you didn't like it very much. Well, if you didn't like being treated
in a disrespectful manner by an authority figure, why would your
daughter feel any differently?

Many girls understandably rebel against hypocrisy. When this

happens with parents, the power struggle can be about anything, big or small. What usually happens is that she gets angry and bottles up her rage. When she finally explodes she looks immature (slamming the door perhaps), and that infuriates her even more because she knows it confirms the negative image her parent has of her. What a girl wants to know is how to formulate an argument and not be accused of talking back; otherwise, she'll end up shutting down.

HOW TO STOP THE EYE-ROLLING

If your daughter excels in the art of eye-rolling or sighing, this may be annoying to you. Here's my suggestion for addressing the problem. At base, your daughter wants something from you—either she wants you to do something or she wants you to appreciate her opinion. This is what you say:

"Sydney, here's the deal. You want X from me. When you roll your eyes and sigh when I'm speaking, there's no chance you'll get what you want out of me because your behavior is so irritating. But if we can have this conversation without eye-rolling, there's a chance we can come to some kind of agreement. Eye-rolling, you have no chance. No eye-rolling, you have a shot. So excuse yourself, think about what I've said, and when you're ready, we can have the conversation again."

Of course, sometimes eye-rolling happens when you want them to do something, not when they're coming to you with a favor to ask. Teenage girls are masters of making your requests seem like Herculean labor. As long as they aren't overtly rude and they're doing what you tell them, ignore the eye-rolls and foot-dragging. As annoying as it is, they're generally just trying to goad you into an argument as a way to avoid doing what they have to do. If they really want to discuss it with you, schedule the argument for after they complete your request. I do it all the time with my sons. I schedule arguments for later in the day because it always seems like these fights happen when they have chores to do or we need to leave the house.

Agenda 3: You're Worried Something's Wrong

When you're worried about your daughter, your first goal is to encourage her to share her thoughts or feelings, and to demonstrate that you're a nonjudgmental listener (note that I didn't say "nonopinionated") and a good resource for advice and comfort if necessary. If you can create this foundation, it will get you to the second goal: helping her develop critical thinking skills so that she can come up with realistic strategies to confront her problems effectively. You'll never accomplish the second goal without the first.

Unfortunately, you can't depend on your daughter to come to you when she's upset. The older she gets, the less she'll want to involve you in her problems (often because she considers you a main source of them, or she thinks you won't be able to help her). If your daughter wants to talk to you but couches it as "no big deal," don't believe her. If she actually wants to talk to you, she's already telling you that she thinks it's a big deal; she just doesn't want you to freak out. Any time your daughter wants to talk, pay attention. And if she doesn't say anything, she will send some signals that she wants your help without actually saying it. Here are some signs to watch for:

1. She hangs around where you are but doesn't say anything.
2. She says she doesn't feel well and wants to stay home, but there doesn't seem to be anything physically wrong.
3. You're about to drive somewhere on an errand, and she volunteers to go with you.
4. She asks to watch a show with you.
5. She slips a casual reference to her problem into the conversation.
6. She begins to revert back to younger behavior.
7. She tries to get other people out of the house except you.

LanD Mine!

If your daughter does any of these things, don't immediately lean in and intensely ask, "Is there anything wrong?" or "What's bothering you?" Just a casual "What's up? Anything you want to tell me?" is good. If she says no, follow it up with "OK, but if you change your mind, I'm here."

How to Respond When Your Daughter Tells You She's Having a Problem

Don't act like a truth cop. Don't ask her a million questions right away in an attempt to verify the accuracy of everything she tells you. Don't barrage her with questions about who was there, where were the adults, what did she do, and so forth. The facts will come out over time, but your daughter's emotional truth is what is important, and you should support that.

Don't force the Hallmark moment. If you go into a conversation with your daughter expecting that she'll completely open up to you, thank you for reaching out, and give you a hug, you're setting the bar way too high. The very nature of having the conversation can be so intense for your daughter that all she can do right afterward is walk into her room and listen to music.

Don't use the slang your daughter uses. There's nothing more ridiculous to a teen than an adult who tries to be hip by using teen slang. Slang changes so fast that it's impossible to keep up anyway. Nevertheless, some parents think that if they use it, they'll relate to their daughter better. Not true. It only looks like you're trying too hard (remember the Hip Parent?), and there's nothing worse to a teen. If she uses a word you don't understand, ask her to explain it to you. She may laugh at you, but it shows that you're really listening and you want to fully understand what she is describing.

Selectively share your own stories from when you were her age. That means don't start conversations with "When I played soccer," "When I was in high school," or "When I was applying to college." Instead, share something in response to something she's talking to you about. Perhaps try out, "Maybe I went through a similar experience, too."

That said, maintain boundaries by trying to avoid telling her stories about your adult experiences. Even though the purpose of such storytelling is to empathize ("I know what you've been through because something similar happened to me"), be careful not to preach or make it about yourself as an

adult. Your friend problems as an adult will likely not have the same tone or context as your daughter's friend problems. Keep the focus on what she is going through.

Don't tell her how you would have handled the situation unless she asks you. You're different from her. Maybe you're extroverted, or you've developed the skills to advocate for yourself, while she's more introverted. If she shares something with you and you respond with "You should have" or "Why didn't you?" you'll come across as telling her that whatever she did wasn't good enough. Develop a plan for going forward, instead of making her feel that she has already doomed herself.

Don't say things that only increase her anxiety. For instance, avoid saying things like "Whatever you do now will affect the rest of your life" or "This is your future we're talking about." Girls already feel this pressure.

Stop trying to fix the problem. Sometimes your daughter just wants to voice her concerns about something and isn't looking to fix it right away. Ask her, "Are you telling me because you want to get it off your chest, or do you want advice? You can always change your mind, but I just want to be clear about what you want right now." If you don't know if you're a "fixer" kind of person, ask your spouse or your siblings. And don't argue with them if they say you're a fixer.

If she asks for advice, don't turn it around and say, "What would you like me to say? What do you think is best?" Yes, you want your child to think through her problems, but when she actually asks you what you think, she really is asking you. She wants you to be the adult and tell her what you think. Don't assume she is going to agree with you exactly, or that she will follow your advice word for word, but do trust that she will take your opinion into account and use it to help her decide her course of action.

Give her ownership of what she does (both good and bad) and let her make mistakes. Unless she's going to do something that will hurt herself or others, the fact that it's her idea means that she's working toward independence. Encouraging that

is more important than making sure she tries the "best" (that is, *your*) solution.

Remember to accept silence. You're her parent. This means that when you discuss difficult or uncomfortable topics with your daughter, she may not respond right away. Don't think you always need to fill the silence. You can ask her about it after a while by saying "You got really quiet when we talked about X. Why was that?"

Don't make fun of her problems. You may be tempted to make fun of the situation in a well-meaning attempt to make her realize that her problem isn't the end of the world. If you do, you will look like you're mocking her. Of course, you might understand that elementary school drama will not carry throughout your daughter's life, but nonetheless, treat her reality with respect. Keep the joking comments to yourself and substitute supportive questions.

Here's what to say when your daughter approaches you with a problem:

"I'm so sorry that happened."

"Thank you for telling me."

"Together we're going to think through a strategy where you feel that you have regained some control in the situation."

You don't have to say these things in this exact order. At some point, just get those concepts across. Here are two more responses that the girl editors and I came up with:

"I don't know how to help you. But I know what you're going through is important. I know it's hard for you and I'm really sorry you're going through this. What do you need from me?"

"I went through something maybe similar when I was a teen so I'm really sorry you're going through this. But I do know that you have a different life than mine so I can't relate one hundred percent. I do know you have a right to privacy and thinking and feeling things in your own way."

Girls choose carefully which adult they're going to talk to and for what reason. Take a moment right now to reflect on whom your daughter has confided in and why you think that is. One thing is certain: Girls won't talk to people who they think will patronize them or overreact, no matter how good their intentions may be.

Land Mine!

Don't say, "Why did you wait so long to tell me?" Even if you have no intention of coming across as accusatory, you will. If you really want the answer to that, say something a few hours later like, "Hey, I've been thinking about what you told me and I was wondering: Is there a specific reason why you didn't tell me before?"

It's important to allow her to have a wide range of feelings. If she's feeling so angry that she wants to release her anger by punching a pillow or a punching bag, or going into her room and yelling at the top of her lungs, or playing really loud music, or even playing a violent video game, let her do it. Your daughter needs a healthy outlet to express her anger without feeling like you think she's a violent, crazy person for having her feelings. I know a lot of parents say that they're cool with these displays of emotion, but check yourself to make sure you're really acting that way in the moment.

Don't Cry

When you watch sappy movies, TV shows, or even ads and you feel those tears welling up, don't hold back. However, crying when you're angry at your children doesn't help you maintain your authority at all. Girls tell me they don't usually feel sorry for you. They can resent you because they think you're manipulating them or you are putting all of the responsibility on their shoulders. So after you stand your ground, go into your room, shut the door, and then cry there.

You never want to see your parent cry. I don't want to hurt her so I told her in moderation what I was doing but it hurt me too because I didn't feel comfortable telling her. She needs to

> figure out her emotions. When I figured out I wasn't respon-
> sible for emotional reactions it was like taking the world off
> my shoulders. And then I could express myself more.
>
> —Lauren, fourteen

LYING AND RECONNAISSANCE

> Is there a statute of limitations about what you can tell your
> parents about something you've done?
>
> —Tessa, eighteen

Many children and teens lie. I won't say "all," because it's true that over the last twenty years I've worked with girls who have not lied to their parents. But that's, like, ten out of ten thousand. I've also been on the receiving end of girls lying to me. Girls that I've worked closely with who I thought would never lie to me. Then they did. Even though I knew better, my anger sometimes stopped me from handling those situations effectively. I lashed out. They got defensive and shut down. It wasn't good for anyone.

There are different reasons girls lie, and understanding the motivation for the lie is crucial. I'm not excusing dishonesty, but it needs to be seen in context so you can hold your child account-able for the right reason in the right way. I understand that most parents understandably define honesty as a virtue, connect it to their family values, and communicate this belief system to their children—with the expectation that their children won't lie. But according to one of my absolute favorite parenting books of all time, *NurtureShock* by Po Bronson and Ashley Merryman, al-though parents list honesty as the trait they most want to see in their children, studies show that 96 percent of kids lie to their parents. By the way, no researchers seem to have ever asked about the percentage of parents who lie to their kids. I've lied to my sons, and each time I've done it I believed I had a very good reason for deceiving them. From our children's perspective, they're lying to us for the same reason we lie to them. Because they think they have a very good reason.

Getting a handle on why girls lie can be difficult because it's

easy for parents to assume either that their own daughter won't lie to them since they have a good relationship with her and "she's a good kid," or the total opposite—that she is always lying to them and can't be trusted. That's not the way I see it. I think young people believe that being honest is complicated. It's not that they're confused about what the truth is; it's that they are constantly balancing social dynamics against that truth. Teens love to put off dealing with consequences and they want you to be happy with them. That's one really understandable motivation for lying. Or, how can they be trustworthy to their friends and yet always keep you in the loop? How can they experiment with risk taking and self-discovery if you need a live update of all the goings-on in their lives? The landscape of adolescence is not fertile ground for truth telling. So keep these things in mind:

To be a good liar, you must be socially intelligent, highly verbal, and able to control "leakage" (the inconsistencies that reveal the lie).

Different lies need different responses. For example, lying to cover up unethical behavior is completely different from a child lying when she feels overwhelmed.

Don't take your daughter's lies personally. If you take her lies personally, your anger, embarrassment, and frustration will stop you from teaching her to develop the internal motivation to be truthful—to herself or to you.

Girls lie to their parents about completely different things than what they lie to their peers about. This may sound obvious, but when a girl is caught lying to her peers, her parents can have a hard time believing it when the behavior sounds so different from what they know of their daughter.

One of the most common and completely understandable things parents say to their kids is this: "If you make a mistake [or do something wrong], I'd rather you be honest with me than lie about it." When a parent says this, they're appealing to their daughter's sense of honor in relation to the family's moral code and correctly communicating that lying after you've done something

wrong makes the situation worse. For some girls, this strategy works. But for the vast majority I work with, it doesn't—at least not in the moment when they make the decision to deceive. Why?

If you look at it from the girl's perspective, you can see the answer. The rewards for being truthful—her parents are happy with her, and she gains the personal satisfaction that comes from being an honest person—are abstract and long-term. In contrast, the rewards for lying are concrete and immediate.

For example, your daughter is out with her friends and shoplifts makeup, and you ask her later where she got it. Here's her thinking: *If I tell the truth, my parents are obviously going to be mad. They might forbid me to hang out with these friends, I will have to come clean to the store manager, and I will have to pay to fix the problem. If I lie, I don't have to have a stressful conversation with my parents, and there's no chance I'll have to own up to the store about my theft. I feel bad about doing it, but since I know I never want to do it again I don't need some kind of extra punishment. No one else needs to know, and everything can go on like normal.*

In parents' minds, when we say "Just tell me; you won't get in trouble," we aren't defining trouble the way our girls do. Talking to parents and having them be disappointed and then talking to the store manager and feeling guilty are all part of your daughter's definition of trouble. If you see it this way, taking the chance to lie and avoid the whole situation begins to make sense.

I'm not saying that your child is a dishonest person. I'm not saying she has poor character—remember, 96 percent of kids lie. What I have realized is that how we respond when they lie—or falsely accuse them of lying—is a direct reflection of how healthy our relationship with them is, both now and for the future.

CHECKING YOUR BAGGAGE

- What was the biggest lie you told to your parents when you were young? Why did you lie? Did they find out?
- Has your child ever seen you lie? I'm not talking about lying about how good the chicken was at your in-laws' house when it tasted like leather. You know what I'm talking about.
- Have you ever lied *for* your child?

HOW CAN YOU TELL WHEN SHE'S LYING?

Some parents believe they have the magical power to look their daughter in the eye and make the truth spill out of her using their stern, unflinching parental lie detector. But a good liar can pass this test easily. A good liar is cool and collected and continues to hold her ground no matter what.

The truth is, parents often can't tell when their children lie. They just think they can. Worse, kids who are good at lying are particularly good at the "look them in the eye" test. What is most frustrating for kids is when parents think they're lying when they're telling the truth, but believe them when they're lying. It drives kids crazy that parents can't tell the difference. Ironically, it's much more likely that a parent will catch a bad liar, and then mistakenly believe that child is less honest all the time. This is a huge mistake that doesn't just hurt your relationship with your child but can also have larger negative consequences within your family.

> I cover for my sister a lot. She rarely lies, but sometimes about drinking, ... One time my parents found an empty bottle of vodka upstairs and assumed it was mine but it was hers, and she didn't correct them.
>
> —Hannah, eighteen

Doesn't this phenomenon harken all the way back to *Ferris Bueller's Day Off*, when Jeanie is always caught in her lies, but Ferris gets away with absolutely everything? Most siblings display some variation of this. They're in cahoots against you sometimes, they go out on a limb for one another sometimes, and sometimes they throw the other under the bus. Parents rarely see any of what's behind the scenes, but they still get caught in believing that one child is always more honest than the other. If a child is blamed for something she didn't do, she starts feeling like her parent doesn't trust her. That expectation encourages her to lie or deceive because she's already dealing with a parent who thinks the worst of her. All of this leads to the child distancing herself from the parent. She pulls away by putting a smile on her face

and/or shrugging her shoulders, which a parent can interpret as disrespectful or indifferent.

CHECKING YOUR BAGGAGE

- Do you use the "look them in the eye" test?
- As the judge, have you already decided the verdict?
- If you have more than one child, do you believe one is more honest than another? What are you basing that assessment on?

WHAT MAKES A GOOD LIAR?

Every lie is based on a grain of truth. If she gets caught, a girl might use this "truthlet" to justify her actions. This is why she can be so self-righteous when she's caught.

Girls recognize who they can lie to and to what extent. If they smell an ounce of hypocrisy on an adult, it's easy for her to lie because she doesn't respect the person. She also believes that the adult would have a harder time calling her out. Conversely, lying to someone whose integrity she respects is way harder.

In either event, a good liar usually resorts to the following tactics and rationales:

1. She overloads you with details so you leave the conversation completely confused.
2. She approaches you when you're distracted or tired.
3. She collaborates with accessories to back up her story.
4. She truly believes she has a higher purpose that justifies the lie.
5. She's angry with you for something else, so she feels justified in lying.

WHY GIRLS LIE TO YOU

REASON 1: SELF-DELUSION

Lying about chores, lying about homework, lying about applications, saying they're all done when they're not. It is so easy to blow holes in these lies, so why do girls still tell them? I want to share with you something Anthony Wolf, PhD, explains about lying in these situations. He calls this a "lie of the future self." The girl lies because she genuinely believes that in the future she'll do the things she's supposed to have already done. So when girls say "Yes, I walked the dog," "Yes, I folded my laundry," or "Yes, of course I wrote that thank-you note to Grandpa," they don't think they're technically lying because they believe they'll eventually do it.

REASON 2: MANAGING PARENTAL INTERFERENCE

Most girls I work with believe that parents overreact to problems, and they want to manage their problems themselves. Their best strategy is to keep you on a need-to-know basis by limiting and manipulating what you know. From schoolwork to after-school activities and athletics, girls will go to great lengths to keep parental interference to a minimum. From the parents' perspective, this doesn't make sense, because who better than a parent—the person who wants the best for them—to help and give guidance? Parents can help only if they know about the problem. But the reality is that parents' reactions often only cause more anxiety, frustration, and anger for the girl.

These sorts of lies can include all kinds of scenarios: The person your child was supposed to get a ride from didn't show up, so she got a ride from a person you don't like instead but there's no way she's going to tell you that. Or, she's having a really tough time with school or her sport or her play or anything, but she doesn't let you in on the problem because she already has a plan to manage it. Telling you would just be cumbersome and annoying. Plus, you might talk to the coach or teacher or tutor, which would only make the whole thing bigger and more embarrassing.

When it comes to managing parental input, girls usually tell lies because they already have a strategy for handling the situation. They don't want to introduce you as another factor of the problem. So if you find out your daughter is lying about something like this, don't blow up at her. Instead, ask her about her ideas for working through the problem, and affirm her independence. Ask if there is anything you can do to help her go through the steps of her plan.

REASON 3: PROTECTION

Girls often lie to protect a bigger truth or secret. For example, one of her friends may have serious family problems but she doesn't want to tell you that because she doesn't think it has anything to do with you, she's fine when she's over at that person's house, and you'd probably stop her from going over there if you knew how messed up things were. She also feels loyal to her friend. Another type of protection could be a girl lying or withholding information to protect some of her truest beliefs or her insecurities. She fears that if she reveals some aspect of her identity to you—her sexual orientation, her anxiety about the sports you make her play, her serious difference of opinion with you about politics, and so forth—you will make incorrect assumptions about her. She lies because she fears that opening up to you about a specific thing will actually lessen your trust in her or your belief in her good character.

> Girls lie in general to make themselves look better. They might lie about things that embarrass them or are insecurities so they don't feel bad about themselves, and keep others from knowing or noticing them.
>
> —Emily, fourteen

One of the things that came up often when I talked to girls was that they lie to their parents about their eating. Lying about disordered eating or about an actual condition falls under the category of "protection" because your daughter could be in self-denial, or

could think that she has everything under control, but the bottom
line is that she does not want you to worry, to judge her, or to take
action on the matter and therefore make it undeniable.

> Oh, eating is a huge one for girls. How did I forget that? I lie
> about my eating sometimes to my parents. Like if I'm not
> home and they ask what I had for lunch I'll just be like, "Oh I
> got a sandwich" or something.
>
> —Hannah, eighteen

It's possible your daughter is in a time where she very carefully
analyzes and monitors her own eating, so much so that she is willing to lie to you about something as trivial seeming as whether
or not she ate dinner. If you find out she is lying about her food
habits, do not compartmentalize the issue in the same box as your
daughter not cleaning her room. It is much more likely something
that she considers with more seriousness, which is why it is important you realize that this lie is to protect her identity and her
fears, not to avoid claiming some kind of responsibility (for more
information on concerns about eating disorders, see chapter 6).

REASON 4: FREEDOM AND INDEPENDENCE

> I know that my younger sister has lied to my parents a couple
> times saying that she was over at a friend's house when she
> was actually at a nightclub. I think she got away with that
> because [my parents] raised my sisters and I with very strict
> rules and have just expected and trusted all of us to be "clean"
> in that respect.
>
> —Casey, sixteen

Girls want freedom to go where they want to go, and they believe
they can assess danger and risk more accurately than their parents. Parents want them to be safe, and they believe *they're* better
at assessing danger and risk in their daughters' lives. This is especially true as girls get older, spend more time riding in one another's cars, and are increasingly exposed to the party scene,

including alcohol, drugs, and sexual encounters. Of course, girls who can drive or who have friends who can drive know that parents don't want seven kids in a car piled onto one another's laps. Or when the driver is texting or searching for her favorite song. But girls believe they know who's a good driver and who isn't, and they want the independence that comes with not relying on their parents for rides. Therefore, they believe they're in a better position to gauge the safety of getting into a particular person's car; parents don't understand the specific situation, so their perspective is unreasonable.

> Older girls told me that the majority of their lies told to parents are about alcohol, drugs, and their sexual behavior. They figure if they're still around to tell you the lie, everything must have been OK, so there's no need for you to know how much they actually drank or how close they came to blacking out. They'll say that they drank less than they did or that they didn't drink at all, because there's no reason to freak you out. Or if they did something one time—say, smoked a cigarette—but hated it and don't plan to do it again, then they have no reason to tell you they did it one time because it might only make you mad about something that in their head is already resolved.

Of course, the other reason girls lie in these situations is that they know the possible consequences of their actions but believe they'll never encounter them. Girls can have a selective memory; when they're thinking about their lying track record, they may be remembering the times they got away with lying rather than the times they got caught and were punished.

Teens think they're invincible—or so adults love to say. Undoubtedly this is true, but before we move on, look in the mirror. Do you talk on your phone or text while driving? Have you ever drunk a couple of beers or glasses of wine and driven home, even when your kids were in the car with you? It's important to consider that young people aren't the only ones who are in denial about possible consequences hitting them upside the head.

RECONNAISSANCE STRATEGIES

You can call it a support system or parental covert operations. It doesn't matter how on top of things you are as a parent, you need other trusted eyes and ears to back you up. The best operatives are people who really like your kids, people who for better or for worse know what your kids are capable of, and people your kids respect and are a little afraid of making angry or disappointing.

The best way to create your own network is to connect with the parents of your daughter's friends and associates. Whether she participates in an activity, a team, the theater, or the robotics club, get to know the parents of the other kids involved. (Actually, you don't have a choice because you'll be hanging out together watching your children or carpooling with them.) You don't have to be BFFs, but you do need to know how to get a hold of them when necessary, and you have to let go of any embarrassment or hesitation you might have in admitting you're having a problem with your kid. Every parent will have the experience at least once of not knowing something important that's going on. So get over any hesitation you have and embrace the idea that you will be asking other adults for help.

It's also good to develop your child's paranoia (to an extent). The more she thinks you're talking to her friends' parents, the less confident she'll be that she can deceive you. Whenever possible, get as complete a list as possible of cellphone numbers for your daughter's friends and their parents and keep them in your cellphone.

YOU'RE CLOSING IN ON HER

We are up against experts. If they have an ounce of social intelligence, they figure out how to trick us and wear us down or bypass us altogether. That's why they're often so good at deceiving us.

This is especially true when your daughter knows you're close to catching her doing something that you'll be displeased about. When your daughter is close to being caught, there's almost nothing she won't do to get you off her back. Imagine this picture: You're the advancing army, and you have arrived at the castle

walls. She's in the castle, and she's going to fight you to the death before she lets you see what she's been up to in that castle. As you begin your final attack, hot oil is dumped on you. Fireballs are next. Flying cows. Tar bombs. Whatever she can find. Nothing is considered off-limits to push you back, including her secret weapon—your love. Here are three examples of brief exchanges between a daughter and her parent that show you how they do it:

DAUGHTER: "Why don't you trust me?"

PARENT: "I do trust you."

DAUGHTER: "OK, good." (*End of conversation. Puts earbuds in.*)

DAUGHTER: "Why don't you trust me?"

PARENT: "I mean, it's not that I don't trust you. I just want to know what was going on."

DAUGHTER: "OK, well, I told you." (*Walks out of the room or puts earbuds in.*)

DAUGHTER: "Why would I still be trying to prove to you that I'm telling you the truth if I were lying?"

PARENT: "I don't understand why you're getting so angry."

DAUGHTER: "I'm not angry. You're just being completely illogical and you drive me insane." (*Takes out phone and texts.*)

Realize right now that you can love your daughter and still stand your ground. You can call her out for lying, being disrespectful or dismissive, and trying to manipulate you and still have a good relationship with her. Whether you're married or not, or parenting with someone who has a different approach to parenting, you must present a united front. You can't let your daughter manipulate either of you.

YOU CAUGHT HER—NOW WHAT?

If you confront her in front of her friends, she'll be resentful and 100 percent focused on showing she has as much control as possible over you in the situation. You're not giving in or letting her get away with something if you wait until she's alone. In fact, waiting is a punishment unto itself. Remember when you got in trouble? Often the worst part was knowing you'd been caught and waiting

for the ax to fall. The only time you should talk to her in public is if she lies to you with her friends—if she's involved in a group effort to deceive. Then walk out of the room with phone in hand so they can listen to you call the other parents.

If you have good reason not to trust her, tell her why. Describe the specific actions that led to your suspicions, explain how you feel and what you want, and let her know what she can do to gain back your trust. Remember, your daughter may give you incremental information. Whether she's in trouble with you or she's had a bad experience that she wants to share with you, she'll probably parcel out the story in chapters, if not sentences. Give her the space to do so—within a reasonable limit. I say to girls that they have a day to "remember" anything that happened that they had "forgot" to tell me in our initial conversation. Anything told to me within that twenty-four-hour period counts as telling the truth and not withholding information. Anything after the twenty-four-hour period counts as withholding information. This window enables them to come up with a good cover story with their friends, but it also gives them time to think about all the possible consequences of their actions.

If you've gotten to the place where you really don't trust her, you need to say specifically why and then say:

> "I don't want to have the kind of relationship with you where I doubt everything you say, but that's where we are. When you lie, you're forcing me to be much more involved in your business than I'd otherwise be, and I know that's the last thing you want. I want to trust you. I want to respect your word. I need to know: What is so important to you that you're willing to make this kind of sacrifice?"

Discipline

Overall, my general strategy when disciplining children (either my own or my students) is to frame my response in this way:

1. Tell them exactly what they did that was a problem.
2. Tell them that those specific actions are against what I believe in (as their mom or a teacher).

3. Tell them specifically what privilege will be taken away and for how long.

4. Give them a "way out"; that is, a way to make amends that will make them and me proud.

YOUR DAUGHTER WILL TAKE
YOU SERIOUSLY IF . . .

For any of this to work, you must practice what you preach. You can't be hypocritical. Don't lay down your values, expect her to follow them, and then act differently yourself. If you gossip about other people (especially other children she knows), don't expect her to do anything different. If you lie or sneak around, expect her to do the same. If you make a mistake and don't own up to it, don't expect her to hold herself accountable. If you're defensive and refuse to apologize, she'll be self-righteous. It doesn't mean you can't make mistakes and admit that to her—in fact, that in itself can be a great bonding moment for both of you. Being a credible role model depends on you consistently demonstrating the core values you believe in and want her to practice.

Here's a short list to remember in an emergency. If it's helpful, you can put it in your phone's notes or in your wallet for immediate access.

1. *Is this situation really a crisis?* Is someone going to be hurt or killed if you don't get immediately involved? If not, focus on modeling social competency and dignity in the moment.

2. *Strategic timing and location:* Are you and your daughter in a place and time where she can listen to you and you can listen to her?

3. *Affirm feelings:* Say, "I'm really sorry that happened to you." Ask if she's just venting or actually wants advice.

4. *Don't tell her what you would have done if you were in her situation.*

Technology, Social Networking, and Girl World

My dad is always checking email—I'm always checking email. My mom is always on Facebook—I'm always on Facebook. My mom takes pictures of everything that moves, and I Snapchat constantly. And then, my parents wonder why I'm online all the time.

—Sadie, eighteen

I can't move without my mom texting me at school. Like, "How's your day? Is everyone being nice to you?" She never stops, and don't even get me started on how often she emails my teachers.

—Bella, eleven

There is an unspoken code. How many times you post things is big. You don't want to post more than once a day because it looks like you don't have anything else to do. If you're the only thing on my feed that's weird. If it's Facebook you shouldn't change your profile page more than once a month. And I'm a lot more choosey about what I put on Instagram. It's a running advertisement of yourself.

—Eden, fifteen

One of the weirdest things about working with teens is that I can trick myself into forgetting how much older I am than they are. But technology shoves that reality into my face. As in, one of my high school interns recently showed me the online dating service he had just signed up for and was joking that one of the girls he "matched" with was sitting in his school's cafeteria the next day.

Think about the girl you are reading this book for. Take a step back and ask yourself:

How is she managing her relationships online?
How does she respond online when someone is angry with her, or vice versa?
How does she express humor online?
What image is she presenting to the world on social media?

Do you know? If you don't know, are these questions stressing you out, or are you thinking you're somehow a bad parent (or teacher or counselor or whatever you do) because you don't know? I don't know everything that my children post online. We can't. And with all due respect, if you're reading this right now and telling yourself that you do know everything your child is doing online, you're probably wrong. But you don't need to know everything. You just have to be curious—not in a controlling, freaked-out, *"What are my children doing online?!"* way, but a *"This gives me insight into their lives and gives me an opportunity to apply my values in a way that they can apply in their day-to-day lives"* way.

If you do that, you can go a long way toward teaching your child how to manage herself competently and with dignity. But before I talk to you about how much oversight you should have over your child's online social life, or when you should get her a phone, or what happens if "all" the other girls have some device that she really wants and you really don't want to get for her . . . before all those questions we have to look at how girls see technology and, specifically, how adults talk to them about it.

Where to start? You may not like this but we're starting with us—adults. Wherever you fit in the spectrum of tech awareness (somewhere between your kids programming your phone and being a software engineer), here are some things to keep in mind:

- Don't come across as assuming that kids behave more irresponsibly than adults do online.
- Don't describe what anything a young person posts as insignificant or shallow.
- Don't panic. You don't have to keep up with every new social media platform, game, phone app, and viral video to effectively guide your daughter to responsibly use any kind of technology.
- Do be curious and continually educate yourself about what technology your children use most.
- Do communicate that we care deeply that our children conduct themselves online based on the same ethical rules we expect them to follow in real life.

Your daughter lives in two worlds simultaneously—the real world and the virtual world. What happens in one impacts the other, and vice versa. The information stream is constant. We go from Facebook to Twitter to Instagram every day. (In fact, because people use so many social networking platforms, and they change all the time, I'm going to use the acronym "SNP" throughout this book.) Even if your child disconnects, she understandably believes that she can't ever stop what people are posting about her online.

I assume you know all of this, but it doesn't matter if you know it right now. You have to remember it in the moment your daughter is having a meltdown and her fingers are furiously flying on her phone and you have no idea why—or you do know why, but the reason seems ridiculous to you. In that moment, you must remember that to her, it's like all those people in her school and community are all around her, they know her deepest secrets, and they're all judging her.

Everyone is going to pretend that it doesn't affect you but it does. It's like being under surveillance. Even at home you still have to fit into all the standards that everyone else has. It's so weird.

—Lizzy, fourteen

HOW DO WE MAKE A POSITIVE DIFFERENCE?

We start with acknowledging our own double standards and (though usually well-intentioned) unrealistic advice. We have to recognize why so many kids blow off anything adults say about "responsible technology use." We need to admit we have a serious credibility problem. And we have to stop sounding like cheesy public service announcements. Does the following sound familiar?

> "Once you press send, it's out there forever."
> "Your future employers/college admissions people can see what you post."
> "Anyone can access your information."

Every child knows this. Every person who uses social media knows this. You know this. Does it stop most of us at all times from posting information that reflects poorly on us? Nope.

But our biggest problem is that the way adults act online contributes to the unhealthy ways our kids act online. It's hard to admit but we can be really hypocritical when it comes to what we do online and what we tell our children to do online.

I am fourteen and have trouble talking to my mother for a few reasons. She is constantly on the phone, texting, calling, emailing, or checking Facebook. I really want to talk to her in the car because it's a personal space, but I can never bring something up. I've tried but she tells me she has important business and scheduling to take care of. Also in the car, I will ask if I can play my music on the loud speakers, she'll say yes, but then turns it off or to mute as soon as she starts texting or calling. So I will put in my headphones, and many times she's remarked by doing this that I am being antisocial or rude. I want to open up, but time is limited and my trust with her was broken a long time ago (also media related) and there's only a bit of faith in me left that I can talk to her.

—Alicia, fourteen

LanD Mine!

Whether your kids are five and you're at the playground or they're eighteen and you're at their high school graduation, we are all checking our phones. I think so many of us do it because we feel that we have no time. If we are sitting down with "nothing" to do, then we want to take advantage of the moment. But these moments aren't meaningless. These are moments in our child's life. And I know recitals and plays and graduations can be mind-numbingly boring but we have to be present for them.

Here's a list of things we do that make it harder for our kids to take us seriously:

1. *We are constantly online.* "Mom, I already told you that. You weren't paying attention." Sound familiar? We need to admit that most of us constantly check our phones when we're bored or jump every time we hear our device chirp. Just like our kids, we convince ourselves that we always have a good reason for checking our email, Facebook, Instagram, and so forth. We leave our devices by our beds, we reach for them as soon as we wake up, and we take them with us to the dinner table.

2. *We obsessively "check in."* There's nothing wrong with wanting to be in contact with your daughter. But if you're "checking in" with her throughout the day, you're modeling that she needs to do the same thing. More dangerous, texting her constantly may mean she ignores your texts—not a good thing when there's actually a reason that you need to be in contact with her immediately.

It's eleven in the morning. I've only been up since seven thirty. I've literally received fifteen messages from my mother since that time—the most important of which informed me that she was "driving through Richmond" with my "sisters sleeping in the back of the car" and that "Gma's flight is delayed, but not really that much." Really, Mom? Was it that crucial I

know my sisters' nap schedule? Shouldn't you be paying attention to the road?

—Katelyn, eighteen

3. *We criticize what our children post about, but they are exactly the same things we post.* Why is what our children post about the party they went to last weekend more superficial than what *we* posted about the party we went to last weekend? Why do we warn them about protecting their privacy and then post pictures that clearly show where we are? Our kids' lives on social media are as legitimate and relevant to them as we perceive ours to be, and adults are often more lax about security settings than teens are.

4. *We stalk our child's friends.* When necessary, it's great to get in contact with the friends of our child. But we need to define "necessary." "Necessary" means situations when you can't find your child or when her phone is dead and you need to give her important information, like, "I'm running late at work so stay where you are and I will pick you up in twenty minutes."

Having said that, it's crucial to your sanity and sometimes your child's safety to be able to text a child who knows where your child is or can figure out where your child is. Just try to be aware that relationships can change, so you want to have the contact information for one child that you are pretty sure is close to your daughter.

If you have a good relationship with your child's friends (which doesn't mean you know everything about them, but you have mutual respect and goodwill), then those friends might reach out to you if your child is in trouble, which is definitely a positive thing. But don't abuse this privilege. Stalking children online or demanding that they "friend" you will backfire. Kids are extremely aware of any parent who uses social networking to spy on them or get overinvolved in their lives. They also believe that these parents will gossip about what they see online and label some kids as bad influences. You may read this and think, "Who cares? The more information I know about the kids' online social lives the better." It's not that simple. If you are seen as an *overinvolved, microman-*

aging crazy parent, you undermine your trust with your child, and her peers will be reluctant to tell you anything.

> Some parents will think that they are much better friends with their child than other people and therefore these rules don't apply to them. I've known a few parents that Snapchat and comment on Facebook with their kids' friends because they think the kids think that they are cool and like the parent hanging out and talking to them. The child always feels awkward and apologizes at school for what his mother or father is doing.
>
> —Rachael, nineteen

5. *We believe that every person our children meet online are dangerous predators.* We need to give our children a little bit of credit. Our children are "meeting" people they don't know online all the time, especially if they play games online. If they have a headset when they play games, they are definitely talking to other people. Some of those people are annoying; some of them say racist, sexist, homophobic, or rude things. I hate that people do this, but that doesn't mean they're planning on kidnapping your child. The vast majority of young people who meet people online and then choose to meet them in real life fit a specific pattern: a thirteen- to sixteen-year-old neglected and/or abused girl who desperately needs attention and love because she isn't getting it from the people in her real life.

> And oftentimes if your child feels threatened or creeped out, he or she will get themselves out of that situation!
>
> —Nicole, seventeen

> There have been some incidents lately in my town, which is supposedly very safe.... Predators were looking for vulnerable people who were alone. Basically, what I'm trying to say is that the emphasis should be removed from online predation and transferred to real-life predation. Girls need to be made more aware of real-life threats that can happen

anywhere, because that's where the real danger lies. Online, we're shielded by a screen. We have time to think things over and react accordingly, especially since there is no physical threat—this is not the case outside of the digital world.

—Sophia

6. *We take way too many photos.*

MOM: "It's my profile."
SEVENTEEN-YEAR-OLD TESSA: "Well, it's my face!"

We have to bring it down a notch when we want to take pictures of our kids—especially when they're asking us not to. It's not fair to get angry at them for being frustrated when you don't listen to them and take the pictures anyway. If you want to post a picture of your child, ask their permission and then respect their answer.

The parents of the kids I babysit for are always asking for pictures while we are out doing things. It's like whenever we leave the house the kids are supposed to smile.

—Sasha, seventeen

Furthermore, when your child posts something on their SNPs, you can comment but keep it classy, light, and general. You can even lightly embarrass them. After all, anything you contribute on their SNP is either going to be seen as cute and/or good embarrassing, or horribly intrusive. Here is an example of a good comment:

"That's my girl! I am so proud of you!"

If your child posts something that you don't think belongs on the Internet, you can write, "No comment." If you feel strongly that your child has made a serious online mistake, do not comment for the public and instead talk with your child in person. Tell them why the post bothers you, and ask them to erase it. (See

page 336 for what to do if you see a picture your daughter posted that you think is *way* too sexy.)

DRUMROLL... WHEN DOES SHE NEED A CELLPHONE?

It's the $10 million question in raising kids today.

Here's my list:

- She rides public transportation or a school bus, so she needs one for safety, or to document anything crazy that goes down. If she's really young, say, third grade or younger, and riding the bus, give her a really simple phone.
- She's going to a concert or any event where there will be a lot of people and it'll be easy to get lost.
- She's going to a party where she may want to or need to leave.
- She is participating in activities after school, so she needs to be able to call you, or vice versa, if anyone has a change of plans.
- You want to be in contact with her about schedule changes.
- She drives a car.

However, you don't just hand her a phone. Appreciate your leverage here. You have something she wants. This is a great teachable moment about family values, honoring agreements, and understanding financial responsibility.

Wait until you want to upgrade your phone so that the person who's getting the new phone is you. She gets your old one. When you're in the store, have the salesperson explain how much it costs to add the phone to your plan and what limitations will be on your child's phone. Then ask how much money it will cost if your child goes over the plan. Explain to your child that she'll be responsible for paying the cost of going over. Then ask her to recite back to you everything she just heard.

Walk out of the store with your new phone. Before handing over your old phone—with her hands reaching for it as if it's manna from heaven—have her repeat back to you one more time what you said about the rules. Then say, in your own words:

"Do you understand that you must obey these rules even if you think they're stupid? Do you understand that under certain circumstances I may feel that I have to check what you post online? If the phone breaks or you lose it, you'll pay for its replacement. These are my ironclad rules. There's no negotiation about these rules. Do you understand the terms?"

Then realize that no matter how vigilant you are about holding her accountable, if you get her a plan that streams data, you *will* incur "overage" charges because she won't keep track of her use. And she will crack the screen. And you will want to tear your hair when you get the phone bill because it's so much higher than what you agreed to. Then you can call your provider and block data on your daughter's phone, but then you also have to block her phone from streaming data from your modem at home—which will work until she goes to a coffee shop where she can use their service. All to say it's impossible to completely shut her down . . . but you can make it more difficult.

It's understandable to want to give up. But we aren't going to.

Plus, it's not all bad. There are some really good things about using digital devices to communicate with our children, beyond making it easier for us to pick them up. For example, your daughter tells you she's had a bad day. She goes to school still worried about it. So you text her something during the school day like, "I'm thinking about you." But remember you don't text her throughout the day. Just once to reassure her. You can also text her after a fight and you lost your temper. As in, "I'm sorry I lost it. If you want to keep talking I'm here." Or, what about if your child teaches you something or makes you see something a different way? You can write, "I'm really grateful that you open my eyes."

All good things.

HOW DO YOU TEACH HER HOW TO USE IT IN A WAY THAT DOESN'T MAKE YOU WANT TO RIP IT OUT OF HER HANDS?

It's not just about her being "nice" online with her friends. Representing yourself on social media is an increasingly important part of anyone's self-identity. In our personal interactions online a lot of us function in extremes. We swing between posting horrible things impulsively or obsessing about every word and emoticon we write. Technology allows us to throw more intense self-righteous temper tantrums, which is why many of us have received an email from someone who is angry with us that's filled with WORDS IN ALL CAPITALS, and comments on websites and articles are crazy rants.

Manners

There's never an excuse for bad technology manners. Whether you're a teenager or an adult, it's rude to text when someone is talking to you. When you're around other people, especially if there's a reasonable expectation of social interaction, you need to show interest in their presence. Few things annoy me more than watching a kid sit completely unaware of her surroundings because her parents let her talk on the phone, text, or play games. Allowing your children to use their phone or any handheld device during meals or while sitting in the corner of your cousin's wedding is enabling them to be rude and socially incompetent. For the record, I completely understand wanting to conduct a conversation without interruptions from whining children. I myself am not above putting my children in front of a movie while I have dinner in the next room with friends. But if they are included in any kind of social gathering, you must expect them to participate.

At whatever age your child begins to socialize with other kids online, in whatever format, it's time to have the first conversation tying safety and ethics to their online behavior. That talk needs to be age-appropriate and concrete.

If your daughter is young (under ten), here's a sample script on safety that hopefully strikes the right balance:

"As much as I wish this weren't true, there are some people in the world who say really mean things online or even want to hurt kids. This doesn't mean everyone is like that, but some people are. What's great is that you have grown-ups in your life who love you and you can talk to if anything happens online that you feel bad about. So let's think about two people you want to talk to if that ever happens. . . . Me and Uncle Dave? Great! You know what? No matter how smart you are, it can be incredibly easy to give away personal information without even realizing it. For example, if you record something in your room and post it, do you say something or have things in the background that give away your personal information? If you're playing online games and someone you're playing with says they go to a school nearby and are in a certain grade, it's easy to believe they're telling the truth and then give them more information. If you make a mistake about that, it's way more important to tell us than worry about us getting mad at you. If someone starts talking to you like that or using bad or scary words, go get an adult. If an adult isn't around right away, then write down what you heard and then tell one of us."

Ethics: Not Using the Phone for Evil
YOUNGER GIRLS

"You can joke around with people just like you do when you're face-to-face with someone, but what is important to me is that you don't make someone feel bad or post information that embarrasses them. If you do, because I understand mistakes happen, I expect you to apologize. If any of these things happen to you, I want to know about it so we can think through what's the best way to handle it. Did I miss anything, by the way? Are there other things that you think could happen that you're worried about?"

OLDER GIRLS

"Now that you're getting older, I need to check in with you again about communicating with people online. Above all, the same rules are true today as they were when we first talked about it. You don't use these platforms to ridicule other people, because some-

one else's embarrassment is not and should not be entertaining to you. You represent yourself truthfully and authentically. If you use someone else's phone or SNP, you have their consent before you post anything. You must also have permission to post any videos or pictures of other people. I'll be checking once in a while to see if you're honoring our agreement. I think you will, but just so there aren't any surprises, if you violate the terms of our agreement, I'll take your technology away until you earn the right to have it back."

TECHNOLOGY CONTRACT

Technology contracts have become a popular way to state the family technology rules and then use them as a handy reminder when those rules are being bent. I've done them with my kids. But the only way the contract can work is if your children are involved in developing the rules and are a reinforcement, not a guarantee, of the rules. *And* the adults need to follow the rules, too. Start by sitting around the kitchen table and asking your children what your values are and how your values apply to technology. On the next page is a sample one to get you started.

If you're a religious family, make this an opportunity to show the relationship between family and religious values, and sign it in front of your religious leader. If you aren't religious, consider signing it in front of a notary. Either way, you want your children to understand that your family stands for treating people with dignity and that your word is your bond. Last, frame the contract and put it near the place you all relax/play games/watch movies as a visible reminder.

We, the Edwards family, believe our family values include integrity and compassion. Every member of the family understands that our use of technology must reflect our values. Therefore we:

- Will pay attention when someone is talking to us instead of paying attention to the device in our hands.
- Won't spread gossip.
- Will only use someone's password and identity with their consent.
- Will only sign someone up to a website with their consent.
- Won't use any social media platform with the purpose of creating, viewing, or participating in the humiliation of others or getting revenge.

If any family member is found acting in violation of this contract, the following will occur:

- First violation: Computer or cellphone privileges ended for X [amount of time].
- Second violation: Computer and cellphone privileges ended for X [amount of time].
- Third violation: One of the person's most valued privileges is taken away. *Remember, an iPod is a privilege and so is participating in team sports—no matter how good your child is.*

While we understand that any of us can make a mistake, we believe that living according to these values is critically important.

Signed on this day _____ of this year _____

Child _____

Parent(s) _____

LEARN FROM THE KIDS

Many of the teens I work with have come up with their own ways to cut down on technology use when they are hanging out with people in real life. One of the most common ways is to do the following:

When spending time with friends or family, try making a "phone stack." In the middle of the table form a stack of everybody's phones to ensure that nobody slyly slips their phone out of their pocket to check their messages or sneaks off to the bathroom to post a picture on Instagram. To offer more of an incentive, if you are out at dinner, the first person to grab their phone has to pay the tip.

WHEN SHOULD I LET MY CHILD GET AN SNP?

> *Recently I tried to change my age on FB to the correct age because I made a FB page when I was 11. So now it says that I am 19 instead of 17 and I can't change it until I'm 18.*
>
> —*Tessa, eighteen*

Of course, you don't have a lot of control over whether your child sets one up or not, because all she needs to do is click "Yes, I am thirteen." But this doesn't mean you should just give up. We just have to acknowledge that if they want to sign up for an SNP, they have the ability to do it. Over and over again, what I have learned in my work with teens is that if you acknowledge the power they do have, they will be much more likely to listen to you.

Say your child has been begging for an SNP page and you decide to let them have one. This is what you could say:

"First I want to thank you for asking me because I know if you really want to get one, you could without me knowing—or at least it may take me awhile to find out. Now let's talk about the particular SNP you want to have. If it says you have to be older than you are, I want you to wait because I don't want you to lie. If you are old enough, I want to be there when you set the privacy settings,

and we will decide together what they'll be. Other than that, the rules of using the SNP are the same for all the other technology you use. Just humor me and tell me what they are."

Young people use different SNPs for different reasons. Your child will probably go through phases where she has multiple pages on the same SNP, pages on different SNPs, or uses one a lot more than another and then drop that one and use another one. Here's how a few of my teen editors described it in their communities:

> There are a lot of unspoken rules that come with social media. On Snapchat, people get annoyed if your snapstory is over 100 seconds long. On Instagram, you can't post more than once a day. It's also irritating when people post the same type of selfie in the same position over and over again, or if they incessantly post about their significant other. Also, hashtags are generally only used for the purpose of irony. In terms of Facebook, people don't really post statuses anymore, and game requests are generally pretty frowned upon. I feel like these unspoken rules are pretty consistent among teenagers in general, but then again, that's a hasty generalization. It could just be my town or region. The unspoken rules of technology change as time goes on.
>
> —Sophie G., sixteen

> Twitter was a good way to find out what was happening in the community, however, the downside is that everyone knew what you were thinking as soon as you post that tweet. Oftentimes people would use Yik Yak because that was a way to post opinions, often very insulting ones, without being "tagged."
>
> —Marianna, fourteen

Most teens set up an SNP that is their "public" online face. There's nothing wrong with that—they're actually learning how to express themselves in different venues. Right now, young people usually use an Instagram account as a public face—what they want

everyone to see. That's why they're so obsessive about choosing the right images to post because it's all up for judgment by others. Then they have a Snapchat account that is more private, fleeting, and spontaneous. Snapchat, unlike Instagram, is not perceived as a permanent display of your image or status. It feels less "judgy."

> Lots of my friends have one Instagram account setting that has tight privacy so that only the people they want can see what they post, as opposed to another setting that has lax privacy so everyone can see—including parents and strangers.
>
> —Tal, fifteen

Please don't read this and think you now have to search for every SNP your child is on or get some surveillance, monitoring, scanning, and filtering program someone is trying to sell you. Relationships of trust are always going to be more important than surveillance with your child.

As powerless as this may make you feel, take hope: Guess who *is* effective in getting younger teens off inappropriate SNPs? Older brothers and sisters. Never underestimate older siblings' ability and desire to protect their younger siblings, even if those older children act badly themselves. Also, recognize that they know better than you do what's going on online.

> My older brother won't let me use Facebook. He told me I was too young and he wouldn't even friend me. He said that I should do it when I'm older.
>
> —Arval, twelve

> My brother helped me make a Facebook account when I was nine years old when the website was just starting to become popular. At that age all my online "friends" were relatives and the website wasn't anything of much importance to me. But as more and more of my real-life friends became active on Facebook, this online presence became a social necessity—if you weren't posting about your social excursions, you essentially didn't have a social life. The website morphed into an unhealthy way to form an identity for myself, where posting

online to seem "cool" became more important than spend-
ing genuine time with my friends. I deleted my Facebook
page after a couple of years and while at first I felt like my
social life was done for, I discovered that I began to create
more meaningful relationships with people in "real life" and
had much more time on my hands to spend in important and
creative ways instead of spending that time worrying about
maintaining this Internet identity.

—Sydney, seventeen

EVIL SNPs

There's always some of them floating around making people miserable. A few years ago it was called Formspring. More recently
it's been Yik Yak and ASKfm. They're like viruses that run wild
through a community going after the most vulnerable and insecure. Disturbingly, my colleague Danah Boyd discovered that
some of the kids who posted the nastiest things were the same
people who had posted the "question" that started the attack. You
may think this is insane—why would someone want to cyberbully
themselves? It's sad to say, but getting this kind of attention can be
important to some people.

Yik Yak will go away and be replaced with something equally
nasty. If your child likes these types of sites, it's important to understand her motivation. I'd ask her,

"Can you help me understand why you like [name of horrible site
here]? What does it feel like when you read posts from people attacking someone else? Can you tell me what you think worries me
about you using this site?"

DELETING SNP ACCOUNTS

It's not unusual for teens to voluntarily take a break or delete their
SNP accounts. They do it when they feel overwhelmed with their
online lives or when they're scared they're going to be attacked.
I can relate—there have been several times when people have

hated something I've done or written and then trolled me on my Twitter account. I've wished I could delete my account, but I've resigned myself to not looking at Twitter until the wave of raging tweets goes away.

> I've definitely considered deleting Facebook and Twitter—I never use them—but I keep thinking that if I want them in the future, I'll have to refriend and re-follow everyone. That would be a mildly awkward situation, so I keep them just in case. Also, Facebook is fun for purposes such as sharing/ looking at prom pictures and communicating with class-mates/teammates. Having those accounts doesn't really affect my life in any way, since I don't use them. However, for an English project, I didn't use entertainment technol-ogy (phones, TV, computer) for the entirety of a week. That definitely had an effect on my life: I thought deeper, spent my time more wisely, explored my passions, read more, and was consciously grateful for everything in my life. Since then, I've continued to be an Instagram addict, but I still try to make my life more meaningful every day.
>
> I deleted a few social media accounts in middle school, In-stagram and Snapchat. I knew people who were being bullied through social media and I was afraid that people would use it to attack me. So to avoid the possibility I deleted my ac-counts. I soon realized how out of the loop I had become so I decided to sign back up and I have not had any problems with cyberbullying when I signed back up.
>
> —Syndey, eighteen

HOW MUCH SPYING CAN YOU DO?

The question I always get after "When should I get my child a cellphone?" is "Should I monitor what my child is texting and doing online?"

First let's read the responses of my teen editors when asked "Does a parent ever have the right to check his or her child's text/ Facebook messages?"

No, it's called independence and there is no way they can control or sensor everything so they might as well teach how to be respectable and smart and what expectations they have for Internet use! But that's like sneaking into a journal . . . invasion of privacy. Just talk to your kid.

—Maya, fifteen

I think this is only OK when parents believe that their children are in danger or are partaking in risky activities. My parents have never checked any of my messages, and I would be really frustrated if they did; that would be a sign that they didn't trust me or respect my privacy. However, one of my friends' parents does check messages. I felt like I was constantly being watched and monitored when I texted her. I think the best way to avoid this uncomfortable situation as a parent is to educate your child on Internet safety repeatedly, so what's OK and what's not OK will be instilled in their memories.

—Sophie

Yes, if the child is being bullied via text or Facebook message and the child doesn't know how to handle the situation correctly. Or if inappropriate content is being sent that could come back to haunt the child in the future (like nude photos).

—Tal

I think it's only OK if the parent thinks their child is in trouble or doing something they shouldn't be doing. If the parents are checking your messages constantly without reason it shows how little trust there is.

—Jordyn

You can see there's a range of opinions here. I know a lot of parenting experts would disagree with the teens above. The standard line is parents have the right to see everything their child is doing whenever they want. I get why people say this. We want a simple answer to overwhelming or complex problems. But it doesn't work

like that. Our relationships with our children are *relationships*. No matter what experts or the hypervigilant parent in your neighborhood tells you, it's actually really hard to know everything your child is doing all the time online. This is the way I think about it. Monitoring your child's online life is not about controlling your child's online life. It is about teaching your child to communicate online ethically and authentically. It is about creating a relationship of mutual respect with your child where they'll tell you if something is running off the rails.

Every child is different, but in general I now believe that if your child has conducted herself according to your rules, by the end of her freshman year of high school you can allow her to have a password of her own, and you can stay out of her social networking—until and unless you see or become aware of something that makes you worry.

I've really changed my opinion about this in the last four years. My thinking has been greatly influenced by a colleague I mentioned earlier, Danah Boyd, a senior researcher at Microsoft and a fellow at the Berkman Center for Internet and Society at Harvard University (plus a lot of other things). She defines "privacy" as the combined ability to control a social situation and to have agency to assert control over that situation. Young people want that control and agency. Here's how I suggest you think about it. Your daughter's privacy is her most precious treasure. When you violate her privacy, it feels like you're stealing something invaluable to her. Now, there are times when you have no choice but to violate her privacy, but you need to be very thoughtful and considerate when you take such a huge step. Because you can't do it that many times without it seriously backfiring on you—that is, she stops trusting you entirely and starts lying and sneaking behind your back.

It's not that young people want to be public everywhere, or want their lives to be broadcasted all over; what they really want is to participate in a public place that's meaningful to them and their peers. Imagine living in a city where there are a lot of parks, and you know that one of the parks is the place where all your friends hang out. You want to be able to go there and be a part of that community, and you would want to have the ability to

present yourself and participate in that community as you like. Your child's chosen social network (whether that happens to be Facebook, Instagram, Tumblr, Twitter, or whatever) is that park.

Young people are deliberate about how they present themselves and who they let see what. But the other insight I've learned from Danah is that young people assume that everything online is public and actively create structures to exclude certain kinds of information from being generally available. Contrary to the stereotype that kids don't value privacy online, they do—intensely. They value it so much that they'll come up with incredibly creative ways to hide in plain sight what they really feel. Even if you're a parent who checks their social networking posts, you may look at the images they're posting and have no idea of the meaning behind those images. You may even misinterpret the meaning of the post.

Really, teens have been doing this forever. How they choose to dress and the music they like are the most obvious ways they present themselves. But what's important to recognize is that the way your child chooses to present herself online is extraordinarily meaningful.

All of this gets us to this fact: Unless you are a tech security expert or a hacker (or both), you have no privacy. Neither does your daughter. From our family's financial information to what we post online, we have all given up our privacy. But as one of my students said, just because we may not have privacy doesn't mean it's OK to violate people's trust. It's your moral responsibility to respect people's dignity and therefore their privacy.

And all of this gets us to anonymity. We all know that being anonymous or the illusion of anonymity makes it easier for people to behave badly. The question is how do you talk to your child about it? Here's a script:

> "I know it feels like it can be anonymous online and I know that you know you really aren't. But you shouldn't want to be anonymous. You should stand by your words. You should be ready to own what you say in real life and what you post online."

"I Need It for an Alarm!"

Nice try. My boys use that excuse all the time. There should be no phones in her bedroom at night. She shouldn't be looking at a screen shortly before she goes to sleep because the light from the screen messes with her sleep cycle.* Plus, it's about 100 percent likely that she'll experience a conflict online that keeps her up all night. Now let's think about how that may look to you. The next morning you can't wake her up. Eventually she comes downstairs, barely eats breakfast, and is in a foul mood that you attribute to being a moody, lazy teenager. In frustration, you say, "How do you plan to do well in school if you aren't taking it seriously? Life doesn't wait for late people." She just looks at you like you're crazy and blows you off, making you even more irritated.

IF YOU WANT TO TAKE IT AWAY

If you're worried that something is wrong, your first instinct shouldn't be to grab that phone out of her hand. Ask your child what's going on like this:

> "I'm so worried about you because [give one or two reasons, not ten] that I am thinking about going through your phone and SNPs, but I'd much rather hear it from you because I respect your privacy and it's more important that I hear from you what's going on."

Here's a list of signs or symptoms you can look for to tell if something is wrong:

- She is sad and distant, exhausted, or anxious.
- Her brow is constantly furrowed, and she seems worried

---

* From *The New Puberty*: New studies show that the pineal gland—a small, mysterious endocrine organ in the brain that produces several hormones—is highly sensitive to certain wavelengths emitted from digital screens. This partly explains why teens who use computers, tablets, and smartphones late at night can have a difficult time going to sleep, as these devices stimulate the pineal gland and disrupt its production of melatonin, the sleep-inducing hormone.

about whatever situation she is texting about. Her fingers are flying and she seems desperate to get her message through.

- You can hear the constant beeping sound of group texting, and she seems stressed.
- She'll be shifty about her phone (like it'll always be face-down, she'll answer as if she's been electrocuted). She's not happy about answering it.

And if all these signs definitely point to something being amiss, consider mandating a break from technology. It could even help her to relax and forget about the drama.

My mom took my phone out of my room at night. I thought it wouldn't help, but I actually slept better. I don't know how to tell her I think she was right. We have been getting into a lot of fights recently and I don't want to give in to her.
—Ashley, fourteen

If Other People Are Making Her Miserable
If the drama that's coming through that phone is making her miserable, it's still going to feel like punishment when you take it away. When you disconnect your daughter in any way, you are going to get serious pushback, so make sure you have a good reason to do it. She's going to be mad, resentful, and worried that she's missing out.

"I know this feels like a punishment. But I am trying to give you some time to just take a break from the drama. You need to breathe. Let's you and I do different things together. Like we could go to a movie or we could go to the field and I can throw the ball back to you. I know you'd rather have the phone but I want you to take a break."

If She's Made Someone Else Miserable
"I can't allow you to have something that you use to make other people upset. Even if you think you had good reason to do it, or it wasn't that big a deal, it was to me. You need to think about what you will do to make the situation better for the people you hurt."

SHE DID NOT . . . YOUR DAUGHTER MESSED UP ONLINE

Can we just admit that everyone at some point is going to do something online that they shouldn't? Haven't you cc'd someone on an email and you *really* didn't want to? Sent a negative text about a person to *that* person by accident? And then you have that awful moment when you realize what you've done and visualize crawling through the computer to somehow take it back? Just writing this is making me have flashbacks. So, guess what, it's going to happen. Here's how this usually happens with girls your daughter's age and how you can help her through it when it happens to her.

If She Accidentally Posts Personal Information

You may be really frustrated, but don't say things like "How could you not have realized that the picture you posted on Facebook showed our home address?" Honestly, it's really easy to make these kinds of mistakes. Your daughter knows by now that it wasn't an intelligent thing to do. The first time it happens, I'd say:

> "Look, we made an agreement about how you could post things onto the Internet. I know what you did was an honest mistake, but it's important to take responsibility for your actions. To the best of your ability, you are going to remove the post. You are also going to ask your friends if anyone forwarded it to any other social networking site and you're going to do whatever you can to pull that down as well. I really do get that this was a mistake and you didn't intend to do it, but you also have to understand that if it happens again, I may have to take away more computer privileges because you're showing me you aren't ready to use it safely."

If She's Perpetuating Drama

Make no mistake, forwarding humiliating or degrading information is not being an innocent bystander. She has made an active choice to make the problem bigger. If she participated in the creation of negative information or forwarding of that information about someone else, she has to apologize to the target in person (see page 220 for apologies), and she has to send an email to all

the people she knows saw that information and acknowledge that what she did was wrong. It would look something like this:

> To everyone in the ninth grade,
>   Last week I forwarded information about Allison that wasn't true. I shouldn't have done it. I have apologized to Allison in person, but I also needed to write to you so you would know it wasn't true and I am sorry that I sent it.

You will be standing over her and watching her press "send" while she does this. And yes, she will hate you for making her do it. Too bad. Someone has to take a stand about this stuff, and that someone is you.

If She Embarrasses Herself

There is nothing you're going to say that she hasn't already thought herself, so avoid anything along the lines of "How could you have been so foolish?" She's going to feel humiliated, dumb, possibly defensive (like, "that never would have happened if . . ."), hurt, and paranoid that everyone knows about what she did. Don't say, "Everyone will forget about it tomorrow. Don't let it bother you." That's impossible. Just hold her and tell her how sorry you are. No matter what she did or how embarrassed you are by it (under no circumstances should you say you're embarrassed), this is the time to tell her you will get through this as a family. Everyone makes mistakes. It's how you conduct yourself after messing up that shows what kind of person you are.

Then try to talk to her about how she's going to walk down the hallway the next day. After comforting her, have her give you her phone for the next seventy-two hours. She may balk at this suggestion because she may be trying to convince herself that there's something she can do or say that will fix it. Let her know that the way she's going to fix it is by holding her head high in real life. To have any chance of that, she has to disconnect from what people are saying to her or one another about what she did. Hearing that stuff would just make her feel worse.

If Someone Teases Her About Whatever She Did

Tell her to take a deep breath. Then suggest that she say something along the lines of "I made a big mistake, which I'm really trying to deal with. You bringing it up makes me feel worse. I'm not sure if that's your point, but I promise you that I would never make you feel bad if you were in my situation, so I'm done talking about this."

GIRLS GOT GAME

Does your daughter play video games? If she does, she's not alone. Lots of girls play games. For some girls, games provide a crucial social outlet and community—one that is as or more meaningful than their offline community.

The realization that games had become an essential part of young people's social lives dawned on me gradually. I had to broker a truce between two fourth-grade girls because one of them had hacked into the other's Club Penguins account and changed the account holder's penguin color from purple to a salmon color. It turned out that this was just one of several things the aggressor had done, but changing her penguin's color was the targeted girl's last straw.

Then I just observed and listened. I heard elementary school girls passionately talk about Minecraft and Clash of Clans. High school girls delightedly terrified me by showing me a game genre called creepypasta (I have always hated scary movies so I was totally freaked out). Other girls boasted that they could beat any boy they knew in FIFA (the soccer game). Over time it became obvious to me that video games were an increasingly important part of children's and teens' social lives. At the same time, I was hearing from many educators and parents that they hated video games because their content was violent or hypersexual (or both), and they contributed to children's screen addition. But when I asked adults to give me more specific information about these games they had such strong opinions about, they didn't really know that much.

Then I read Jane McGonigal's book *Reality Is Broken*. She uses Bernard Suits's definition of a game as "the voluntary attempt to

overcome unnecessary obstacles." McGonigal's book was the first one I read that backed up what kids say to me. I had played video games myself when I was eleven and in sixth grade—it was my favorite thing to do after school. But I'd often wondered what it was about gaming that made people willing to devote so much of their lives to an activity that promises no tangible reward. McGonigal's premise is that a good game fulfills what human beings need for happiness: satisfying work, the hope of being successful, social connection, and meaning beyond oneself. When I read that, I stopped reading and realized the connections between games, my work, and how much better we'd all be if our educational systems were designed around these four concepts.

Games make you want to work, overcome obstacles, and think through things in a different way to achieve your goal. Ironically, the fact that games are entertaining is both the reason so many people dismiss their value and what makes them so compelling. For those children who attend schools with burned-out teachers who teach to the test, gaming is literally a graphic example of school's irrelevance.

Usually when we talk about gamers, we are referring to boys. But girls play games. It's important not to make assumptions about what girls play. Through the informal research I've done with girls around the country, I've learned they are playing all kinds of games.

Unfortunately, many popular games have terrible gender and racial representations because until recently the industry had done little to create positive social norms within games. Some "gamers" can be as bad as, if not worse than, the most stereotypical sexist jock. One of my least favorite websites actually chronicles the horrible things that guys say to girl gamers. It's common for girls who play these games not to wear their mics while they're playing so the other players don't recognize that they're female. Some will play with their mic only if they're playing with friends.

Why can't you just tell your daughter to stop playing her favorite game? If your daughter is very invested in a game, she may be losing a community and a tremendous amount of hard work. I know that doesn't seem like much, but it is. It's like any project you work on for a long time.

One of the best ways to understand is to play the games she plays. At the least, sit down with her while she's playing it so you can watch. If she's shy or feels easily overwhelmed by the social dynamics and drama of school, building an online community may feel more comfortable to her. But if she's playing a game to the exclusion of having any other interests or developing friendships in real life, that's maybe a cause for concern. Your reaction should be to ask yourself why she's so driven to find meaning and fulfillment in those games. It's time to educate yourself about the specific game or games she's most drawn to. Look them up on Wikipedia or Reddit. Look up what players are posting about the games, and watch scenes from the games on YouTube. Don't take the advice of people who don't know the specific game.

As important as those relationships are to her, she's most likely going to run into conflicts with other people in her online community, just like she would anywhere else. Let's look at Minecraft. It's an amazing game. Second-grade kids *love* to play Minecraft. Teachers love Minecraft. As kids get older and go to more sophisticated servers hosting more mature, complex Minecraft worlds, every one of those planets has its own "lore" and its own traditions and rules that people have to follow. If you are accused of not following those rules, people can get angry at you and there's your drama and conflict.

I know video games (especially ones with violent or sexual content) can make parents and teachers uncomfortable. And even after we educate ourselves about the games our kids play, we still may have the same opinion about screen time and content as we did before. But that's OK, because when we've done our research and then lay down the rules, we will do so from a place of knowledge, not anxiety.

Video games are a complex, important, and permanent part of our culture. They give young people the opportunity to learn how to balance their responsibility to treat others with dignity with their right to express themselves freely, be creative, work in a group, and contribute to something that is valuable to them. Young people need to learn from the adults in their "real lives" that they have a voice and a responsibility to make games better

and to challenge those in the gaming community who may not represent their values and core beliefs.

YOU HATE THEIR MUSIC (OR THINK YOU SHOULD)

"Has anyone had the experience of an adult telling you they hate your music? That it sends the wrong message? That it's too violent? Hypersexual? That it's disrespectful to women?"

Of course, when I ask teens these questions, all hands go up. Just as their parents' hands would have if I had asked them when they were teens.

Music is and always has been powerful, and never more so than during the teenage years. Think about the music that brings back your strongest memories—isn't it from when you were young? Think about the music you loved growing up. What were your favorite artists?

Music means something to us because it touches the most profound aspects of our lives: love, lust, jealousy, alienation, confusion, anger, loneliness, insecurity. And, more often than not, the times we feel these emotions most strongly occur in our teens.

What's different about music today is how it comes into our lives. It has interlinked with all the other forms of technology to combine into one relentless stream. And, more than any other time in human history, music is about selling things to the listener. Mainstream music is a constant advertisement for the "Act Like a Woman" box. (See page 46 for information on the "Act Like a Woman" box, and page 280 for the "Act Like a Man" box.)

That's why it's absolutely critical to engage in the music your daughter is listening to in just the way I'm suggesting you engage in all the other forms of technology she uses. This can be really hard for some adults. Why? I think it's for three main reasons: (1) you feel overwhelmed by the crassness of the message; (2) the images and sounds put you into sensory overload; or (3) you kind of like the music, too.

You can find almost all the music your daughter is listening to in two ways. One: Type the name of the song followed by the

word "lyrics" in your favorite search engine. Two: Type the name of the song followed by "official video" into YouTube to view the music video for free.

Also, you don't have to limit yourself to music, because that is by no means the only form of media that can be analyzed. Your daughter also needs to become an informed observer of television shows, movies, video games, websites devoted to TV shows, blogs, gossip/teen magazines, and advertisements. In other words, her brain should always be on.

"I JUST LIKE THE BEAT"

"I just want to disconnect and not think about anything." "I just like the beat. I don't want to think about what it's trying to tell me." I have arguments with my students and my own children on this exact issue. And I agree that it's annoying to get to a place where you can't see a movie or any kind of show, or listen to music, and not analyze it. Notice the product placements, the sexist or racist or other offensive things in it. So this is what I say:

> "Yes, it is annoying. I can see why you don't want me talking to you about this topic because all you want to do is listen or watch it without thinking too much about it. And I'm not asking you to stop listening. What I am asking you to do is think about it, so you're not just following along mindlessly. I want you in control of yourself, not other people in control of you."

It doesn't mean that I don't sing along or dance. Yes, I do. Why? Because the music is good—that is, it's catchy. It's really easy not to pay attention to the messages in the songs, so you can listen to it. You can even dance along, but you have to know what it's telling you so you can withstand its influence.

MOST ARTISTS AREN'T ALL BAD OR ALL GOOD

Every once in a while, the adult media label an artist, a type of music, or a video game as a really bad influence on the nation's

youth. Don't buy into that. Things are almost never that simple, and if you believe it and try to talk to your daughter from that standpoint, she'll dismiss you for your unfounded judgments and assumptions. It is common for an artist to create an amazingly poignant song about racism, child abuse, or domestic violence and then to turn around and perform a song that has women shaking their butts in his face while they throw money at the camera. It's common for women artists to talk about how they are into female empowerment and positive self-esteem for girls, and then sing about how all they want is for people to envy them and they'll take away another girl's boyfriend because they're hotter. You don't have to keep up with each and every artist and what he or she is doing. You just have to keep this in mind when you are talking to your daughter so she takes you seriously.

DO I OVERANALYZE THINGS?

Many of my students love to ask me this question, and I understand where it comes from. If you do what I'm asking you to do, it seems like you'll never be able to watch or listen to anything mindlessly again. I get that. I also admit that I do have a tendency to analyze things—a lot. But do you know who does it more than me? The companies who package any and all media your daughter consumes. My one brain is nothing compared to the army of marketing people working to sell the consumer the feeling that they must have whatever they're seeing. This is about who has control over your daughter's brain—is it your daughter, or other people whose single purpose is to make her a manipulated consumer?

TALKING TO HER ABOUT ANY OF THIS

All of what I just wrote doesn't take away from the fact that media can be deeply personal and powerful for young people. Music can be positively transformative. Asking them to share their music and other preferred forms of media with you can be like asking them to share their diary.

Before you can have any chance of a successful dialogue with your daughter, it is critical that you process and manage your own emotional reactions. You can't sit across the table from her with a look of disgust on your face and hope to have a successful conversation. Try this instead:

> "I know I've been complaining about your favorite music/video game but I've decided that I really need to learn about it and why you like it. After that, I'd like to talk about it. I have media coming at me all day, and I want us both to be more aware of what messages are coming at us. I want us to be informed, so I'd really like for you to show me what you like and tell me why. Then I want to ask you a couple of questions so I can understand it better."

ENOUGH ALREADY

In the following chapters, you'll see how technology is woven into every aspect of girls' lives. Technology and how it is used in the media are constantly changing. That's not a good thing or a bad thing—it's just our reality. You have to pay attention because it either empowers your daughter to be more engaged, curious, and thoughtful about her world or it turns her into a mindless consumer of ideas and products.

The Mirror

In middle school, young girls will remark openly on their own bodies with disgust and frustration; the girl who dares to be content with her body doesn't feel comfortable saying anything, or will even fabricate some claim of displeasure just so she fits in with the rest of her peers. After a while, she no longer needs to make up these claims: She actually believes them.

—Grace, seventeen

When I go out in public I have to put on makeup or else I will feel like a complete trash bag walking down the street. Fourth grade was when it started. My babysitter wore it all the time. She was perfect.

—Alex, fifteen

Girls can own one body part (like I love my eyes but I hate my butt) and two girls in the same friend group can't have the same thing they like about themselves. You can't say I like my butt because Sydney is the butt girl in the group.

—Ella, thirteen

Unfortunately, no matter how many editions of *Queen Bees* I write, girls will still attempt to fit into an idealized standard of

beauty, and this will undermine their self-worth and identity development. Most of us know that. But we often overlook how girls' interactions with one another contribute to their feelings of inadequacy. From best friends to acquaintances, most girls are constantly comparing themselves to the girls around them—and feel inadequate and even worthless as a result. What we want is for girls to understand that they are surrounded by a powerful culture that objectifies, commodifies, and demeans them, and that they actually need each other's support to develop into powerful, substantial young women.

I have no doubt that we can help girls reach this goal. Here's how we are going to do it. We must be honest with ourselves about how we define femininity and how our actions and the way we talk about ourselves reflect that. We have to understand where we got these ideas about femininity and how we transmit those values and beliefs to our girls. We must recognize the coded language girls speak to themselves and one another that undermines their sense of worth. Then we need to teach them how to change those scripts. And we have to appreciate that this generation of girls is not only getting an unprecedented barrage of messaging about what the culture wants girls to look like, they are also given the forums for judging and being judged on how well they are conforming to this impossible ideal on social media.

Can you stop your daughter from wearing revealing tops, tight pants, or shoes that make her six inches taller? Does she hear you when you tell her that she's beautiful? What do you do if she feels ugly and fat and your words to the contrary make no difference to her? How do race and class impact your daughter's definition of beauty?

And what if you have something completely different going on that is just as confusing? What if your daughter wants to wear only big sweatshirts (remember, she could be doing that to hide her breasts)? Or what if she wants to wear clothing that makes it hard to tell she is a girl? No matter what, how do you raise a girl to believe she is truly valued inside and out—to withstand the relentless messages she'll get throughout her life that she isn't?

Yes, this can seem overwhelming. But we're going to do it. And we're starting at the mall.

Your thirteen-year-old daughter has just been invited to a party, and she's convinced she must have new shoes. Your selective memory kicks into gear and you temporarily forget about the last time you attempted a shopping expedition with her. Off to the mall you go. As soon as you walk in, you're bombarded by videos of models flashing on monitors, neon signs proclaiming the brands your daughter covets, and perky store assistants barely older than your daughter offering their assistance. You begin to feel exhausted, defeated, and slightly paranoid that the whole situation is conspiring against you. Which, of course, is true.

Then it happens. She sees the pair that she *must* have. You groan. They look ridiculous, they're too expensive, the heels are too high, and they're too sexy. You hold up a pair you like: "What about these?" Your daughter rolls her eyes, then begs, then barters, "Just let me get these shoes and I promise I'll walk the dog, clean my room, and do the dishes every day for a month!" When you are less than persuaded, she launches into an outright self-righteous tantrum to the strains of "You're so mean!" You begin to feel the watchful eyes of the other people around you. You look at a mother with a daughter who looks about your daughter's age, and that girl isn't freaking out. Why can't your daughter behave better? The saleswoman hovers and you hate her for how nice she's being to your daughter. You think of all the girls in your daughter's school, so many of whom are wearing the shoes your daughter wants. Your resolve starts to crumble. If all the parents are allowing their daughters to have these shoes, maybe it's not that big of a deal. But you don't want to be that parent who can't hold their own against their kid. You think of the article the PTA just sent out to all the parents about kids dressing too sexy. But they're just shoes, after all, and they *are* 40 percent off. There are bigger issues to worry about with your daughter . . . and so it goes until you find yourself handing over your credit card.

OK, on the face of it, this is a ridiculous fight over shoes, but why is this situation so contentious? First, it's hard to see your daughter grow up. Those shoes could symbolize your daughter's developing sexuality, and you could understandably (and correctly) think she's growing up too fast. Even if you think of your-

self as a fairly relaxed parent, it can be unnerving to see that your daughter wants to be sexy . . . and, even worse, that she can pull it off. But those shoes are equally meaningful to her. Why is she acting like it'll be the end of the world if she doesn't get them? What may be hard to remember in situations like this is that those shoes are a lot more than just something she wears on her feet.

It's *never* just about the shoes.

In her mind, those shoes are the key to maintaining or gaining social acceptance—and not having them means complete social destruction. She believes that if she gets them, her life will be better. She'll take a selfie with the shoes and post it on Instagram . . . and she knows that all of her friends will "like" the post and tell her how cute she is. Plus, the girl who has been annoying your daughter recently posted a picture of the same shoes on Instagram, saying she really wanted them.

But all you know is that you are dealing with an insane person. Is there anything you can do to help you daughter regain her sanity?

What you should know:

- Issues of beauty for girls start at really young ages, so don't be surprised if your six-year-old starts comparing herself to other girls or noticing who's "beautiful."
- Girls know they're manipulated by the media to hold themselves to an impossible standard of beauty, but they hold themselves to it anyway. They could probably school you on Photoshop and airbrushing, but they still look at those pictures and feel inadequate.
- The constant commenting on girls' social media pictures makes them even more insecure and fixated on their looks.
- If they aren't obsessed with their appearance, it's often because they have found another way to express themselves through a talent or skill that is the foundation of their identity and sense of worth. But getting them into an activity is not a magic bullet.
- The way a girl decides to "mark" herself—from piercing her nose or lip to coloring her hair to wearing her favorite

clothing brands—identifies how she sees herself and to what group she belongs. Her markers reveal her relationship to the "Act Like a Woman" box and her opinions about living in Girl World.

FEMININITY: THE RULES OF THE BRAND

Being feminine sucks because I don't always know how to do it. Everyone else seems to just know.

—Anonymous

You will always find flaw after flaw. When I get into that mind-set about how awful I see myself I will research the problem like it's a major school report. Sixth grade was the first time. I was really into tutorials.* So I can look like what society wants.

How we think about gender is always changing, but I think it's fair to say that we are going through a lot of transition right now. On one hand, we're in a time where some young people are demanding a remarkable broadening of the definition of gender, sexual orientation, and identity. Young people are identifying as transgender or asexual, and demanding that adults respect these choices. Many kids aren't passionate about the issue, but accept these changes and the transgender movement without hesitation. At the same time, most girls I work with are still straitjacketed by traditional expectations of appearance and behavior, based on fitting into the "Act Like a Woman" box. In the same school it's not uncommon to have a few students who refuse to answer to a gendered pronoun or who have transitioned from male to female or female to male in the same classes as girls who are killing themselves to look like the hyperfeminine and sexualized celebrities they obsess over. These two realities are coexisting in parallel universes.

---

*   Some of YouTube's most popular videos are tutorials, where girls go to watch and learn how to put on makeup or do their hair.

So, if you're confused, that's more than fair. I'm confused about a lot of this. But two things are clear: Girls have a right to challenge these gender norms and come into their own in the way that feels most comfortable to them, and the overall culture is still telling your daughter to conform to the "Act Like a Woman" box. As I said in chapter 1, whatever she thinks about them, she still absorbs the messages about what it looks like to be a girl. I asked Blue, who is in eighth grade and transitioned from female to male, to describe what it's like. And a helpful definition: "Cisgender" is a term to describe where individuals' experiences of their own gender agree with the sex they were assigned at birth. *Cis* in Latin means to "be on the side of" and is used often to complement *trans* ("on the other side of") when it relates to gender.

> Most [adults], at some point, end up getting their head around the non-cisgender concept, but some are simply very stubborn and don't wish to accept it, or how I wish to express myself. I just want them to make an effort to understand, and maybe then they'll see that there's nothing too confusing about the concept of gender. I think I would have to be most proud of how I have held up with the offensive comments I get from people. I am a very sensitive person, and it is really hard for me not to take comments personally, especially when it is a subject I already struggle enough with on my own. . . . When I am out in public, I am constantly wondering how the people around me perceive me. I try exceedingly hard every morning to achieve the look I am most comfortable with, though most people seem to use female pronouns, even though I have been out for about two school years (some even forget to use my preferred name). . . .
>
> This year, people have been treating me as more of a male than last year, and people are beginning to accept me for that. Though I am not alienated by the girls I know, I am treated more like the gender I identify as than female. Some of the guys in my grade have started to treat me more like one of them. The fact that people are exploring their gender is a very exciting notion to me because for the longest time I

was convinced that I was the only person at my school that identified differently from the gender that I had been assigned at birth.

THE PERFECT GIRL

Girl World often feels like one big beauty competition to girls—one that's rigged against them no matter how "well" they do. And in Girl World, everyone is automatically entered in the contest. How does a girl technically win? By looking like she is standing right in the middle of the "Act Like a Woman" box. However, in my experience, winning always comes at a high price. Either she has to deal with people who like her only for her looks, are jealous, or assume she's arrogant and her life is perfect. Or perhaps she drinks the Kool-Aid and believes she's only worthwhile for how she looks, and sometimes believes she is better than others because of her appearance (and then as she ages desperately tries to maintain her looks because she feels worthless as they fade). So you actually lose a lot when you win.

Picture the perfect girl . . . what does she look like? Keep that image front and center in your mind's eye. Does she have long hair? Is she thin? Does she have light, maybe white, skin?

> *People think being pretty is going to make your life way easier but it's not that simple. My mom puts a lot of pressure on me to always look right. She always tell me it's important to look good and present yourself well but sometimes I think that's what is most important to her. As long as I look good, she's happy. And I'm not happy, I'm pretending—but when I tell people that, they don't believe me. They say sarcastic things like, "Yeah, I know it must be really tough to be you." It's like if you're pretty you're not allowed to have any problems.*
>
> —Gillian, sixteen

I'm sure it wouldn't surprise you that this girl typifies the classic white American definition of beauty: tall, thin, blond, and beauti-

ful. If this girl—the one so many girls want to be like, the one girls envy—can feel unworthy, can you imagine what other girls feel?

I often ask girls (including girls that fit the "perfect" image), "In an average day, how many times do you think about your weight and/or your appearance, and what percentage of those comments are negative versus positive?" They laugh at me for thinking they have positive comments. For some, these moments of insecurity are just that—moments when they feel good or bad, secure or insecure. But for far too many others, these moments dictate an entire self-concept of who they are and what they can be.

> I have never met a person who thinks she's pretty. You sit and pick apart every flaw. The combined list of how you don't measure up really adds up.
>
> —Joni, fifteen

I teach countless girls who are beautiful by anyone's standards, yet they're absolutely convinced that their flaws are all anyone sees, because they're either constantly evaluating themselves according to the girls they see in the media or online, or the "perfect" girls around them. So when your daughter tells you how incredibly ugly she is, how fat her thighs are, or how big her nose is, you have to realize that she believes it—no matter what you tell her.

> There are so many things that girls have no control over that absolutely end up affecting them when they compare themselves to others: too tall, too short, mental and physical disabilities, even teeth, for crying out loud! In a thousand insidious ways, almost all of us let these uncontrollable factors attack our self-worth. It's truly horrible in the way it convinces us to judge aspects of ourselves that we cannot change. We just need to see how we all get so tricked.
>
> —Tessa, eighteen

You may have wondered why your daughter doesn't seem to care when you tell her she's beautiful. You're being blown off because you unconditionally love her. That's why she says, "Mom, that's what you have to say; you're my mom," which implies that if you were more conditionally loving, your opinion would matter more. This doesn't mean you shouldn't say it, because you should. But it's important to know why she's blowing you off. The sad truth is that the girls who really need to hear that they are beautiful are usually the girls whose parents undermine their sense of worth.

BREAKING THE CODE

The closer you are to someone the more that they are going to tell you what they don't like about themselves, and they are going to compare themselves even more to each other. If you're comparing yourself to every girl, you can't trust them. Talking to each other makes it worse.

—Alex, fifteen

Alex's comment is as frustrating as it is true. The constant back-and-forth between girls about who is pretty and who has the best body—or the best anything—acts like a poison to girls' self-esteem. It makes girls seem like they're materialistic and obsessed with their appearance and other people's judgments of them—or are ruthlessly judging others themselves. If you're having this experience, regardless of your understandable feelings, you need to acknowledge what she's up against. If she's going through puberty, her brain chemistry is already highly attuned to wanting the reward of social approval by her peers.* Now add in the fact that every picture posted of her, every selfie she takes and posts, is not only a way for her to create and maintain her online and real-life identity, but a tool for other people to judge her.

---

* Laurence Steinberg, *Age of Opportunity*, page 74.

One of the best ways we can counteract this dynamic is by educating girls about how they talk to one another in a coded language that undermines not only their self-esteem but their friendships. The following, which probably won't be a surprise to you, are the ones I think are the most undermining:

- If there's something about their physical appearance they do like, most girls will never admit it because they're afraid other girls will accuse them of being vain.
- If there's something about their physical appearance they don't like, they're obsessed with it.
- Girls need constant reassurance from each other that they look good—but they're never sure if their friend is telling the truth.
- When you're with your friends, you should always put yourself down, especially in comparison with them. Picture what happens when one girl tells another girl how great she looks. Does the recipient of the compliment thank her? Rarely. Instead, the response is usually some variation of "Oh, no, I look so fat and horrible. I can't believe you would say that. You look so much better than me."
- Leap to your friends' defense when they put themselves down; they'll leap to yours when you put yourself down. So you say you're fat? "OMG, you look so good!" Girls compete with one another about who's the fattest: "You're so much thinner than me! Compared to you I'm such a cow."
- Don't do any of the above too much because then it will look like you're begging for compliments all the time and that's annoying.

Particularly painful and problematic is how intensely girls compare themselves against the friends in their group. This is how the "Act Like a Woman" box's definition of beauty infects the girls' friendships, pulling them away from one another as they either compete for a place near the top of the hierarchy within their friend group or as they struggle to meet the standard for staying in the friend group. The pursuit and attainment of the

elusive standard of beauty is one of the most critical components of girls' power structure. Girls are keenly aware of these dynamics, and, unfortunately, few of them feel there's anything they can do to stop them. I think the tremendous pressure to maintain these friendships convinces girls within a group to conform to one look.

> The Queen Bee always asks "What are you wearing?" but not like "What are you wearing? You look cute" but "OMG, what are YOU wearing?"
>
> —Gabriel, eleven

The Queen Bee doesn't invent the look, but she's a conduit of information on the look from the media to the rest of her clique. The irony of all of this is that a Queen Bee is copying, too—she's just really good at looking like she's not imitating anyone around her. A Queen Bee strictly adheres to the rules and quickly corrects those who break them and stray outside the set definition of cool. The fear of censure is so strong that it can largely dictate who gets into the "higher" cliques, and it encourages all girls to be Wannabes.

> It's not that they're all beautiful, but those girls all look alike. They seem like they're all sisters. They have the same body structure and they're all petite.
>
> —Lynn, sixteen

Six Questions to Ask Your Daughter

Do her friends compliment her? If so, what about?

If they do compliment her, how does she respond?

Does she believe what they are saying?

Does she feel like she has to compliment her friends?

Can she honestly say what she's proud of or likes about herself?

Are her friends proud of her accomplishments? How does she know?

Helping Girls Break the Code

- Stop the negative self-talk by countering it with a positive message. For example, "My legs are so fat" turns into "My legs are strong." It doesn't matter if your daughter doesn't believe what she's saying at first. The goal is to interrupt the pattern.
- When someone compliments her, her answer should be "Thank you!"
- If she gives a compliment, she can't get angry if she isn't complimented in return. She needs to think of the compliment as a gift, not a transaction.
- If a girl gets angry at her for being vain, she needs to ask what she's doing that makes her come across as vain. If she is proud of something she's done or something about herself that she likes, she gets to express that. If she is putting other people down, constantly or consistently talking about herself, then she needs to accept that feedback and do her best to modify her behavior.
- If she gives a friend a compliment and the friend responds by putting herself down, she needs to say, "Hey, I really meant that compliment. You are X, and you should be proud of it so don't put yourself down."

RACE MATTERS—NO MATTER WHAT RACE YOU ARE

One of the things I always felt growing up as someone of mixed racial heritage was that I didn't fit in anywhere. On the one hand, I was presented with the white image of beauty as the blue-eyed, blond-haired, tall, skinny, big-breasted All-American girl. On the other hand was the Asian image of beauty as petite, slender, long dark hair, exotic features, and pale skin. The only thing I had in common with any of those images was that I was fair-skinned. Otherwise I never felt like I measured up. It's also true that Asian women try to look more white. My mother, for instance, puts tape on her eyelids to make them look rounder. One of my Korean friends once

*told me I was lucky that I had pale skin because when she
went to Korea, people told her she looked like a "country girl"
because she's naturally tan. There are also operations that
some girls get to make their eyes look more "white," and some
girls get nose jobs to make their noses look more "white."*

—Ellie, twenty-one

It's frustrating how often well-intentioned adults avoid talking about racism with their children. Most white parents tend to say some variation of "We aren't racist. We believe everyone is equal." That's not enough. It is the definition of white parent privilege that you don't think you need to talk to your daughter about race and racism as she grows up. For example, if you're white and have a young daughter who likes to play with dolls, it's your responsibility to look at the dolls being marketed to your daughter and buy dolls that represent the diversity of girls in real life.

Has the underlying culture of beauty shifted in recent years? It's a mixed answer. While it's becoming more common to see nonwhite women on magazine covers, we need to take a closer look at these images in the media. Almost all nonwhite models share the same caramel-colored skin and long, straight hair. So it raises the question: Do Asian, black, Latina, East Asian, Native American, or any other girls of racial minorities in their communities see themselves reflected in the faces of the women they see in the media?

To my mind, "beautiful women" of all races with light skin, the "right" curves, and straight hair are not proof that our culture is race blind. Our girls are still getting toxic messages that certain physical traits are more worthy than others. Yes, it's great that a few more women of color are included in our perception of beauty. Yes, it's good that your daughter is probably looking at beauty tutorials by women who aren't white—but their beauty is still defined by the white standard. The most socially acceptable and easiest way to be considered a "beautiful" woman of color is to be closer to the "white" ideals that the culture demands.

I know lots of famous women say they love their curves, but they're not talking about what my friend and colleague Shanterra

McBride calls their "jiggle." They aren't loving their potbelly or flabby arms, because they don't have them. I'm not sure how much we've progressed if this is what we call "accepting" all different types of women's bodies.

> The Indian standard of beauty is long hair, light skin, graceful, big doe eyes, and curves, but only in the right places. My culture has always thought that the paler a girl's skin is, the more beautiful she is. The prejudice still exists now, even among the girls in my group. My mother is always telling me not to be in the sun to preserve my relatively pale skin. My friends talk about other Indian girls, deriding them because they're dark. I used to hang out with a clique of all Indian girls, but we were full of contradictions. We say that we have friends in other groups, but we don't. You had to pretend that you belonged to many different cliques, but the reality was that you could only belong to the group to be accepted by the group. Wearing an Indian anklet is cool, but discussing the partition of India and Pakistan isn't. The Indian clique was exclusive, but the only way I can be proud of my heritage is not to be part of the Indian clique. Part of this is selfish because, like all girls, I want to be more special than everyone else, and I couldn't be in that group. Nevertheless, life in that group was a whole lot of pretending. The ones who take the most authentic pride aren't part of their cultural group. One of my closest friends is Japanese and she thinks the same thing.
>   —Nidhi, sixteen

Race and racism impact girls' sense of self and their friendships. Ask your daughter to imagine a girl who is being teased or looked down on because she's too skinny, too fat, too flat-chested, has no butt, or doesn't have the light skin or straight hair of other girls. Then ask your daughter if she could give advice to that girl, what would she say to her? Now your daughter needs to tell herself those same words. You don't want your daughter feeling ashamed or less worthy because of how messed up the world is. Moreover, she needs to see this issue in a larger context so that she doesn't

feel alone, and she realizes this problem is bigger than her. That way she begins to understand the context for the comments and feels empowered to stand up for all women, including herself.

"ACTING WHITE"

Even in the most diverse schools, kids of different races or ethnic groups often have a set hallway and designated lunch tables that they occupy year after year. For some kids it's about needing some downtime to hang out with other kids who share a common language or culture. But if a student doesn't want to hang out there and maintains friendships in other groups, does she still fit in with her same-race clique? Not always. In fact, these "floating" girls tell me they often get grief for "trying to be white." In schools with racial and economic diversity, the students of color are often torn: Where do they sit in the hallway or cafeteria? Where is their loyalty? For these young people, it can feel like they must make a choice between personifying their "race culture" (or how their dominant culture is portrayed in movies, TV, music, and so forth) and what their real lives actually reflect.

> Adults all believe that since I am black, I can't live in the suburbs and talk like I do. They all expect me to talk like I come from a bad neighborhood. It gets really frustrating because people are surprised when they see that I'm smart and have a good home life.
>
> —Nia, eighteen

> The white students in my school act really arrogantly. But I still wanted to try and get involved in my school through student council, but then I had the other problem of some of my Mexican friends didn't want me crossing over to the other side. I still did it—I want more Hispanic students in leadership at my school and I want to be a role model but it's hard.
>
> —Lissa, sixteen

Unfortunately, I have had experiences with parents and educators who directly reinforce this message. Before I work in a

community I always have a conference call with the organizers. A couple of times a year, I inevitably have a conversation with a parent or administrator from a majority white suburban community, who "just wants to check in," about what I am going to say. Then just as predictably, I get this comment in the form of a question: "We're just a close community and want to make sure our children aren't exposed to things they shouldn't be. They're not like those urban children you work with who are exposed to more sexual things and more violence. We don't have those kind of influences." Meanwhile, their kids are at home playing a video game where they're killing prostitutes on their flat-screen or they're laughing at the latest pornography they've downloaded to their smartphone.

BAD HAIR

If you're reading this and were born with naturally straight hair, did you know that perming "white hair" curls it, but perming "kinky hair" straightens it? That those long braids some women wear are made from hair extensions, cost hundreds of dollars, take ten hours to complete, and are braided so tightly that women often get terrible headaches? Or that a girl is told she has "good hair" if it's like white hair and "bad hair" if it's kinky?

Listen to some of my students:

I have to sit for an hour every morning while my mother yanks my hair. It makes me cry because it hurts so much.

I hate having to do my hair! I wish it were softer!

Sometimes the perms can really burn your skin.

You get your hair braided and they braid it so tight I get a really bad headache.

People always say nappy hair is bad and I have nappy hair and there isn't a thing I can do about it. It makes me feel bad.

RACISM WITHIN

Just because you are a member of a minority group doesn't mean you can't hold racist or bigoted viewpoints about your own group.

> *I hate when people say "You're pretty, for a dark-skinned girl."*
> —Monica, sixteen

> *You want to be the light-skinned girl with the good hair. You stare in the mirror and think, "She's so beautiful. I wish I had her color skin. Why isn't my nose thinner? Why am I so ugly?" In my Dominican community where I teach, the girls are either very dark or light skinned. The darker-skinned girls are just like the African American girls. They touch the light-skinned girls' hair and say, "I wish I had her hair. She's so pretty."*
> —Sonia

> *I don't have a big butt. People compare me to a white girl. I'm teased a lot for being too skinny. I wanted to hang out with people who would accept me for not being so curvy.*
> —Aliesha, seventeen

Why am I writing about this? Because girls say racist comments. Because girls are friends with girls of other races and need to be taught not to make racist or racially insensitive comments. And in response to those racist comments, white girls need to know that they don't have the right to say to a girl of any minority "You're just taking it the wrong way." Or use the word "ghetto" or the n-word or any other racist term and think it doesn't matter because no one confronts them about it. Because girls need to support one another so the one minority girl doesn't have to carry the entire responsibility to speak out when someone is demeaning her based on race.

MAKING HER MARK

Markers control girls' minds whether we like it or not.

—Jade, seventeen

A marker is the signifier of how your daughter accepts or rejects Girl World, her place in her community's social hierarchy, and her place in her group. Her choice of clothes, hairstyle, and overall style are all markers. So are the sports she plays, what clubs she belongs to, how well she does in school, or how much money her family has. Markers for a particular clique might be more specific; for example, the soccer team clique might all wear a particular sports headband in their hair.

It can be hard to appreciate markers for what they are—a wealth of information about a girl. Whether she has one look and sticks with it throughout her childhood and teen years or she suddenly does a complete overhaul, how she presents herself gives you a window into what she thinks about her world and her place in it. Don't see markers as a sign of disrespect but as expressions of her identity development. Your children want your affirmation. A girl wants you to be proud of her and the choices she makes. She wants to be accepted by you for who she is, odd clothes and strange makeup included. If you don't accept her, she'll feel rejected at the precise time in her life when creating and exploring her sense of self through her image is her greatest priority. When you tell her that her tongue piercing is distracting (and you're a little worried about the dental bills), you may believe you're only looking out for her best interests, but she can't hear what you're saying. That's why she fights back so hard. She feels as if she's fighting for her soul and you're one of the forces trying to take it away from her.

> **What were your markers or your style when you were a teen? Why did you choose them?**
>
> **What part of your body or appearance were you most self-conscious about?**
>
> **Did you ever look at certain people when you were growing up and think they were better than you because of the way they looked?**
>
> **How did adults make you feel about the way you looked?**

SELFIES

There is really only one "rule" for selfies, and that is to look good or sexy. For selfies, girls will pucker their lips (duck face), or stick their tongue out. Some girls try and show their boobs as much as possible. Others make a face that looks like they are in pain or extremely confused. Whatever the pose is it usually is not a normal facial expression, and if you saw someone posing like it in public you couldn't help but laugh.

—Rachel, fourteen

I don't think there's a better example of a marker than what kind of selfie a girl takes and what she's doing in that picture. Selfies are how she takes all her markers, all the ways she wants the world to see her, and then puts it out for the public. But that's not all. It's also where the development of her ideal online identity (what she wants others to think about her) combines with all of the messages from the "Act Like a Woman" box. Many girls I work with have a signature look they always use when they take a selfie, and they usually assume that pose whenever someone takes a picture of them.

Some girls take selfies by themselves in a bathroom, but that's usually seen by other girls as being desperate for attention. Other girls take selfies in the school bathroom with their friends. Girls will text purposefully ugly selfies to their friends, ones with dou-

ble chins, no makeup, weird faces, bad angles, and embarrassing hair—but they're usually not going to post them on a social
networking platform like Instagram, because that's where they
display their public image. On the other hand, some girls will
post only ugly pictures of themselves, possibly because they want
to make it harder for the invisible, judgmental public to make
nasty comments about them. You can see it as a defensive attempt
to seem like they don't care what others think. Or perhaps they
truly like to post silly pictures of themselves. But no matter what,
girls take selfies to fit the image they want of themselves, and then
many of them connect that image to increasing and maintaining
their popularity. So educate yourself about the selfies your daughter takes. Does she have a pose she strikes or a facial expression
she makes as soon as someone points a camera in her direction?
What do you think she's trying to convey in that moment?

> Stereotypically a girl who takes a lot of selfies is a middle
> school girl and a "girly girl," but that isn't necessarily true.
> There are a lot of sporty girls who take selfies a lot, probably
> because in my school the sporty girls are the cool kids, so
> since they feel so popular they want to show themselves off
> often. Girls take selfies either because they think they look
> good, or they want someone to tell them they look good. It's
> also a competition on Instagram, to see who can get the most
> likes. Girls like when their selfies get a lot of likes because it
> makes them feel better, and it makes them feel prettier, and
> that they're almost winning the popularity contest.
>
> —Vanessa, thirteen

When sending selfies to boys through direct messages and
texts, girls try to be effortlessly sexy, with noticeable but not over-
done cleavage, slightly pouted lips, big eyes, and a slender neck.
But getting the "right" selfie takes time. It may take twenty times
to get the perfect "spontaneous" selfie. By the way, girls aren't the
only ones sending selfies. You want to listen to a funny conversation? Ask girls what selfies boys send them. Apparently many boys
frequently send pictures with messages like these:

just waking up (shirtless)
getting out of the pool (shirtless)
about to shower (you guessed it . . . shirtless)

There is a lot of pressure to be sexy online for most girls. But some take it too far at an early age. I say if you're still in middle school, strive to look cute, not sexy. You will look back at your attempts at being sexy and cringe. Trust me. No one wants to see a 13 year old in a skimpy bikini posing with her butt half hanging out.

—Peyton, seventeen

I think there is pressure to look sexy online. Everything is based on likes and things like that. If you look better you get more likes. If the selfie is being sent to a close friend the pictures often don't need to look good and can be taken quickly. These selfies are also often taken without makeup and show things that could be embarrassing if others were to see (crazy faces, messy hair, etc.). If the selfie is being sent to a new friend, the selfie becomes more formal and normal. These selfies generally have smiles and are captioned with proper grammar. When I send a selfie to a guy that I find attractive, it often takes a few tries. I have noticed that females often pose lying down or on places such as a couch to make it seem like they aren't trying too hard even though the selfies have lots of thought put into them. When someone does not want the other person to see their whole face, this is often when they have no makeup on, they will sometimes take a picture of one part of their face. These include most commonly lips and eyes.

—Alex, fifteen

LAND MINE!

Look at the pictures you have posted on your own SNPs. What do they say about you? How do you think your daughter would answer that question about your pictures?

HOW TO TALK TO HER ABOUT HOW SHE LOOKS

Whether your daughter wears all black, wants to get a tattoo, or is obsessed about looking like the people she idealizes in the media, here are some suggestions for talking to her about her appearance. *Remember: This is a process.* You get to have a lot of these conversations with her as she grows up. Of course she isn't going to love all of them. But even asking the questions below will hopefully get her thinking. And that's what you want: a girl who critically thinks about these issues so she'll pay attention to her feelings and have the words to articulate those feelings.

If She Dresses to Look Exactly Like Her Friends

"Hey, I've noticed that you and your friends dress a lot alike. Am I crazy? Can you tell me what that's about? Who is deciding what the look is? Is there something you could wear that your friends wouldn't approve?"

If She's Super Scary

Let's say your daughter is wearing all black, and her eyes are heavily rimmed with black. Your first impulse is to say "What is wrong with you?" Instead, put aside your feelings about what the neighbors will think. You've got to seriously watch your tone here because you need to come across as respectful and curious, not hyperanxious and embarrassed. Remember what I said on page 98 about really listening to her? This would be a good time to take me up on this. Ask "Why the black lipstick? Why do you want to get your eyebrow pierced?" Anytime she's defensive, say "I really want to know. If it's important to you, it's important to me."

If her appearance is really hard for you, you can say:

"OK, I respect your choices, but I'm not going to lie to you and say this isn't hard for me. How about a compromise? Wear the makeup you want but I'd really appreciate it if you didn't wear the ripped shirt with the zombie on it to the family reunion."

It's OK to admit that you don't like your daughter's choices, but it's important to understand why they are so important to her

and affirm them anyway. And, really, what's the big deal about a zombie T-shirt?

I'm aware that many parents will pose the "slippery slope" argument: If you "let" her choose her hairstyle, makeup, and clothes, you lose authority. You truly lose authority when you aren't consistent and respectful. But her fashion choices are not a free-for-all. You and your daughter need milestones. There's a fine line between handing down rules that create power struggles between you and your daughter and rules that create safety, provide structure, and signify maturity milestones in her life. So if your tween daughter is begging you to wear makeup, tell her that before she's allowed to wear makeup, she has to learn how to take care of her skin. Then get her some good, not too expensive, facial products. And, as a compromise, let her get one lip gloss. Think of it this way: I'd have a much easier time letting my daughter wear something weird than something really conformist that shows she's just absorbing all these "Act Like a Woman" box messages around her.

The Stakes Get Higher: Your Daughter Is So Sexy You're Embarrassed to Let Her Leave the House

Here you really have power with younger girls, because it's up to you to buy the outfit for the hip-hop dance recital. You are the one who chooses the Halloween costume. In the Resources in the back of this book, there are links for videos you can watch together that show little girls speaking out about these issues. When you watch these videos together, you're showing her that she's joining a group of really cool, smart girls.

But let's fast-forward a bit and imagine you now have an eighth-grade daughter and you're sitting in the living room on a Friday night. Your daughter walks down the stairs and quickly darts past the living room but not quite quickly enough. You can see that she's wearing a really short skirt, knee-high boots, and a shirt held up by two strings. You want to go ballistic. This is how you have the conversation.

First, prepare mentally. Take a deep breath and let go of any anxiety and/or anger. Remember, she isn't wearing this outfit out of disrespect for you.

Check to see if she has any friends with her. If she does, ask to speak with her privately, but don't say "I want to speak to you privately," because then you'll have embarrassed her in front of her friends and she won't listen to you. Instead, say something like "Hey, can you come into the kitchen for a minute? I need to ask you something." Keep your tone casual! Check in with her about her plans. Then say something like this (in your own words):

> "You probably don't want to hear this, but I'm going to tell you how I feel about the way you're dressed. [Wait until she stops rolling her eyes.] I know that if I forbid you from wearing what you're wearing right now, you could change as soon as you leave the house. This is what I'm worried about. You look older and sexy, which may be the point. I'm worried that people are going to treat you as if you're older and you'll feel pressured to maintain that image. I want you to be proud and confident when you walk into a room. I want you to feel that how you are presenting yourself is true to who you are. After you leave here, ask yourself if your clothes are making you act differently than you feel is the real you."

Then, the next morning, over breakfast, ask her if she did think about it. If she says yes and tells you anything, this is great! It matters less what she thinks at the moment than whether she actually thought about it and is processing that with you. If she blows you off, tell her that while you can't force her to talk, part of being her parent is that you will bring up these issues on an annoyingly consistent basis.

If you've ever seen a girl dressing in a way that you think is too sexy, have you ever asked yourself "What kind of mother lets her daughter out of the house dressed like that?" First of all, there's a double standard because I've never heard a parent say "What kind of dad lets their daughter leave the house dressed like that?" We have to stop blaming moms. Second, that girl who's dressed so inappropriately in front of you could have left the house in sweatpants. Or she could have thrown a bag with her "cute" clothes out the window and picked it up when she left the house. Or she could have left the house and gone to find something "cute" to wear at a friend's house. So . . . be careful about throwing stones.

Halloween Immunity and Having the Conversation Again

Have you noticed that some girls will use any excuse to dress up in sexy costumes? Halloween is the most obvious example, but girls will do it whenever they feel they can get away with it. Note that I don't mean get away with it with you but with their peers. These situations are cease-fires in girls' battles with one another when they get to dress as sexily as possible with less fear of recrimination. That is, people are less likely to say "Did you see the way she was dressed? What a slut!" It's the freedom to be a "bad" girl.

> I love Halloween! You can be a devil, angel, or a French maid. It's an excuse to be sexy without worrying about what anyone else is saying.
>
> —Lynn, sixteen

> We had celebrity day and everyone used it as an excuse to wear short skirts and low-cut shirts, and no one could say anything about it because you can dress up however you want without people calling you a whore.
>
> —Nia, eighteen

When your daughter dresses up as a sexy kitten for Halloween or wants to wear revealing clothes every day, she's test-driving her developing sexuality and she's experimenting with what it feels

like to present herself sexually in our culture. Those are two different things. Understandably, both can make you anxious, but neither one is "bad." Again, what you want is for her to go through the process being self-reflective. And that's why you have open conversations with her.

> "Because I'm your mom [or dad] I'll admit that what you're wearing sort of freaks me out because it's so revealing. [She tells you she doesn't want to talk about it.] Just hear me out. One of the reasons I'm freaking out is because you're growing up. You have a right to come into your own and that includes your sexuality. That's my issue and I need to deal with that. You look great and there's nothing wrong with wanting people to notice. But, the other reason I'm nervous about how you look is because the culture we live in gives you so many double standards. On one hand, it tells you the most important, valuable thing about you is your body. Then when you follow those rules, you go out into the world and people will only value you for how you look, or they'll disrespect you. Some girls get so wrapped up in the whole thing that their behavior starts to match as well—so they act like they are less intelligent and confident than they are. So when you walk out the door I want you to be proud of yourself and how you look, and aware of how this system is designed to mess with you. I want you to be in control of yourself so no one else is. That's why I am freaking out. Thanks for listening. I love you."

Then she'll say, "Dad/Mom, I know this. You've told me this stuff a thousand times. I've got it." And then she'll walk out the door and your stomach will be in knots. But as excruciating as these moments can be, the one thing I know is if you have conversations with your daughter like this, your words are in her head when she needs them most. (I'll discuss this issue in more depth in chapter 12.)

But maybe you don't see it this way. I have students whose mothers want them to dress "well" or "nicely"—meaning sexily. I have this experience quite a lot, but one situation stands out for me. I worked with two high school girls who were getting in trouble at school for wearing short skirts, knee-high socks, and high

heels. If you walked up the stairs behind them, you could easily see up their skirts—which they prepared for because they always wore sexy underwear. They were constantly getting dress-coded (see page 185), the female teachers were incredibly frustrated, and the male teachers were afraid to look at them. When I talked to the girls, I learned they were from Miami, and they insisted that in their culture they were dressed nicely and specifically the way their mothers wanted them to dress. In addition, one of them had a horrible relationship with her mother and was trying to rebuild it. Dressing the way her mother wanted her to dress was a way to bond with her.

Obviously you can disagree, but here's what I see. If you're coming from a culture that encourages women and girls to present themselves primarily in a sexual way, several things happen to your daughter:

- The boys who have been raised to value women only for their bodies will be the ones who are the most attracted to her and go after her. They may be charming, they may come from "nice" families, but that is what's going on.
- These boys dismiss girls' opinions, especially when those opinions are different from what they want.
- These boys are conditioned to devalue her intellect or anything else about her except how she looks and what she can do for them sexually.
- Other boys may think she's beautiful but will be too intimidated to approach her.
- Girls will be uncomfortable with your daughter (which is not necessarily jealousy), and many of them will talk behind your daughter's back.
- At school, some well-intentioned male teachers will be afraid to talk to her at all because they don't want to be seen alone with her.
- Female and male teachers will be worried for your daughter but will be confused about how to talk to her, because they don't want to be disrespectful about how she's being raised and possibly get an irate phone call from you.

Bottom line? You have the right to raise your daughter as you see fit. But consider whether the culture you were raised in primarily values your daughter's identity as a sexual object. If so, are you devaluing your daughter's overall worth and dignity by conforming to those cultural mores?

DRESS CODES

With all this drama about what girls wear, wouldn't it be easier to just give them a school uniform and be done with the whole thing? Not really. First, while most schools don't have uniforms, most do have dress codes. And a lot of girls are rightfully frustrated about the way dress codes are enforced. A lot of teachers are similarly frustrated that they have to police what students are wearing—especially the one teacher who takes it on the most. In fact, "dress-coded" has become a verb—like "I got dress-coded today and Ms. Wiseman pulled me out of class. I hate her!"

So what is a dress code? It's more than just "girls can't wear spaghetti straps." Officially, dress codes are the articulated expectations and enforceable rules created by an educational institution to reflect what it wants to "see" in its students, balancing safety, unity, and the individual rights of its students. Here are the standard arguments to support uniforms and dress codes:

- They decrease materialism and social competition.
- They stop children from wearing clothes that are offensive or that promote illegal or unhealthy substances, such as drugs and alcohol.
- They set a standard for students that learning environments should be given respect, and they prepare them for a professional environment as adults.
- They contribute to students' self-respect.
- They contribute to school spirit and unity.

While they do make it much easier to dress in the morning, uniforms aren't a magic bullet to stop the fashion show competition between students. Kids always know who has more money

relative to others, either because the student boasts about it or other people talk about it. If it's important to students to show how much money their family has, they will figure out a way to show it—from their headphones, smartphones, computers, shoes, and jewelry, to what cars their parents drive or what car their parents buy them.

Having rules against product promotion make sense. We don't want our children to be walking advertisements. But you could argue that anything we wear is an advertisement for something, so it's not a foolproof reason.

Setting a standard for a learning environment? Sort of true. But what is much more important is supporting learning standards in which critical thinking is encouraged. It's the same thing for creating spirit and unity—again, I'd take a mutually respectful relationship between faculty and students any day over students wearing uniforms.

Here's the Reality of Dress Codes

Boys and girls usually get dress-coded for different reasons. Boys most often get in trouble for wearing clothes that are "disrespectful." When you ask adults to give examples of what this disrespect looks like, the response is almost always "baggy pants." Or they use the word "urban" (that is, stereotypical black), although I've heard the word "ghetto" used as well—which is clearly racist. Far too many adults start the interaction with boys by using their adult power to dominate them and seeing any resistance as defiance and cause for punishment.

In contrast, and not surprisingly, girls get in trouble for "inappropriate" displays of their sexuality. Girls who go through puberty early and/or are more developed are disproportionately targeted. It is also well documented that African American and Hispanic students get in trouble more often and get harsher punishments than their white peers for breaking any school rule, including the dress code. It is also true that a dress code is always enforced inconsistently because of the human dynamics at any school. Some teachers don't agree or care about the dress code and won't enforce it; some don't like the way students are dressed but don't feel comfortable bringing it up. And that means a student can go through

six of their seven periods during the day only to get in trouble at the end of the day—which seems unfair and inconsistent.

Now think about the difference between girls' physical development. One girl who doesn't have large breasts wears a tank top and teachers aren't going to notice, or they'll feel ridiculous telling that girl she is violating the dress code. Another girl can have her breasts spilling out of her tank top. One doesn't feel like a problem, and the other does. But technically you're supposed to hold all girls to the same standard—easy to say when you're not actually in the situation.

Teachers and administrators are in a tough spot. Many male teachers are uncomfortable talking to a girl who is violating a dress code because they don't want to come across as seeing that girl sexually. Few teachers are trained on how to talk to a boy or a girl about the dress code, but they're told to enforce it. But it is also easy to overlook that for white middle and upper class girls, violating the dress code is an easy and safe way to rebel against the system. Unlike their African American and/or lower socioeconomic female peers, the punishments they get for being out of dress code aren't usually that bad. They don't get suspended. They don't have the situations escalate so the punishment in no way fits the "crime." They get detention, their parents get really mad at the school administrators, and their rights become the central issue.

We know when we are breaking the dress code. I have gone through my day waiting to see how long it will take for someone to dress-code me. And I have tested my teachers, too.
                                              —Simone, thirteen

What I have written above doesn't invalidate the girls' complaints. What I am saying is that punishment for dress code rule breaking is often very different based on the race and socioeconomic class of the girl, and all girls need to know that. Furthermore, a dress code should be an opportunity to build relationships with our children. They can also be easily connected to core academic subject areas in topics that matter to them. For example, if a student is wearing a shirt advertising alcohol or getting drunk,

educators should be teaching media literacy. ("Why do you want to be a walking billboard?") If children want to fight the dress code, let them research their legal rights in a social studies or history class. That way they can learn about the First Amendment and their right (or lack thereof) to free speech through the rulings on school dress codes. If they are outraged that a teacher lectured them about how they were dressed, they should read about the punishments their peers experienced, especially if they are a different race, religion, or class.

Most important, they should be an opportunity to show our children that we care about them. We should never talk to boys and girls disrespectfully about what they're wearing and get into a battle of wills with them. And we should never tell girls that they are a distraction to the boys.

> *Telling boys we are a distraction is not OK. And isn't it more distracting for teachers to pull you out of class?*
> —Gabriel, thirteen

Yes, a girl's appearance can be distracting, but that doesn't mean the boys around her should be held to such a low standard that they aren't expected to treat her respectfully. It also contributes to the dynamic where adults teach girls and boys that girls are responsible and therefore to be blamed if others say and do sexually degrading things to them.

> *I was in fourth grade and I was wearing a tank top and I was in class working and the teacher pulls me aside and says, your shirt isn't appropriate. What will other people think of you? I'm in fourth grade! I kind of knew what she was talking about, vaguely, but why was this a problem? But now looking back on it she was saying I was being slutty.*
> —Simone, thirteen

> *Parents dress-code me all the time! I get it if you want to wear flip-flops in winter that's fine. But if you're butt is totally showing or your bra is entirely showing I get that's not cool.*
> —Holly, thirteen

If you're a teacher and want to let a girl know that she is violating the dress code, take a moment with her, like during passing periods, and quietly say she's out of dress code. If you're a parent and your daughter is getting in trouble for dress code violations, here's what's important to communicate.

"This is difficult to speak about with you but it's important to me that I do. You are getting in trouble for violating the dress code and we have to address that. But way more important to me than the dress code is you. You are a smart young woman with a lot to contribute to this world. Like all young women, you're growing up in a world that dismisses your opinions and rights by trying to convince you that the most important thing about you is your physical appearance. Obviously, you are so much more than that. I want you to be proud and comfortable with how you look. But I also want you to be proud and comfortable about who you are beyond that. Can you think about what is most important in how you want to present yourself?"

If an adult is disrespectful to her, here's something you can say to her:

"If someone talks to you about being out of dress code, do what they say. If you feel that they have been rude to you or shamed you in any way, I still want you to do what they say but then tell me and/or tell the administrator you trust the most. Then we will figure out the most appropriate next steps. If you're genuinely confused about why, or if what you're wearing is important to you and it's not communicating something rude or degrading about someone else, you have the right to respectfully ask why you are in violation of the dress code. If you feel strongly about this, you can research your rights about freedom of expression in schools and bring that to the administration. You may not get what you want but it's important to know your rights, and I will support that."

THE COMPETITION NO ONE WINS

You're getting new jeans for your daughter. Sometime over the last year she's developed hips. You have brought no less than twenty different styles and sizes into the changing room for her to try on, yet she hates all of them. After what seems like hours, she opens the dressing room door and she's near tears. She says to you, "I hate how I look. I am so fat." If you're still wrestling with your own issues about weight, these situations can be lightning rods between you and your daughter. For her sake, get yourself together about it so that you can be an effective role model.

CHECKING YOUR BAGGAGE

Who among us doesn't have some baggage about their weight? And women aren't the only ones messed up. Men have baggage, too. So . . .

- How do you feel about your own weight and appearance now?
- How would your daughter answer that question about you?
- How often do you talk about your weight? Every week? Every day?
- Does your scale decide whether it's a good day or a bad day?
- When someone compliments you, do you thank them or put yourself down?
- What have you said to your daughter about how she looks?

Right after I was born, my mom was anorexic. When I was little I remember my mom looking in the mirror and saying, "I'm too fat!" She would never eat granola.

—Laney, fifteen

I have one friend whose mother is pretty crazy. She's always putting pressure on her daughter to wear makeup. I think her mom was a model so she always needs to be perfect and thinks the daughter should follow in her steps. My friend is

really insecure and thinks she's fat. Whenever we talk about anything it always come back to that. I think the mom is oblivious. It's weird that you can say those type of things to your daughter and not even think about how it would affect her. It's like a chain reaction.

—Lizzy, fifteen

My dad said, "Wow, you've gained a lot of weight lately." He's always commenting to my younger sister about how heavy she is.

—Ivory, fifteen

If your daughter really is eating unhealthily and she's genuinely overweight, you do need to address that. But don't do it by letting your anxiety run your mouth. As in, you see her eating a cookie and you say "Do you really need to be eating that?" which is parent code for "Can't you see how fat you are?" Other messages are just as unhelpful: "I'm only saying this because you'd be so pretty if you just lost weight. Don't you want to look your best?" And please forget about the bribes like "If you lose ten pounds, I'll give you that cellphone you really want."

What does help: healthy dinners, teaching her to slow down while she's eating so she can listen to her stomach when it's full, and enrolling her in physical activities where losing weight is a by-product of the fun she's having and skills she's learning. This is a tough battle; girls often hear "Eat healthy food" as code for "You're fat." If weight issues are an ongoing struggle for you, it's best to admit that to your daughter up front (but remember, there's a good chance she already knows that).

Acknowledge the powerful influence of the media. Even the most emancipated women can't escape the impact of all those messages our culture sends us about what we have to be. Discuss the issue with your daughter. For younger girls, eight through twelve, look through magazines together and ask your daughter to create a collage of what she considers healthy images of women. Then ask her to do another collage of all the unhealthy images she finds in the women's magazines. Help her analyze what's right

and wrong with these images. Then talk to her about the messages she gets about body weight from her friends and clique. Are these messages that make her feel good about herself? What kind of pressure is she feeling from the group to change how she looks?

The message your daughter needs to hear from you is that you love her just as she is, that you acknowledge that the world we all live in makes us irrational about weight, and that any conversation about her weight is based on developing strength and confidence in her body.

COULD YOUR DAUGHTER HAVE AN EATING DISORDER?

My friend knew I was throwing up. She is a follower and always tells me she's jealous of me. The second time she caught me she told me she was jealous that I could throw up. And then she started throwing up. She got to this point that she was skeleton skinny. And I blamed myself. I didn't know what to do. She told me if you stop I'll stop.

—Alex, fourteen

Eating disorders, at their core, are not about weight, but are mental disorders about control that manifest themselves physically. For many girls, a friend who has an eating disorder can be so confusing. If the friend refuses to admit her abnormal or dangerous eating practices, her friends may be worried about her but not know how to talk to her. It can look like they don't care because they don't know what to do. What's more, behind almost every girl's concern when her friend starves herself is the simultaneous worry "If she thinks she's fat, then I'm obese!" And for some girls, her internal voice whispers, "Am I worried about her, or am I really envious that she has enough control that she can starve her body into submission?"

If you suspect your daughter has an eating disorder, either anorexia (she's starving herself or is headed that way), binging, or bulimia (she binges and purges), it's essential to see a qualified therapist who specializes in treating these problems. In addition

to the signs to look for here, you'll find more information in the Resources in the back of the book. We all have a stereotype of the little girl lost, starving herself to please her perfectionist, controlling parents. I can tell you that I've worked with many girls whose parents were truly loving and supportive and didn't conform to this stereotype at all. Don't waste time blaming yourself for your daughter's eating disorder. Get professional help right away.

SIGNS AND SYMPTOMS OF AN EATING DISORDER

Emotional
Sudden change in attitude
Talks constantly about dieting or being or feeling "fat"
Denies problem
Constantly asks for reassurance about appearance

Behavioral
Seems constantly moody
Wears baggy clothes, either to hide weight loss or to conceal body
Compulsive behavior, appears "on edge," talks a lot about food, carries food around, possessive about food
Avoids social functions where food is present
Suddenly stops eating around other people; always claims to have previously eaten
Ritualistic about food (cuts food into small pieces, takes a long time to finish meals, avoids food other people have bought or cooked)

Physical
Sudden fluctuation of weight (loss or gain)
Abdominal pain
Constantly tired, forgetful
Feeling faint, dizzy, cold
Develops lanugo hair (a fine, downy, white hair that grows on the body to regulate temperature)

WHAT YOU SAY MATTERS TO HER

Last year I went bulimic. I starved, threw up, took magnesium. I lost sixty pounds in a month. My dad walked in on me throwing up and he said, "I'm not going to buy you more food if you're just going to throw it up." My dad told his family, and I didn't know he had told them. Then I get all these texts saying I shouldn't feel this way. They were telling me how to feel instead of supporting me.

—Lindsey, fifteen

Here's some advice from girls who have experienced eating disorders about what they do and don't want their parents to do:

- Don't act like it's the end of the world. I do need help but the world isn't ending.
- Keep calm.
- Don't get mad and start yelling.
- Don't shut down like your face has no emotions.
- Don't cry.
- Don't tell me I am a child so the things I am feeling don't matter.
- Don't tell me you give up.

Here's what girls say would help:

"I'm really sorry you're going through this. And I can't know exactly what you're feeling or why you want to hurt yourself like this. But I do know I want to help you and that means listening to you and being by your side as we figure out what you need to feel better."

Moms: You should be proud of your body if you take care of your-self and you look good. More power to you. But there's a big differ-ence between that and being so caught up in body image craziness that you transform your body—or your teen daughter's—into some-thing more resembling a female superhero. On top of that, when it comes to going to school, remember that it is a professional place. I'm not saying you need to wear a suit to drop off your kids. But tiny yoga outfits or tight jeans with little tops are inappropriate. Plus there's this:

Please stop competing with us. It's really uncomfortable.

—Mia, seventeen

BACK TO THE MALL: DEFINING YOUR "SHOE MOMENTS"

At the beginning of this chapter, you were rationalizing your de-feat as your daughter texted her friends about the shoes she just got out of you. But now you know why they mattered to her so much. I'm not saying that you should give in every time she "has" to have something. Far from it. She should never be rewarded for whining, acting entitled, or being rude. What I'm saying is that before you say no, remember why she thinks the stakes are so high. Remember the pressures she's under. If you can empathize, it'll be a lot easier for you to take her seriously, which makes you come across to her as a reasonably sympathetic person. And that will make arriving at a mutually agreeable solution more likely. You want flats, she wants four-inch heels: You compromise on two-inch heels. You just shelled out for shoes last month and don't want to pay a penny more: She has to split the cost with you or do extra chores to pay for them, or it comes out of an agreed-upon clothing budget, beyond which every dime comes out of her own pocket.

A pattern is being established; what will it be? She goes to you for help. You say no. She feels that you "just don't get it." She does it anyway but now sneaks behind your back. When she's thirteen,

it's shoes; when she's fifteen it's an older boyfriend. Or, she goes to you for help. You give her limits but try your best to understand her motivations and the environment she's growing up in that's influencing her. Whether she grows up too fast is in large part determined by your recognizing the cultural pressures she's under, and establishing yourself as someone who listens and respects her problems and works with her to come up with mutually acceptable solutions.

Remember, it's never just about the shoes.

Mean Girls: Teasing and Gossiping

I have this friend Bree and we get into a lot of fights. She takes my stuff and I get really angry and then I'm the mean person. She also jokes about how short I am but it goes on to other things like I'm fat and ugly. I can take the little jokes but they always build. Then I wonder do other people think I am ugly, fat, or mean? I don't look like it but I am very sensitive. Then we got into a fight and she texts me: You need to work on your anger issues. Until you get them under control we can't be friends. This is why no one likes you. You were never my best friend. It was right before school and I'm really worried that she's telling other people not to like me and I will lose all my friends.

—Ava, twelve

Jordan and Keila have been off-and-on friends since the beginning of the year. Then Jordan sees on her Facebook news feed that Keila has posted *I saw you all over Dylan but that's none of my business. Don't want to be petty but you're looking a little desperate.* There are no names, so Jordan's not sure if Keila is talking about her. Jordan messages her:

JORDAN: *Are you talking about me?*
KEILA: *What do you think?*

JORDAN: *Why are you being shady? I thought we were friends.*
KEILA: *I'm just being honest. I don't like seeing you so desperate over a guy.*

Within an hour, Jordan's phone is blowing up telling her that Keila is making up rumors about her. Jordan is sad, confused, and embarrassed, and dreads going to school. She doesn't sleep well and is exhausted and anxious when she wakes up. She gets into a fight with her dad because she's so disorganized and late for school. When she gets to school that morning she sees Keila in the hallway and their eyes meet. Keila rolls her eyes and laughs. Jordan walks up to her and this is their conversation:

JORDAN: "What?"
KEILA: "Nothing."
JORDAN: "Why are you spreading all these rumors about me?"
KEILA: "I'm not spreading rumors about you. I can't help it if people are talking about you."

Keila walks away and joins a group of girls that Jordan thought until this moment were her friends. Keila says something to them and they laugh.

In the first example, can you see how easy it would be for both Ava's and Bree's parents to think the other girl was horrible and defend their daughters? In the second example, would you blame Jordan if she punched Keila in the face? What should you do if you are Jordan's parent and you find out what's going on—because either Jordan tells you or the conflict escalates and the school intervenes? What do you do if you're Keila's parent and you get a phone call that your daughter has been cruel?

We are really in the thick of it now. In this chapter I will look at how teasing, gossip, and reputations impact your daughter. I'll break down different ways of handling gossip and teasing inside or outside the girls' friendships and social groups. I'll give you more strategies to help you become a great support system when a girl comes to you for help. But we won't just focus on your daughter as a target. We will also look at what to do if she's a bystander or a perpetrator.

For some parents it's hard to imagine your daughter being unkind or downright nasty to other girls, especially if she's never shown this kind of ugliness around the house. On the flip side, you may know your daughter is a gossip and be so frustrated with her that you secretly side with her friends if they drop her.

I hate to say this, but I'd understand if my daughter lost all her friends right now. She's so gossipy I think it would be good for her if someone in her group stood up to her. And I can't believe I'm saying this because two years ago if you had told me I'd feel this way or my daughter would act like this, I wouldn't have believed you.

—Meg

I can't believe what I overhear my daughter and her friends saying about this one girl. And believe me I talk to her about it! I get so mad at her but nothing I do seems to make a differ-ence. She really feels like it's not that big a deal to be talking so badly about people.

—Karen

GETTING STARTED

- Around five years of age, children start to use "Just joking!" as a way to tear someone down and then deny they did any-thing wrong.
- The younger your daughter is when you give her a cellphone and access to SNPs, the younger she'll be exposed to gossip.
- Girls struggle between expressing their anger and worrying that doing so will destroy their friendships.
- Almost all girls gossip, including your daughter.
- While we're on the subject, your daughter is taking her cues from you. Just saying . . .
- Like all of us, girls tend to maximize the impact of what someone did to them and minimize the impact of what they did to the other person.
- What I just wrote is especially true when they get in trouble with their parents or other adults.

- This is also the reason that girls will usually blame their behavior on something or someone else. Let's say your daughter is accused of spreading a rumor. Instead of admitting her guilt, she'll demand to know who exposed her as the information source, as if the "snitch" were the person who's really at fault—conveniently forgetting that she was the one who gossiped.

- If she's over twelve, girls have probably called your daughter a slut and/or bitch. It's also quite possible that she has called other girls a slut and/or bitch. You can't count on the fact that you've never heard your daughter say these words to reassure yourself that she doesn't say them around her peers.

THE POWER OF GOSSIP

Gossip is like money. We exchange it, sell it, and lend it out. It's what we have of value.

—Jane, sixteen

Whoever gossips to you will gossip about you.

—Courtney, fifteen

Why do we gossip? Sad to say but it makes us feel good and we forget that they're other people on the end of our words. Whatever the gossip is about, there is an unspoken agreement between the people sharing the information that the subject of the gossip somehow deserves the disrespect. It also feels like many of us have lost any internal braking system to prevent ourselves from joining in the gossip mill. Someone else's embarrassment and humiliation becomes everyone else's entertainment or opportunity to make the person feel even worse. But we continue because we don't think it's serious—until we are on the receiving end.

Many young people I work with don't think gossip matters—again, until it happens to them. I have heard variations of fourteen-year-old Ana's belief countless times.

It doesn't matter what people say. Sure, someone's reputation gets trashed for a few weeks but then the gossip moves on to someone else.

We can't allow children to believe that seemingly small acts of degradation are acceptable as long as it's not happening to them. And gossip and rumors don't affect people equally. They "stick" to people who are already socially vulnerable because of their race, socioeconomic status, ethnicity, sexual orientation, and/or gender expression—all the things the "Act Like a Woman" box is about. They "stick" because our stereotypes about those identities reinforce the believability of the gossip. We see the target of the gossip less as a person in a particular circumstance and more as a reflection of the bias we already have.

We also have to come clean. Many parents and teachers talk about our children's personal lives, and not in an *"It takes a village"* sort of way. Whether it's about bratty behavior, a bad influence, a friend breakup, who wore what at a dance, or who had a big party last weekend, we are not above gossiping about other people's kids. I'm not saying we can't talk about what's going on with our kids. Sharing information about our kids can be really helpful. But there's a big difference between talking about if the kids had a good time at the dance and gossiping about which girls dressed "trashy." We also need to help other adults do the right thing. When we hear adults gossip, we need to say "Is there something about this girl that you're worried about? How do you think we can support this kid?" I don't think this will magically stop a parent bent on trashing another kid, but all of us have a responsibility to redirect them so that the public conversations we have about our children focus on the right thing: their welfare.

What if we hear girls gossip about someone else? Here's what you can think about saying:

"I have to interrupt you all. I'm listening to you gossip and backstab. It's like it's entertaining you to put someone down. It's disappointing me and it's beneath you. It's important that you hold yourself to a higher standard."

GOSSIPING VERSUS VENTING

*You always end up talking to another girl because you're
angry or you just want someone to talk to about what you're
feeling. But then sometimes she tells other people and then
everything gets into a huge mess. I really don't get why we
do this.*

—Pamela, sixteen

What's the difference? "Venting" is when you have had a bad
experience with someone else and you need to get your feelings
off your chest and process what happened so you can understand
the experience better. "Gossiping" and its cousin "backstabbing"
are when you're talking about someone to deliberately make them
look bad. For example, you get really mad at another girl and then
tell another friend what happened and how you're feeling about
it. That's venting. But then both of you stop talking about your
feelings and instead talk about all the other sketchy things she did
and . . . that's gossiping.

Venting is tricky. When your daughter is on the receiving end
there will be pressure for her to agree with everything the com-
plaining girl is saying. As in, your daughter is expected to say, "Yes,
that girl you hate is insane, annoying, and one hundred percent
wrong." But what if your daughter doesn't feel that way? What if
she thinks the other girl in the conflict has a point? Loyal friends
tell each other when they don't agree. They say, "I get why you're
mad but I can see why she's mad, too, because . . ."

Girls don't want to do this because they're afraid the venting
girl will get angry with them. They may be right. The girl may get
angry with them. But if they do it privately and are ready to back
up what they just said with "I'm not a loyal friend if I tell you only
what you want to hear," then they have done right by everyone:
their friend, the other girl, and themselves. But whatever happens,
if she's able to express how she really feels, she hasn't been manipulated by the situation.

Even if your daughter thinks the complaining girl is 100 percent right, she needs to pay attention to what's happening. Does

she feel like it has become a trashing session? Is she or the other girl talking about what they should do to that girl to get back at her? Is your daughter prepared for the possibility that her angry friend could retaliate in some way and will expect your daughter to join? What is her strategy if this happens?

DRAMA VERSUS BULLYING

You know all those bullying assemblies and classes your children have attended in school? Ask them what they thought about them. I wouldn't be surprised if they told you they think they are a huge waste of time. Really sorry to say it, but I'd completely understand if this is your child's attitude. The way we usually talk about bullying to our children is unrealistic. Why? Because most bullying experts talk about it as if one kid is 100 percent evil and the other is 100 percent innocent. That's not most people's experience. We advise children that if they follow our advice, the problem will cleanly go away. And we talk about bullying as if it only happens between children. It is the rare bullying program that acknowledges that it can occur between adults, or that adults can bully children. Our children sit in these assemblies and think we have no idea what we are talking about.

But the biggest problem is we call way too many things "bullying." Every conflict young people get into with each other is not bullying. It's time to get clear about what bullying is and what it isn't.

Bullying is when one person repeatedly abuses or threatens to abuse their power against another person. I think of bullying as stripping someone of their dignity and their inherent worth by attacking and/or humiliating someone based on a perceived inherent trait such as their sexual orientation, their conformance to gender expectations, their religion, their socioeconomic level, their race, or a disability. Not being invited to a birthday party is not bullying. Nor is being excluded from a picture that someone you know posts on Instagram. These acts are hurtful but unless they fit with the definition above, they are not bullying.

Most girls I work with describe their conflicts as "drama." I

define "drama" as a conflict that's serious to the people involved but not taken seriously by other people gossiping about it. Of course drama can be hurtful. Of course we need to help girls work through the drama they are in. But words have meaning, and if we use them so loosely that they lose their significance, that's a problem.

Land Mine!

To stop gossiping (or any hurtful thing people can do to one another), you may be tempted to say, "How would you feel if someone did this to you?" I know it's technically the right question to ask, but in my experience just saying that to a girl doesn't shift her thinking or her behavior. It's just one of those things adults are supposed to say.

TEASING

How do you tell when someone is teasing you in a good way and when they are putting you down but using teasing as a cover? Here's how I do it.

GOOD TEASING

Good teasing is one of the cornerstones of great friendships. Someone who cares about you, knows you well enough, and is comfortable with you can tease and joke around with you—"with" (not "at") being the operative word. With good teasing, there's no intention to put the other person down, and the teaser understands what your "No Joking Zone" is—the specific things you never want to be teased about.* Your daughter will know if she feels liked by the teaser and doesn't feel that the teaser's motivation is to put her down. If your daughter says she doesn't like it, the behavior will stop.

---

* Rachel Simmons, *The Curse of the Good Girl*, Penguin, 2009.

UNINTENTIONAL BAD TEASING

It's easy to tease someone and not know you hurt her feelings. We've all done it, and we've all been on the receiving end of it. It's also hard to know because people on the receiving end can be really good at hiding or even denying their feelings. We will get into why later in this chapter, but I can say right now that it can be hard to tell someone they hurt your feelings. When the intent isn't malicious (which isn't to say it couldn't be insensitive), once the teaser understands the impact of her behavior, she'll sincerely apologize and she won't do it again.

Why Is "Just Joking" So Incredibly Annoying?

When someone says something mean and then follows it up with "Just joking" or "Just kidding!" "No offense!" "I'm just being honest," what they're really doing is hurting you and then denying your right to be upset about it. It gets them off the hook for taking responsibility for their actions. Even more annoying, it allows the person an excuse to make even more fun of you if you complain.

> Sometimes I would make a pretty feeble attempt to tell my friends to stop teasing me that probably came off as whining that no one took seriously. And these girls were supposed to be my friends.... If the girl protests, even weakly, the teasers will say, "We're just joking. Stop making such a big deal of this."
>
> —Jordan, seventeen

> I hate when my friends say "Just joking" to me. They pick on me and pick on me and I try to hold it in and then sometimes I just can't anymore. Then I explode and they say, "Fine, if you're so sensitive then we don't have to be friends!" But I want to be friends, so I end up begging to get back with them. I hate it.
>
> —Samantha, ten

Samantha is completely right. It's bad enough that your friend is making fun of you and refusing to admit it. Worse, your friends

can threaten to break up with you. Then it can feel like you have to make the following choice: Either I put up with the ridicule or I lose the friend. What lots of people do (no matter what their age) is bury their anger. But burying those feelings means that your friend's right to treat you badly is more important than your right to be treated with dignity. You never want these kinds of relationships no matter how old you are.

MALICIOUS TEASING

Malicious teasing isn't really teasing, because that would imply it's harmless. It's really more akin to being cut with words, because the person is being attacked precisely where they feel most vulnerable and embarrassed—the "No Joking Zone" I mentioned earlier. It's usually in "public" and relentless. If the target protests, the perpetrator increases the teasing and ridicule—usually trying to get more people to join in. This is all done to make the target feel ashamed, humiliated, and isolated. Malicious teasing within a clique is about maintaining order or demoting someone who has broken the group's rules. Malicious teasing outside the clique is about maintaining the power of the group in relation to the overall community it is a part of.

Why do girls do this to one another, even when they "know" it's wrong? There are a couple of possible reasons. Mostly it's because girls don't know how to admit their anger in a straightforward, healthy way. Plus, as I talked about in chapter 6, girls are constantly comparing and judging themselves against each other. All of this judging creates a lot of resentment and anxiety, and that leads to gossip and malicious teasing. That's why it's common for girls who are friends to turn on one another, and the teasing can be brutal.

> These girls are my best friends. I can tell them anything. They'll back me up. But if we're so close, then why do they tease me all the time? If they really are my friends, then why do they make me feel bad? Why am I so frightened to say anything?
>
> —Greer, fourteen

Things would be a lot easier if your daughter asked herself to answer Greer's questions. But girls, like many of us, often make excuses for their friends or convince themselves that they really don't care so they won't have to take action. And in any case, it's hard for a young girl to get all of those feelings organized into thoughts, much less be able to ask you about them.

It feels like a no-win situation. She's trapped hanging out with friends who make her miserable, and if she doesn't address the problem, she'll be angry with herself because she can't hold her own against bullies who masquerade as her friends. Keep this in mind later when you ask yourself why your daughter dates someone you don't think is respectful to her. She is learning to ignore her personal boundaries to maintain relationships.

At the least, these dynamics can make it extraordinarily difficult to concentrate in school, and many girls will do anything to avoid the people making them miserable. Here are a few strategies girls have shared with me to avoid their tormentors:

- Being so slow in the morning that she misses the bus. Meanwhile her parents are hitting the roof because she's lazy, not taking school seriously, or being immature because she doesn't realize how missing the bus makes them late for work.
- Refusing to use the bathroom at school all day.
- Taking a longer route to class, even at the expense of being late.
- An unwavering commitment to listening to music with headphones or earbuds.
- Always reading, so she can pretend (or not) to selectively hear what people are saying around her.
- Pretending to be sick.
- Pretending that she's not hungry and she has to study so she doesn't go to the cafeteria.

REPUTATIONS

Tomboy, crazy, psycho, whore, slut, nerd, square, manipulator, raver, theater, sketch, stoner, druggie, golden girl, eating disorder,

social justice warrior, long-term-relationship kid, flirt, tease, athlete . . . these are some of the reputations my editors came up with in about ten minutes when I asked them to name reputations.

Like cliques, your daughter will probably perceive reputations more rigidly in her early teens than in her later teens. Remember Ava? Her reputation by twelve was that she was a tough girl. That was her reputation, and it greatly impacted the way she perceived her options as she tried to figure out her conflict with her friend. She felt she couldn't cry or even show her feelings when little things bothered her. She would try to bury her anger and then it would explode later—and then she'd look like she was 100 percent at fault.

The impact of a reputation can be felt throughout your daughter's teen years, because somewhere along the way, girls start believing it as truth. Who they are (their character, sense of self, and personality) gets tangled up with their reputation. This is one reason why girls are often confused about their own motivation when they know they're doing something foolish and/or dangerous. Because they want to please their friends, boys, and/or you, they will do things against their better judgment to uphold their image.

THE ÜBER-REP: THE SLUT

> *You're either supposed to know everything about everything or be an innocent little angel. There's no in between. I'm confused a lot.*
>
> —Katia, sixteen

"Ho." "Freak." "Skank." There are few other words that carry so much weight, have so much baggage, and control a girl's behavior and decision making more. Though today's generation of girls can talk about "slut shaming" and recognize the double standard that is applied to girls, that hasn't diminished the power of this word.

One of the biggest difficulties of raising girls is to help them be proud of their developing sexuality while making sure they understand how vulnerable they are in a world that constantly wants

to exploit their sexuality. When it comes to the "slut" reputation, girls accuse one another of two things: acting like a slut, and being a slut. The fear of being accused of acting like a slut controls girls' actions in a particular situation. For example, when your daughter chooses what to wear to a party, she's trying to balance looking sexy while not coming off as slutty (that is, being attractive to boys yet not incurring the wrath of other girls).

> I was playing basketball with three friends. One of my friends was a girl and the other two were boys. We had been playing for a while when a girl in our school who was in seventh grade asked us if she could play. We said yes. After a while, she took off her sweatshirt and pants and she was only wearing a tiny tank top and shorts. We kept playing, but the boys couldn't pay attention. I thought she was really showing off and flirting with the boys. The whole thing got really weird. I think she was acting like a total slut.
> —Brett, eleven

When I asked that girl how she felt watching this scenario unfold, her reaction was far more complex. As much as she didn't approve of the seventh-grade girl's behavior, she was conflicted because she envied the boys' attention. Girls often feel they have to choose between being themselves and displaying a sexy costume, which is a huge conflict. If a girl opts for the costume and acts the part, she'll get the boys' attention, but she'll also risk the girls' resentment—and the spiteful talking behind her back. She'll try to achieve the impossible by pleasing groups with two competing agendas. She might also feel that once she interacts with boys in a sexual way, she won't be able to hang out with them without her sexuality being the only thing they value about her. These conflicting emotions and confusion increase when girls accuse one another of acting like sluts.

For younger girls, the threat of being called a slut defines the limits of acceptable behavior and dress. They use it to describe a girl who is perceived as flirting "too much" and dressing "too" provocatively. They're easily and understandably confused about

their own personal comfort level regarding how they come across to others, because they're literally transforming from little girls into women in a world that often perceives them first and foremost as sexual objects. It can be confusing, exciting, and terrifying all at the same time.

"Acting like a slut" is a label a girl gets from her appearance and behavior in "public," such as the school hallway, images of herself she posts online, malls, and parties. It's a reputation that's almost impossible to shake because the accused is the repository of everyone's judgment, jealousy, curiosity, and fear. When I work with girls with bad reputations, they're initially wary of me. Why should they trust me? They've learned to build big walls around themselves to block out the judgment and rejection they so often feel from others.

When I have girls like this in my class, I can usually pick them out by their defiant expressions. The worst expressions come from girls who aren't only on the outside of the "Act Like a Woman" box but are really suffering at the hands of the other girls in the group. At first, talking about these issues can feel dangerous for them. We're talking about things that hurt them, and they have no reason to believe I'll do right by them.

Kate was a student in one of my tenth-grade classes. The first time she came to class she was late, and her expression was both challenging—waiting for me to call her out for being late—and hostile, because she anticipated that the class would be boring. She started off sitting in the back of the room, but within five minutes she moved in front of me. The "Act Like a Woman" box was on the board and the girls were discussing the different roles girls play in cliques. Kate scowled and said something I couldn't quite hear. When I asked her to repeat herself, one of the popular girls said, "Oh, don't pay any attention to her. That's just Kate." Kate's face clouded over and her back stiffened as she repeated herself, "I said that I hate girls. You can't trust them. Girls are petty, stupid, and jealous. Like in this grade, the girls are just jealous because I get more attention from the boys. I know I'm known as a slut, but I don't care." As she spoke, I felt the ripple of anger and resentment in the classroom in response.

There are few things popular girls hate more than being accused of jealousy.

Consider this quote from a senior girl remembering what it felt like to see girls like Kate.

> In seventh grade, I watched a girl who constantly flirted with boys. The problem was that she alienated herself from other girls. She pretty much accepted the slut role that people made her into. The boys she flirted with didn't take their relationships with her seriously. Even though I didn't want to be treated like she was, I wanted the attention she was getting. But whenever I was around her, I felt incredibly prudish and uptight.
>
> —Grace, seventeen

Girls are at best uncomfortable with girls like Kate, and at worst treat her like dirt and refuse to have anything to do with her. In turn, Kate doesn't trust girls, and she has good reason not to. In her mind all girls are bad, and her mistrust of girls clouds her thinking about which boys to trust. Naturally, she seeks out people who'll make her feel better; often the easiest, fastest way for Kate to get the attention she wants is to hang out with boys. The boys who will want to hang out with Kate the most are the ones who need to prove their masculinity by interacting with girls only as sexual objects. Kate, not wanting to turn away the attention she's getting, will do what the boys want. She won't reject someone who isn't rejecting her.

But one of the saddest things about girls like Kate is that while many convince themselves that they can't depend on anyone but themselves or that they are in a position of power over the boys, they still often romanticize love and sex. They're still girls caught up with wishing someone will see them for who they really are and love them. Every time they hook up with someone, there's a little part of them hoping this person is the one who will.

CHECKING YOUR BAGGAGE

- Have you ever felt trapped by a reputation you couldn't shake?
- Were you ever teased? What were you teased about? How did you handle it?
- When you were your daughter's age, did you ever spread gossip and get caught?
- Were you ever gossiped about? How did you handle it?
- Write down a list of your daughter's closest friends. Do you think they support her or discourage her?
- If you were mean, what would you tease your daughter about? How do you think your daughter would respond?
- Do you gossip and tease other people today?
- Does your daughter hear you gossip?

RULES OF ANGER IN GIRL WORLD

All of this stuff—the teasing, gossiping, backstabbing, being labeled with a reputation you can't shake—can make girls really angry. But the challenge is that the "Act Like a Woman" box and Girl World teach girls unhealthy and ineffective ways to communicate their anger. Without even realizing it, most girls and women follow these Girl World rules of expressing anger:

- Keep it inside and suffer silently.
- Keep it inside and beat yourself up with negative self-talk.
- Laugh it off to convince yourself that you don't have to take your feelings seriously.
- Give the person the silent treatment until (hopefully) they notice and ask you what's wrong. When asked, deny your anger by saying "It's fine" or "Whatever," and then get mad at the person when they can't read your mind.
- Finally ask for the behavior to stop, but then having to endure the other person dismissing you with some comment that makes you feel weak.
- Keep it inside until something small (to everyone else)

QUEEN BEES AND WANNABES   213

makes you explode in tears and/or screaming, only to have your feelings be dismissed again.

- Have a "You have no idea who you are dealing with" attitude and then try to destroy the other person.
- Fight, either verbally or physically.
- Use drugs or alcohol to deaden feelings.

All of these ways give way too much power to the other person or the environment (like a group of people encouraging you to get revenge or recording the fight on a cellphone). If we can give girls a healthy way to express their anger, figure out the group dynamics and their part in it, and then apply those insights with a strategy to enable them to speak their truth—they have a much better chance of managing themselves authentically and in a way that makes them proud.

Here's one way to give a girl an outlet and a way to visualize her feelings that I learned about from social worker and teacher Thomas McSheehy. It may seem odd for older girls and teens, but I have a lot of success with it. Ask her to choose an animal that can represent her anger. She can have different kinds of animals for different levels of anger or even mix animals together. Here are some examples girls have given me of what they picture:

Rabid raccoon
Gorilla
Hippopotamus
Python
Wasp

Or my personal favorite:

I have a whole zoo in my head. It's a T-Rex feet with a shark head, and Rottweiler body.

—Charlie, twelve

If she's up for it, let her act out what she would want to say to the person who made her angry. Even if she says things that are really intense, let her get it out.

LanD Mine For GiRLS!

Don't use the word "annoying"—as in "You're so annoying!"—when you're telling someone you're mad. Why? Because there are a million different things a person can do to be annoying. In order to stop the behavior they have to know what they're doing. It's the same thing when you say "You're so mean!" You have to be specific. Again, someone disagreeing with you isn't mean. It's having a different opinion. If they tell you they disagree in a way that puts you down or makes you feel stupid . . . then that's mean.

Now let's give the girl another animal to choose. This time she needs to choose an animal that represents calm, wise power. The goal is for the angry animal to tell the calm and wise animal why she's so angry. The calm and wise animal will hear it, make sense of it, and then guide the girl's brain when she speaks. Although rudimentary, this is the basic way we want the brain's limbic system to process emotions in conjunction with the brain's prefrontal cortex. Examples girls have given me:

Unicorn
Giraffe
Panda
Bear

WHAT SHOULD YOU SAY WHEN YOUR CHILD TELLS YOU SOMEONE IS BEING MEAN TO THEM?

If she starts off by saying something vague, like, "Those girls were bothering me," ask her to give you more specifics so you'll have a better understanding of what happened. Once she tells you, here are a few common things I suggest *not* saying.

"*She's jealous of you. She's insecure.*" This response is ineffective because there's nothing she can do with this information. Even if it's true, that doesn't stop the other kid from

making her miserable. And you never want a girl telling other girls they are jealous of her because that will be seen as a declaration of war.

"Be nice." Accommodating people who are mean to you doesn't look like you're being nice. It looks you're weak and easily manipulated.

"She probably comes from a bad home. You should feel sorry for her." While it's sad that some kids have really tough home situations, that doesn't give them an excuse to lash out at other kids. Additionally, encouraging a child to pity another child or to think herself superior can only bring up more problems.

"Are you sure? Maybe you took it the wrong way." Without meaning to, you can come across as if you don't believe her or you think she's overly sensitive or overreacting.

"Use your words." How? What words? What happens if the person doesn't listen?

"Just ignore it. Walk away." By the time she comes to you for advice, she's probably been trying to ignore or walk away from the problem, but it hasn't worked. That's why she's coming to you.

"Forget about it." The message is, if she can't forget about it, then she must be weak.

Remember, your go-to response is some combination of:

"I'm so sorry."

"Thank you for telling me."

"I'm going to help you think this through so you can come up with a plan to feel a little more in control."

What if your child says "I'm going to tell you, but you have to promise not to do anything"? This is an incredibly confusing moment. You want her to tell you what's wrong so it's understandable to feel if you don't make this promise, she'll shut you out. But you don't want to make a promise that you might have to break because she may tell you something that you have to tell someone else, or you might have no idea what to do and need to get another adult's advice. Instead, this is what I want you to say:

"I would love to make that promise, but I can't. The reason I can't is because you may tell me something that's too big for us to handle alone or I don't know what the best thing to do is. But this is what I can promise: If we need to get another person's opinion, you will know about it and we will decide together who is the best person to go to."

If you include your daughter as part of the process, she can tolerate your decisions, even if she really disagrees with them. When a young person stops talking to you, it means they feel that you failed to appreciate that this is *their* life, this is *their* problem, and *they* are the ones who have to deal with any repercussions. And of course they're right.

THE SEAL STRATEGY

Now we have set the stage for developing an action plan. Whenever I am strategizing with my students about how to think through a situation where there's any kind of conflict, worry, or anxiety, I use SEAL.

SEAL stands for these four things:

Stop and Strategize. Breathe, listen, and think about when and where you want to talk to this person. Do you want to do it now or later—or maybe a little of both?

Explain. What happened that you didn't like and what do you want.

Affirm. Admit (recognize) anything you did that contributed to the conflict, but affirm your right to be treated with dignity by the other person and vice versa.

Lock. Lock in the friendship, take a vacation, or lock the friendship out.

It's totally understandable if you read this and think "There's no way my daughter (or my student) is going to do this." It's likely your daughter (or any girl) is going to believe it's not going to work. There are good reasons for this. First, do any of us want to tell

someone we are angry with them or don't like something they did? No. Most of us dread it. Strategies to put "our feelings to words" always seem weird and cheesy, especially to tweens and teens. Let's face it, they are. We are supposed to talk about our feelings and expect the other person to respect what we're saying? Really? It seems much easier to hope the problem goes away or to have a self-righteous temper tantrum.

Ignoring the problem or throwing a temper tantrum means that you aren't going to be in control of yourself when you finally do face the problem. The fight could become entertainment for other people—something they can record on their smartphones and post online. Girls' anger should not be other people's entertainment.

Of course it's also true that some girls physically fight because they feel they have no choice; they can't look weak in front of other people. I'm never going to say to a girl that fighting is never the answer, because I'm not living her life. But what I will (and do) say to girls is that fighting makes it much more likely the system where the girl operates—for example, her school—will identify her as a problem. And, unfortunately, she will be disproportionately (and ineffectively) punished, especially if she is African American.

The other reason girls are reluctant to use a strategy such as SEAL is that girls, like most of us, usually define success in a confrontation by either being best friends afterward or destroying the other person. SEAL shows girls how to redefine what it means to be in a confrontation. SEAL shows girls a way to think through a situation and structure their words so they have a better chance of articulating their experience and opinion clearly. Most important, this is a practice. Doing any part of it builds social skills capacity.

After you say, "Thanks for telling me" and so forth, follow up with a few of these questions:

> "Let me ask you a few questions so I can understand what you're going through. How is this situation making you physically feel? Like in your stomach or your head? Put the feelings you're having to words. Or draw it. Just get it out."

Then ask her, even if it's incredibly obvious or it's happening "all the time," what she doesn't like and what she wants to change.

Then ask her to imagine any possible pushbacks—the responses that would make it harder for her to accomplish communicating what she wants to say.

After she's gotten all of this out of her system, ask her if there's anything she's done, no matter how understandable, that from the other person's perspective could have contributed to the problem. That's the *Affirm* part. Add that to the things she needs to prepare to say.

Last, reiterate the *Lock* that she doesn't have to be friends with this person. She gets to decide what kind of relationship or interaction is best for her. In any SEAL situation, advise the girl to avoid using words such as "always" and "never." For example: "You always talk behind my back."

After she has thought through this, you can boil it down to answering one question: What are the three things you want to communicate to the other person no matter what happens and no matter what she says? Have her repeat those three things over and over again.

Now let's use the situations I started the chapter with to show how SEAL can work.

The Anger Management Problem

AVA (*Stop and Strategize*): [Ava and Bree live in the same neighborhood. Ava sees Bree outside. Takes a deep breath. Imagines the wise strong animal in her head calming down her angry animal. In this case, because Ava has a history of losing her temper, she should probably start with the *Admit* part.]

AVA: "Hey."

BREE: "Hey."

AVA: "Um . . . this is hard but I know I get really angry and lose it sometimes. I'm sorry I do that and I'm trying to get better."

BREE (*Pushback*): "OK, but you've said that to me before."

AVA (*Admit*): "You're right. I'm trying, but it's hard for me. I understand why you're frustrated." (*Explain*): "I'm not making excuses, but getting those texts from you that I have anger

management problems made me even more mad. I feel like I start off calmly but you don't listen and then it seems like it's my fault for getting mad without admitting that there are reasons why I'm so mad."

BREE: "You always make such a big deal out of everything! This is the reason we didn't invite you to hang out yesterday!"

AVA (*Lock: Take a vacation*): "I think you're right. I think we should take a break for a while."

The Gossiping Problem

JORDAN (*Stop and Strategize*): [Jordan thinks about where the best place to approach Keila would be. She remembers that they both have after-fourth period free on Tuesday and none of their other friends will be around.]

JORDAN (*Explain*): "Keila, we don't have to be friends but saying that I'm throwing myself on Dylan is rough."

KEILA (*Pushback*): "I'm just being honest."

JORDAN (*Explain*): "Yeah, but you're doing it to embarrass me."

KEILA (*Pushback*): "I can't help what other people say."

JORDAN (*Acknowledge*): "But you can stop what you're posting."

KEILA (*Affirm*): "Ok fine. Can we drop this now?"

JORDAN (*Lock*): "Sure."

But let's be realistic. Even if both girls did their SEALs perfectly, it's still possible that the girls on each side would go to other girls and talk badly about them. So girls in Ava's and Jordan's positions need to ask themselves if it's worth it to them to speak out.

This is where you get to your last part of SEAL: Ask. If you say nothing, what are the positives and negatives? If you speak out, what are the positives and negatives? Based on the answers, it should be clear if it's time for her to try out her ideal SEAL—knowing that in the real world her ideal SEAL isn't going to be perfect.

THE ART OF THE APOLOGY

Teaching your child to apologize is one of the most sacred responsibilities you have as a parent. Unfortunately, true apologies are precious and rare. Our public figures apologize when they get caught, not when they realize they have done something wrong. The media often portray apologizing as a loss of face and respect, when, in fact, the opposite is true. We just don't get to see good apologies modeled. We have to change that.

Apologies are powerful because they're a public demonstration of remorse, an acknowledgment of the consequences of hurtful behavior, and an affirmation of the dignity of the person who has been wronged.

A true apology must be:

- Given with a genuine understanding of what the person did. Especially when your daughter is younger, make sure she understands what she's apologizing for. Otherwise, she may very well hurt the other person again. Don't let her put the best possible spin on her actions. ("I didn't mean to say X to her. I think she just took it the wrong way.")
- About the apologizer's actions alone—her apology can't include what she thinks the other person did or said.
- Given without including any "last licks" in which the speaker buries another insult within the apology. ("I'm sorry you're so sensitive that you need an apology. But here, 'I'm sorry.' Feel better?")
- Given without qualification. It's not an apology if it includes "But I only did it because . . ." or "I wouldn't have said that unless you . . ."
- Genuinely contrite—there's nothing worse than an apology clearly rendered only because the girl was told to apologize. ("My mom says I have to apologize," or "I'm supposed to say I'm sorry.")
- Given without the expectation of a return apology. If the listener has the grace or goodwill to say "I'm sorry, too," that's a bonus.

- Rendered with the understanding that it may invoke further recriminations. ("Yeah, well, you really hurt me! I can't believe you did that!")

But apologies in Girl World can be manipulated. Girls with more social power can anti-apologize—which means they are technically apologizing but they don't mean it. They're just apologizing to get out of trouble. Girls in lower positions in the social hierarchy apologize when they inadvertently challenge a more powerful girl. In that case, they aren't apologizing for something they did that hurt someone; they're apologizing for challenging the other girl's right to make her miserable.

WHAT IF YOUR REALLY MEAN GIRL REFUSES TO APOLOGIZE OR APOLOGIZES BUT DOESN'T MEAN IT?

Just remember you're on a long road with her toward becoming a decent human being. You're going to have to model what it looks like. By email or in person, apologize to the other girls like this:

"Jane, on behalf of my family, I want to apologize for what my daughter did to you. That was an incredibly hurtful thing to do, and it should never have happened. If it ever happens again, I want you to contact me. Here's my email and phone number. Thank you for seeing us."

If your teen daughter insists on acting like she's five by not apologizing herself, then you need to treat her like she's five. It's her choice.

ACCEPTING APOLOGIES

If your daughter gets an apology, there's one last thing you have to teach her. Instead of saying, "That's OK. Don't worry about it," she should say, "Thanks for the apology." When you say it's OK, you dismiss your feelings—the fact that you needed the apology in the first place. You know someone is truly your friend if,

when they apologize to you, you believe it. And, if you apologize to them, they believe you, too.

Just a little note on how hard apologies are to give: It's natural to feel defensive when someone has told you that you messed up or you were caught doing something bad. So the child may need some time to reflect on what's happened and what she needs to do. Ideally, give your child a night to sleep on it. That way you have a better chance of having them process and internalize what's happened so they can take true ownership of their actions.

LanD Mine!

When parents see someone else's child being rude or mean, they usually do one of two things: look away or march up to the offending kid and yell at them—often demanding an apology (that, even if the child gives it, will be insincere). But neither of these options is effective. If you run away, the kids feel like you don't care or are too scared. If you get in the kid's face, you can be so overwhelming that the offending child will shut down or fight back by being disrespectful so she can save face in front of her friends. The goal here is for all the children involved to believe adults can handle conflict with calm, ethical authority. So, instead, use SEAL to frame your approach and your words.

WHAT IF YOU'RE WORRIED SHE'S TOO SENSITIVE?

While you never want to discount or minimize someone's feelings or perceptions, it's also true that some people have much thinner skins than others. It's a delicate balance, affirming a child's experience and at the same time allowing them to have difficult, even painful, experiences that will build their emotional strength. And girls can be really different. One girl can be excluded from a social activity, not take it personally, go find another group to play with or hang out with, and never think another thing about it. Another girl can walk down the hallway, see someone look at her

the wrong way, and worry all day about why that person hates her. And yet another girl can see someone look at her the wrong way and, instead of worrying, get really angry and then plot revenge.

What you're looking for is a pattern. If a girl consistently perceives these social aggressions with her peers, it's important to look at what's going on with her that may be contributing to the problem. For example, a natural assumption would be that these girls would always be targets, but that's not the case. Ironically, some of these girls have a tendency to exhibit Queen Bee behavior because they "see" social threats or slights much more easily than other girls and then want to do something about it. Or, she could lack social skills and not realize what she's doing that is alienating to her peers.

Here's a way to help her take a step back from social anxiety:

> Sit down with her and have her relate the experience of feeling upset and anxious, from beginning to end. She can also write it down. When she's done, tell her to rewind in her mind to the place she first felt that the other person was aggressive to her. Ask her "Did the other person intend to be mean to you? How do you know?"
> For sensitive or anxious children, remind them that they're OK right now. They're sitting with you. Then break down the event they described using SEAL, and talk about how they would like to handle the situation step by step, but do not put any pressure on the child to do it in real life.*

On the other side, what happens if your child is accused of being mean or bullying, she denies it, and you truly can't find any evidence that she's done what she's accused of?

There are also family dynamics that sometimes create a situation where a child will complain to a parent about being bullied as a way to get attention. This doesn't happen often, but it does occur. If it's a she said/she said thing, tell your daughter that you believe her and you understand why she would be frustrated, but

---

* This is adapted/inspired from "The Whole Brain Child" by Dan J. Siegel and Tina Payne Bryson.

the other girl's feelings need to be respected. It also doesn't matter that your daughter thinks the other girl is overly sensitive. Just like your daughter has the right to her feelings about things that happen to her, the other girl has the right to hers. Then reinforce your expectation that she won't put the girl down and will tell any other girls to stop.

WHAT HAPPENS IN A MEAN GIRL STORM

When I was a freshman, there was this new girl that a bunch of guys liked. Two girls in the grade made a Facebook group called "Lori Shore is a mega-whore." The next day, another girl told her about the group. Lori confronted the girls. One of the girls flat-out said, "Yeah, I did it and what are you going to do about it?" The other girl was a really good friend of Lori's and kept denying it.

—Hope, sixteen

As despicable as this story is, it involves all the issues we've been discussing. Let's assess which girls did what:

- The Queen Bee, who made the Facebook group (and admitted she did it), is doing it to bring Lori down and to demonstrate her power over the other kids.
- The Torn Bystander keeps denying she was involved. She's intimidated by the Queen Bee and too ashamed to come clean with Lori.
- The Messenger is the girl who told Lori about the group.

If this happened to your daughter, how would you handle it? First things first, you're allowed to hate the Queen Bee or any other girl who is being mean to your daughter. It's easy to see how parents get so angry that they feel justified going over to the other girl's house and screaming at her parents. Honestly, I'd totally understand if you read that story and thought if it happened to your kid, there's no way you'd allow her to go to school the next day unless those girls were expelled.

IF YOUR DAUGHTER IS THE TARGET

Even in this situation, there are parents who believe ignoring it is still the way to go. This may sound like a mature strategy, but it's exactly the kind of parental advice that makes girls feel that their parents don't understand the world they're living in. When girls have problems, they need help right away. Immediately. It's absolutely realistic that every student in the school knows about the Facebook group, and that if the adults at the school knew about it, they may refuse to punish the girls because Facebook isn't associated with the school and the girls did it off school grounds. Imagine if you were Lori. You wouldn't care about anything else but how you were going to show your face at school the next day. Lori isn't thinking in the long term. Next week may as well be next year. Lori knows that everyone else in school, especially the girls who created the Facebook group, will watch her the next day to see how she'll respond. She has to know what to say, how to hold her body, and what tone of voice to use so she can feel some control over this situation.

Let's start with how Lori may approach you if you were her parent:

YOUR DAUGHTER: "Um . . . well . . . can I talk to you for a minute?"

YOU (*Paying bills, looking at your schedule for tomorrow*): "Huh?" (*Your brain slows and the gears start to shift.*) "What's up?"

YOUR DAUGHTER: "It's nothing really. I mean it's not that big a deal, but there are these girls at school who did something on Facebook about me."

YOU (*Paying more attention but keeping a casual tone*): "What are they doing?"

YOUR DAUGHTER: "If I tell you, you have to promise not to freak out."

YOU: "Can you define 'freaking out' so I know exactly what you're talking about?"

YOUR DAUGHTER: "You know, call the school, call their parents. Not let me go on Facebook ever again. If I tell you, you have to promise you won't do anything like that."

YOU: "OK—I can promise I won't immediately start calling people. I can promise I want to help you. I also can promise whatever it is you tell me, we'll think about what to do together and take it step-by-step. But I can't promise I won't do anything else because I don't want to go back on my word with you."

YOUR DAUGHTER: (*Silence. Tears welling in eyes.*)

YOU: "Listen to me, I don't know what you're upset about, but I'm ready to listen. Later, if we do need to tell someone, we'll decide together who and when that will be. So . . . what are the girls doing?"

YOUR DAUGHTER: "They just say really rude things. It's so annoying!"

YOU: "Can you describe specifically some of the things they do or say?"

YOUR DAUGHTER: "This girl at school made up a group on Facebook that she called 'Lori Shore is a mega-whore.' People are saying horrible things about me. People I thought were my friends, but no one is talking to me."

YOU (*Take a deep breath! Sit down next to her and give her a hug.*): "I'm really sorry that happened to you. I can't believe anyone would say that about anyone, let alone you. But thank you for trusting me to tell me. I think the most important thing is to figure out what you can do to feel like you're getting a little bit of control over this situation."

Now we are going to use this situation to walk through a sequence of possible steps your daughter (and you) can take. You can apply this strategy to any situation where your daughter is having a problem with a peer and you all are trying to figure out who to talk to, what to say, and when. Overall, the goal is to have your daughter take the most ownership in addressing the conflict every step of the process. For our purposes, I'm calling the girl who perpetrates the gossiping the RMG (Really Mean Girl).

1. Girl confronts the RMG.
2. Girl (possibly with you) asks an adult who has direct knowledge and interaction for help.

3. You can talk to an administrator.
4. You can call the RMG's parents.

WHAT'S THE DIFFERENCE BETWEEN TATTLING AND TELLING?

"Tattling" means all you want is for the person to get in trouble. "Telling" means that you believe there is a problem you can't solve by yourself so you need to tell a trusted adult; it means your goal is to right a wrong. A person reports a problem because they want the problem resolved. A person tattles because they want the problem to get bigger or more public so everyone knows. The really tricky thing, however, is that it can be hard to tell the difference between the two, because when you report something you're bringing attention to it. It's like the problem was in a dark cave and you're going in there with a big flashlight and shining a light on it. If you report something and people get mad at you, the most important thing to remember is that the people who are now in trouble are not in trouble because you reported them. They're in trouble because they acted in ways that were against the rules. If you want to say something about it, here's a suggestion: "They didn't get in trouble because I told the teacher [parent, coach, or the like]. They got in trouble because they [say specifically what they did]."

Starting: Step One: Preparing Your Daughter

You want to encourage her to express her anger, frame her feelings, and define what she wants out of a confrontation with SEAL. Because this is happening at school, you also want to help her document what happened, including, if possible, taking a screenshot of what bothered her. You never want to assume the worst, but you want to be prepared for it. Your daughter needs to show a history of what happened and the steps she took to address it. If you show specific dates and times, the perpetrator's pattern of behavior, and the steps your daughter took to address this problem, the school will take you more seriously because the situation will be more difficult to dismiss than a she said/she said conflict.

Step Two: Speaking to the RMG

If she feels physically safe, she needs to make at least one attempt to speak to the RMG. The conversation isn't going to be long—a few minutes max—and it can't be in public. Public means, for example, the cafeteria, in front of school when everyone is around, or online. Here's how her conversation might go:

> YOUR DAUGHTER: "Can I talk to you for a minute?"
>
> RMG: "What about?"
>
> YOUR DAUGHTER: "I know you made the Facebook group. I want you to take it down. I know you can blow me off or try to make my life worse—"
>
> RMG: "Whatever. I didn't even do it."
>
> YOUR DAUGHTER: "I'm not arguing with you. I just want you to take it down. I hate it and it's embarrassing but it won't kill me."
>
> RMG: "Sure. Whatever you say."

Remember, any part of this your daughter does is a success. If she writes down her feelings but decides not to confront the RMG immediately, that's OK. SEAL's overall goal is to give a person who feels stuck in their anxiety and anger a way to move. In this scenario your daughter was specific about what happened, how it made her feel, and what she wanted stopped, and she finished by saying something positive. She lost nothing by admitting that the other girl "won." In fact, it can be empowering for the targets to say, "I admit it. You did something to me and it's making me miserable—but I'm strong enough to stand here and call you on it."

Notice that the RMG concluded the conversation by saying "Whatever." Your daughter can't expect the RMG to respond with "I'm so sorry! I had no idea that calling you a mega-whore was going to hurt your feelings! I promise I'll never do it again!" If the RMG did that, your daughter wouldn't believe her anyway. "Whatever" is probably as good as it'll get. The immediate goal is to stop the RMG's behavior. The only way she'll do that is if Lori communicates that she's not easy prey. If the RMG tries to sidestep the issue by asking "Who told you that?" don't let your

daughter get distracted. If the RMG tries this, your daughter can say "It doesn't matter how I know or who did it. If you're involved in any way, I'm asking you to stop."

If the RMG is a friend inside the clique, your daughter can "take a vacation" and spell out exactly what it will take for the friendship to continue. But realize that this could be a huge thing for her to do. Maybe she really likes the girl, or maybe she fears that all the other girls in the group will side with the other girl.

TALKING TO THE TEACHER OR COACH

If Lori has confronted the RMG and the behavior hasn't stopped or has gotten worse, she needs to think about what to do next. And she very well may decide to do "nothing," meaning she doesn't talk to anyone else. Even if you disagree, it's important that you show her that you respect the choice she made. The only thing I'd ask her to do is think about what could happen where she'd think that going to an adult is appropriate.

However, if she does decide that she needs to bring in someone else, it's time to think about how and who. Depending on her age and maturity level, the person to meet with next is the teacher or another authority figure who has direct interaction with the girls (for example, a coach). If she wants to have this conversation on her own, let her. But before her meeting, both of you should be familiar with the school/athletic association, organization's policies, and state law concerning conduct, bullying, and/or harassment.

If she wants you to attend the meeting with her (or she's too young to do it herself), think of yourself as an advocate for your daughter, not a mama or papa bear out for the kill, and approach any school professional with an attitude of collaboration and respect. Don't assume, unless you have direct evidence, that they're part of the problem. As most teachers and administrators interact with parents only when something is wrong, they can be a little wary of you. Parents are often perceived as overly emotional micromanagers who too quickly call conflicts between young people bullying and/or are defensive and unwilling to take responsibility for their child's actions. In addition, far too many parents go over

the teacher's head as soon as something goes down in the class-room that they don't like. Believe me, doing that will make the problem bigger rather than smaller.

In preparation for this meeting, I want your daughter to go through SEAL again while you write down what she says. If you are planning to attend the meeting, there should be an agreement that if at all possible, your daughter will do most of the talking during the meeting. If she is too uncomfortable, reassure her that at her request you will speak for her using the things you have just written down.

Once you are in the meeting, she should thank the teacher for being there and then implement SEAL. In this conversation, the goal is to communicate that the conflict is stopping your daughter from feeling safe and focused. She has already made different at-tempts to solve the problem, but the situation hasn't improved. Get a firm deadline for action from the teacher. Here's how the conversation might go in person or by email between your daugh-ter and the other adult. Well, I'm including a kind of response I train educators to implement.

> YOUR DAUGHTER: "Ms. Wiseman, can I talk to you privately after class today?"
> ME: "Sure, is this something we are going to need some time for or just privacy?"
> YOUR DAUGHTER: "We might need some time."
> ME: "No problem. Why don't you come back after last period today?"

Notice that this is the *Stop and Strategize* part of SEAL.
After last period . . .

> ME: "Hey, Lori, what's up?"
> YOUR DAUGHTER: "Well, some girls did something to me."
> ME: "Can you tell me what they did?"
> YOUR DAUGHTER (*Explain*): "[The Really Mean Girl] and her friends made a Facebook group that calls me a whore."
> ME: "I'm so sorry! Coming to school today must have been really hard. Thank you for telling me because I get that you really

didn't want to come to school today. Let's just talk for a while and figure out what we can do so you feel better."

YOUR DAUGHTER: "I just want it to go away."

ME: "I totally understand. Let's figure out together a strategy for dealing with this. Tell me what you've done so far."

YOUR DAUGHTER: "I told her to stop, but she wouldn't listen."

ME: "I can talk to her. Let's decide together what you would like me to say."

YOUR DAUGHTER: "OK, but I don't want her to know I told on her."

ME: "No problem. I can say I found out about it on my own."

Your daughter should then give the teacher a copy of everything she's written about the incident.* After the meeting, both of you should email the teacher, thank her for the meeting and for being a resource for your child, and reiterate your daughter's understanding of what will happen as a result of their meeting. Request to hear back within forty-eight hours, because everybody works better with deadlines. If the deadline passes, your daughter should ask the teacher two days later about what's going on—which you will follow up with another email for confirmation.

For any teachers reading this, please note: If you have created a positive learning environment in your classroom, chances are good that your students will come to you for help with serious personal issues. It's one of the rewards of being a great teacher; you can literally transform or save lives. It can also be really scary, because you may not have been trained for handling the problems your students have. Just remember you're the bridge for your students to a person with more expertise. You don't need to have a counseling degree to do that—all you need is a relationship with the child. So when a student comes to you, use the same script for when a child comes to the parent looking for help. "I'm so sorry that happened to you. Thank you for telling me. Together we're going to work on this." If the student requests that you don't tell anyone else, follow the same strategy I outline on page 226. Don't

---

* This situation involves Facebook, but if the RMG uses an SNP that quickly disappears or she deleted it so there's no "proof," your daughter can still write down everything she remembers and show that to the teacher.

underestimate your importance in this situation. If you handle the situation effectively, your student will believe that going to an adult for help can be a positive experience.

PARENT TALKING TO AN ADMINISTRATOR

If you're unsatisfied with the teacher, it's time to get an administrator involved. I wrote extensively about this in my *Queen Bee Moms* book, but in sum you're contacting an administrator to establish the following: There's a consistent pattern of behavior where your daughter is following reasonable and stated protocols of requesting support and that support wasn't forthcoming or effective. As a result, your daughter's ability to concentrate in school (or on the team) is suffering. In your email requesting this meeting, ask them to confirm who will be in attendance and what their goals are.

Especially for younger children, sit down with your daughter the night before and have her tell you what the kids have said and done to her. As much as she can, she should tell you exactly the words the bullies said. While she speaks, you should write it down. Then, when you get to the meeting, she should try her best to say what she told you the night before. But she needs you as a backup because sometimes it's too hard to say what happened or the bad words that were said. That's why kids sometimes say "I don't remember" when people ask them what happened. Ask her what her goals are for having this meeting and have her practice saying them out loud.

Land Mine!

Don't demand to know what the punishment has been or will be for the other child. Remember, your only goal is to have your daughter feel that she can concentrate in school and that the adults are there to help her.

TALKING TO THE RMG'S PARENTS

No matter how tempting it may be to call the RMG's parents and scream at them about their evil child, this is not an effective way to handle the situation. Even if the other parents do exactly what you want—get off the phone with you, then scream at their daughter and ground her for a month—guess what happens next? The next day your daughter goes to school with an RMG bent on revenge. At some point, the RMG's and your daughter's paths will cross without adult supervision around. The harassment will escalate.

It's better if you handle this through the school or whatever organization the girls are involved in. But there may be a time when you have to talk to the parents. If you're in that situation, assume that the RMG's parents don't know what their kid is doing. Go to them asking for their help in solving this problem, not accusing them of bad parenting or having bad kids. And try to keep in mind what it would feel like to be them. They're not crazy for getting defensive or anxious. That's why it's now *your* time to implement SEAL. Dads, you are more than capable of making this call. Don't shy away from this opportunity to show your daughter she can rely on you as a sane advocate on her behalf.

YOU: "Hi, I'm Lori's mother. This is an uncomfortable call to make, but I need to talk to you about something that's going on with our girls. Is now a good time to talk?"

RMG'S PARENT: "Well, I'm really busy right now but sure."

YOU: "Thanks *(which you try to say sincerely, not sarcastically)*. We need your help and I have to tell you, parent to parent, this is really hard. Your daughter created a Facebook page that said my daughter was a whore."

RMG'S PARENT: "What?! Are you sure? How do you know it was my kid?"

YOU: "Lori has talked to your daughter to try to get her to stop, but she hasn't. Lori is dreading going to school, so I really need your help to make this situation better."

RMG'S PARENT: "But why do you think my daughter did it?"

YOU *(Take a deep breath and remember the goal)*: "Because Lori

has talked to her about it. We've really tried to work it out between the girls, but that hasn't helped."

RMG'S PARENT: "Well, what do you want me to do?"

YOU: "Lori would like the Facebook group pulled down immediately, but she's worried that because I'm telling you what happened your daughter will be mad she got in trouble. Can you
help us so that won't happen?"

RMG'S PARENT: "I can try but I can't guarantee anything."

YOU: "Thanks."

Look, this conversation may not go great. You may get off the
phone and say to yourself, "Well, I know where that girl gets it
from." The point is you are going through a process in which you
are handling yourself maturely and the parent is now on notice
about what's going on. And if you have a parent who responds well
in this situation, this is a person to appreciate.

If You Get a Call About Your Daughter's Behavior

It's six P.M. and you're blissfully alone, heading up to your clean
bathroom to take a bubble bath (or more likely, desperately trying
to get dinner on the table and telling your kids to stop fighting),
when the phone rings.

LORI'S MOM: "Is this [the RMG's] mother?"

YOU: "Yes . . . what can I do for you?"

LORI'S MOM: "I need to talk to you right now about your daughter."
(*Her voice trembles with self-righteous anger.*)

YOU: "OK . . . what is this about?" (*You glare at your daughter, who
is beginning to clue in that this conversation is about her and it's
not about her latest community service project.*)

LORI'S MOM: "I just need to tell you I have never been so disgusted
in my entire life! I know girls can be mean, but your daughter
is absolutely the worst. I have no idea how you're raising her but
if my daughter did what your daughter did, I would ship her to
reform school."

YOU: "Excuse me?"

LORI'S MOM: "Your little angel created a Facebook group calling

my daughter a whore. My daughter is crying herself to sleep every night and won't go to school because she's so humiliated." (*Your head begins to throb and your eyes narrow. Where is your daughter? You walk into the living room and find her talking on her phone. You begin to wonder, "Is my daughter capable of doing something to terrible? Am I a horrible parent? Does everyone at the school meeting I am about to leave for already know about this?" Put all those thoughts out of your head and immediately acknowledge the other parent's feelings.*)

YOU: "As hard as this is to hear, thank you for calling and I'm really sorry. Can you tell me what happened and when? Can you give me more details?" (*Write them down.*) "Let me talk to my daughter, and then I would like to call you later tonight. When is a good time?"

Because Lori's parent usually wants to vent, these calls can take a long time. If you don't have the time, apologize, tell Lori's mom why you can't talk, and let her choose another time to talk. Then call exactly when you agreed.

I listen to them and then listen to my daughter. It's her responsibility. I think it's wrong to be accused without seeing the accuser. I also don't use pronouns. For example, I will say, "A call came in. . . . It reported X. Do you know anything about it?" Then I think my daughter has to make a choice. She can continue her crappy behavior or she can change. Now, this doesn't work all the time because I'm so pissed off.

—Peggy

If Your Daughter Is the Bystander

Remember the other girl involved? How responsible is she if she didn't help create the Facebook group but did join it?

First of all, you may not hear anything from her about it. You'll hear it from other parents, or you'll get called into the school yourself. Either way, even if she wasn't directly responsible, she made a choice to contribute to the problem. If you do find out, here's how you use SEAL to frame what you want to say.

YOU: "So I heard about the Facebook page. You want to talk about it?"

YOUR DAUGHTER: "No, not really."

YOU: "Well, I want to talk about it. Was there really a group calling Lori Shore a mega-whore?"

YOUR DAUGHTER: "Yeah, things just got totally blown out of proportion. It's so stupid! I really didn't want to do it. I wish [the RMG] would back off a little, but she never does."

YOU: "What does [the RMG] have to gain by doing it?"

YOUR DAUGHTER: "I don't know, [the RMG] just hates her."

YOU: "But there must have been a reason in her mind that this was something she needed to do."

YOUR DAUGHTER: "She's just really mad at all the attention Lori's getting from the boys. She thinks Lori's getting really stuck up about it."

YOU: "Now I want to ask you a question. Do you think what happened to Lori was justified?"

YOUR DAUGHTER: "What are you talking about?"

YOU: "If [the RMG] is right and Lori's really stuck up, is [the RMG] right to create that group?"

YOUR DAUGHTER: "I don't know."

YOU: "Actually this is an important thing for me to know. Did you think [the RMG] was right to do what she did?"

YOUR DAUGHTER: "It wasn't right, but this whole thing has gotten totally blown out of proportion."

YOU: "If you didn't think it was right, then we need to talk about why you didn't do anything to stop it, because your actions contributed to the problem. So what do you need to do right now to make it right?" (*Possible options include using SEAL to frame a conversation with the RMG, apologizing to Lori and her parents, Internet/cellphone restriction.*)

If Your Daughter Is the RMG

When you confront your daughter about her nasty behavior, tell her the facts as you know them. No matter what her excuse or justification is, she should be punished in a way that communicates how seriously you take this issue. It's hard to admit that your daughter has behaved like a jerk, but it isn't a reflection of poor parenting if you admit her misbehavior. Quite the opposite. Guess

which parents teachers complain about? The parents who think their daughters are little angels and blame everyone else for corrupting their little darlings.

Say you just hung up with Lori's parent and you ask your daughter to meet with you privately—away from her siblings. If possible, both parents should be involved in this conversation so she can't take advantage of any information gaps between the two of you. If you're divorced and have any kind of working relationship with your ex-spouse, please apprise them of the situation so they can be part of helping your daughter take responsibility for her actions.

YOU: "OK—as you may or may not know, I just received information about you creating a Facebook group calling Lori Shore a whore. Did you in any way participate in making and/or creating this group?"

RMG (*Crossing her arms and grumbling*): "This is so stupid! That girl just blows everything out of proportion!

YOU: "I need you to answer my question."

RMG: "Well, I knew about it, but it wasn't my idea. It was Monica's."

YOU: "Did you have any part in writing it?"

RMG: "Fine! Whatever you say!" (*Rolling her eyes.*)

YOU: "Well, there are a couple of things you need to know about what I think about this. Most important, I don't really care whose idea it was. I hold you responsible for participating."

RMG: "Fine! Ground me forever!"

YOU: "Not quite. First, I'm going to need your phone, which I will keep until I think you've learned to handle technology more responsibly. You will also be forbidden from using Facebook for the next month and I will be checking your page to see when you last logged in. I'm going to call Lori's family and see if we can come over, and you will apologize to Lori in front of me and her parents."

RMG: "You're totally insane!"

YOU: "When you do something that is unethical, it's my responsibility to you to hold you accountable. I love you with all my heart, so I can't stand by and do nothing about this. You must have the courage to right this wrong. I know it's going to be difficult to do this, but I'll be beside you the whole time. While I

believe what you're telling me, you need to know that if I find out that you're more responsible for this than you are telling me right now, then that will mean additional consequences. There is a chance I won't find out, but there's also a chance I will."

RMG: "Fine. Believe whatever you want. I don't care!"

YOU: "This is a hard situation, so think about it tonight and if you remember anything else about what happened, you can come back to me and I won't consider it lying. After tomorrow morning, however, I will. The last thing that I really need for you to get is that if Lori's life becomes more difficult because of this conversation or anything the school decides to do, I will be forced to take much more severe actions. I'll put it to you this way—I understand if you're really angry about this, but under no circumstances are you allowed to seek revenge. You aren't in trouble because Lori told. You're in trouble for what you did to her."

Then call Lori's parents and ask them if you can come over to apologize. If they say yes, set up a time that's convenient for them to go over there. If they say no, then have your daughter write a letter of apology, which you should drive over to her house and watch her as she places it in the mailbox. Then email the parents to tell them that the letter was dropped off.

In the next chapter I'll give you ways to apply the strategies in this chapter to other common conflicts, such as being treated hot and cold or being whispered about as you walk down the hallway. I wish I could give you a magic spell that would make girls stop gossiping and tearing one another down. But you know I can't do that. What we can do is have your daughter create, maintain, and communicate her personal boundaries to other girls through difficult experiences like these. We can teach her to give and accept apologies in a way that transforms her relationships. And as I tell my students, if you can handle these situations using SEAL, no matter what the outcome, the sting of cruel words will lose their venom. You gain a degree of mastery and pride just knowing you got through a difficult experience and came out the other side.

Power Plays and Politics:
Speaking Truth in Girl World

Lila has just come in from fifth-grade recess and can't find her backpack. She knows she left it underneath the stairwell, but it's not there. As the other students collect their books to go to class, Lila looks for it in the hallway, the bathroom, and the classrooms, but she can't find it anywhere. She starts to panic. She has to turn in her project for Mr. Thompson, and he won't believe that she so suddenly and conveniently couldn't find her backpack. In desperation, she goes back outside to the playground to retrace her steps like her mom tells her when she loses something; there it is, sitting in the middle of the playground. Lila is confused. She knows there's no way she left her backpack there. She hears laughter behind her and turns around to see Jackie and Abby giggling and staring at her. When they see her looking at them, they hurry away to class.

Three weeks ago, Abby couldn't believe how lucky she was to get two concert tickets to see her favorite band. And even though she hasn't been hanging out with Christina like she used to, of course Abby invited her. The night of the concert, Christina comes over early and they're getting along great. They have fun together at the concert—that is, until Christina gets a text from Isabella, the

girl she's been hanging out with more recently. Isabella is at the concert with her own group of friends. At intermission, they all agree to meet, but, as soon as they do, Abby completely regrets it. Christina barely acknowledges Abby's existence in front of the other kids. They go back to their seats, and Christina gets more texts. She tells Abby she needs to get something from Isabella and leaves—and doesn't come back. Abby texts Christina, but doesn't get an answer until the end of the concert, when Christina tells her, "Don't worry about me, just text me when your dad gets here." When Abby's dad does get there, it takes twenty more minutes to find Christina. Abby lies to her dad about where Christina is— which makes her feel even more angry. The next day, Christina refuses to admit she did anything wrong.

Let's go back to what I wrote in the introduction: Dignity is not negotiable—not your daughter's, not anyone else's. Treating yourself and others with dignity isn't hard when everyone is getting along; it's when you are angry that your character is really tested. The power plays in this chapter are great examples. You're in a situation where you're pretty sure and then very sure that people are just messing with you to make you miserable. Doesn't it make sense to beat them at their own game? It's so tempting. . . . I know.

WHAT YOU SHOULD KNOW

- Just as these experiences are rites of passage for your daughter, they are also rites of passage for you as a parent. Don't underestimate how painful they can be for both of you.
- Remember, most girls aren't stuck in one role, which means your daughter will likely have experiences as the one who excludes, the one who watches but doesn't say anything, and the one who's excluded.
- Reconciliations are often fleeting. Two girls previously in a fight may say that they've worked it out, only to have one attack the other again. This is especially true when the girl in the weaker position believes everything's OK.
- Technology makes power plays much easier to conduct.

UNINVITED TO THE PARTY

I don't care how old you are—few things will make you as insecure as not being invited to a friend's party. The party girl gets to be Queen Bee for the day as she decides (in consultation with her best friends) whom to invite and whom to leave out. (If she's allowed to invite boys, as I'll explore further in chapter 10, the drama escalates to a fever pitch.)

> MARY: "Did you get Amanda's text about her birthday party? It's going to be amazing!"
>
> ANA: "I didn't get it yet . . . but my phone's been acting really weird this week."
>
> MARY: "Oh, I'm sure you're invited. I'll go find out and let you know."

That afternoon . . .

> MARY: "Amanda says that her mom is only allowing her to have a few people. You know, like her really good friends."
>
> ANA: "That's OK."
>
> MARY: "Maybe I can talk to Amanda and get you invited."

How should Ana process this? On the following page I have diagrammed each girl's feelings, motivations, likely outcomes, and a better outcome (called "Makes herself proud") for a few typical power plays. I suggest girls use this grid whenever they have a conflict with friends to sort out competing interests and the roles girls play. Show your daughter this format and help her through a few examples so she understands how they work. Understanding other girls' motivations can help her figure out what she wants to do when she encounters a power play, such as not being invited to a friend's birthday party.

In the preceding example, Amanda is a Queen Bee (that is, the person with power, at least temporarily), Mary is a Messenger (in the middle), and Ana is a Target (the person left behind). Here's how the birthday party drama would look:

	Ana	Mary	Amanda
Feelings	Rejected	Torn but feeling important because she's in the middle	Enjoying being the center of attention
Motivations	Torn—wants to be invited but doesn't want to beg	Torn—wants to help friend and affirm her own social place	Wants to have her birthday her way
Likely result	Feels she's at the bottom of the totem pole	Feels important	Gets what she wants
What she learns	Has to change herself if she wants to be accepted	Her Messenger position is powerful	Has control over others
Makes herself proud	Recognizes it isn't a reflection on her	Feels torn, but doesn't make this an opportunity to feel important	Realizes she's hurt others' feelings and opens party to others

If you're Amanda's parent, you want to do something special for your birthday girl, but you don't want to make other children feel bad in the process. This is an opportunity to work together with your daughter to show your values in action. If your daughter goes to a large school, you're not obligated to invite everyone in the class, nor is it good modeling to throw a party you can't afford or that will show that you have way more money than everyone else. If she goes to a small school, make sure the invite list isn't including everyone but one or two girls.

Start by empathizing with her and saying you can understand why she would want only the people she likes best at her party and that she wants it to be nice, but that it's very important that she makes decisions that are inclusive of others. Don't force her to invite certain girls, but encourage her to explore how she'd feel if she were left out. Suggest she do something less grandiose so she can invite more kids rather than do something exclusive. Make up the guest list together and stick to it. If a delegate comes to your daughter on behalf of the girl who wasn't invited (Ana) and your daughter changes her mind and invites her, be aware that this

turn of events usually backfires. Ana might come to the party only to have your daughter be mean to her because she was "forced" to invite her. Then you have that horrible experience of hanging out with Ana in the kitchen, waiting for one of her parents to pick her up and glare at you for being a bad parent.

If your daughter is a Wannabe in her clique and it's her birthday, the Queen Bee and Sidekick may look like they're deferring to her when making up the guest list. Don't be fooled. This is a tactic. They'll almost certainly try to get your daughter to exclude people they don't like or pressure her to invite boys. Please understand that no matter how mature and kind she is, if she's having a party or going somewhere like a concert, there's very little chance she'll be able to control herself from talking about it at school. You can't invite everyone to everything, and girls have to accept that they aren't going to be invited to everything all the time. That said, there have to be some general rules for navigating these situations. Here are mine and this is how I'd communicate them to her:

1. "I expect you to keep the talking about your party to a minimum. I know I can't control every word that comes out of your mouth, but I need you to be aware that other people may feel hurt or excluded because they weren't invited. You're allowed to invite friends, but you aren't allowed to make others feel bad in the process. This is my law."

2. "I expect you to honor both the spirit and letter of the law. This means you can't do anything obnoxious like obviously try to cover up that you're talking about the party with your invited friends by falling silent, starting to whisper, or running away when someone who wasn't invited comes up to you. I consider that unacceptable behavior."

3. "If I find out that you have used this party, which is my gift to you, to make someone feel bad, I will cancel it." (If you issue this threat, you must make good on it, no matter how your child whines, apologizes, or promises to never do it again.)*

---

*   This is from *Queen Bee Moms and Kingpin Dads.*

During the party, it's important that she be gracious to all her guests, meaning she's not allowed to invite people and then ignore them at the party, nor intimate that they're only there because "Mom said I had to invite you" or "Dad made me ask all the kids."

Of all the parents in this "uninvited to the party" scenario, Mary's parents are least likely to know about this drama. If you find out what's going on, you should help Mary figure out her motivation: Is she getting in the middle because she feels bad that Ana isn't invited or because it makes her feel important as a Messenger? If she's the star of the story, she's more likely to intervene on Ana's behalf, in an effort to solidify her position in the clique. You both should ask yourselves why it's important for her to be in this role of Messenger and center of attention. If her description centers on her empathy for Ana, then you have a great opportunity to ask her questions about what she gains from being invited and going (perhaps she feels popular), and what she loses (determines she's making decisions based on popularity or on her friend's feelings).

If you're Ana's parent, you should respond to your daughter's exclusion with your version of "I'm so sorry, thank you for telling me, what would you like to do about it?" This is also a good time to share a personal story if this has ever happened to you. This is one of those times when you don't need to do anything about what your daughter just shared. She just wants to vent. She doesn't want you getting on the phone with the birthday girl's parent and begging for an invitation. *Nor should you.* Under no circumstances should you call the parents of the party girl to angle for an invitation. If you do this, you're teaching your daughter that social status is more important than her personal dignity. As painful as it is to see your daughter excluded and as bad as she feels about it, *it's more important to affirm her ability to cope.* When the party day arrives, do something with her that she wants to do so she's reminded that there's life outside the party. Now, if your daughter wants to use SEAL to address the birthday girl (for example, if they have been friends for a long time and she is really surprised and hurt that she's not invited), this is what she can say:

YOUR DAUGHTER: "This is really uncomfortable for me to admit, but I know you're having a party and you didn't invite me."

BIRTHDAY GIRL: "Well, my mom said I could only have, like, four people [or other excuse]."

YOUR DAUGHTER: "I'm not talking to you so you feel guilty and invite me. But I was pretty surprised. I just wanted to ask you if there's something I did that made you not want to include me."

Then, she needs to be prepared to listen because there may be a perfectly logical reason why that girl didn't invite her. Like maybe the birthday girl doesn't like her because your daughter hasn't been nice to her. Remember, the goal is not to get an invitation. Instead, the goal is to have your daughter think through the problem and address it.

WHISPERING

Your daughter walks down the hallway and two girls start whispering as soon as she passes them. Does she say something to the girls? I think if it happens once, she should let it pass, because she may be making an incorrect assumption that the girls are whispering about her. But if it happens more than once, then she should consider addressing it, using SEAL as a way to prepare what she wants to say. Remember, while she's doing her preparation, put no pressure on her to do SEAL in real life. Ask her what it feels like when she sees the girls in the hallway. Have her put it into words. The thing you need to get across to her is that while she can't control girls whispering, she can control what she does. Using SEAL, she can do the following:

Stop and Strategize: She decides she's going to say something to them the next time it happens.

YOUR DAUGHTER (*Explain*): "I really wish you'd stop whispering when I walk by."

OTHER GIRLS (*Pushback*): "We aren't whispering about you!" (*Laughing.*)

YOUR DAUGHTER (*Affirm*): "Well, that's what it looks like to me."

OTHER GIRLS (*Pushback*): "You're being so dramatic!"

YOUR DAUGHTER (*Lock Out*): "If there's something you need to tell me, then you need to tell me to my face."

OTHER GIRLS (*Pushback*): *Continue laughing.*
YOUR DAUGHTER (*Lock out*): *Walks away.*

I know—it's terrible to walk away from people who are laughing at you. But in this situation they're doing it anyway so at least this way your daughter is standing up for herself.

YOUR DAUGHTER'S FRIEND IS TREATING HER HOT AND COLD

It is 4:30 p.m. and I have just dropped off a girl who came to play with my daughter for the first time. This is the conversation I overheard while I was reading in the living room and they were doing art in the dining room.

PLAYDATE: "The reason I didn't want the teacher to tell anybody I was going to play at your house is because my other friends might dump me. I can't be your friend, but I can still have playdates with you."
YOUR DAUGHTER: "Just don't tell your friends and they won't be mad at you."
PLAYDATE: "They won't be mad, they will make fun of me."
YOUR DAUGHTER: "Why will they make fun of you?"
PLAYDATE: "Because they think you are weird. Another classmate told me she felt sorry for me for having a playdate with you."

This woman's daughter shouldn't turn herself inside out trying to be nice to this girl. It will only come across as trying too hard and chasing her. At best, the old friend will treat her well when they are one-on-one, but she'll turn her back on her when she's around her new friends.

This is how she'd SEAL it:

Stop and Strategize: How does she feel about what the girl said? Where does she think is the best place to talk to her?
Explain: "When you were over at my house, you told me that people are making fun of you for being friends with me. I

want to hang out with you, but I don't want to worry about when you will be my friend and when you won't."

Affirm: "I want a friend who treats me nicely no matter who's around."

Lock: "I would really like to keep being friends."

If the girl agrees and then goes back to treating your daughter hot and cold, then I would ask your daughter to consider the "take a vacation" or "lock out" option.

What if the girl says "It's not my fault. You always want to hang out so I never feel like I can see my other friends"?

As much as this may hurt your daughter's feelings, she needs to respect what the other girl is saying. If the other girl says that she wants to play with someone else at a certain time, then your daughter needs to respect her friend's boundaries. No matter how old your daughter is in situations like this, she can't force people to be friends with her. And the more she tries the more they will back away from her. She has to give the other girl some space.

HOW DO YOU TALK TO YOUR DAUGHTER IF SHE IS IGNORING HER OLD FRIENDS?

Take her somewhere you can talk privately while also doing another activity, like taking the dog for a walk, and say, "Hey, I'd like to check in with you about your friends because it's really common for people to change friend groups." Whatever her response, you want to get across that she has the right to change friends but she can't be mean about it. Then ask her to explain to you what you mean by "mean." If she gets defensive, demands to know who's talking about her, or launches into why everyone else is being oversensitive, remind her that people have the right to be upset when they feel rejected.

THE THIRD WHEEL: DIVIDED
LOYALTIES AND THE TAGALONG

Jennifer and Kimber are in sixth grade and are very good friends.
Sometimes they play with Sara, a girl who really wants to be in
their group. Kimber and Sara used to be really good friends, but
now Kimber thinks Sara is boring. Jennifer invites Kimber to her
house for a sleepover on Saturday night. Sara overhears them talking about it and asks if she can come. Jennifer tells Sara that she's
sick of her and that she should make her own friends. Kimber
doesn't like what Jennifer said to Sara, but she doesn't say anything.

On Sunday morning after the sleepover, Jennifer and Kimber
are playing when Jennifer's mother marches into the room, obviously angry, and asks to speak to Jennifer alone. Right outside the
room, Jennifer's mother tells her that Sara's mother called her and
told her what happened at school. Jennifer's mother is really angry
with Jennifer and she's now forbidden from having sleepovers for
a month. The first thing Jennifer does is to complain to Kimber.

JENNIFER: "Can you believe what Sara did? She cries to her mom
    and now I get in trouble. This sucks!"
KIMBER: "Yeah, I can't believe it."

On Monday, Jennifer and Kimber are walking down the hall at
school when they see Sara.

JENNIFER: "Sara, what did you think you were doing? You ran to
    your mom so I would get in trouble! My mom thinks I wouldn't
    let you come over because that's what your mom said. Now I
    can't have anyone over ever again!"
SARA: "What are you talking about?"
JENNIFER: "Don't pretend like you don't know what I'm talking
    about."
SARA: "I'm sorry. I didn't know. I mean, I'm so sorry. I was upset
    but I told my mom not to tell anyone. What can I do to make
    it up to you?"
JENNIFER: "You already did enough damage. Come on, Kimber,
    let's go."

Using the grid again, let's break down each girl's role.

	Sara	Kimber	Jennifer
Feelings	Excluded, rejected, upset, maybe angry	Depends on what kind of bystander she is: torn would feel guilty; powerful would feel justified and angry	Angry and defensive; wants to put Sara "in her place"
Motivations	Wants to be liked and is hurt by the other girls' rejection	Torn between friendships and doing the "right" thing	Got in trouble; doesn't want to be forced to be Sara's friend
Likely result	She'll apologize to the group, change her personality to fit with the group, or find other friends	Weakens friendship with Sara	Bullies Sara to stop hanging out with them and bullies Kimber to follow her lead
What she learns	She'll get in trouble if she admits that her feelings are hurt or confronts powerful girls; won't talk to her mom again	Jennifer is a strong Queen Bee; don't cross her	Bullying people works
Makes herself proud	Stands up for herself by telling both girls how their actions make her feel; walks away proud of herself; knows that she should make new friends because the old ones come at too high a price	Tells Jennifer she doesn't like how she treated Sara and gives suggestions for handling the situation better	Takes responsibility for her behavior and apologizes to both Sara and Kimber

If you're Sara's parent: In this situation, Sara has learned that people in positions of power can bully weaker people and that if the victim of the bully "tells," it'll come back on her. When a parent finds out their child has been slighted, they sometimes forget what kids know well: If you get the bully in trouble, at some point she'll find you, and no one will be around to help. In this

situation, involvement should be limited to strategizing with her about what she wants to do and then affirming that she has the strength to carry it out by herself. It's a fine line because your daughter needs to know that you're watching her back, but she also needs to know that you have confidence in her ability to take care of herself. That means not calling the other girl's parents to complain about your daughter's exclusion and keeping her complaints to yourself when she confides in you. If you keep trying to fix life for her, she'll think that she can't do it herself, or that she can't trust you with her feelings. This becomes proof that going to you makes the problem worse.

Your first step, as always, is to empathize with your daughter. It hurts to be excluded, especially if you're labeled as a tagalong. It's hard to admit that other girls see your daughter as a nuisance. But, if she is, you need to talk to her about it. Otherwise, sixth through eighth grade will be even more painful for her. Review your daughter's Bill of Rights for Friends (see page 264) with her. Ask her if she knew that Kimber and Jennifer felt this way about her. If she did, why does she still want to hang out with them?

The hardest question that both you and your daughter need to think about is this: Why is this happening? Whatever the answer to that, the next question is equally difficult. For example, if your daughter is annoying her friends because she's not as into boys as they are, is this something she wants to change about herself? I would say no. She should be interested in boys at her own pace and in her own time. On the other hand, if your daughter is annoying because she interrupts people and is constantly getting in people's business, that may be something she needs to look at and change.

It's critical to get your daughter to understand the difference between her actions and her personality. She might want to change how she acts, but she shouldn't try to change who she is. Talk out why she thinks she and Kimber grew apart. Are they into different things? If so, is Sara feeling any pressure to "catch up" to Kimber's interests? Remind her that every girl has her own schedule, and that Sara shouldn't give in to pressure to fake being into boys, clothes, or whatever else Kimber thinks is a more "ma-

ture" interest. At the same time, Sara needs to recognize that it's fair for Kimber to have her own interests and to want to hang out with girls who share them. She shouldn't ask Jennifer to invite her, but she can tell Kimber how she feels when she's left out. And she needs to do it in person, not online. For example:

SARA: "Kimber, can I talk to you for a minute?"

KIMBER: "Sure . . . what's up?" (*She probably knows something's up.*)

SARA: "This is hard to say, but I'm pretty sure that you don't want to hang out with me as much as you used to and I want to know if we can talk about it?"

KIMBER: "That's so not true! I don't know what you're talking about!"

SARA: "I'm not saying this to make you feel bad. I just want to talk about it because you're a good friend. Can you tell me why you don't want to hang out? I promise I'll do my best to listen to what you're saying."

It's painful to realize that a friendship may be ending, but remind your daughter that a lot of friendships have natural ups and downs, and that she and Kimber might be more in sync later. On the other hand, if Kimber is more interested in being part of a clique than being a good friend, Sara needs to assess whether this is a friendship worth trying to keep.

If you're Kimber's parent: What would you want Kimber to do in this situation? Girls do have the right to choose their friends. They just don't have the right to make the girl they don't like feel like dirt in the process. On the other hand, a girl can be too "nice." Of course, you want your daughter to be kind to others, but you don't want her to feel that she must always put other people's needs before her own. Being too much of a "people pleaser" can lead to people taking advantage of her.

Even if you don't agree with what she did, empathize with her first and let her raise her initial defense on her own. See it from her perspective and don't show anger that she hasn't done the "right thing." These situations are complex and demand your thoughtfulness. During adolescence, girls' loyalties are frequently

divided. If Kimber sides with Sara, she'll earn Sara's undying loyalty, but she'll "betray" Jennifer. Betraying Jennifer makes her extremely vulnerable, because Jennifer will seek revenge by getting
other girls to gang up on and exclude her. If she betrays Sara,
there's no social liability, and most likely Sara will forgive her later.
If you were twelve, in Kimber's situation, dealing with Jennifer
and her friends all day, every day, what would you do? Going with
Jennifer is often the only answer that makes sense. Jennifer is intimidating. Acknowledge how hard it is to stand up to someone
who seems to hold all the cards.

Your next step is to get Kimber to take responsibility for her
actions. Girls are masters at convincing themselves that their bad
behavior is a result of someone else's actions. Jennifer believes she
never would have been in that situation if Sara hadn't complained
to her mother. Almost anyone in Kimber's position will back down
and do anything to stay in the good graces of the powerful girl in
the group. The girls' social hierarchy supports Jennifer's denial of
responsibility because the other girls won't challenge it and the
parents aren't there to know what really happened.

Girls often get angry with the person in Sara's position, but it's
just a diversionary tactic. Don't let your daughter get away with it.
This is a great time to teach your daughter about the need to treat
others with respect. She needs to admit that she should have stood
up for Sara. Then, ask her about Jennifer. Does she want to be a
person other people push around? Does she want to be a person
who says nothing when another person is bullied? Ask her how
she would like to handle the situation in the future. Encourage
her to talk through with you what she would like to say to Jennifer
and Sara.

If she's really brave, the best thing she can do is apologize
to Sara in front of Jennifer (see "The Art of the Apology" on
page 220). She should say to Jennifer that she didn't feel right
about what happened to Sara. (She shouldn't say "what you did
to Sara" because, first, Jennifer will get defensive, and, second,
Kimber needs to take responsibility for her actions that backed up
Jennifer.)

If you're Jennifer's parent: You may be angry and embarrassed,

but focus your energy on the lessons Jennifer can learn from this experience. Because another parent is blaming your child for bad behavior, it's easy to feel that your parenting skills are being questioned. Take Jennifer's behavior seriously, but also look at this as part of the unfortunate yet realistic parenting process. Thank Sara's mom for telling you and apologize for Jennifer's behavior. Then, get Jennifer's side of the story (which will likely initially focus on how she was pushed to be mean because Sara wasn't listening to her). Empathize: "There's nothing wrong with wanting to spend time with Kimber alone, but that doesn't excuse or justify treating Sara the way you did." Just as if you were Kimber's parent, emphasize that it doesn't matter how she feels about Sara, because it was wrong to be cruel. Tell her how you want her to act instead: "You don't have to be friends with everyone, but that doesn't justify being mean to people. The next time you are in this situation, I want you to first ask yourself why hanging out with this person is such a problem. What is making you not want to be with her? What is making you want to show her that you don't like her?" Ask her to call Sara to apologize for her rudeness (see "The Art of the Apology" on page 220) and follow up to make sure she did. Have her call Kimber, too, and apologize for putting her in the middle. Last, say something like, "I know you might be mad at Sara for telling on you, but I don't want to find out you're making her life worse because of this."

BFF: BEST FRIENDS FOREVER OR A DAY?

I'm convinced that best-friend relationships can be the most intense relationships girls will ever have and that nothing can threaten these friendships more than power plays.

Other girls and boys perceive BFFs as living in their own world. They have their own language and codes. They wear each other's clothes. They may even have crushes at the same time on the same person. (That may seem strange, but what better way to start exploring the scary boy-girl world than with your best friend?) It's common that the BFFs will break up around seventh grade (if not before) when one wants to expand her social horizons.

From then on, they may make up, then break up, then make up again. Sometimes it becomes a friendship where they only hang out one-on-one when they're at each other's house, but the minute they're around their peers, one of them will barely recognize the existence of the other. Or worse, one of them will be mean.

> I have a friend who is so nice to me when I'm alone with her but in public she's so mean. The problem is our parents are friends. I like to be with her alone but I'm sick of her other side.
>
> —Kelly, thirteen

Sometimes your daughter will be the dumper, sometimes the dumpee. When your daughter is on the outs with her friend, discourage her from demonizing her friend or the friendship by focusing only on the negatives, and don't you do it, either, because where will you be when they're back together next week? Again, remind your daughter that friendships have a natural ebb and flow, and that she doesn't need to burn her bridges behind her. Help her appreciate that people can grow apart and still be genuinely nice. Don't minimize her broken heart over a lost friendship. Emphasize the importance of talking one-on-one and not relying on email and texts. It's always better to face these situations in person; this way, not as much is "lost in translation." There's little you can do to "fix" the situation, but this is your chance to hone your listening skills and help your daughter realize she can survive the pain and difficulties of the situations that naturally arise from these kinds of relationships.

EXILED FROM THE PROMISED LAND

It all started in October. I began to feel left out of my group. One of the girls in the group, Brittany, was moving, and I wanted to be closer to her before she left. Every time I went near her, she ran away. I was very upset. So I expressed my feelings to her. She told me that I was following her. I agreed, I was. After we talked, I was happy because I thought I wouldn't be left

out again. I was wrong. Then a soccer teammate of Brittany's told me she saw Brittany and my friend Brianna imitate me before their soccer game.

I decided I would hang out with Kim. The next day, I went to lunch with my head high, but when I walked into the cafeteria, Brittany and the other girls in my group were taking up all the seats. I was very hurt by what the girls did. I cried uncontrollably. I just couldn't stop crying. When I talked to the guidance counselor, she suggested that we talk to one of Brittany's best friends, Krista. Krista was one of my close friends, too. Krista offered to have a party inviting Brittany and the others that were in my group. At the party, Brittany and I apologized to each other and we're now friends again. The party turned out so well that I looked forward to Monday. The next day at school, nothing had changed. Brittany, Krista, and the others in the group were still sitting at the opposite side of the table. So I said to Kim, "Fine! Let them sit there, I don't need them." And to this day, I have not talked to any girl in the group. Kim has stuck by me during the hardest time of my life. I'll always have eternal gratitude for Kim. She's a true friend.

—Amy, fourteen

You're in. No, you're out. One day your daughter will go to school and her group of friends will have decided that she's no longer one of them. Or it may happen to one of her best friends in the clique. The reasons may look superficial to you—maybe she has the same shoes as the Queen Bee and everyone knows the Queen Bee told everyone else not to copy her because purple Pumas are *her* signature item; maybe your daughter's hanging out with the "wrong" person, she took the "wrong side" against a Queen Bee or a Sidekick, and/or she committed some other act of high treason. Sometimes there's no easily identifiable reason except that the leaders of the group decide she no longer belongs. Whenever and for whatever reason it happens, it's devastating. Girls come away from these experiences learning that girls—even the ones you think are your true-blue friends—can turn on you on a whim.

As is the case here, this is also a time when girls can learn the meaning of true friendship.

Amy's mom told me her daughter's seventh-grade year was completely horrible. She watched her daughter go from being relatively happy to miserable. Here's how I would help Amy and her mom. They need to break down what happened, so Amy (with her mom's guidance) can figure out the best next steps. When I asked Amy's mom to describe her daughter, she was compassionate but honest in her assessment: "She can be bossy and sometimes self-righteous." She talked openly with her daughter and supported her. She even called Brittany's mom because she thought Amy might have contributed to the problem.

Unfortunately, Brittany's mom chose to act more like Brittany. For more information on how to talk to other parents, see chapter 7, but suffice it to say that these are difficult yet critical conversations to have. You'll be more effective if you approach the other parent as an ally and resource than you would as an attacker.

If you're Krista's parent: When a counselor has a good idea of the power dynamics between girls and the relationship pattern between them, sometimes it can be effective to bring the girls together for a facilitated discussion. But, in this situation, it wasn't a good idea to bring Amy and Krista (instead of Brittany) together. Doing so sends the message that Brittany is either operating below adult radar or is above the law. As a result, Krista's party became an opportunity for Brittany to steamroll over the other girls and call all the shots. If your daughter is in Krista's position and asks you if she can have this party, she may feel so excited about being the social nexus that she'll tell you what's up. If it's clear that she's doing this mainly to cement her social status, nix the party. If Krista explains that she was only trying to patch things up between Amy and Brittany, ask her why she joined Brittany in snubbing Amy at school. You need to get her to admit to herself what she is getting out of this situation. (Girls are never nicer to each other than when they're fighting with someone else.)

If you're Brittany's parent: Brittany may be feeling anxious because she's moving—but, though that may be a reason for her behavior, it doesn't justify it. Maybe she snubbed Amy because she wanted to confirm her status as Queen Bee; that is, she's doing it

just to prove that she can. In your discussions with her, talk about what's making her feel anxious and out of control. Your job is to make her see the connection between what she's anxious about and the things she's doing to feel more in control. Empathize with her about what's motivating her to act out in this way. Then, insist she apologize to Amy. Follow up to make sure she not only made the apology but also is continuing to act consistently afterward. (Freezing Amy out at school clearly violates the spirit of the apology.) Watch out for this: Many girls agree to a truce or reconciliation and then start a war all over again as soon as they get the opportunity.

THE BETTER OFFER: BLOWING EACH OTHER OFF

Amber and Michelle are in high school. They used to hang out all the time, but recently they haven't been spending as much time together because their interests are changing and they're hanging out with different groups—Amber is hanging out with a more popular group, while Michelle still hangs out with their old group. Amber likes Michelle, but when she's with her, she feels as if she's missing out on the fun things her new group likes to do.

Amber and Michelle make plans to hang out on a Saturday night. Michelle is supposed to come over at seven o'clock. At five, one of Amber's new friends, Nicole, calls her and asks her to go to the movies. She also tells Amber that Will, a really hot guy in the group, is interested in her; he's going to the movies, too.

At this point, Amber has three options.

1. She can tell Nicole she wishes she could go, but she already has plans with Michelle. She tells Nicole to have a good time without her.
2. She can blow off Michelle with a lie and go with Nicole.
3. She can try to have her cake and eat it too by getting Nicole to invite Michelle to the movies as well.

I've role-played this scenario hundreds of times with girls in my classes, and I've had only a few stick to the plans with Michelle. About 20 percent invite Michelle along, and the rest lie. There

usually isn't a moment of hesitation before they decide to lie, and the lie usually blames the mother: "My mom is so mean! She won't let me go out because I have to do chores for her/babysit/finish my homework." ("My grandmother died" is another popular option, which never ceases to amaze me—don't these girls think the truth will come out?)

Whichever choice they make, girls learn critical lessons from this situation.

- If Amber sticks with her original plan to hang out with Michelle, Nicole may not respect that Amber is doing the right thing. And if Amber sticks with the original plan, she may resent Michelle for "keeping her down" and worry that Nicole will think she's not cool enough to hang out with again. Amber learns that "doing the right thing" isn't all it's cracked up to be, no matter what her parents may say.

- If Amber lies, Michelle will usually find out about it. (In our role-playing, we make the girls run into each other at the movies so that they learn that if you lie, you usually get caught.) Michelle will think that Amber is two-faced, but she'll also be confused about what she should do about it; would she have done the same thing in that situation? Michelle may not have the same social aspirations, but it's a clear indication that Amber has been anointed by the powers that be (Nicole), so it will be harder for Michelle to confront Amber now that her value on the social index has increased.

- Nicole brings a person like Amber into her group for a reason. Amber is most likely a Pleaser/Wannabe or Torn Bystander. Michelle is hurt and rightfully angry at being blown off, but the social pecking order is reinforced. Michelle learns that she should try to change herself to be more like Amber and Nicole so she won't get left behind. If she tells Amber how she feels about being blown off, Amber will probably accuse her of jealousy, so Michelle learns to keep her mouth shut.

- Nicole, despite her high social status, often feels that the only way to maintain friendships is to make people prove

themselves to her. She's just as trapped as everyone else, maybe more so. Girls in Nicole's position can get so caught up in maintaining their high status that they may not even develop a solid sense of self to lose in the first place.

Let's diagram the situation:

	Michelle	Amber	Nicole
Feelings	Betrayed, rejected, and angry	Confused, defensive, and flattered by Nicole's attention	Say what? Amber should feel grateful she's being accepted into the group
Motivations	Wants things to go back to the way they used to be with Amber	Wants the status of hanging out with Nicole and the attention of the guy	Wants to demonstrate her power
Likely result	Gets into a fight with Amber where she has to justify her feelings and then gives up on Amber	Couches any apology by accusing Michelle of being jealous and holding her back	Dismisses Amber's friendship with Michelle and flatters Amber with more attention
What she learns	Popularity is more important to Amber than their friendship	She can't have friendships with Michelle and Nicole; she has to choose one	She's in control
Makes herself proud	Talks to Amber and responds effectively to the accusation of jealousy. She feels good about how she handled herself.	Apologizes to Michelle and decides which friendship she wants and why. Is able to stand up to Nicole.	Apologizes and stops.

If you're Michelle's parent: Don't make her feel better by talking about how badly Amber or Nicole behaved. You need to help your daughter feel better about herself because she is who she is, not by putting someone else down. (Besides, chances are you'll

come home in a week and see Amber hanging out with Michelle and then she'll worry that you don't like Amber.) Acknowledge how difficult this is right now, but point out that in the long run, her situation is probably less difficult than Amber's. Michelle doesn't have to change herself to be accepted by her real friends; Amber does.

Encourage Michelle to tell Amber how she feels and brainstorm how to respond if Amber tells her she's just being jealous. ("I know you think I'm jealous, but that's not the issue here. The issue is that we agreed we were going to hang out. Good friends don't blow each other off the second a better offer comes along.")

If you're Amber's parent: The biggest problem you have is a daughter who's willing to do things against her better judgment to increase her social status. Acknowledge that Nicole may be more fun to hang out with, but she needs to keep any commitment she makes, regardless of whether a better offer comes along. Ask her what she's giving up in the process. If she says, "Nothing," review her Bill of Rights for Friends (page 264). What does she want and expect from her friendship with Nicole? Can she be herself with Nicole or does she edit herself to please Nicole? If she assures you that Nicole is a really good friend, don't press the issue, because you don't want her to feel she has to defend Nicole to you. Let her think about it on her own.

If Amber were your daughter, there's a chance you'd know about her plans with Michelle. If she changes her plans to go with Nicole, she has to figure out how to get past you (because you'd make her keep her plans with Michelle). You become the biggest obstacle in her way, and she might lie to get around you. Once she lies, you won't know where she is and/or who she's with. It's at this point—though Amber may feel more secure in the life raft than ever—that she's actually swimming in shark-infested waters because she's with friends who aren't going to respect her boundaries, even if she articulates them, which is doubtful because she doesn't want to be uptight.

In any case, Amber owes Michelle an apology, and if at all possible, she should tell Nicole how she feels. If she went with Nicole and blew off Michelle, then she needs to tell Nicole: "Look, I

need to tell you that I made a big mistake. When you invited me out, I actually had already made plans with Michelle and I blew her off. I feel bad about it and I don't want to do that again. So next time, I'd like to invite Michelle."

If she invited Michelle along and Nicole was mean to her, then she needs to tell Nicole that she won't hang out with her if she's going to treat other people like that. Rest assured, there's a self-ish reason to do this, because if Amber stands up to Nicole now, Nicole will be a lot less likely to turn on her later. You need to im-press upon her that there's real danger in trying to please everyone around you all the time, because it usually results in pleasing no one and losing yourself in the process.

If you're Nicole's parent: Your daughter will appear in control. Do some soul-searching before talking to her. What motivates her to build and sustain friendships like this? She didn't technically do anything wrong; she just tried to persuade a friend to hang out with her. But when I do this role-playing scenario in class, the Nicoles can be very convincing because they make Amber feel like she's losing out on the opportunity of a lifetime. It's often pre-sented as a choice that's not a choice: Either you can come with me and you'll have the keys to the kingdom, or you can stay home and spend forty years in the social desert. You need to hold her accountable for her behavior, and perhaps hold yourself account-able for encouraging it, too. Are you perhaps a little too invested in your daughter's popularity?

FISHING FOR COMPLIMENTS

Clara is your daughter's good friend. Recently, though, Clara has been getting on your daughter's nerves because she is always com-plaining about how fat and ugly she is. For months, your daughter has tried to reassure Clara about her appearance, but nothing she says makes Clara feel better. Your daughter comes to you com-plaining about Clara and says she's really tempted the next time she puts herself down to agree with her. Worse, your daughter tells you hanging out with Clara is making her question her own weight and appearance.

Ask your daughter, "What do you think is motivating Clara? Why does she say she's fat when she's not?" (If your daughter says, "She's insecure," dig deeper to find out what lies behind this insecurity.) Ask her to describe the physical feeling she has when Clara starts putting herself down. Have her think about the place and time she could talk to Clara with the best chance of her listening.

Here's a sample SEAL dialogue you and your daughter can use as a starting place to create her own.

Stop and think about her feelings and *strategize*.

YOUR DAUGHTER: "Clara, I need to talk to you about something important."

CLARA: "OK, sure. Are you mad at me or something?"

YOUR DAUGHTER: "No, I'm not mad at you, but I need to talk to you about the things you say about yourself."

CLARA: "OK . . ."

YOUR DAUGHTER (*Explain*): "When you say you're fat or put yourself down about how you look, I tell you you're not, but it doesn't make a difference. I want you to feel good about yourself, but I don't want to feel like I have to do this all the time."

CLARA: "I'm sorry. I'm sorry. I know it's so stupid."

YOUR DAUGHTER (*Affirm/Lock*): "Don't apologize for feeling bad. As your friend, I want to be able to help you, and I think the best way to do that is to figure out what's going to work here beyond the two of us. Who do you think could help?"

CHECKING YOUR BAGGAGE

- When you were your daughter's age, did you blow friends off if a better option came along?
- What and how have you communicated your values about friendships and commitment to your daughter?
- What do you think your daughter would say if I asked her the same question about you?
- Do you have close friendships where you can tell people when you're upset with them and they'll respect what you're saying?

- How do you handle power plays when you see them occurring in your own life?

WHAT YOU CAN DO TO ALLEVIATE THE FRUSTRATION OF POWER PLAYS

You may feel that it's not worth making a federal case of not getting invited to a birthday party or letting your daughter blow off one friend for another. You may have heard someone say, "We need to let the girls work it out." Remember what the difference is between bullying and drama, but acknowledge that both can still hurt. Remember that involvement isn't all or nothing. You don't want to micromanage. But you have to be behind the scenes using these opportunities to show what you stand for as a parent. These may seem like trivial issues, but they aren't. They lay the groundwork for girls faking their feelings, pretending to be someone they're not, pleasing others at their own expense, or otherwise sacrificing self-esteem and authenticity. The skirmishes that in earlier years are limited to hurt feelings can transition into parents' worst fears: vulnerability to drinking, drugs, and bad relationships. You can use these early power plays to help your daughter figure out why it's worthwhile to be true to herself and to think through what real friendship is all about.

You should also appreciate that sometimes the values you teach your daughter will be in conflict with the way she feels she needs to act in order to feel comfortable in her clique. Let's suppose that you've always taught her that championing the underdog is the right thing to do and that she should stick up for people who are being bullied or picked on. If your daughter stands up for an unpopular girl and the result is that her friends in the clique are angry at her, she's bound to feel burned by your teaching her to do the right thing. To her, she only ends up feeling punished. She needs to know that you understand how she feels. Acknowledge that sometimes doing the right thing will bring her grief in the short term, but in the long term, it's more important to be true to her character and values and it's the only way she can truly be in control of her life. Tell her you're proud that she took the rougher

road and that sooner or later, she'll feel just as proud of her actions as you do.

This is how I explain it to my students:

"I'm not going to lie to you and say people are going to thank you for doing the right thing. If you complain about this stuff, people very well may turn on you. They may make your life more difficult. You have to decide what price you would rather pay. If you decide to speak out, the price will possibly be some kind of social rejection, but you will know that the people who stand by you are your true and loyal friends and that you treated yourself and others with dignity when it was hard. If you decide to say nothing, people won't get in your face. Things will be calm on the outside. But there is a cost, and it is your dignity. Another cost is people being able to take advantage of you or believing that even if you don't like something that's going down, you won't say anything about it. It's up to you to decide which price is higher."

Talk to your daughter about what she should expect to give and get from her friendships with others. Every friendship will have its ups and downs, so there are benefits to encouraging your daughter to take a longer view so she doesn't burn all her bridges. That said, you should help her identify patterns of inconsiderate behavior that suggest she rethink the relationship. Help her clarify her expectations with the Bill of Rights for Friends.

BILL OF RIGHTS FOR FRIENDS

- What does she want and need in a friendship? (Trust, reliability, loyalty, telling her when they're angry with her in a respectful way.)
- What are her rights in a friendship? (To be treated respectfully, with kindness and honesty.)
- What are her responsibilities in a friendship? (To treat her friends ethically.)
- What would a friend have to do or be like for her to end the friendship? (Not listen to her, not honor her values and ethics.)

- Under what circumstances would she go to an adult for help with a problem with a friend? (When the problem feels too big to handle alone.)
- What are her friends' rights and responsibilities in the friendship? (To listen even when it's not easy to hear.)

Then, ask the hardest question: How do her experiences with her friends compare to her Bill of Rights? If they aren't similar, why does she have those friendships?

If and when your daughter makes the decision that her friends aren't right for her, it'll be a very lonely time for her. She may know that she has made the right decision in ending a friendship, but that'll be only a small comfort. It takes incredible strength of character to decide to break up with a friend who doesn't respect her Bill of Rights and even more strength to remain resolute. Praise her courage. I present some examples from my teaching on how to do this in the next section.

"WHAT IF?" AND "HOW DO YOU?" Q&A

The following are common questions girls ask me when I am teaching them about the role of power plays.

Q: What if one of your really good friends is someone everyone talks bad about, but if you stand up for her everyone will hate you, too?

A: This is a particularly difficult situation because it feels like there's no way to win. I would begin with baby steps. The next time someone trashes your friend, pretend there is something really interesting about ten feet away from the group and go over to it. This is another way of saying "Walk away." If you see a post or message trashing your friend, train your brain and your fingers to immediately press delete—no matter how much you "really just want to find out what they're saying." Just try it once and see if you can actually do it. Once you have accomplished these two goals, you can start preparing for the second goal, which is to talk privately to the person who is the most focused on hating your friend. Then you would use SEAL.

Q: What is the best way to approach a friend who you feel doesn't like you anymore?

A: You can't make people like you. Back off a little and give your friend some space, for about a week. Then, the beginning of the second week, be casually friendly with the person. Like, "Hey, what's up?" when you see her in the hall, in class, or at lunch. After a couple of days of that, if you still want to, I'd ask her to hang out and see how she responds. If you do hang out and you have a good time, then that's good and you can think about putting energy into maintaining the friendship. If it doesn't go well, then the space you've gained will make it easier to walk away.

Q: What if I feel like I can't trust people because they'll make fun of me? I have so much on my chest. What do I do?

A: Just like it's not good to distrust all people, it's not good to trust all people. Overall, it's never good to make judgments that begin with "all" and "always," because both are rarely true. What you need to do is write a list of any people you think are trustworthy and slowly build relationships with them—both people your own age and adults. From that list you need to find someone you feel comfortable sharing your problems with.

Q: What do I do if I have a friend who constantly embarrasses me in front of other people?

A: You have to give the friend one chance to seriously hear how you feel. The next time she embarrasses you, wait until you are alone with that person and say:

YOU: "Remember two hours ago when you teased me in front of those guys about how awkward I was in front of my ex? It seriously has to stop. I know I laughed, but I did that because I didn't know what to say at the time because I was so frustrated."
FRIEND: "I didn't mean anything by it. It was nothing!"
YOU: "It wasn't nothing to me so please listen to me about it because otherwise it's really hard to hang out with you and not worry about what you're going to say."

FRIEND: "Fine . . ."
YOU: "Thanks, so did you like the movie . . . ?"

And if they still do it, I seriously think it's time to "lock out" the friendship. Or at least take a vacation.

Q: How do you tell a good friend that her new "best friend" is a terrible influence and is using her for her connections?

A: The biggest risk you're taking by saying something is that your friend will tell her BFF what you said and then you have a big problem on your hands. If you think that's the most likely outcome, I wouldn't say anything. Why? Because even in the best of circumstances, there is a low chance that your friend will hear what you're saying. I'll put it to you this way: If or when your parents tell you they don't like a friend of yours, what's your response? I doubt it's "Mom, Dad, thanks so much for bringing this to my attention. I had no idea she was such an untrustworthy person. I'll stop being friends with her right now."

But if you really think it's the right thing to do, this is what I'd suggest you say to her: "I admit it's hard to see you being such close friends with someone else. But beyond that, when I see her do X, it seems like she's using you for Y. I totally could be wrong but as your friend at least I thought I should talk to you about it."

Q: What do you do if one of your BFFs was also best friends with your enemy and then your BFF turned against you? You want to be friends again but the whole time she was just getting info out of you.

A: Ask yourself what this girl has that makes it so important to you to be friends with her. Then ask yourself "Do I trust her? Why would I trust her? Why do I want a friend who uses me? What am I getting by being friends with her and what am I sacrificing?"

Q: What do you do if one of your best friends that you've been friends with forever has totally changed and you don't like it?

A: Usually in situations like this one, the friend is acting to come across as less intelligent, and more into style, fashion, guys, and flirting than she was previously, and you don't like it. First, you have to come to terms with the fact that there's probably nothing you can do to make her change back to the way she was before. But you *can* say something like this:

> YOU: "Jaden, you and I have been friends for a really long time. Part of me still really wants to be friends with you, but when you act like [explain exactly what she's doing that you don't like], I don't like it, because it seems like people only know you as that kind of person. I want them to see the things I like in you, like you're funny and smart."
>
> JADEN: "Why are you so mad at me? I haven't done anything to you! It's not my fault that I like to do different things now."
>
> YOU: "I'm not mad. I'm telling you what I think. As your friend, I want us to be able to talk honestly with each other. It would have been much easier if I had said nothing and kept these things to myself. But I don't think real friends hide what they're thinking."

Q: What if the girl denies that she's mad, or if she tells you she's angry but refuses to tell you why?

A: This is a classic power play. The reason a girl does that is because in Girl World, she has to control the way she expresses her anger. If the girl denies she's mad, this is how I'd respond:

> "OK, you're saying you're not mad but if you change your mind later and decide you are angry, the only thing I'm asking is that you come to me directly instead of talking to other people about it—because I want to work it out with you."

Then, don't wait around for her to change her mind. Let her think about it and make her own decision.

If she has established that she's mad but won't discuss it further, you might talk to her like this:

"I'd really like for you to tell me what I've done to upset you. I don't want to guess because I might be wrong. When you're ready to tell me, I'm ready to hear it."

Q: What if you try to talk to your friend about why you're mad or why she's mad at you and she accuses you of flipping out?

A: First of all, using SEAL to communicate substantially decreases the likelihood that you will "flip out" (that is, cry, yell, get all red and splotchy, and so forth). But if you get that accusation, this is how I suggest you respond.
   Take a deep breath.

YOU: "Lauren, why do you think I'm flipping out?"

LAUREN: "I didn't do anything, and you're acting like I killed your dog!"

YOU: "I'm telling you that I don't like it when you embarrass me around Mike and Jack."

LAUREN: "OMG! I am totally not doing that! You are being so overly sensitive!"

YOU (*Remaining calm*): "I'm asking you to stop. That's all I want. You can do what you want but that's what I'm asking. If we're going to be friends, I need you to take this seriously."

Q: What if you think a friend's apology is insincere?

A: She says something like "Fine, if it's that important to you . . . I'm sorry."
   You say, "Thanks for the apology, but I have to tell you that the way you said it came across as if you think I don't deserve an apology. I don't know if that was what you meant, but that's the way I heard it."

Q: What do you do if someone apologizes to you and you think she means it and then she does the same thing again?

A: You need to reread the Bill of Rights for Friends and compare your friendship standards with what is actually going on in your relationship. It sounds like your friend is acting inconsistently with what you say is important in a friendship.

Q: What if my friend refuses to accept my apology?

A: Sometimes people have a hard time accepting your apology because they think you're apologizing insincerely. If you have apologized before, acknowledge that, and really try to be more mindful of your future actions. But sometimes people would rather hold on to the hurt and anger they feel than accept the apology. People like this say things like "I forgive but I never forget," which really means they don't trust the apology so they really haven't accepted it. All you can do is take ownership of your actions, apologize sincerely, and walk away. Nothing you are going to do beyond acting respectfully will change their feelings—and sometimes that's not enough. Just keep in mind that while it is frustrating to have someone refuse your apology, it's way worse to not apologize at all.

Q: What if I'm just not a confrontational person? I will never be able to talk to someone like this.

A: People getting angry at you is not the end of the relationship. You actually will only know who your true friends are once you have gone through a conflict and your friendship has come out the other side—not with words unspoken, assumptions intact, or your true feelings still buried, but where you have had a conflict in which you have actually shared what you really think and listened to your friend's own emotional truth. Then you know you have a true friend. One who you can believe in. One whom you can depend on.

DO ASK, DON'T TELL

It's very hard as a parent to hold your tongue when you can see your daughter being used or mistreated in power play situations. You'll be sorely tempted to tell her what to do and summarily banish the Mean Girls who steamrolled her heart. But remember, these situations give her a chance to test her own strength, hew to her own standards, and affirm her self-sufficiency. And when your daughter is the steamroller, you'll be tempted to control her behavior by grounding her or taking away her privileges. That may

be appropriate, but it's not enough. Your most important goal is not to punish her for her actions but instead to get her to take responsibility for them.

CRITICAL THINKING

Here's a general strategy for communicating with her about girls' power plays:

- Even if you think she's behaving abominably, appreciate the awful pressure of the clique and her fear of losing her social status.
- Ask her questions to articulate her motivations and those of her friends. (Drawing a diagram similar to the ones in this chapter can help.)
- Have her review the Bill of Rights for Friends (page 264) to clarify whether she thinks her behavior or that of her friends has stepped outside bounds.
- Articulate your values and ethics and how you would like to see them reflected in her behavior. Ask her what she thinks your values look like in the situation she is facing.
- Brainstorm and role-play with her about how she can respond so that she stands up for herself while communicating her feelings respectfully, and emphasize the importance of one-on-one communication so she can clearly ask for what she wants. Remind her that success in these situations is not being best friends with everyone or the girl she wants to get back together with, and it isn't about getting even. It is simply about handling herself well so she will be taken seriously and can be proud of herself at the end of the day.
- Hold her accountable when she makes mistakes.

What I have diagrammed in this chapter is a methodology for your daughter to develop the critical thinking skills she needs to think her way through these difficult rites of passage. If she is able to accomplish that goal, she will develop social competency—the necessary coping skills to navigate her personal relationships and

the social hierarchy. From social competency comes high self-esteem. I see high self-esteem as the end goal of all the work you and I are doing to raise healthy girls with a strong ethical foundation who can make sound decisions. This is hard, and you have to manage your own reactions as you watch your daughter muddle her way through. Just don't forget that it's only in going through the process that your daughter will reach her full potential.

WHAT SHOULD SCHOOLS DO?

This year, two girls got in a fight and one sent an inflammatory email. Then, they got into another fight, and the first girl copied and pasted the original email to a new one so it looked like it had just been sent. Somehow, our IT person figured it out, but if you had told me when I first got into education that I would be dealing with this, I wouldn't have believed you.
—Brian, principal

Fact: No matter how wonderful a school, how nice the neighborhood, or what kind of school it is (religious, single-sex, charter, or the like) conflicts happen in schools. Abuse of power happens in school. Bullying happens. There is no school that can avoid these issues. It only is common sense that conflict, bullying, and power plays will sometimes end up being a school problem. Good educators know this, and they aren't afraid to acknowledge it. They understand that young people can't learn when they are preoccupied with their social lives and don't have faith in the adults in the school to create and maintain a fair and just learning environment.

If children don't feel welcome at school, if they feel like people are cruel to them and the adults can't or won't address the problem effectively, they will disengage from school. But unless you work in schools on a day-to-day basis, there really is no way to fully appreciate how complicated and multilayered these conflicts can be, especially with the majority of the conflict's content hidden on everyone's phones but profoundly impacting the visible social dynamics occurring in the classroom. It is not unusual for

school administrators to spend hours trying to figure out which students started the latest smear campaign against someone else in the school.

Schools, and by default school administrators and educators, are on the front lines of the battle to teach young people how to use technology ethically. To say the least, this is an incredibly difficult task—one that no one in education today got their professional degree in. I know I didn't. But I, like many people in education, have had to become an expert. We all want to be proactive, but the nature of the technology means we will always have to be on the lookout for its newest incarnation.

First, let me give you a few examples of what school people say who don't know what they're doing or don't want to do the right thing:

"Sorry, our hands are tied. It didn't happen on school property and they didn't use their school email, so we can't do anything."

"We have a zero-tolerance policy against bullying." (As if that fact will magically stop bullying from happening.)

"I didn't see it so I can't do anything about it."

Here's what happens when there's an actual problem in schools like this. All the students know that the adults either can't or won't create a safe environment for them. The target has to go to school knowing that no adult can or will protect them, and so, of course, they feel anxious, depressed, and isolated. The perpetrators know that they are in control.

The consequences of ignoring these situations are teens and children who hate going to school and believe the educators who are supposed to keep them safe are incompetent at best, and that there is no point in standing up to bullying and harassment. The adults don't get it—they just have assemblies and put up kindness banners. How in the world can children fight the battle that grown-ups won't?

But not all school administrators are like this. There are a lot

who are doing their absolute best. In my experience, those people understand the following:

- They acknowledge that conflict and bullying can happen in their school.
- They make an effort to know their students by walking the hallways of the school and attending different types of school events, not just the high-social-status ones like football games.
- They realize that what happens in the school affects what happens outside the school and vice versa. For example, many of the schools I work with include the following in their technology contract: *Bullying often occurs outside of the school's physical grounds yet these actions impact the safety of our students as though they have occurred on school grounds. Any bullying behavior demonstrated at school or outside of school that affects our school community will be addressed by the school.*
- They believe "to discipline" means "to teach." They understand that there are various levels of culpability, and it takes time to figure out who has done what and to what extent. This takes a great deal of skill and finesse because while you are uncovering the facts, you're dealing with angry parents and defensive, embarrassed kids who are often trying to hide what they've done.
- They understand the relationship between transparency and confidentiality. The people in a position of leadership in a school need to share enough information with their community so that people feel informed about how issues of bullying in any form will be handled, but be clear that in specific cases, the people involved and any disciplinary actions against them will be confidential to respect their privacy.

In my experience, there are waves of how these things go. The first wave is gathering the data and interviewing the people involved. The second wave is giving out the disciplinary action—that is based on an understanding of the various

levels of individual responsibility and accountability. The third wave is the reaction of the parents in the larger community. Sometimes it's a ripple and sometimes it's a huge wave.

—Stewart, head of school

LaND MiNe!

When you're sitting on the bleachers at your child's athletic event or waiting in the car pool and another parent tells you a horrible story about bullying and describes the counselor as incompetent or says the head of the school "did nothing," there's a chance they're right. But there is a larger chance that the parent has no idea what they are talking about. This is not to take away from any child's bad experience with an uncaring or ineffective school staffer, but in my experience parents who know nothing about actual events spread gossip while the school personnel are working their hardest to figure out what happened and what the best response should be. The problem is that principals, teachers, coaches, and counselors cannot divulge to the community at large the exact circumstances of their decision making without compromising their integrity and breaching confidentiality.

Schools can't be safe places of learning without your help. If you have a bad principal who won't take the leadership role necessary, go to that person with a plan of action created by different stakeholders in your community (including the students) so she's compelled to make the necessary changes.

Support school administrators and educators when they take a stand—especially when your child has been identified as part of the problem. Back them up when parents start the rumor mill. If you think the school personnel are part of the problem, at least demand that people demonstrate civil thoughtful disagreement.

Be very, very nice to your school's computer specialist. He, along with the custodians and the office person who greets you, is often the most underappreciated person in the building—and the most important.

Boy World

Getting involved in a girl fight is like putting your head up when you're surrounded by sniper fire.

—Will, fifteen

A guy has to be funny and act cool. He can look like a nerd, but he has to play basketball and have social skills.

—Theo, fifteen

If you're a pretty boy, that's bad because you can't put too much attention to your appearance. There's no way to win. Too much attention . . . you're like a girl. Too little and you won't get girls.

—Jake, sixteen

We don't gossip unless it's a real emergency.

—Rob, eleven

Your daughter lives in a world with boys. I know that's obvious, but it's important to remember because boys and Boy World are inextricably tied to all the drama in Girl World. Their presence in her life and how she learns to manage herself with them is critical.

You have to take it seriously. No matter how young your daughter, how innocent her interactions with them, or if you feel like she's still too young to have a "boyfriend," you need to acknowledge this part of her life so that you can help her navigate through it. You are laying the groundwork for her to form strong, healthy relationships with boys, as friends, work partners, competitors, or possibly people with whom she'll develop intimate relationships.

What should you do when your third-grade daughter comes home spitting mad because kids at school are teasing her because her best friend is a boy? Or your seventh-grade daughter is devastated because her best friend just got together with someone she has a huge crush on? We have to spend some time understanding what's going on with boys. To start, let's look at a common statement adults say about boys:

> "Boys are so easy compared to girls! They don't get into drama. They don't have any of those problems like girls do, and if they get mad they just fight it out and it's over."

When we say boys are "easy," we are saying to them, by extension, "If you get upset or sad about something in your life and you let other people see that, there's something wrong with you." We are encouraging boys to suppress having emotions about the relationships that matter most to them. And then we make the mistake that if a boy doesn't talk to us about his feelings, he doesn't have any. We believe this for various reasons. We don't give them a language for talking about their worries and experiences like we do with girls, for one. And we really don't think enough about what our culture—and ourselves by extension—demands and expects of boys and how it frames their emotional lives, decision making, self-esteem, and social competence.

When we do notice boys, it's usually because they're somehow failing or they're acting out in ways that appear thoughtless, reckless, disrespectful, threatening, or frightening. As a result, by the time boys reach adolescence, most have adopted an appearance of calm detachment and seem to be disengaged from their most meaningful relationships, their future academic or professional

success, and any desire to make the world a better place. This is the "slacker" attitude that people so often note in describing boys. Our reactions to this attitude are equally problematic because we usually dance between two extremes: getting angry with them because they're unfocused and "lazy" or dismissing the problem as "typical boy behavior" (that is, not anything that needs to be addressed).

The reality is that most boys' days are filled with many of the same social challenges that girls face, and what they learn from those experiences matters now and for their futures, as it does for girls. We just aren't trained to see it because boys' problems can look deceptively simple, and we can't interpret the signs when they're calling out to us for help. Frankly, we find it really challenging to admit how much we contribute to boys' alienation. But make no mistake—under that detached facade, boys are desperate for meaning in their lives and for relationships they can count on for support and love.

I'm going to ask you to be mindful of how we contribute to boys' seeming detachment. Let me give you one example: what we say to boys when they get dumped. The common response from adults is "There are lots more fish in the sea." It would be unlikely for someone to say, "Wow, I bet that feels awful. It's OK if you want to cry about it. Breakups are tough." His real feelings aren't acknowledged because people want to replace them with "Look at all the other girls you can have now."

A girl, on the other hand, may be told "You're so much better than him," and the "more fish in the sea" part is usually framed as "You'll find the right guy for you" or "You just have not met 'the one' yet." Very few adults would say to a girl "There are so many guys out there, why would you want to pick just one?"

It's also important to recognize that girls can be mean to boys and vice versa. Our collective attention on Queen Bees and Mean Girls has meant that boys' verbal and psychological aggression is overlooked, and the pain they experience is dismissed. Just like girls, technology enables boys to wage psychological warfare on their peers. You give a boy a cellphone with a camera at a high school party or a locker room and he has a weapon of mass destruction.

We owe it to boys to do better. We owe it to the girls who are growing up with these boys to do better. Because you don't want girls having to put up with insecure, intellectually stunted, emotionally disengaged, immature guys. Worse is when some boys' insecurity combines with arrogance and privilege. Then we're dealing with guys who believe that they have the right to amuse themselves by degrading other people, and that their amusement is more important than behaving with common decency.

WELCOME TO BOY WORLD

To help you get a handle on this, I'm going to give you a primer on Boy World in much the same way I did with Girl World.

WHAT YOU SHOULD KNOW

- Boys easily and often can have their hearts broken.
- In general, boys and girls have a completely different sense of humor. What's funny to a boy may be absolutely idiotic to a girl.
- Some boys are extraordinarily good at dismissing and insulting girls to the point that the girls give up saying what they think.
- Boys have a hard time taking girls seriously if the girls who surround them act less competent than they are and/or are obsessed with their weight or clothes.
- Ironically, boys can be intimidated by girls who are really competent; that is frustrating and confusing to girls.
- Boys, just like girls, aren't allowed to complain when they see someone being ridiculed or humiliated. If they do, instead of being called "uptight," they're called "retarded" or "gay" or other words you probably don't like.
- Most boys think the worst thing that can happen to them is to be publicly humiliated.
- Most boys aren't violent and abusive. A few are and the rest have no idea how to stop them.

HERE'S MY BOY WORLD DEFINITION OF MASCULINITY

Nothing is ever serious. You can't try too hard or care too much about anything. You laugh off emotional and physical pain. The right girls like you and you like all attention girls give you. You're competitive about everything, and, by five years of age, you can discuss professional sports with authority (especially fantasy football).

In my boys' classes, I conduct the same "in the box" exercise as I do for girls. I begin by asking them to describe a guy with high social status. This is a person everyone knows. If he has an opinion, everyone listens and agrees. Then I ask them to answer these questions: What does he look like, and how does he act? What is a boy or man who doesn't have high social status like? Is this someone who is likely to be teased, ridiculed, or dismissed? What does he look like, and how does he act?

These are their answers, incorporated into the "Act Like a Man" box.

Backs down	Strong	Funny (nothing is	Doesn't like to
Weak	Verbal	serious)	play video games/
Short	Tall	Good style/right	bad at video
Poor	Tough	gear	games
Acts like a girl/	Athletic	Good at video	Gay
flamboyant/	Likes girls	games, but not	Snitch/tattletale
effeminate	Girls like him	obsessed	Learning or
Bad style/wrong	Money		physical
gear			disabilities
Whipped			
Awkward			

Just like in Girl World, not every guy reacts to these rules in the same way. Some guys really drink the Kool-Aid. Others openly despise or rebel against the rules. Some guys are in the middle. But one thing is always true. In order for a boy to come into his own, he has to come to grips with how these messages exist inside his head and how they influence what he thinks, says, and does. For example, boys want to have strong friendships, but many boys don't feel they can talk to even their closest friends when they're upset because they'll be teased and the information will be used against him in the future. Asking for help is often the same as

admitting you're weak and sensitive. I'm not just talking about so-cial problems boys experience. When boys have learning disor-ders, they don't ask for help because it seems weak and shameful. But overall, one of the most profound things the box teaches is that the easiest way to prove your "in the boxness" is to demean and dismiss girls and out-of-the-box boys.

Land Mine!

When it comes to our boys, we still say things like "Don't throw like a girl!" and "Stop screaming like a little girl!" Some people dismiss the problem of these comments by saying "But it's true. Most boys throw better than most girls. Little girls scream at a higher pitch." When people say those things to boys, they set up a parallel in boys' brains between acting incompetently or in a way that people can ridicule and being like a girl. If you want boys to respect girls, and if you want girls to feel capable, you have to stop saying things like that, and you should politely and firmly ask the adults in your child's life who may be saying things like this to stop.

DO BOYS HAVE CLIQUES?

In our school there is a group of junior guys who act just like they're a group of middle school girls. There's a Queen Bee that all the guys are afraid of. I'm not joking. They don't do anything without checking with him first. One day, I saw one of the guys sitting outside on a bench waiting for class. I wanted to talk to him because we used to be a lot closer but since he's been hanging out with this guy he doesn't want to. So I came up to him and tried to talk to him and he wouldn't and he was all nervous. So I looked around and there was the guy coming over to our direction. It was so messed up. He used to be such a great guy and now he's so arrogant. It's really hard to believe he's the same person and he'd let this guy have so much control over him.

—Ellie, seventeen

Boys can have cliques. They just call them "groups." But it is true that, in general, boys do have more flexibility with their friendships than girls—although I have countless examples of boys being just as exclusive as girls. And in moments of conflict when boys have to prove where they fit in the "Act Like a Man" box, these roles come to life and control boys just as profoundly as girls.

POPULARITY IN GUY WORLD

Recall from chapter 1 that one of the most common questions girls ask me is "Why are the popular girls popular? In all the years I've taught, no boy has ever asked me that question. It's not because guys are unaware of the power of popularity and social status. It's because the definition of popularity is incredibly obvious to them.

To most boys popularity doesn't mean that people like you. It means people know you have power and it's not worth confronting you in a conflict. It's like having shiny armor that gives you protection to do what you want—and some girls (especially the ones who like shiny things) think you're hot. Of course, what armor also does is hide your weaknesses. Before you realize it, you're so dependent on it that you feel like you always have to wear it.

THE BREAKDOWN

Most guys I talk to believe there's an elite 10 percent who look like they fit into the "Act Like a Man" box at the most, followed by the 75 percent who make up the general population, 10 percent who hang out at the bottom but have a strong group, and the last 5 percent—an outer perimeter of kids who either get how the system works and don't want any part of it or who have such poor social skills that they can't fit in anywhere. Every group has a corresponding girls' group to the point that some are entirely coed, but for the most part there's limited social interaction between these larger groups of guys.

For older teens, there are a few notable exceptions when the groups tend to intermingle. The most common one is when people are drinking or smoking pot. Here's a quote from one of my editors

who helped me when I was writing *Masterminds and Wingmen*—the companion book to *Queen Bees* about the social lives of boys.

> I have proof of it from yesterday! In my school everybody stays within their own group. However, yesterday, my friend (slacker) was telling me before a party at night that he, along with 2 hipsters, 1 jock, 1 musician, 2 drug dealers, and another slacker, all got together to smoke pot. At first I was super-amazed to find out that some of these kids smoked pot, but also that the jock—who you'd think would be "too cool" to hang out with others who weren't from his group—was actually willing to hang out with the hipsters and vice versa.
> —Brian, sixteen

When you combine the "Act Like a Man" box, popularity, and the group breakdown, you're looking at something that spans generations. As in, the men you've grown up around can probably relate to all of this. (Whether they remember it or will admit it is another issue.) But this generation of boys does seem to have a unique relationship to this Guy World social structure. Being in the top 10 percent of the traditional "Act Like a Man" box doesn't always translate to being in the top 10 percent of the social hierarchy of a specific school. Being a musician, a skater, a hipster, or even a drug dealer—these are all paths to high social status. Especially in big, diverse schools, there isn't one social hierarchy but an infinite number of them. But, here's the catch: No matter what a guy does or has that brings him high social status, that status can lead to a sense of entitlement with girls.

THE 10 PERCENTERS

For the top 10 percenters, conforming to the "Act Like a Man" box is law. If a guy is in this group, he isn't an individual; he's a piece of a machine. Just like girls who have the highest social status, these kids usually strictly follow the unwritten rules and judge others with the same rigidity.

There are four defining characteristics of this top 10 percent:

1. They look like they're good (not necessarily actually being good) in at least one Guy World sport—football, basketball, soccer, hockey, or even lacrosse or water polo (depending on your geographic location).
2. Their hair, clothes, walk, swagger, flow, and slang are the same. That look becomes their social uniform.
3. Their parents are so invested in their sons' statuses that they allow "bad boy" behavior by supporting it outright, looking the other way, making excuses for it, or denying it altogether.
4. Maybe most important, these guys have an intense desire to be in and remain in that 10 percent group.

Listen to what guys say:

They constantly put up a front, and they build it up in school. They walk around with this scowl and attitude of, I'm so cold and tired of everything. If I go up to a normal person and say, "Hey, what's up?" they'll say, "Hey, what's up?" back to me. But with the kids we're talking about, they don't mingle in the other groups because they think, Why should I?

—Ethan, sixteen

It's like a cult. Every year a couple graduate, so they add a few. It's a continuous cycle.

—Auguste, eighteen

At my school I'm in that 10 percent elite, but I honestly feel like I have to fight for it. I'm not the meathead jock who plays lacrosse and football and gets the praise handed down to them. To be up in the 10 percent elite, I have to be bold and make some moves that I personally wouldn't make but have to in order to fit in. We [the 10 percenters] are the ones with the parties and the booze, the hot girls, and I feel like if I wasn't fighting to be in this group I would just blend in with the rest of the crowd and high school would be pretty crappy. I wish I didn't care as much about my social standing, but no matter what any guy says, they truly care.

—Cole, seventeen

THE MAJORITY

While the 10 percenters feel self-conscious about socializing out-side of their tribe, the 75 percent of guys in "the majority" usu-ally feel that they can easily hang out with kids in other groups. The 75 percent is made up of different groups of about five to ten kids each. Of course, regardless of their social status, all guys are subject to the pressure to live up to our culture's standards of masculinity, so the guys in the majority can be self-conscious, but they aren't constantly thinking about their image in terms of the "Act Like a Man" box the way 10 percent guys are. The only time a guy in the majority intensely cares about his image is when he decides to fight his way into the 10 percent, but that's an excep-tion, not the rule.

> The 75 percent is much more open to change. I try to move around in the 75 percent group. What I've found is that it's a lot easier to be sitting at one table with one group in the 75 percent and go to another table the next day because they aren't as territorial as the upper 10 percent.
> —Will, fifteen

> I'm in a pretty high group. Not the highest, but pretty high. This may sound weird, but honestly, what I'm about to say really meant something to me. In tenth grade I had gotten into theater, and one day the theater kids invited me to a party, and that felt incredible. Some people would say that those kids invited me because I'm in a higher group than they are, but that's not true. They're happy to keep to their group. When they did that, it was a huge feeling of acceptance.
> —Hunter, seventeen

THE BOTTOM RUNG

Adults often assume that guys on the bottom rung are miserable, lonely, depressed, and the target of the most bullying. It's not true. Guys in this group know their low social position, know they can appear odd to others, and usually don't care as long as they have

at least one strong friendship. Many of them believe that because they aren't even in the running for high social status, they have more dependable friends. That's debatable, but what is true is that the members of the group are usually very connected to one another and don't feel like they have to constantly prove themselves to anyone.

THE OUTER PERIMETER

The outer perimeter (OP) is made up of guys who, in their peers' eyes, exist apart from the entire social system. It's populated with anarchists, pranksters, politicians, obsessed single-subject or single-sport high achievers, and kids seriously lacking in social skills. (Obviously, I'm grouping a lot of people in the OP who have very different characteristics and can be at the highest or lowest level of social status.)

Guys can choose to be in the OP because they understand the "Act Like a Man" box (even if they may not exactly call it that), see no value in joining the social system, and have strong friendships outside of school. That means these guys can also be exceptionally good at blending into the background. Other kids don't think they're irritating; they just don't know what to make of them, and sometimes don't know they're there.

There are also guys in the OP whose position is inflexible. These guys can struggle with reading people—such as trying to figure out what people mean versus what they say--or how to join a group of people and talk to them. Sometimes people can get irritated with them because these guys obsess on one topic or because they can't get the hint if people don't want to hang out with them.

> With these guys, [playing] video games goes beyond being a pastime, a distraction, or a way to blow off steam. It becomes an obsession, one that won't really help him make friends. It becomes the guy's sole method of interaction with others.
>
> —Robert, fourteen

*Since I am really bad at making friends, I have to keep any
that I make. Right now I have one friend, but they don't want
me making other friends. I don't know what to do. I'm stuck.*
—Michael, sixteen

If someone is on either side of this struggle, as a guy on the
OP or someone dealing with a guy on the OP, it can be really
frustrating. You can see *Masterminds and Wingmen* for advice on
this problem.

THE RULES OF ANGER IN BOY WORLD

Just as there are cultural rules guiding girls when they're angry,
the same is true for boys. Your daughter needs to know this because it will help her understand boys better when they are in
conflict with her or vice versa. Here's the general breakdown:

- Internalize and suffer silently.
- Blow it off and say "It's not a big deal. Don't worry about it.
  I'm fine."
- Laugh it off. Convince himself that whatever he experiences
  or observes is funny or nothing he can or should do any-
  thing about.
- Refuse to admit he's angry.
- Rely on other boys to help him manage his anger and justify
  physical outbursts by saying "You can't push me like that. I
  just lose it." Or even better, his friends will say it for him.
- Verbally dominate the other person.
- Physically dominate the other person, but only if he has
  numbers or he knows he is tougher or not afraid to fight if
  the other person doesn't back down.
- Drink alcohol or do drugs to deaden feelings.

The rules of anger go right to the heart of why boys are conditioned not to complain when they are being ridiculed or bullied,
or when they see someone being bullied. I have asked many boys
"What would it take for you to intervene if someone was getting

bullied?" Their response is inevitably "They'd have to be really hurt," "Like someone was going to die," or "Something would have to happen like what you see on TV."

We have to counteract boys' belief that coming forward is necessary only when someone is at risk for or is actually being assaulted, because by then it's too late. Just like girls, boys need the education, awareness, and skills to express their anger in a constructive, healthy manner. They need men around them who can do that, women who can hold their own with them (especially as the boys get so tall they literally look down on their mothers), and the belief that they don't have to hold all these feelings in or lash out.

WHAT HAPPENS WHEN GIRLS GET MAD AT GUYS?

When a girl says something negative, she's expressing her feelings. When a guy says something negative, he's an asshole.

—Brandon, sixteen

When girls are mad, it's all about the numbers. What numbers? The number of other girls they bring with them to destroy you.

—Alan, fourteen

Girls in a group get mad at one guy and then they corner him and attack him. If a group of guys did that to a girl, everyone would hate them.

—Jacob, thirteen

When teachers get mad at you, it's really boring. When girls get mad at you, they surround you and then give you a no-nonsense lecture.

—Malesh, eleven

Ganging up on someone when you're mad: It makes so much sense. Fueled with self-righteous fury and backed up by your

friends is a really safe way to confront someone you're mad at. Of course, this strategy exacerbates the conflict because the other person feels attacked and defensive—which means it will be impossible for him to hear anything the angry girl is saying.

Girls do this with boys for understandable reasons. They anticipate being blown off for being uptight, and they want backup if the boy has a history of making fun of her.

This problem is so pervasive in some schools that it infects the entire atmosphere of the community. A pattern emerges where the other boys rationalize not calling the guy out because "it's not worth it," and the burden of expressing the anger falls on a few girls, who become labeled as the "uptight complainers"—and I am being really polite in how I am writing that. Although the girls don't like admitting it, this experience is frustrating and exhausting. They lie low for a while until there's a buildup of smaller insults that make them blow. But the blowup is usually about something that can be easily dismissed—and does not reflect the other indignities that preceded it. A cycle emerges where the complainers explode in anger, usually with other girls surrounding them. The targets of their anger feel attacked, so they dismiss or ridicule the complaint. This, in turn, reinforces to everyone else that it is futile to speak out, and the complainers shut up until something else makes them blow up and the whole thing begins again.

All of this results in some boys who believe they have the right to put people in their place, who think making fun of someone is funny, and who silence boys by questioning their heterosexuality (the totally predictable use of the word "gay") and call girls "bitches" and "sluts." Their behavior continues unchecked—until it becomes so untenable that an adult, such as a coach or principal, must intervene.

Once girls get into high school, these issues become even more complex because the boys who dismiss the "angry complaining girls" can be reinforced by other girls. A girl who calls a guy out, and in particular uses the label of "sexist," "racist," or "homophobic," becomes the "political" girl who is always making a "statement." It only takes one boy to relentlessly dismiss her and the

other boys to say nothing for a girl to believe that being the out-spoken "social justice warrior" will only result in boys' ridicule or silence.

That is, unless you back up the boys who are going after the girls. Then you can be as outspoken as you want to be. Other girls, who want to prove they belong in the "Act Like a Woman" box, won't back up the "uptight angry girl" (even if, deep down, they agree with her), and they will use her intensity to make them seem more relaxed, friendly, and inoffensive. Unfortunately, this strategy usually works for a while because the boys who want to fit into the "Act Like a Man" box like girls who aren't calling them out and making their lives difficult.

> *She will feel stuck many, many times in her life. She won't know why she feels like she can never say anything but she will know it's an unwritten truth. She knows the most desirable girl goes with the flow, doesn't make too much noise, and when she does make noise it's laughter.*
>
> —Emily

I realize that some girls and young women may read this and say, "That's not the way it was at my school." If this is true, be grateful. But recognize the responsibility to model for girls and women who weren't that lucky. Don't look down on them when they lose their voice. Show them by your words and deeds what it means to be a courageous, competent, substantive woman of dignity who isn't afraid to say what she thinks and doesn't put down other girls.

APOLOGIZING IN BOY WORLD

Just like girls, boys struggle to give and accept meaningful apol-ogies. As I said in chapter 7, girls can have a really hard time trusting apologies—from both boys and girls. They don't trust apologies from girls because many have seen girls apologize and not mean it or continue to hold a grudge. They've seen boys apolo-gize, but their tone is clear—they really don't mean it. By the time

girls get to high school, girls don't trust a lot of boys' apologies because they've had the experience of a boy apologizing and then going right back to what he was doing before. Why would boys apologize and not mean it? I think it's for one of two reasons. One, boys are conditioned to not take girls' feelings seriously. Two, boys often find girls' display of emotions overwhelming. An emotional or, way worse, crying girl is at the top of the list for what must be stopped. So they say anything (that is, apologize) to placate her or "calm her down," sometimes without listening, to get the girl to stop.

HOMOPHOBIA AND BEING A MAN

Throughout this chapter, I've been talking a lot about boys calling each other "gay" without fully explaining the power of that word. Many schools have gotten better about clearly stating they won't tolerate homophobia. Collectively we have gotten better. But it doesn't mean homophobia isn't still used as the invisible hand in Boy World, guiding boys to assigned roles of perpetrator, bystander, or target. Some boys threaten and/or perpetrate violence to prove their power and control—their masculinity—daring other boys to stop them.

A boy who witnesses these acts has a choice. He can be a passive bystander by looking the other way; he can be an active bystander who backs up the bully with words and deeds; he can run away; or he can stand up to the bully. Standing up to the bully by physically fighting him can be scary, but it isn't a social risk—that's condoned behavior in Boy World. Standing up to a bully by saying his actions are wrong, however, challenges the foundation on which Boy World is built.

The irony of this cultural definition of masculinity is that it represses courage—not the kind where a boy will fight someone if challenged, but the moral courage for a boy to raise his voice and stand up for what's right. Kids calling each other "gay" and "fag" and parents not understanding its wide-ranging implications create an environment in which we all suffer. Starting around fourth or fifth grade, boys are called "gay" or "fags" not just when they are

acting like girls but when they speak out against bullying. You see a kid in school being teased and you want to say something about it? If you do, any boy by sixth grade knows he's going to be labeled gay for doing it. This dynamic is so powerful and pervasive that most boys don't realize its viselike grip on their behavior.

We also must get ourselves straight (pun intended) about homophobia. It should go without saying that everyone—gay or not—has the right to be treated with dignity. This dignity is not negotiable. You do not have to change your religion or your politics in order to have the basic human decency to respect another person's right to exist in this world.

What's so frustrating and ironic about this is that calling boys gay for speaking out makes no sense. Guys who speak out about social injustice don't want to have sex with other guys—but that's what the bullies are saying when they try to silence others with "Don't be gay." So are we saying that a real man is a heterosexual man who says nothing when he sees someone being degraded?

We must individually and collectively change the definition of masculinity to include standing up for social justice. Real men speak out when they see someone being targeted. If you're a parent, talk to your children about this tonight before they go to bed or do it on the way to school tomorrow. If you're a teacher, start the class tomorrow making sure that your students know your classroom is a sanctuary. And if you're straight, you have an even larger responsibility to speak out—because you won't be so easily dismissed for trying to advance "an agenda."

Seen in this light, homophobia becomes much more than whether you "tolerate" or "accept" homosexuality. Homophobia is one of the cornerstones of the culture of masculinity. If you want your daughter or son to be treated well by boys and men, you have to actively take a stand against homophobia.

DO THE RIGHT THING

Most boys really want to do the right thing; they just have no idea how. They want to be courageous, loving, emotional, strong men. They want to be good dancers who can sweep someone off their feet. They want to make the people they care about proud of

them. But how can they when most of their role models are men who are idolized for being tough and always in control, and when they themselves are vilified and emasculated when they demonstrate characteristics associated with women and girls? Where are the role models who look like the strong men they want to be but who are also emotionally articulate, engaged, and morally courageous?

If we believe that most boys are out-of-control, uncaring, and thoughtless members of our communities, and if we believe that the best response to this problem is to toughen them up and punish them, we'll create a self-fulfilling prophecy. But if we demand the best from boys, hold ourselves accountable for what we do that contributes to Boy World, and reach out to them with respect, we will raise morally courageous men.

Talk about this chapter with your son—and with your daughter. Show her the "Act Like a Man" box and ask her how it corresponds to her experience. Does she know boys who fall into the categories in this chapter? Ask her to imagine what it would be like to be a boy. Talk to her about homophobia, and how it affects not only attitudes toward the gay community but how people behave. Talk to her about how issues of race and religion intersect with boy culture. Most of all, help her appreciate that boys are in their own life raft. Just like girls, they're looking to break out and be appreciated for who they are. If your daughter can empathize with how difficult it is in Boy World, she can work toward seeing boys as equal partners on the path toward healthy adulthood.

Girl World Meets Boy World

My dad told me that if a boy hits me then he likes me. But I can't tell the boy that so I still don't know what to do.

—Madeline, eleven

One time a boy punched me in the nose so his parents made him come over to my house to apologize to me and bring flowers. But then everyone in school started teasing us. So then we had to hate each other and now I punch him.

—Abby, ten

Boys are asking us out but we aren't going anywhere.

—Molly, thirteen

THE DRAMA BEGINS

Emily and Kristi are seventh graders, and both are in love with Jason. Each spends considerable quality time with Jason. They send him notes, write his name on their notebooks, call and text him, hang out after school to see if they can bump into him, and "accidentally" walk by when his team practice is over. When the competition for his affections becomes unbearable, they make a

pact that both will stop liking him. Of course, neither girl has any intention of keeping her word, but each also believes that the other will. Each is also convinced that she reserves the right to be angry with the other if she goes back on her word, but both girls quietly do everything they can behind each other's back to win Jason's affection.

Things become much more complicated when they discover that four other girls in their grade like Jason as well. Making matters worse, one of the four girls, Liza, threatens Emily and Kristi's position as the front contenders for Jason's affections. Emily and Kristi's response is to go after Liza, assured that they're in the right because (a) Liza knows they like him, (b) Liza is throwing herself at Jason, and (c) they staked their claim first. Within a day, the grade is abuzz watching the drama unfold. Messengers are dispatched. Queen Bees are consulted. Delegations confer.

In the situation described above, the parents of Emily, Kristi, and Liza are largely clueless that anything's going on. Jason's parents figure something's up because their son's phone is going off all evening. I've talked to many parents like Jason's. They perceive their son as a deer in the headlights with these girls barreling toward him like a Mack truck.

> It's like the movie Inside Out when the guy starts freaking out and goes into girl alarm mode.
>
> —Keo, eighteen

Is this true? Are the Jasons of the world clueless and terrified as girls vie for their attention? If one of these girls were your daughter, would you know about this drama? Should you? Why do girls turn against one another over a boy they may barely know? How does girls' competition for boys influence your daughter's friendships with girls and her future intimate relationships?

In this chapter, we're going to examine how Girl World and Boy World work together. You may have to witness your daughter being blown off by a close friend for a boy, or become suddenly

insecure when all the other girls obsess about boys and she's more interested in soccer or basketball. You'll see your daughter question her self-worth if she doesn't think she fits the model (pun intended) she thinks the boys want. She'll fall madly in love and not know why. Or she'll know why, but she'll think she has no chance because everyone else is so much prettier than she is.

WHAT YOU SHOULD KNOW

- Around ten years of age, girls' bonding often extends beyond navigating their friendships with other girls to include drama with boys.
- If one girl is getting attention from boys or is more "boy crazy" than her friend, it will strain the relationship and put pressure on the other girl to play catch-up.
- At some point, almost all girls will pretend to be less smart, strong, or capable around a boy they like. A girl may be embarrassed by her behavior but not know how to stop.
- Her girlfriends will see this, be confused or embarrassed, and talk behind her back. They may also wonder if this is the right way to get boys' attention.
- As in their friendships with girls, girls often communicate unclearly with boys because they don't want to make things uncomfortable.
- A girl will have a crush on someone who doesn't treat her or other people well. She'll know this, but won't stop liking the person.
- Not all girls are boy crazy. Some girls aren't that interested until they're older, or they may be sexually attracted to girls. Some girls will refuse to choose who they're attracted to based on gender or never be interested.*

---

* An asexual person is a person who does not experience sexual attraction. This may be difficult for some to believe because we assume sexual attraction is innate in all of us, but we can't decide for other people. Moreover, young people are increasingly talking to me about and connecting with this identity. For more information, go to asexuality.org.

- Regardless of her sexual orientation, your daughter will likely have strong friendships with boys. Some of those friendships can become sexual, but that doesn't take away from the depth of the friendship.

"FRIEND BOYS" AND BOYFRIENDS

I'm sure you remember this concept from your teens. There were boys or girls who were friends and then there were boyfriends and girlfriends. Girls still make those distinctions. Most girls have strong friendships with boys that they value highly, and, ironically, girls don't seem to be as constrained by gendered behavior within these friendships. These friendships are defined by the fact that the girl has no problem clearly communicating what she really thinks. As Mike, age sixteen, puts it, "My girl friends will tell me when I'm acting like a dumb ass." But far too many girls don't communicate like this with boys. As I'll discuss in this and upcoming chapters, girls often hide their true selves as soon as the boy goes from being a boy who's a friend to a potential or real boyfriend.

Girls will tease each other about the boys they are friends with. If your daughter has close male friends (this seems to be especially true with boys she grows up with and/or who live in the neighborhood), tell her that she doesn't have to lose those friendships if people are teasing her. I have talked to many confused girls who don't want to lose these close friendships but can feel them slipping away under all the scrutiny and pressure to pair up.

> One of my best friends is a boy I grew up with. My friends tease the two of us all the time and I don't know what to do about it. He's like my brother and all these people want us to be boyfriend/girlfriend.
>
> —Rachel, twelve

At the risk of repeating myself, it's really important to remember that girls have individual responses to boys. Some are totally boy crazy and have been since kindergarten when they chased the boys around the playground trying to capture them and put them

in "jail." But that doesn't mean that all girls are like this. They can be anywhere from very interested to sometimes interested to never going to be interested. What's important to understand is that your daughter can often value herself and other girls based on the belief that she has to be interested in boys. Starting around third or fourth grade, you need to say to her, "Honey, girls can think all different things about boys. Some are boy crazy, sometimes interested in boys, and some only want them as friends. But whatever you think and feel about boys is totally fine. No matter how old you are, that will never change." Then keep reminding her that however she feels, it is completely acceptable. Also, don't tell her that a boy is mean to her because he likes her. You never want to send the message that people who "like" her, have a crush on her, or are attracted to her have the right to be mean to her.

CRUSHES

Sooner or later, your daughter will probably have her first crush, and it'll feel like she's been hit between the eyes, with butterflies in her stomach and cheeks burning. Girls fall in love with someone "who is so hot, you don't understand," and then, overnight change their affections to someone else. These are typical descriptions of crushes from the girls in my classes:

> I feel like I'm going to throw up. And I'm sure right in front of him.
> I get butterflies in my stomach.
> I get excited, can't breathe, and then I start to giggle uncontrollably. It's humiliating and also fun at the same time.
> I'm so nervous. I'm sure I'll do or say something stupid.

But sometimes the problem with crushes goes back to the "Act Like a Man" box, because girls who buy in to the culture tend to be drawn to boys who fit in the box. When you add in the difference in biological maturity between most middle school boys and girls, it's easy to sympathize. Compare and contrast. Do you remember what boys were like in sixth and seventh grade? Maybe two grew proportionately. The rest were awkward and gangly. Now I want

you to picture a typical eighth-grade girl and an eighth-grade boy. If you were a girl, who would you fall for? Exactly—the 2 percent of guys in your class who look like they belong in the box, or . . . older guys. Even though the awkward ones will be the hottest at the high school reunion, girls don't know that, and even if they did, why should they care? Girls want someone who's cute and cool now.

We also have to hold up a mirror here. Parents often love boys who look like they fit in the box. They like to have them as sons, and they like if daughters bring them home as friends or boyfriends. I'm not saying all those boys are jerks. Far from it. But for many of them, the power and privilege leads to the belief that they don't need to treat girls with respect.

> Those guys develop an ego. One of my best friends did this. The girls were all over him and he treated them like trash. They accepted it and came flocking back.
>
> —Jake, sixteen

One of the things girls have to learn is why they're attracted to boys who aren't going to treat them with dignity, or why they go back to these boys when they know from previous experience that it isn't good for them.

OBSESSIONS

WHY ARE GIRLS OBSESSED WITH CELEBRITIES?

> The girls in our class are completely in love with famous people. They have shrines in their lockers and they doodle their names all day. When they talk about this guy that they don't even know in real life, they start to scream. It's really really weird.
>
> —Keith, ten

Do you remember your first crush? Maybe it was someone you actually knew. Did you have a crush on a celebrity? Did you think you actually knew that person?

Why do girls do it? It's an easy and timeless answer. Because

liking boys can be so stressful and weird, it's way easier to fall in love with someone who you have no chance of actually meeting. That way, you are free to fall in love as intensely as you want, without actually having to deal with all the unnerving feelings of developing sexuality. That's why girls make shrines, are possessive of the person they love, and forbid other girls from liking the person, as if he were someone they actually knew. Plus, an imaginary boyfriend can be anything you want. If you were a girl in fifth, sixth, and even seventh grade, wouldn't you look at the clueless boys around you farting and jumping on one another, and choose the guy in your head instead?

OBSESSIONS WITH PEOPLE WHOM THE GIRLS ACTUALLY KNOW

> I was obsessed with this guy named Scott. I have no idea why. I look back and laugh at this now, but at the time I was totally serious. I would write [in my journal] the different things he had done that brought me closer to the conclusion that he liked me. I would show off, try to be near him. Every day during recess, my friend and I would play tag near where he played soccer with his friends and count the number of times he smiled at me. It was pathetic.
>
> —Julia, twelve

> Obsession in middle school is worse because you have nothing to compare it to. Someone who humiliates you, you like even more. I was obsessed with a guy in seventh grade. I dated him and then he broke up with me. Then he fell in love with someone else and I hated it. But then she did a little Mexican hat dance on his heart by hooking up with five guys and I felt a lot better.
>
> —Angie, seventeen

> In fifth grade I was obsessed with this guy. I naturally told my friends I was crazy about him and they spread it around that I liked him. He stayed as far away from me as possible and wouldn't say a word to me after that.
>
> —Nina, thirteen

LanD Mine!

What not to say to your daughter about boys:

"You're not at that stage yet."

"You're too young."

"He only wants one thing."

POWER BROKERS IN PUBERTY: MATCHMAKING

For all the difficult things I write about, early adolescence is an exciting time to be a girl. Some girls eagerly anticipate when they'll be old enough to have boyfriends and all the accompanying drama. But they're also cowards (which is totally understandable). They want to check out the whole boy thing and be involved in the drama, but without putting themselves on the front line. So in many different ways, girls push one another to be the first one to jump off the cliff.

For example, Julia, eleven, is on her way to math class when one of her best friends rushes up to her.

ANI: "I was just talking to Jeremy and he says that Matt likes you! That's so cool! You guys would make such a cute couple! I knew he liked you!"

JULIA: "Are you sure? What did Jeremy say exactly?"

ANI: "He said Matt thought you were really pretty and nice."

Julia is so happy because she's had a huge crush on Matt since the beginning of the year but hasn't known how to tell him. After class, she discusses with her two closest friends what her next step should be. Later that afternoon, they send Matt the following text:

Do you like Julia?

Between classes Julia's friend checks her phone every thirty seconds until she gets an answer.

If Matt's answer is "Yes" and maybe even a request to meet after school, this means high drama. Julia gets to figure out every nuance of what she should do in full consultation with her friends, who offer their opinion and analysis. She will be the center of attention the entire afternoon, and it will seem to her that all is right in the world.

But more often than not, Julia and every girl in her situation is quickly disappointed, because the meeting with Matt isn't nearly as good as she anticipated. Where is the romantic boy from her favorite movies and boy bands? Why is this boy answering in monosyllables? Why, if his friends are around, is he acting like he doesn't know her? To make matters worse, without being aware of it, Julia's expectations of Matt are also based on her closest friendships. Remember, girls' friendships are often characterized by endless conversations. It's hard for the awkward first crush to measure up to the intimacy of girl-girl friendships, or even the camaraderie of friendships with boys. That's one of the primary reasons why the first thing a girl does after hanging out with her crush is to call, text, or IM with a girlfriend to analyze every word of the conversation. In these early romances, she may spend more time talking to her girlfriend about the boyfriend than to the boyfriend himself.

A lot of girls' first crushes never even get to the stage where girl meets boy. Some follow dramatic trajectories from first inklings of attraction through flaming breakup without the boy even knowing he was the object of affection ("It is so over with Jason"). Some girls run through a series of "boyfriends" without any of the relationships advancing, as one girl put it, "all the way up to holding hands." What's often true of a lot of these early experiences is that the reality is disappointing compared with the anticipation.

But let's go back to why Julia and Matt are getting together in the first place. It may have been a crush at first sight, but Julia and her friends could have collectively decided that Matt is a worthy object on which to experiment. Girls love to be in one another's business as they dissect the boy mystery. What better way to deal with boy anxiety than setting up a friend? No matter who made the initial push, the whole group can analyze every stage of the

relationship, from the first mutual flirtations to the inevitable conflicts that send the whole thing crashing down in flames. As girls go through this phase in their lives, their friendships solidify around these dramatic moments. Not surprisingly, the social hierarchy is operating at full force.

> In the social hierarchy, although I am not the super Queen Bee, I'm fairly close. I'm not hated by anyone (hopefully) and have many good friends. The people I've set up are not outcasts or dorks, but they aren't the Queen Bees. The people close to the Queen Bees are the matchmakers.
>
> —Kim, fifteen

> The Queen Bee set me up and I didn't feel like there was anything I could do about it.
>
> —Molly, eighteen

> It was really hard to like a guy my friends didn't think was cool enough. I liked him because he was nice. But he wasn't that cute. They made fun of him all the time. It made me feel bad but I didn't know what to do.
>
> —Raquel, fourteen

Queen Bees are careful to regulate the popularity of other girls. When they set up another girl, one of the ulterior motives is to bind the girl more closely to the Queen Bee. The girl set up for her first boyfriend, and her moment in the sun, is now beholden and bonded to the Queen Bee. In Julia's situation, she is likely a Pleaser/Wannabe or Messenger, and Ani is a Banker or Queen Bee. Note that both girls' stock goes up when Julia gets her first boyfriend. One way to solidify your place on the social totem pole is to be a Banker or Messenger whose information on who likes whom is vital to the unfolding drama. If you're wondering what your daughter texted in those three thousand messages she sent to her friends last month, a situation like this easily provides the answer.

The Queen Bee can also influence when the girl stops liking

the boy. Real conflicts between girls occur when the girl who is set up begins to act independently.

What if Julia didn't like Matt or really didn't want a boyfriend? It'll be hard for her to resist the encouragement of her girlfriends, the gratification of being the center of attention, and the excitement of this new kind of intimacy. So she's forced into relationships that she might really rather not have. When a girl is twelve or younger it's generally about a crush, and the scope of what she'll most likely do with this boy is limited. But the consequences are there: She's learning to stifle her personal boundaries with boys so she can maintain her friendships with girls and fit into the "Act Like a Woman" box.

THE BIRTH OF FRUIT CUP GIRL

Of all the topics I have ever taught girls, Fruit Cup Girl is definitely one of their favorites. I came up with this term after teaching a group of seventh graders who'd had a big blowup after a field trip. Why? Because one of the girls (let's call her Mia) had a huge crush on a boy but was too shy to talk to him. Her two best friends decided to take on the cause, and they set their sights on putting them together on an upcoming field trip. The big moment came during lunch when they orchestrated having the boy sit next to Mia—while they sat at the next table so they could overhear everything. When Mia was finally alone with her crush, she had no idea what to say. So without even thinking about it, Mia pretended she couldn't open her fruit cup and asked the boy to do it for her.

That was the conversation opener, and, from Mia's point of view, it was a good one because everything went well from that moment. So well that they sat next to each other on the bus ride back. At the same time, however, Mia's friends noticed how "weird" she was acting with this boy. She was laughing really strangely, acting like she was incredibly stupid, and pretending she was clueless. For the next two days, every time Mia was around this boy, she acted like this, causing the girls to get more irritated with every passing minute.

That's when rumors started circulating that Mia had done

"things" with the boy on the bus ride home. Mia was very upset about the rumors and then she found out one of her friends was behind the gossip bomb. The morning I had my class with them, Mia was understandably furious at her friends for betraying her, but the friends were also angry at Mia for acting stupid around the boy.

That's how I came up with Fruit Cup Girl (FCG). This girl personifies girls' internal conflict between expressing personal authenticity and codified gendered behavior that they believe gets them attention from boys. But girls aren't clueless—it's just usually one of those things you know but don't have the words to explain. Girls know they're not supposed to act incompetent, but this is really where you and your daughter can see the power of the culture (everything you know but have never been sat down and taught) controlling girls' behavior, even the girl she sees in the mirror. To help girls think through FCG, I go through the following cost-benefit analysis with them.

Benefits of Being Fruit Cup Girl
- She gets the boy's attention.
- It's easy. She can do it without thinking about it. Somehow she knows how to play the part (even while criticizing herself for doing it).
- It works.

Costs of Being Fruit Cup Girl
- She can feel ridiculous.
- Girls and guys can and will make fun of her.
- She can feel like a fraud.
- She fears the only way guys will like her is if she acts in stereotypically feminine ways (weak, laughing at their jokes, and so forth). She's afraid to show her real self.
- She's afraid people won't take her seriously.
- She conditions herself to be Fruit Cup Girl whenever she's around a boy she likes.

FCG gets the guy, but feels like a fool. By the way, the vast majority of boys don't really get or like FCG, either. While they

don't want girls beating them at everything or making them feel stupid, they also don't want a girl who seems incredibly superficial and brainless.

> I constantly see girls act superficially around guys! It's amazing how girls instantly become charming and flirty when a guy steps into the room, as if they can't let down their guard for a split second and just be themselves. Although I hate to admit it, I'm sure I've done this before.
>
> —Jenny, seventeen

> Girls feel they're not perfect enough and try to make up for that by acting. Same with me.
>
> —Jessica, thirteen

But the larger issue is that FCG makes girls feel ashamed to be girls. You look at girls acting like FCG and you understandably don't want to be associated with that because you know boys don't respect it (which, of course, doesn't stop some of them from hooking up with her). The big problem with that—beyond the fact that we want girls to be proud of being a girl—is that as girls get older, this dynamic is the reason why girls won't help an FCG girl who's in trouble with a boy and/or intoxicated.

When girls are younger, being an FCG is the easy way to get a boy's attention. By eighth grade, girls know that acting like that is going to get you only so far without inviting ridicule. Older girls still bring out FCG to get boys' attention, but need an excuse to openly fall back on her. That's where drinking comes in. As long as a girl has a beer in her hand, she has an excuse to be FCG. The metamorphosis from Fruit Cup Girl to Beer Cup Girl sets the stage for girls to use alcohol and drugs as excuses for doing what they want to do but are too afraid to do sober because they'll get a bad reputation.

> When I was twelve, I remember wondering why girls had to act so fake around guys. They would stand around in clusters and scream and giggle and shoot looks over at some guy.

Maybe one of their friends would come over and give you a message. If they act like that now, I would think they were trying to hook up. It's obvious. No one acts like that much of a moron unless they want to hook up.

—Patrick, sixteen

To inoculate against your daughter succumbing to FruitCupGirlitis (or to the least have people take her seriously), teach her these three seemingly small things:

1. Sneeze naturally. She's not a kitten.
2. Do not speak a declarative sentence as if she's asking a question, meaning her voice doesn't rise on the last word she says.
3. If bothered by the presence of an insect or small animal, walk away or calmly remove it with a container or paper towel.

FIGHTING OVER BOYS

Recently, a teacher gave me the lowdown on an ongoing challenge she was having. The girls in her class were off-the-charts cliquey and mean. They had already been talked to several times with no improvement. The teacher described one girl by saying "I'm sure Morgan's the Queen Bee; I've been trying to catch her all year and haven't been able to."

When I met this girl, she was tiny, pretty, and didn't say a word in class. Meanwhile, there was another girl named Brianna, also tiny and pretty, who talked constantly in class and asked for my advice afterward. Of course, being a sucker for anyone who asks my advice, I thought Brianna was sweet and Morgan was mean. I was wrong. They were both mean. They had been waging a protracted dirty war against each other all year, and the pivotal battle peaked at a boy-girl school event in the spring. At this event, where adults were everywhere but no one was officially chaperoning, Morgan and two of her friends met up with three popular boys who Brianna thought were "hers." When Brianna found out, she began

a systematic campaign to get the boys to switch their allegiance back—and she was successful.

Practically the entire grade was polarized between these two girls, with savage consequences threatened for any displays of disloyalty. Morgan vowed revenge, although she justified her actions because it was "equal to what she did to me." The only thing that stopped them was the end of the school year. The next year, many new students joined their grade, and they had about a day to decide which girl they aligned with. It's situations like this that seem so "middle school" but truly negatively impact the environment of the grade and even the school. Imagine being a new student: Instead of focusing on finding new friends you really like, you are immediately thrown into a cutthroat war between two rivaling students.

When girls are younger, fights over boys are usually limited to telling the boy bad things about the other girl or telling the girl something to make her feel terrible under the guise of "I think there's something you should really know." For example, an eighth-grade girl recently asked my advice for the following situation:

Q: I like this guy and he likes me, too, but he's still talking to this other girl. She doesn't know that he likes me. Shouldn't I tell her?

A: Yes, you should, but you have to be honest with yourself about your motivation. If you're telling her because you feel bad that this boy is manipulating her, then by all means say something. But let's be clear that she isn't the only one being manipulated here—so are you. If you're telling her because you want her to know that he likes you more or she should back off your property, then, no, I wouldn't. I would tell the boy you're not going to allow him to use both of you and that until he stops doing that, whatever you've got going with him is over.

I agree talking to the boy is the best in this situation. Talking to the girl would seem to be trying to start something or trying to take the boy for yourself. That wouldn't really change

the boy's thought process or behavior. He still gets one or maybe both girls and now they are just fighting. Holding the boy accountable is necessary because he is the one manipulating.

—Keo, eighteen

CHECKING YOUR BAGGAGE

- Close your eyes and remember your first crush: Where were you when you first saw this person? How did you feel?
- What makes you most nervous about boys and your daughter?
- What do you want to teach your daughter about boys?
- Were you ever dumped by a girlfriend or boyfriend? Where and how did it happen?
- Who, if anyone, did you go to for support?

Just as you've brought your baggage from your own experiences with friendships, you'll do the same thing when your daughter begins to be sexually interested in people. Somewhere in your daughter's adolescence you'll go from telling her what to do, with a good chance she'll do what she's told, to guiding her and recognizing that she needs space to make her own decisions.

HER BILL OF RIGHTS WITH PEOPLE SHE LIKES

Lots of girls get all red in the face as soon as you bring up the whole romance thing. Here are some suggestions for how to have those conversations. Remember, this may be a great time to see if she's interested in talking to that ally. You don't have to wait until your daughter likes someone to have this conversation. As soon as you see your daughter or her friends being interested in any of this you can start to have these talks.

Have a discussion to clarify what she wants and has the right to expect out of any relationship. Your goal is to help her understand how her feelings when she likes someone may impact her Bill of Rights. Ask her how she feels when she likes someone (don't

use the word "crush" because then she'll think you're patronizing her). Then, ask her what her Bill of Rights should be with someone she likes. If the discussion is too uncomfortable for her, suggest she write it down in her journal. It should look like this:

When I like someone, I feel . . .
   Nervous
   Excited
   Butterflies in my stomach
   Distracted

When someone I like treats me with dignity, they . . .
   Respect me and other people
   Don't make fun of me with bad teasing
   Listen to what I say
   *Don't treat me differently in front of other people than when
      we're alone*

The question you need to get your daughter to think about is this: If she likes someone and they don't act according to her Bill of Rights, what should she do? She should reread her Bill of Rights for Friends (see page 264) and then ask herself why she would hold a person she likes to a lesser standard than she would a friend. How can SEAL help her strategize and frame her words? Reassure her that you're there to listen or to help.

> A girl sometimes discounts her Bill of Rights with boys because she thinks if she lets him get away with more, he'll like her back. What she doesn't realize is that that will only make him respect her less.
>
> —Nidhi, sixteen

DADS, PAY ATTENTION!

If and when your daughter starts to like boys, you have a crucial opportunity to reach out to her. If you establish a rapport with her, she'll see you as a critical resource for the boy perspective. If your inclination is to sum up what your daughter should know about

boys in the sentence "All boys want is sex," think again. Even if you believe this is the case, your saying that will totally shut her down. She needs to hear about boys from your vantage point. For example: "I know this may be uncomfortable, but if you ever want to talk about guy stuff, I'm here anytime to talk."

When she opens up, this is a great time to talk about the first person you liked and/or your first relationship. Your daughter needs to be reminded that you were her age once and you may have gone through similar experiences. Feel free to tell her what confused you about girls and how you figured things out. Invite her to ask questions about what a boy might be thinking in certain situations.

Most of the time there is so much focus on the special relationship that mothers and daughters share that dads kind of get pushed to the sidelines.

> *Girls want their father's approval. There's something really powerful about being "Daddy's little girl" and most girls don't want to tarnish that image. At the same time, it's also difficult to talk to fathers because it seems like they don't know what to say and they can seem kind of clueless. Dads seem to have a really hard time letting go of the image of their "sweet little baby girl" and fear what will happen when guys start to find their "little girl" attractive, because dads know how guys think and "no one better be having those thoughts about my daughter." It's good to warn daughters that not all guys may have the best intentions, but it's also important to let her know that there are some good guys out there, because your dad can't be the only exception to the rule. I've noticed that my friends who grew up with their mothers and have really bad relationships with their fathers end up having bad relationships with their boyfriends. It often seems like they date guys who share some character traits that their fathers have.*
> *—Ellie, twenty-one*

Remember Frank, the widowed dad from chapter 2? He's a great example of someone who almost lost an opportunity to be present in his daughter's life but didn't because other adults in his

family reached out to him and he was open-minded and -hearted to his daughter's changing needs. He went from a relationship of conflict and misunderstanding with his daughter to one of understanding and deeper connection.

THE GAMES BEGIN: THE BOY-GIRL PARTY

It's happened. Your daughter has just received her first invitation to a boy-girl party. Should you let her go? I would let her go if she wants to. If, however, there's a hint that she doesn't want to go but is feeling pressured, always give her the out of denying permission, so she can "blame" you for not letting her. If she does go and she's open about it the next day, try to have a conversation with her about it. Don't start by asking if she had fun (that's like asking how her day was), but ask her what she thought about the party. Ask if people acted the way she thought they would or if they acted differently. (If she answers that some of the girls acted like FCGs, you have a great opportunity to ask her why she thinks girls act like that.)

Now, suppose your daughter is in seventh grade and relentlessly begs you to allow her to invite boys to her birthday party. Remember why this could be so important to her: Having a boy-girl party is a huge asset in ascending the social pecking order. Girls will get upset over a boy, someone will make out in your basement, and your daughter will be at the center of it all. I guarantee tears and fights culminating in a Messenger going back and forth between two cliques brokering a peace accord. What could be better?

Then why, you ask, would you volunteer to be the sacrificial host here? You don't have to, but if you want to try, you must use this as an opportunity to demonstrate parental responsibility. If you agree to have the party, make sure your daughter understands your parameters for invitations and the importance of diplomacy in issuing them, especially if she can't invite everyone. This is a tough call for girls, as they know their stock goes up if they have a boy-girl party.

Before the party, clarify with your daughter where you'll be during the proceedings. Will you stay upstairs with occasional policing reconnaissance missions? Circulating is one way you can

minimize drama. It's also an informal but clear statement about who is in charge. Go over your house rules for appropriate behavior and what will happen if kids behave inappropriately. Adopt a zero-tolerance policy for cigarettes, drugs, alcohol, and nasty exclusive behavior. Most important, make a plan with your daughter for how she can ask for your help if things get out of hand and she doesn't want to lose face and risk losing a sense of acceptance among the other girls.

YOUR ROLE AS PARENT: THE ETERNAL "OUT"

One of the cardinal rules you want to establish with your daughter for a boy-girl party is that she can always use you as the "out" and blame you for any rules she may secretly want enforced but doesn't want to take the rap for in front of her friends. Two examples: "My mom and dad will kill me if you bring that in here," and "My parents absolutely freak if anybody goes upstairs to any of the bedrooms."

This rule isn't just for parties, however. Make sure your daughter knows she can always pin it on you if her peers are pressuring her to do something she doesn't want to do: "Sorry, but my mom doesn't let me go out on weekdays." "Sorry, but Dad would go ballistic if I went over to your house without any parents there." It's a fair deal: You're the fall guy, and she stays safe.

> I did it a lot freshman year, and it worked!
>
> —Vivian, fifteen

> For any "Hip Parent" types, if your daughter uses you like this, it won't make you lose face with her friends: Valid excuses (which these almost automatically are) don't get a second thought from them.
>
> —Katelyn, eighteen

> That's so true. Unless they are on the very extreme side of not letting their son/daughter out then the parent excuse works no questions asked.
>
> —Keo, eighteen

OFF TO THE MALL: RUNNING IN PACKS

It's normal for teens to run in packs. It's also normal that once in packs, kids do things they never would do alone. You can't stop your daughter from running in packs, but you can guide her about how to behave in these packs.

Having a check-in time is important. Make an agreement about when she'll check in with you. (I think it should be written down and put in the alarm of her cellphone—here's a time when cellphones are good!) If you say she needs to be home at ten o'clock, then you have every right to expect her home by then. If not, apply appropriate consequences.

LATE-NIGHT PHONE COMMUNICATION

Here's yet another reason for your daughter to hand over her phone at night.

When you were a teen, did you ever wait by the phone at night for someone to call? When the phone rang, somehow your mom or dad would answer before you could get to it? Then you would have to suffer the humiliation of your dad saying things to the caller like "Do you know what time it is? No, she doesn't talk to people at this time of night!" Today, if your daughter goes to bed with her cellphone, she misses this experience because she'll get all the calls she wants without parental interruption. Don't deny her that experience! Take her cellphone with you when you go to bed, and if someone calls or texts or snapchats or whaetever, respond with "Hi, Dylan! Yes, I have Piper's phone. It's a little late to be texting, isn't it?"

THE STOMACH CHURNER: SHOULD YOU ALLOW BOYS IN THE BEDROOM?

Maybe the rest of the group took off, and it's just your daughter and the guy she currently is obsessed with. Or maybe he came over to study. Are you uptight if you forbid your daughter from having boys in her bedroom? Who cares? My opinion is that

you shouldn't allow your daughter to have boys in her room. Of course, having this rule may not stop her, but it's important to make the rule anyway. When I ask teens what they think about this question, most of them don't know what's the best, either. Some think when girls are in middle school, boys should not be allowed, but freedom should increase when they're older. Others have the opposite opinion.

There are several reasons to have this rule. First, if you aren't home and she's with a boy she's attracted to, she may feel nervous about "going upstairs" with him. She can blame you, the "eternal out," again. Second, when she tells the boy he isn't allowed upstairs or she's obviously nervous about it, it transfers critical information to him about you: This is a house with rules and your daughter respects your rules; therefore, he should, too. You are reinforcing your values about personal space (yours and hers) and it gives her the feeling that you're watching her.

What if she's attracted to girls? For years, girls have been hiding their sexual relationships with other girls under the guise of being friends so they can be alone in their bedrooms or be private in a way that their parents would never let them be alone with a boy. In this context, I don't think your daughter's sexual orientation matters. If you don't want her to be in her bedroom with the person she's sexually involved with in any capacity, then you get to set that rule. Just recognize that she is highly incentivized to break that rule or find somewhere she can be alone with this other person.

Teens in same-sex relationships may have fewer public places for them to be comfortable being physically affectionate. Give some thought to how you can balance affirming your child against setting rules. If you do that, she may not agree with you about the rule, but she'll respect the process you went through to come to your decision.

REJECTION: GETTING DUMPED

No matter how old you are, and no matter how many times it happens to you, being rejected is awful. But a girl's inexperience

can blind her to the warning signs of an impending rejection. It ends up being a cruel surprise. And it's not just being upset about the relationship being over. It's also embarrassing. They may have the same friends or see each other every day at school. She could feel that her image in her school community is tied to the relationship. Last, rejections are almost impossible to keep private. Technology makes it feel like a public event open to everyone else's commentary.

When someone breaks your daughter's heart, what can you do to make her feel better? Honestly, there's really nothing you can do to make her pain and feelings of rejection go away, but you can give her a hug, if she lets you, or tell her you're available to talk anytime. Let her sulk and lick her wounds in her room, and let her cry; when she does want to talk, just listen and don't rush in with your judgments. Empathize with her feelings, even if you don't believe they could be that intense. Give her some time. Offer to do something fun with her, and, if she says no, wait for a while and ask again.

> I'd be incredibly depressed and I would take it out on my family. They would probably think I was back in some phase or something. Which of course would be really annoying. Chances would be that my mom would know that I was dating him, but she'd probably be happy that I broke up with him. If I thought I was in love with him, she would think I wasn't. So then I wouldn't want to go to her. Girls are going to talk to someone else or keep it inside.
>
> —Nidhi, sixteen

Support your daughter without tearing the other person down. That way she learns that she doesn't have to put someone else down to take care of herself. Also, if she gets back together with them (which is quite possible), she'll still feel she can go to you without looking weak.

> In sixth grade he wrote a script to break up with me and read it to me in the lunchroom. He said, "Erin, it's over, I can't be

with you anymore," and I said, "OK," and he goes, "No, you're not following the script! Your line is, 'I need you, don't leave me.'" In seventh grade I gave him another try. That time he recorded himself breaking up with me.

—Erin, eighteen

A breakup's silver lining is that it creates great girl-bonding moments. The intimacy that comes out of these experiences can be unexpectedly rewarding. Especially if the dumped girl has been blowing off her girlfriends for her now ex-boyfriend, those friendships can experience a honeymoon period. The dumped girl can pour out her sorrows, anger, and confusion to her friends while they analyze the ex-boyfriend's baggage and problems.

HOW DOES SHE BREAK IT OFF?

I broke up with my boyfriend over the phone and my mom got so mad at me. I said, "What do you want me to do, ask you for a ride so you can drive me there? I can't break up with him while you're waiting for me outside. There's no way I am doing it at school because everyone will see. How else am I supposed to do it?"

—Katelyn, eighteen

Modern technology makes it so difficult to break up these days. You can always see what your exes are up to, if they're hanging out with other people, if they look hotter than ever, if they seem to be having a better life than you ... and it's depressing. They might even manipulate their feeds because they know you'll see it—wearing the shirt that they know is your favorite, writing things that they know you'd find obnoxious. Plus, technology allows you to access your ex at the slightest moments of weakness. When you're feeling a little lonely, or start feeling sad, it's way too easy to text your ex and fall right back into wanting them and despairing over your breakup. These moments of relapse totally undo the

progress toward the independence that you wanted from the breakup.

—Sydney, seventeen

You really have to be careful how much explaining you do when you break up with someone. I know it's necessary but at the same time the breaker-upper may come across as willing to take the person back if they changed. So if she really wants to break up, she has to be clear about it. It's not fair to leave them with false hope.

—Alex, eighteen

As I mentioned earlier, your daughter might run through several relationships, with varying degrees of seriousness. Remember that even though you think the relationship is superficial and/or that they haven't done much more than hold hands, ending these things is so hard—and it's painful to be on the receiving end. So you need to clarify for her that if she ever wants to break up with someone, she should do it respectfully, clearly, and on her own (meaning no Messengers doing her dirty work for her or breaking up online). She can use the same SEAL strategy I've outlined in earlier chapters. She should *Strategize* where to do it privately and *Explain*: "When you tease me in front of your friends and won't listen when I ask you to stop, I feel like you don't respect me." When there's no reason other than that she just wants to move on, she can say, "I just don't like you that way anymore." Recall that this is very tough for girls; she may be tempted to be unclear. "I'm not sure we should see each other anymore" or "Maybe it isn't a good idea for us to keep dating" are fuzzy statements that invite misinterpretation. Finally, she should *Affirm* and *Lock*. She doesn't have to say anything cheesy and patronizing, but communicate that she can set her boundaries while treating him in a way she can be proud of.

BREAKING UP ONLINE

Getting dumped online is the worst! This is what this guy emailed me. "It's not you. It's me. I don't like you. You're bossy and I don't like the sound of your voice. I used to like you and now I don't. Sorry. PS I want my PlayStation back." Then he forwarded it to all his friends before he sent it to me. So by the time I got to school everyone in the school knew.

—Zoe, eighteen

I broke up with a girl once by text message and it was a huge mistake. You can't tell the person's reaction. I really shouldn't have done that.

—Dylan, fourteen

Technology has created a whole new system for breaking up—and that's not a good thing. Think about it. What better way to go through the discomfort of getting out of a relationship than doing it online, where you don't have to face the person, and if they do anything you don't like, you can forward their response to all your friends to justify your actions?

Going from worst to least objectionable, here are the most common ways my students are breaking up online:

1. Changing their relationship status on an SNP from "In a relationship" to "Single"
2. Texting/email
3. Leaving a voicemail on a cellphone

Here are some guidelines for breaking up:

1. No one should find out they got dumped by having their ex (who they don't even know is an "ex" yet) change their relationship status on any SNP from "In a relationship" to "Single." It's just cowardly and mean. Adding to the humiliation is the likelihood that five minutes later all the "friends" are going to see it and

then post things on the rejected person's wall like, "I'm soooooo sorry!" "When did it happen???????" "WHATTTTTTT!!!!! U MADE THE CUTEST COUPLE!!!!!" Or, even worse, someone commenting, "Finally . . . good for you to get rid of her."

2. Text messaging is unacceptable. It's impersonal and disrespectful. The more formal option, email, has the benefit that it can give the person being dumped the opportunity to read it on his or her own time and decide when to contact you back. However, email still isn't that great of an option because it, too, is impersonal, and people are more than capable of dumping someone meanly and forwarding any part of the exchange to other people. Also remember that any email or text can be misinterpreted, even at its best.

3. Voicemail. You've taken the risk that the person may pick up, unless you deliberately call when you know he or she will miss the call. If that's the case, voicemail is like text messaging. You're rejecting a person without giving him or her the respect to have the conversation.

The best way to end a relationship is to do it face-to-face, without other people around. Of course, if your daughter doesn't feel safe with the person, or if she is worried that she might be manipulated into changing her mind, then she might try a different way—perhaps over the phone. But seriously, not online. It's also good to keep in mind because online breakups can be shared or transmitted (via screenshots, forwarding, copied texts, and so forth) with a large network of people, making the breakup that much more public. Doing it in person lowers the potential for the breakup to be viral drama.

How should your daughter go about it? Well, a good time to break up is before a school break. A bad time to break up is on the person's birthday. I know this is hard because I am asking your daughter to reject someone in a clear and direct manner. By the very nature of what she's doing, she'll hurt the person's feelings. Accept that as fact, but remember that she can control how she conducts herself, and she should treat him with dignity. She can do so by preparing what she's going to say and being clear so there are no false hopes that they'll get back together.

They [the person who gets dumped] are going to trash you no matter what, so timing is important here. Don't do this when you're about to see them in the next few hours, so don't do it in the middle of school. After school, like when they can go to practice and run out their frustration, is good.

—Alex, eighteen

You can't take steps backward in a romantic relationship and say, "OK, we're just like we were before we started dating." Before dating you were on the path to dating. You need to give the other person space and let the friendship re-form between the people you are now.

—Faith, seventeen

WHAT DO BOYS AND GIRLS MOST WANT TO KNOW ABOUT EACH OTHER?

At strategically placed times in my courses (that is, when our students are capable of having a meaningful conversation without putting one another down or yelling over each other), we bring the boys and girls together and have them write down anonymous questions to ask one another. Of course, some of our students can't resist asking questions that are meant to shock, and we weed those out first or ask the question in a more appropriate way. Then we let the boys have the opportunity to answer the girls' questions (without the girls' commenting) and vice versa.

So, what do boys want to know about girls? These are their common questions and the girls' most common answers:

1. *Why do girls like jerks?* Girls' reason: Because he's hot and can be really cool when he's alone. My reason: He fits in the "Act Like a Man" box. He's the Misunderstood Guy who looks like he has things under control. Girls find it especially attractive if he shows them his sensitive side and feel that only they can understand him.

2. *What are girls looking for in a boyfriend?* Or *Why do girls say they're looking for someone who listens and respects them and then date the guys that don't?* Girls' reason: We don't know. My

reason: The "Act Like a Man" box gives them bad boyfriend criteria.

3. *Why do girls always go to the bathroom together?* The girls and I agree: It's a big-time bonding opportunity. Girls check in with each other and gossip. If they're on a date, they discuss if they're into the date, or, if not, strategize how to get out of it.

4. *Do girls think about sex like boys do?* The girls and I agree: Sometimes, and they talk about it with one another in detail. When girls say this, the boys giggle nervously.

5. *Why don't girls tell you what they're really thinking?* Girls' reason: We do, but you don't listen. My reason: For one of three reasons: (1) girls think they are, but they're communicating in a way that makes their opinions unclear; (2) they're so conditioned not to that they develop severe anxiety just at the thought of telling boys something they may not want to hear, and they shut down; or (3) they're putting up a front.

6. *How do you tell a girl you like her?* The girls and I agree: Directly.

7. *Why do girls ask so many questions when you're dating them?* Girls' response: We don't, but every time we want to ask anything, you all freak. My reason: Because talking and sharing personal information makes girls feel they're getting to know you.

8. *Why do girls wear tight clothing if they don't want the attention?* Girls' response: Don't even go there! We have the right to wear what we want, when we want. My response: Girls do want attention, but not the kind that makes them feel like a piece of dirt and/or a slab of meat. When girls wear revealing clothes, don't make the assumption that they want to have sex. Wanting to feel sexy is not the same as wanting to have sex.

What do girls ask about boys? Here are their common questions and boys' responses:

1. *Why are boys such jerks in front of their friends and totally nice with you when you're alone?* Boys' reason: We don't know what you're talking about. Girls want too much when we're with

our friends and it gets on our nerves. My reason: To get their friends' respect, boys put up a front that they're tough, in control, and funny. They may feel more comfortable showing their vulnerable side to a girl because a girl won't tease them.

2. *How should I tell a boy I like him?* The boys and I agree: Directly.

3. *Why do boys get mad when you don't want to date them?* Boys' reasons: Because girls give mixed signals, play games, and never know what they want. My reason: Some boys believe that girls don't have the right to say no. Much more likely is that the boys' feelings are hurt, but they don't want to show it because it makes them look weak.

4. *When a boy talks to you, why does he look at your chest?* Boys' reason: Because we can't help it, especially when girls wear things that make it impossible to look anywhere else. My reasons: (1) He could be objectifying you because that's how he generally sees women; (2) he could be distracted by your breasts because he's attracted to you but really does like you; (3) you are wearing clothes that really do show off your cleavage, so don't pretend you're not.

5. *Why don't boys talk about their feelings?* Boys' reason: Because we don't make a huge deal out of things like girls. We have nothing to talk about. My reason: It's a sign of weakness. They feel that girls have power over them if they give personal information.

6. *Why can't boys ever be serious?* Boys' reason: Girls take things too seriously. My reason: "Serious" to boys often means emotional, which equals weak and vulnerable or up for public humiliation.

COMMON QUESTIONS YOUR DAUGHTERS ASK ME ABOUT BOYS

Q: What if a boy says, "I'll tell you who I like if you tell me who you like." Should I tell him?

A: The only reasons to answer this question are (1) if you are talking about each other; or (2) if you want the person you like to

know and you want them to find out through a Messenger. But if you send it through a Messenger, you can't control the information the person gets. So even though this is unbelievably uncomfortable to think about, wouldn't you rather have the person find out directly from you?

Q: How do you get someone you like to notice you?
A: You can stare until he notices and then smile. And you can still flirt and not be Fruit Cup Girl. If you share something in common, like you both write for the school paper, you can use that as an opportunity to talk.

Q: What do you do when you have a friend who has done things with boys that you don't agree with? I want to be her friend, but I don't want to live in the shadow of someone like her. She wasn't always this way.
A: When you prepare to talk to her using SEAL, you have to get your judgments out of your head. For whatever reason, what she's doing with boys probably makes sense to her right now. So, if you tell her something like, "Do you realize that everyone thinks you're acting like a slut?" it's going to backfire because she'll only get defensive. Think about it: If you were her, wouldn't you get defensive, too? I would focus instead on what you liked about your friendship and the way she used to be and say something like:

YOU (*Explain*): "This is sort of hard to talk about, but you're my really good friend and I'm worried about what you're doing with guys."

FRIEND: "I know you don't approve, but you're not my mom and I don't think there's anything wrong with what I'm doing. I'm having fun."

YOU (*Affirm*): "This isn't about whether I approve or not [and, by the way, it isn't]. But as your friend, I have to tell you when you're doing things that I don't think are a good idea. I need to tell you that I don't want to hang out with you when you are hanging out with X guy."

FRIEND: "Then don't! I really don't need you worrying about me."
YOU (*Lock*): "Friends are supposed to worry about each other. I'm just telling you what I think. If we can hang out, just the two of us, that would be great. I miss our friendship."

Q: If my best friend has a new boyfriend and I like him, what should I do—just grin and bear it and pretend not to care?

A: Yes. You are absolutely not allowed to flirt with him to try to get him to dump her and go out with you. That is against the rules of how women should treat one another—best friend or not. Now keep in mind, this rule applies with a current relationship. Girls don't have the right to stop their friends from dating exes.

THESE EXPERIENCES ARE IMPORTANT!

These early boy-drama experiences set the stage for your daughter's expectations for and understanding of her personal rights in intimate relationships. As she gets older, these relationships become more mature, and her friendships will become even more important as safe places to reflect on and analyze new and often confusing experiences.

11

Pleasing Boys, Betraying Yourself

Dear Rosalind,
Please help me. There's a boy that I really like and he likes me
also and we went out and were boyfriend and girlfriend but then he
broke up with me and he told me that he wanted to listen to his mom
and not have a girlfriend because he can't sleep at night and it's a
distraction to him. So I said OK that's fine. Then I found out about
three days later he was dating a girl named Katya and he kept it
from me and they didn't tell me and Katya is my BEST FRIEND
and I knew her since fifth grade and we are now in eighth. We made
a promise to each other that we would never date a guy that we went
out with.

Thanks! Jasmine

Dear Rosalind,
There is this guy that I really like and he says he likes me a lot too
and then the other day I found out he was making out with one of
my closest friends and it was like a dagger in my heart and he calls
me and tells me that he's sorry and that I wasn't supposed to find
out. I spent 1 hour crying in the bathroom and I don't know what to

do cause we are very close friends and now he pulls this on me and
it made me sad and mad. What should I do?

Yours truly,
Alisa
Please help me!!!

If your daughter was Jasmine or Alisa, how could you help her think through this situation without condoning an attitude of "Girls can never be trusted"? How can you give her the skills to use SEAL to have a conversation with the girl and the boy who have betrayed her? And this is only the beginning. How can you channel your own concerns, fears, and frustrations as she develops these relationships so she'll listen to you instead of tuning you out? Because, let's be honest: If you knew your daughter was being knowingly used by boys or betrayed by her best friends, wouldn't you be slightly upset that she was putting up with that? Wouldn't you wonder what in the world was wrong with her? After all, you didn't raise her to be a doormat, did you?

All of these issues reflect major challenges girls face as they get older. This chapter looks at how Girl World tricks girls into pleasing boys and betraying the friends who truly support them. You'll learn how you can help your daughter stop the cycle. This chapter, and the one that follows it, will be intense for some people. So I'd like you to keep two things in mind as you read. One, I've made a conscious effort to write the earlier chapters in a way that middle school girls can read. These two chapters are more appropriate for eighth grade and high school girls. If you're reading this and are under age fourteen, ask your parent, ally, or an older sibling to read it first and see if it's relevant for what you're going through. Two, up to this point, I've described each issue, asked you to think about them from your own experience, and then provided strategies. I do the same here. So if you start getting really anxious about what you're reading, remember, solutions are coming.

WHAT YOU SHOULD KNOW

- Getting validation from boys boosts a girl's self-confidence and confirms that she's in the "Act Like a Woman" box.
- Girls understand that their social status and identity can be tied to relationships with boys.
- In trying to please a boy, she may betray and sacrifice her friendships with girls.
- At some point, most girls will lie, connive, or backstab to get the boy they want.
- Your daughter may lie and sneak behind your back to be with her partner.
- Girls, just like everyone else, have trouble defining the difference between acceptable flirting and sexual harassment. In the moment when she may most need to distinguish between the two, she won't be able to.
- Denial is a reasonable response to your daughter's developing sexuality. For her welfare, get over it.
- Your daughter can become trapped in an abusive relationship even if she's confident and self-assured and there's no history of violence in your family.

For most teenage girls, guys are everything. Boys validate their existence; they define who they are and where they stand in the world. You can talk to boys differently than your girlfriends. Until they screw you over, they can be really fun and comforting.

—Ling, seventeen

Being in a clique is an easy way to meet boys. Whichever clique she belongs to, there's a boy group that goes with them. If she strays outside of the accepted group of guys, then that's a problem.

—Portia, eighteen

Relationships usually don't develop by going on one-on-one dates, but rather when both cliques hang out together. By the end of high school, it's common for boys and girls within a large group to

have hooked up with almost everyone in the group. This doesn't mean they're having sex with one another, but sexual interaction is often a part of the group dynamic.

> When I was in high school, the clique I was in had two Queen Bees, which divided us up a lot but we were still all friends. One of the Queen Bees made a hookup map with the other Queen Bee as the center (the "sluttiest" girl) to show how we all connected through our hookups.
>
> —Charlotte, nineteen

The girls' social hierarchy can dictate how much flexibility a girl has in her choice of who she "likes." To a certain extent, a powerful Queen Bee has dating immunity, as she can like whomever she wants, because the guy she anoints as her current love interest will automatically become cool. At the same time, she'll be careful to be interested in someone who has some of the "Act Like a Man" box qualities because she has her image to protect.

> It's gossip central [if a Queen Bee dates outside the box]. People will joke and say, "Is he paying her?" Or they'll ask her "What are you doing?" They won't be supportive of it until she breaks up with him.
>
> —Dawn, fifteen

Girls learn that one of the fundamental criteria for group acceptance is dating someone who has the group's approval. There's powerful pressure for a girl to discount her feelings and her own personal standards to date someone who superficially looks the part even if he doesn't treat her well.

MATCHMAKING AND THE OLDER CLIQUE

By fifteen, most girls have one or two very close friendships—the kind people develop when they go through boot camp together. But their friendships with other girls resemble an extended, although more sophisticated, version of their friendships in late adolescence and junior high. It's hard to convince older girls that

their individual behavior is still affected by what they learned in the clique from earlier years. It's still there; it's just more subtle so it flies under the radar.

Older Queen Bees focus their attention on boys as the final arbiter for measuring their power among girls.

> The summer before my sophomore year, my best friend set me up with her boyfriend's best friend. I felt obligated to go out with him, but I didn't like him. He was extremely sexually aggressive, and he really scared me. Alyson said it was "cute" to have two guys who were best friends go out with two girls who were best friends. I would consider Alyson a Queen Bee and I would be the Pleaser. When I told her what the other guy was doing, she said that I was being a prude, so I just shut my mouth and kept going out with him. I was miserable. Finally, I talked to her boyfriend about it. He understood and apologized for setting us up. He helped me break up with my gross boyfriend. It's really hard to be the girl being set up. I said no numerous times, but she kept pushing!
>
> —Ella, eighteen

Here you can see the direct connection between girls' friendships and girls' unhealthy experiences with boys. Ella, in spite of being miserable, dated and couldn't break up with a boy she was frightened of because she wouldn't risk going against her friend. She was more afraid of displeasing the Queen Bee than of being with a sexually aggressive boy. People often link girls' poor sexual decisions and even their vulnerability to sexual violence with their difficulty in standing up for themselves with a boy. Yet Ella found herself with this sexually aggressive boy because she was unable to hold her own with a girlfriend.

WHEN BOYS ARE THE BETTER OFFER

In previous chapters I discussed how girls often jockey for position within their cliques by blowing off friends for a better offer—a better party, a more popular friend, or a chance to see a new movie with the more popular friend. As girls get older, more and more

the "better offer" involves boys. A girl makes plans to hang with her friends at someone's house, then "he" calls or texts, and all bets are off. This is where older girls follow the invisible rules of the "Act Like a Woman" box, which values boyfriends over almost everything else. According to its rules, girls are allowed to blow off girlfriends for a guy. Girls don't like it. They'll complain and talk behind the back of the friend who blew them off, but they will almost always take her back.

> We all do it to each other. It's understandable. It's part of the code. If she ditches us, then we talk behind her back and say she has no self-esteem and how pathetic she is, but we'll take her back. Sometimes it gets out of control [with the boy] and we never see her anymore.
> —Melanie, fourteen

> We have to forgive each other if we hope to be taken back.
> —Ellie, twenty-one

Ironically, girls often blow each other off for the same reason girls blow off their parents—it's safe. A girl knows her parents won't reject her if she decides to go out with her friends instead of staying home and playing Scrabble with them. Likewise, her friends won't reject her because she's choosing a boy over them. It's the rare girl who will stand up and tell a girlfriend how hurt and angry she is that she was dumped for a boy. And if she does, she often gets accused of holding the girl back or not letting her have her own life. There's a point in most friendships where the girl being blown off decides she won't take it anymore, and it can cause huge fights between close friends. Girls get the message that their friendships don't count as much as romantic relationships. They learn to discount themselves and to value themselves as lesser than males.

> This happens A LOT, and when the relationship with the boy ends, the girl is left friendless.
> —Lily, fifteen

BOYFRIEND STEALING

By high school, girls' friendships are often made or broken over boys, and this can have a chilling effect on the support girls can expect from one another. Some girls become so mistrustful of other girls that they tighten their circle of friends, confiding in only one close friend or deciding that only their diary is trustworthy. When a girl betrays another girl by hooking up with her boyfriend, she has violated a sacred bond between girls. No matter who in the new couple took the initiative, girls rarely blame the boy as much as the girl, if they blame him at all.

> Girls will excuse his behavior by saying that the girl was all over him, she was being a slut and what was he supposed to do?
>
> —Amanda, seventeen

Many girls are conditioned to believe that boys are less capable of fidelity, so they don't hold them to the same standard they would a friend. Since girls' friendships are often more intimate than the sexual relationships they are having with a boy, the feeling of betrayal often runs correspondingly deeper. Girls excuse boys' behavior. They don't excuse girls' behavior. This double standard has repercussions in other aspects of intimate relationships, as we'll see shortly.

Two things happen when girls can't trust each other. First, they miss out on having strong relationships now and in the future. Second, when girls don't watch out for one another, they often walk away from or ridicule a girl who is caught making bad decisions with guys. The sad and frustrating truth is that so many girls forget or never learn how invaluable they are to each other. But look what happens when they do:

> I have about five close girlfriends who have stood by me during this long process of trying to break free from my ex- and now-again "boyfriend" (this word would entail responsibilities, none of which he possesses, so I have trouble referring

to him as such). Rather than tell me I'm stupid and weak and shouldn't care so much, they have tried their best to understand that the relationship is hard to break free of because he was my first everything. No matter how much pain he causes me, my friends understand that he has played an important role in my life and understand why it's a long and winding road. This, to me, is major support and tolerance.

—Brooke, eighteen

I had a friend stay up all night with me as I finally talked about how mean my boyfriend was. She told me I didn't have to put up with it and there was nothing to be embarrassed about. I really think she gave me the strength to break it off with him.

—India, seventeen

CHECKING YOUR BAGGAGE

- Close your eyes and remember your first serious love: Do you remember the first time you saw this person? How did you feel? What did it feel like to be alone with that person?
- Did you ever have a friend get together with a person you liked or dated?
- What has your daughter learned from you about relationships? What have you modeled, for better or worse?

HOOKING UP AND DATING

Do girls still date? As in have relationships? Why are people talking about "hook up culture" so much and why does my daughter roll her eyes whenever anyone brings that up? Does it count as a date when people go out in a big group of friends?

First, let's define some terms. As you'll see from the comment below, definitions have probably changed a lot since you were a teen. With my students, "dating" means going out—one-on-one. Dating is rare and it's a big deal. Much more common is the umbrella term "hooking up," which usually refers to a spectrum of behavior, from literally hanging out to making out to

having intercourse—but the common denominator is it's always no strings attached, whereas dating refers to a more long-term, exclusive relationship.

> Group dating is the best. It makes dating a whole gray area. Group dates are safer because you don't have to be alone with the person and if you decide you don't like him, you can ignore him.
>
> —Isa, sixteen

> This whole hooking up thing is a gray area. It allows people to not communicate straightforwardly or bank on the fact that the other person is too uncomfortable to communicate.
>
> —Aliesha, sixteen

I know that many adults are extremely uncomfortable with the term "hooking up" because it implies that young people don't value these experiences as much as they should. Adults, rightfully so, are worried that young people won't make good decisions about who they hook up with and what they do when they're hooking up. But that adult discomfort often comes across to young people as an accusation—that they are either naive or promiscuous and have no respect for themselves.

I talk to young people about hooking up at every high school I go to and, yes, sometimes "hook up culture" is used as a way to normalize sexual manipulation and coercion. It is often a way for one person to callously use another person and have no sense of obligation to even "look them in the eye" the next day. I have students who only hook up with someone because they think it will increase their social status. None of these things are good. Adding to all of this is that there are way too many girls unable to communicate what they want and don't want with their partners—no matter if they are with that person for two minutes or two years.

But it is also true that some girls want to hook up with someone and not think it's that big a deal. They are coming into their sexuality, they are attracted to someone, and they want to act on those feelings without feeling guilty or ashamed for having a ca-

sual sexual interaction. I don't have a problem with that if the girl can truly be an advocate for herself, maintain her personal boundaries, and communicate those boundaries in the moment.

RELATIONSHIPS ON ANY TERMS:
PLEASE, PLEASE LIKE ME

I hooked up with someone who told me from the beginning that he was not interested in monogamy. I said it was fine because I thought I could be happy with what I could get, but I wasn't. When he hooked up with friends of mine, I'd get so jealous and so angry, but I couldn't tell him why.

—Zoe, seventeen

Think about the many dynamics that intersect when girls become interested in boys. They want true love the way they see it in the media. They want boyfriends to show off to their friends and to increase their social status. They want to explore the excitement and drama of romance. In the course of achieving these goals, they learn that they can get away with blowing off their friends for a boy, that it's hard to trust a friend around their man, and that maybe the more valuable relationship is with the guy.

Combine that with what they learned in early adolescence about maintaining relationships no matter how they are treated, how they learn from the culture to express their anger, and how they depend on online platforms as the way to communicate, and you can see how girls face major challenges to having healthy relationships with boys. Pleasing boys governs what girls say and their perception of their power within a relationship. The desire to please affects the way they date, how they communicate what they want or don't want, and even the way they dump a guy. Girls are looking for an insurance policy against their own insecurity. When Girl World is set up to increase your daughter's insecurity, she'll seek validation from a boy and can become desperate to please him.

SEXTING: GIRLS BETRAYING THEMSELVES?

It is not a coincidence that this section comes right after a sentence about girls becoming desperate to please boys. Sexting can bring together all sorts of dynamics that we've already talked about—technology, boy and girl power dynamics, teasing, the works. It's also the case that sexting isn't always this terrible thing we wring our collective hands over. But it's really hard to see that, because we get so freaked out and tell girls that their lives will be over—that they won't be able to get into college or get a job—if they are "caught" in a sexually inappropriate picture.

That's why it's critical that you recognize all the nuances of sexting before you have to deal with its consequences in real life.

Let's get our definitions straight: "Sexting" is the transmission of explicit texts and/or photos over some platform in the social media world. The sense among the young people I work with is that it happens a lot and there're a few types. The first is flirting, usually by sexually suggestive text but sometimes by sexy pictures. They are generally seen as harmless. They are sent between people who are attracted to each other but haven't necessarily done anything, people who have hooked up in the past to some degree, or people in a relationship. The second kind of sext is sent to get someone's attention or is sent because someone asked for it. The last kind of sext is done to shock the recipient, like when a boy sends a close-up picture of his penis. (That's called a "dick pic," and I'll talk more about that later.)

Picture a beautiful sixteen-year-old girl wearing a cable-knit sweater, her long hair pulled back, who does really well in school, dutifully babysits her younger brother, and is on a competitive sports team. Now I want you to keep in mind that this nice, intelligent girl does not think it's a problem to be sexually texting the guy she likes or even sending a sexy picture of herself. And when the mother of the boy she was sexting with called her mother to complain, the girl didn't think she had done anything particularly horrible. Her takeaway from the experience?

I'm just not going to text like that with that boy again. But will it stop me altogether? No . . . why should it?—Gabby, seventeen

I know countless girls who fit this profile.

Here's another scenario: You are already asleep, and your daughter is up late in her room. She's in bed but on her phone, and she's simultaneously texting and snapchatting a boy she likes. He says, *im lonely. send pics?* and all of a sudden she has to make a decision.

Let's break down the choices she's weighing in her head. First, there's the pressure of time. If she waits too long to respond, the boy might know she is freaking out. She's going to have to decide quickly so that it appears she keeps her cool. If she says yes and sends the pictures, she has given over some of her power to this boy, and made herself vulnerable at his hands. If she says no, however, she has to break the flirty illusion that she was down for anything. If denied, the boy might stop texting and snapchatting her, or might label her as a prude, or might counter her "no" with, "I thought we were friends" or "It wouldn't be a big deal if you just sent them." In your mind, this choice is probably so easy. Why in the world would your smart and self-respecting daughter send pictures of her body to this teen pervert?! And why would she even want to be his friend? *Of course it's obvious to you.* But I am asking you to get inside your daughter's head, and the heads of the millions of other adolescent boys and girls who have sexted, to figure out why they say yes.

Girls would rather not rock the boat by saying no, especially to a boy of high social status who is well liked and outwardly nice. Plus, they perceive sexting as low-risk, "not a big deal." And really, there are so many situations where sexting doesn't backfire that the idea of it getting out of hand doesn't occur to kids.

But even if there is nothing *inherently* wrong with sexting in a situation where you can assume complete trust and that both individuals will keep the sexts solely between the two of them, sexting is obviously risky. It's a problem because there is *never* a guarantee of safety in sexting. Apps that might make sexting seem foolproof, like Snapchat, actually aren't safe because there's an app called Snapsave, which can save received Snapchat messages without the sender being aware of it. Such apps, as well as the carelessness or callousness of kids receiving sexts, turns something that could

be an innocent expression of teenage sexuality into a much bigger and darker deal.

Let's talk about the boys' roles in sexting. To some boys the collection and exchange of sexts is basically the teenaged version of baseball card trading. It's all about the chase, about eliciting sexts from the elusive hot girls. And it's about boys having power over one another—as one boy put it to me, "I have the Derek Jeter card and you don't." In this sense, something that should be so important—a girl's body—can become trivialized and traded around an inner circle of boys. To me, the trivialization is as damaging as the trading. Boys will try so hard to get these sexts from girls—they charm, they plead, they flatter, they pressure— but since there is no emotional investment, their interest fades as soon as they get what they want. Of course, not all boys are evil in this way. There are usually a few core players at the center of the sexting network. These guys are serial offenders, and usually the ones most likely to pressure a girl into sexting. They are practiced at getting what they want and will lie to a girl to get sexts—as well as lie to her to keep them. And who are the boys and girls who are most likely to be involved in this type of sexting? The ones who need to prove they belong in the "Act Like a Man" box and the "Act Like a Woman" box.

There is no magic formula to figure out which sexting incidents will blow up and which won't. The only golden rule is that some explode and some never become public. But if sexting goes public, the most likely consequence is widespread embarrassment and social humiliation. Make no mistake: The overall experience can be devastating. Girls face more serious social consequences than boys if they get "caught" sexting, meaning that their sexts get shared and possibly that adults are alerted to the situation. That's because when sexting becomes public, overwhelmingly it is in cases of girls sexting boys. Additionally, the culture described above about boys trading, sharing, and collecting sexts does not have a mirror image in girl culture. It is almost impossible to imagine girls grouped together rating, miming about, and forwarding the sexts of a boy classmate. Whereas boys publicize the sexts they receive to raise their social status, girls keep sexts

they receive to themselves, as if their pride is in the secrecy of the relationship.

Both boys and girls send sexts, but in my experience their styles differ dramatically. While girls tend to pose provocatively, they usually include their face in the picture; a boy will take a close-up of his penis as a way to be funny or a picture of his abs. Girls are more likely to be grossed out by the genital picture and will go to an adult sooner—which means the event stays private. That's why we have this belief that girls are usually the only people who send sexy pictures.

If you find out your daughter sexted and you are trying to figure out why, you don't have to look any further than what you already know about her. If you know her to be bright, caring, socially thoughtful, and confident in her self-esteem and body image, then she was likely sexting with good intention, albeit questionable judgment. If you have perceived your daughter as desperate for attention and low on self-confidence, on the other hand, it is more likely that she sexted to seem desirable, either for validation or attention.

If you find out that your daughter has sexted, and that the person who received the sexts (most likely a boy) shared them with other people, remember this before you fly off the handle at her: The receiver chose to share the sexts with others. It was that person's choice. Your daughter took a risk, but unless she sent the same sexts to everyone else in her class, the only person responsible for all those other people finding out was the original recipient.

Here's what to do if you find out your daughter sexted and is facing public shame. Give her a huge hug and tell her you love her. You can always add in, "I'm so sorry. Do you want to talk about it?" Don't talk to her about how her future is ruined and that she won't ever get into college or get a job. She's already heard that from fear-mongering adult "experts" who have spoken at her school. If she feels safe to do so, she should go to the person she sexted and ask that person to delete the sexts and to tell his friends to delete them, too. She might say to him, "I don't feel shame because I sent it to you. My mistake was in trusting you, and your

mistake was that you didn't care or took advantage of my trust."
It's entirely possible that he will do nothing about it, and also not
delete the sexts. But at least in confronting him, she takes control
and makes it clear that he is responsible and culpable.

Once she has done all she can do to limit the public nature
of the pictures, she can start to rebuild her confidence, and you
can have a calmer conversation about why she pressed send. If it
was simply a mindless impulse, remind her that not everybody
has the good intentions she has. Assure her that you are proud
of her being a trusting person, but communicate that you very
much hope that she shows her trust in different ways in the future. On the other hand, if she sexted because she desperately
wanted to get a boy's (or multiple boys') attention, you need to give
her guidance to build her sense of self apart from the reactions
she gets from males. Let the conversation be a way for the two of
you to talk about determining who is trustworthy, and encourage
your daughter to think about what sexting means to her in terms
of her self-worth, her body image, and her desire to be liked. If
your child seems to feel too uncomfortable to talk with you, ask
whether she'd rather speak to another adult you both trust.

Another scenario might be that your son or daughter is the
one forwarding pictures they received to others. If your child received a sext and sent it on to friends, he knowingly participated
in someone's embarrassment. Say "I know you didn't originally
send the picture, but I'm holding you responsible because your
actions contributed to someone's humiliation. You will delete the
picture from your phone and wherever you posted it, and you will
tell everyone you sent it to that your parents know who they are.
You have to apologize to everybody affected and you will lose cellphone and computer privileges for two weeks." You have to be
steadfast in this, because your child has broken someone's trust
and knowingly embarrassed that person.

Some lawmakers are already working to decriminalize sexting
or allow officials more discretion regarding how a young offender
is charged. And, fortunately, sexting prosecutions are pretty rare,
even though the media loves to report them. This means it is up
to you to talk to your kids about sexting. Do not use the threat
of legal retribution as your best evidence not to sext—kids won't

listen to that and won't think it applies to them. Nor should you argue point-blank that sexting is stupid and wrong. Understand that sexting is common in your adolescents' lives, just as it is common in many adult lives, and that to help your child reach a better opinion about it, you might need to take a different approach than a flat-out, no-questions-asked "NO."

Instead, talk to your daughter about how she might withstand pressure to sext from a boy she knows and likes. Practice with her what she might text back to *im lonely. send pics?* to be humorous but firm. Perhaps remind her that no reasonable fifteen-year-old girl in real life would stand in front of a guy she liked, take off all her clothes, and ask, "Now do you like me?" Nor would she think it was acceptable for that boy to bring all his friends over to weigh in on the decision—yet that is what sexting becomes. Continue to ask your daughter to think about what self-worth means to her. Discuss how she'll respond if another person in her school goes through difficulty with sexting. Will she be a supportive by-stander? Turn your fear of sexting (the same fear that *all* parents have!) into a constructive conversation with your child. More than anything, remember that it will be OK.

LET ME MAKE MYSELF PERFECTLY UNCLEAR

By the time they're ready to date, girls have had years to hone their understanding of the fake compliment. Girl World compels girls to compliment one another, so girls realize how hollow words can be. Picture yourself in the fitting room at a clothing store; the saleswoman tells you with a fake smile how great you look in a skirt that obviously makes you resemble a large bran muffin. You know she's lying, but there's some small part of you that wants to believe her. When a boy compliments a girl, it's the same thing. She wants to believe him, even if her gut tells her that there's an ulterior motive. She'll feel grateful and then obligated to him.

> *Your insecurity kicks in. At some point the fact that the guy wants something sexual doesn't matter because getting the validation is more important.*
>
> —Zoe, seventeen

Many of us feel that our negative emotions aren't as worthy as guys'. This is certainly true for me and it's aggravating. When I finally tell my boyfriend how I feel, I immediately apologize. So girls end up saying yes when we really mean no. I think a lot of girls also feel like they need to keep up this mystique—it's in everything we do. We cover ourselves in makeup, we wear clothing just short of being completely revealing. Most of us (including myself) never let down that barrier when it comes to our emotions. We don't say "It hurts me when . . ." Or "I feel like . . ." We just aren't speaking up and very few boys listen when we do.

—Anna, sixteen

Communication is another place where the expectations girls bring from their intimate relationships with girls inform their relationships with boys. Girls define a great relationship as one in which the other person knows what you're thinking and you can finish each other's sentences; you're totally in sync with each other. This is essential to girls' closest friendships. They think they're going to get it with the boys they like, and when they don't, they feel betrayed. They want to be understood without having to explain everything.

Isn't it easier to hope someone will guess how you're feeling than gathering your thoughts in your mind and bringing it up? Even now I watch my mom do the same things with my dad.

—Jordan, eighteen

I wanted to break up with this guy and I just couldn't. It was so hard! I sat down with him and gave him a million excuses why I couldn't go out with him anymore. "I'm having a lot of personal problems right now, I just can't handle it right now." The more he questioned me, the more excuses I made up.

—Ella, eighteen

"I didn't want to hurt his feelings," "I didn't want to be rude," "I didn't want to assume what he was thinking," and "I didn't want

to tell him what I wanted because I didn't want him to not like me" are all examples. The result is often a seriously mixed message, and it's more of a problem in relationships among older teens because the stakes are so much higher.

> Recently I went on a date with a guy that I have had an on-and-off thing with for about six months. Today was our first official date. Right when he gets to the movie he hugs me and gives me a kiss on my cheek. When we sat down he tried to kiss me on the lips. What I haven't mentioned is the fact that this is my first kiss. I didn't tell him that though. All he wanted to do was make out and that bothered me a little. If we are on a date I understand if he wanted to kiss me but he kept whispering to me, "you are soooo sexy," and "you are way too hot." And when I finally gave in and made out with him, I got really into it and sort of lost control. Before I knew it he was trying to stick his hand in my shirt and he grabbed my butt. This bothered me A LOT and I pulled away. At the end of the movie I gave him a kiss good-bye, but I'm not going out with him again. —Caroline

I didn't talk to Caroline's date about the date, but I would bet any amount of money that he thought the date went well. She was sexually attracted to him, she was excited to be on the date, she did want to make out with him. But she didn't know what her personal boundaries were or how to communicate them until she felt like it got out of control. From his point of view, the only thing she communicated is that she was into him but didn't want him going up her shirt or down her pants at that moment—because she kissed him at the end of the date. Her date thinks she wants to keep going—just at another time and maybe not in public.

FLIRTING VERSUS SEXUAL HARASSMENT

Flirting is a time-honored ritual. It's how teens test their fledgling romantic social skills, and it can be a lot of fun. It can also be another haven for miscommunication. Hardly anything about teens is subtle, and flirting is no exception. Walk down any school

hallway and you'll probably be disconcerted by the way teens overtly display their bodies, talk to one another in sexually explicit ways, and constantly touch each other. It's a huge part of teen culture, but that doesn't mean that all teens like it.

This is the environment where sexual harassment occurs. When does flirting cross the line? Flirting makes both people feel good, and sexual harassment makes the recipient feel small, uncomfortable, powerless, and/or intimidated. What is relevant to your daughter is that sexual harassment can create a hostile educational environment.

When I give presentations on sexual harassment at high schools, I ask the students to give me examples of sexual harassment separated into categories of verbal and written, visual, and physical examples. These are their responses:

Verbal/Written	Visual	Physical
Sexually explicit posts on social media	Hand gestures	Pinching
Catcalls	Licking lips	Grabbing
Showing lewd pictures	Staring at body parts	Hugging/kissing
Calling someone "bitch" or "ho"	Flashing	Blocking a path
"Can I get some of that?"	Grabbing crotch	Rubbing Grinding (when boys grind their bodies against girls at dances)

Then I ask the students if everything on the list is always sexual harassment. The answer is always no, but it never fails to spark a heated argument. The key to understanding why sexual harassment is so confusing is appreciating that it's defined differently by different people, and that calling it harassment places a huge burden on those who speak up about it (targets) and who subsequently may be labeled uptight complainers.

Several criteria determine whether an action is considered sexual harassment: what relation the person doing the action has to the target; how comfortable or uncomfortable the target feels; the

boundaries and personal space of those involved; and the threshold for harassment. If the target is attracted to the other person, she might have a higher threshold for what she considers sexual harassment.

Girls and boys each have distinct and different reasons why it's often hard to tell a harasser to stop. The following are two stories that may shed some light on these difficulties.

GIRLS ARE SILENT BECAUSE ...

Jim, Craig, and Jess are friends who have history class together. One day during class, Jim convinces Craig to text Jess the details of the various ways they want to have sex with her. Craig realizes, by the look on Jess's face as she reads it, that she's upset, but she doesn't say anything. Craig immediately realizes how stupid it was to text her and just hopes she'll blow it off. However, when she leaves the classroom, she tells her friends. She didn't realize that boys she considered friends would think about her like that. With the encouragement of her friends, she tells the principal, who then suspends both boys. The boys are infuriated. If Jess is as upset as she claims, why didn't she say anything to them when she first got the note? Why did she go to the principal first instead of telling them?

Why didn't Jess tell the two boys off? First, she was so flustered (guy friends of hers think that way about her?) that she couldn't think of anything to say, much less the perfect comeback. Second, these boys didn't pick her by chance. They picked someone they weren't intimidated by. They didn't pick a girl who would have gotten right back in their face. Jess is a quiet pleaser. It would be hard for her to stand up to them. Jess is programmed to not want to make a big deal out of it. What if people think she's uptight, frigid, or a bitch? She's confused about the boys' motivations (maybe they meant it as a joke, or even a weird kind of compliment?) and her own reactions (maybe it's good that someone thinks you're sexy, even if the note makes you feel bad). With the "Act Like a Woman" box controlling her actions, Jess says nothing to their faces. Only when she has the support of her clique does she feel she can take any kind of action.

BOYS ARE SILENT BECAUSE . . .

I was teaching a coed class on sexual harassment with juniors and seniors. The girls had just explained how violated they felt when they walked down the hallway and boys tried to put their hands up their shirts. When I asked if there were any boys who had been sexually harassed, a handsome guy raised his hand. He was on the track team and when he was practicing, girls would call out suggestive things to him as he ran by or would slap his butt. He didn't like it.

The same girls who'd complained of harassment moments earlier now screamed with laughter. This is the double standard boys are up against. Some girls and boys don't believe that boys can be sexually harassed because they "always want to have sex with anyone at anytime." If a boy complains, he's called gay.

It comes down to this: Boys can never say they don't want sexual attention for fear of their masculinity and heterosexuality being ridiculed, and girls worry that if they say they don't want sexual attention, they'll be called frigid or a bitch. Both boys and girls are conditioned to never say no.

> Aggressive girls corner boys when they're drunk and have their way with them when the boy doesn't want to hook up.
> —Ben, eighteen

> A girl in my school sent a really dirty email to my friend about all the ways she wanted to have sex with him, but she never would have gotten in trouble for sexually harassing him. Never.
> —David, seventeen

Let's go back to my school presentation. Examples of sexual harassment are written on the flip charts, and I think the students are getting it when a boy stands up and challenges me. "What about people's First Amendment rights?" he asked. "Don't people have the right to say what they want? If they want to talk about a girl in the boys' locker room, that's their right. How does that hurt the girl?"

I pressed him. "Why would you want to have the right to say something that would make someone else feel bad? Why is it so important that you have that right? Do you think people will like you for exercising this right?"

"You're trying to control the things we say," he answered. "You can't do that."

"You're right," I said. "I have no control over what you say, but don't you want people in your community, including yourself, to be able to walk down the school hall and not be preoccupied with what someone is going to say to you?"

A teen girl gave an eloquent summary of how locker room chat does indeed violate a girl's rights:

> The First Amendment gives you your personal rights as long as, in practicing them, you don't take away someone else's. A guy should have the sense of responsibility enough to know that talking to a bunch of random guys about a girl will have repercussions on that girl, and those repercussions will violate her rights of expecting safety and comfortable surroundings in a school environment. He will indirectly take away her sense of safety and security in an environment where she should be concentrating on studying. However, it's not that indirect because he knows that she will get a disrespectful or some type of sexually harassing response from the guys in the locker room based on what he tells them.
>
> —Nidhi, sixteen

Sexual harassers sometimes don't realize the impact of their behavior. There are also people who do realize and don't care, or who intentionally use sexual harassment as a way to intimidate. How can your daughter tell the difference? It's actually a lot like the different definitions of teasing I discussed in chapter 7.

- An unaware perpetrator doesn't realize the consequences of his actions, but will stop if told in an effective manner.
- An insensitive perpetrator harasses to impress his peer group and can dismiss girls' feelings by laughing or making stereo-

typical comments—for example, "You are so emotional. You are so uptight."

- An intimidating perpetrator most likely intimidates boys as well through verbal and/or physical bullying, but he can have excellent social skills.

Some people think sexual harassment is totally blown out of proportion by the media and overzealous school administrators and teachers. We've all read about the five-year-old boy suspended for kissing a girl in his class. Forget about the extreme cases. The goal, as I say to students, is to have a school environment in which people feel safe and comfortable so they can focus on their education. If there are students who feel uncomfortable because other people are doing something in a sexual manner that they don't like, shouldn't we address the problem? We all have to be honest. Girls and boys both act inappropriately with each other all the time—usually because they're trying to figure out what is appropriate. Girls will rub up against boys at the same time they're pushing them away and saying "Get off of me!" and they mean both. Boys are often deaf, blind, and dumb when girls send clear but nonverbal messages such as tensing and pulling away when they're hugged. While it would be better if all girls could tell a boy directly when they don't like his behavior, we collectively don't help young people understand each other better because we so easily and often blame and attack either side when a problem becomes public.

Our goal should be to create a way for girls and boys to live together in a civilized, respectful way. The challenge is to educate girls and boys about the obstacles they face that make listening to each other so difficult. They have to know how the "Act Like a Woman" and "Act Like a Man" boxes guide their behavior, and take responsibility when they behave in confusing, threatening ways.

OLDER GIRLS VERSUS YOUNGER GIRLS

The senior girls don't like freshmen hooking up with "their" [senior] guys. The girls of higher social status feel like this girl who isn't as cool or pretty as they are is taking "their" guys. They feel threatened. If they're close to the guy, the girls make comments to the guy when the girl isn't around or they'll try to hook up with the guy not because they like him, but because they want to get the "lowly" girl away from him.
                                                        —Ella, eighteen

By far one of the most frustrating and recurring problems I deal with is senior girls bullying a freshman girl because they have decided she doesn't know her place. In some senior girls' minds, that girl's place is underneath their feet apologizing for her existence.

This isn't something that happens *all* the time, but it is a problem. What's going on is the seniors are jealous and threatened because their male peers think the freshman girl is really hot or "frosh meat" (the "o" in the word indicates that sophomores are included). But the senior girls rarely admit that to themselves, let alone anyone else. It's much easier for them to humiliate the freshman girl. Here are things senior girls have done to freshmen in some of the schools where I work:

- Laugh at a freshman girl at a party because she's drunk and vomiting.
- Laugh and yell "Slut!" and "Skank!" as they watch a freshman girl go into a bedroom with a senior boy.
- Create a rules list for all the freshmen (which includes not hooking up with senior guys or ex-boyfriends of senior girls), stating that if they don't comply, their lives would become a "living hell."
- Opening a can of sardines and rubbing the contents into a freshman girl's bed (this was at a boarding school).

What's absolutely amazing to me about this is the consistent belief among these groups of senior girls that this year's freshmen

girls don't have any respect for them. "It's not like when we were their age," they say. "We didn't dress like whores. We didn't throw ourselves on guys. We treated the seniors with respect. These girls deserve what they're getting." There's little empathy. They have no sense that treating these girls so horribly isn't the right thing to do. It's all about the older girls' right to teach the younger girls their place.

On the other hand, if your freshman daughter is hooking up with a junior or senior boy, especially an "Act Like a Man" box boy, there is a good chance he's attracted to her precisely because she won't be able to hold her own with him. You can imagine how angry girls can get with me when I say that, but this quote sums up what boys tell me perfectly.

> I guess there's a possibility that an older guy in high school would hang out with a freshman because he actually liked her but not very often. What freshmen girls need to realize is that when you go out with a guy like that, his friends tease him relentlessly about it. And we talk behind his back because it's so obvious why he would do that—and it's not because he likes you or respects you. It's because you'll do what he wants.
>
> —James, eighteen

THE BAD BOYFRIEND OR GIRLFRIEND

This is my criteria for a bad partner:

- When they argue, their perspective and feelings are questioned.
- Tells him/her they need to lose weight or makes other denigrating remarks.
- Questions his/her intellect and makes him/her doubt themselves.
- Blows him/her off by saying he/she's uptight.
- Calls her a slut or a bitch.
- Insults him/her.

- Humiliates the partner.
- Does all of the above and then says "I'm just joking. You know I don't mean those things."

Please notice that this list is basically the same criteria as those for a bad friend. All relationships have drama, but any time your daughter is in a relationship where she is made to feel "less than" or smaller, where her perspective is questioned, she shouldn't be in that relationship. Later in the chapter, I'll offer some advice on how to help her handle that kind of situation.

HEALTHY RELATIONSHIPS

This chapter has focused on the negative aspects of relationships since these are the issues girls most often ask about. But not all relationships are bad, and your daughter may have a wonderful boyfriend. (And, although you might not want to admit it, she can even have a healthy and responsible sexual relationship with that person.) Remember, girls develop their personal standards for relationships from watching you, their friends, and the world at large.

A healthy relationship is one where the people respect each other and can be themselves without being criticized or corrected. When the person is mad at you, they still treat you with dignity. If the person has a moment where they don't treat you with dignity, they stop and apologize. And, of course, all of this goes both ways.

Security Blankets

There are always a few couples who date exclusively throughout high school. Parents and teachers think they're cute, and other students refer to them as married. But often one of the two eventually wants to hook up with other people but is unwilling to let go of the security blanket that the old relationship has become. If the boy wants to play the field ("I really think we should see other people, but I still want to see you, too") and the girl doesn't want to let go, she may feel that she has to go along with what he wants. She'll put up with his being nonexclusive in the hopes that he'll come back, because it's better to have something than nothing. She'll say she doesn't need or want monogamy when she really does. She doesn't communicate what she really wants, and instead hopes for the best.

The result is that they're still a couple, but they aren't technically going out. They can use this technicality to treat each other like dirt. They can still have sex with each other, but it will be casual sex to one and not to the other. The girl in this situation is in a terrible bind. She's upset about the status of the relationship but knows that she has no "right" to complain. If she does, her "agreement" will be thrown back in her face ("You said it was OK if we saw other people"), her feelings will be dismissed, and she'll have no one to blame but herself. The only thing she can do is create dramatic situations where she either drinks too much, does a lot of drugs, or does something reckless so he can come to her rescue. And he will, because he does still care for her, and her request fits in the "Act Like a Man" box. He feels special because he's the only one she wants to rescue or soothe her. The result of these dramatic moments are long (I'm talking hours), tear-filled conversations, often at a party, where the happy couple locks themselves in a room to discuss their relationship problems.

CHECKING YOUR BAGGAGE

- Did you ever date someone your parents didn't like? How did you react to their disapproval?
- Have you ever been sexually harassed? How did you handle it? How do you think your daughter would? How would you want her to?
- Did you ever go along with something a romantic partner wanted because you didn't know how to say no?

WHAT YOU CAN DO TO HELP

OK—I just described some difficult situations girls get into. Now I'm going to give you my best suggestions for how to address Girl World meets Boy World issues.

1. Teach your daughter to not blow off friends for a boy. This is an ironclad rule that begins when she's little. It doesn't matter if it's the love of her life; keeping her commitment to what she's promised is more important. Ask her about the unwritten code that says it's OK to blow off a friend for a guy. Where does it come from? What would happen if she told a guy she liked that she'd already made a commitment to someone else? Why would she like a guy if he wouldn't accept that she already had other plans? What's important to focus on with your daughter is that breaking or keeping plans has nothing to do with how much you like the person or vice versa. Keeping commitments is about honoring an agreement you made—regardless of the relationship you have with the person.
2. Help your daughter create criteria for dating on her own terms and on her own timetable. Remind her that every girl has her own pace and interest in guys, and wherever she is with that is fine.
3. Help your daughter frame her difficult conversations with boys using SEAL. For example, here's what she can say to a boy she wants to break up with:

Stop and Strategize: She thinks about what exactly she doesn't like and where she can tell him.

Explain: She articulates what she doesn't like. For example, "I don't feel respected when you're around your friends and you make fun of me or you laugh along with your friends when they're making fun of me. I don't want to hang out with you if that is going to happen."

Affirm: "I realize talking to your friends about it before going to you looks like I was going behind your back, and I'm sorry for that."

Lock: "Right now I feel more comfortable not hanging out or calling/texting/IMing each other." (He should feel respected as a person but still know that the relationship is over.)

Unfortunately, breakups are rarely clean and dignified. Most people aren't going to feel comfortable having an extended conversation about why your daughter doesn't want to date them any longer. Most will run away and lick their wounds privately. Sometimes they'll get angry and retaliate, doing things like this:

My friend dated a guy for only, like, two months when he went crazy. After she broke up with him, he was devastated. Apparently he felt the need to get back at her so he went on her Facebook and commented on every single picture she had taken on a trip with him with some version of "ruined," "fucking whore." This wasn't like one or two pictures, it was a full 60-photo album. Needless to say the album had to be deleted.

—Margaret, eighteen

Or he could do it the old-fashioned way by spreading rumors about her. If your daughter has this experience, here's an example of what she can say:

YOUR DAUGHTER: "You've been saying that I'm a slut/frigid bitch who wouldn't give it up. You've been posting pictures I sent you that I trusted you to keep private. You are calling me a whore. I have the right to break up with you without you attacking me. I can't stop you from doing it, but you need to stop immediately.

If you feel I disrespected you or you didn't have the chance to talk last time, I'm open to it, but only if you treat me respectfully."

4. Help your daughter respond to sexual harassment—this includes applying the same standard of behavior to boys. Just as she wants boys to respect her body, she must respect theirs as well. And remember, just because it's something you see every day doesn't mean it's right.

Because sexual harassment is so common, there is a good chance that the person who harasses your daughter doesn't realize his behavior is a problem. And if at all possible (meaning your daughter feels physically safe with this person) she should make the first attempt to stop it a one-on-one conversation with the harasser, using SEAL.

YOUR DAUGHTER (*Explain*): "Todd, can I talk to you for a minute? This is difficult for me to say, but I really need to talk to you and for you to take me seriously. When you hug me in the hall, I often feel like I'm being felt up. I need you to ease up a little. (*Affirm*): "We're friends so I want to be honest.

If he gets defensive or accuses her of sending mixed messages:

YOUR DAUGHTER: "You're my friend, and as your friend it's important for me to tell you when something is bothering me, that it's respected, and that you feel I'm doing the same for you. I'm sorry if you think I've sent mixed messages, so the next time you feel I'm doing that, you need to tell me directly."

If he knows that what he's doing is a problem:

YOUR DAUGHTER: "Todd, I need to talk to you. I want you to stop making comments to your friends when I walk by your locker. Maybe you believe girls like that kind of attention, but I want to be clear to you that I don't.

If he laughs at her:

YOUR DAUGHTER: "Let me be absolutely clear. I want you to stop. I have now asked you several times to stop. If you won't, you will force me to go to [best person in the school] for help."

If he does it again, she should go to her adult advocate in the school for assistance.

What if she does any or all these things to him? It is more than possible that your daughter could be on the giving side of things. She could be the one who gets dumped and goes after her ex. She could be the one who isn't respecting his boundaries. Just as you would with a son, sit down with your daughter and be clear about your expectations. She can't trash this boy online. She can't make fun of him if he breaks up with her. So just as you would talk to your daughter about her strategy when she is on the receiving end of these conflicts, you must be clear with her that being hurt and feeling rejected don't justify revenge.

YOU DON'T LIKE HER BOYFRIEND

Many parents have shared with me how unbearable it is to watch their daughter date someone they believe is unworthy.

Or is he? Before you pass judgment, invite the boy over to dinner and attempt to get to know him a little better. He may have more piercings than you would like, he might have horrible posture, or he may be shy. Forget all that. Does he treat your daughter respectfully? Is he polite? Does he seem to value her opinions? Many kids with green hair and tongue studs turn out to be terrific guys.

I'd make a huge effort to get to know him better by inviting him over to dinner. If I still didn't like him, I'd give her a factual list of why, like if he smokes or he's lazy about grades, not that he burps at dinner.

—Nina, seventeen

I have a policy that my best friend and I devised which originated sophomore year when I dated this guy named Rick who I was really into, but he could never get it together to call or see me. I knew he liked me, but he was just dumb. But my parents would always be on my case about it, and thus I would end up defending him! We then created the "Defending Rick" philosophy, which has come to describe just about every relationship I've encountered since then. The worst has been with Dylan (the one I'm struggling to break free of) because I've had to defend him in order for people to understand why I've let him back in my life after he broke my heart nine months ago.

—Carmen, eighteen

OK, you've tried your best and you still can't stand him. The thought of him makes your skin crawl. What can you do? Try to keep your mouth shut and wait for her to come to you. Girls want their parents and people they respect to approve of their boyfriends. When asked, you can be honest, but first check your baggage. If you don't like what he wears, forget about it. If you don't like the way he talks to your daughter, that's something else entirely.

If you dislike him for a superficial reason, you can say: "I may not like his choice of clothes, piercings, or hair color, but I respect your right to make your own decisions and I have faith that you want to be in a relationship with someone who treats you with respect. But please come and talk to me about it anytime and don't feel uncomfortable bringing him around."

If you dislike him for a good reason, you can say: "I would like to talk to you about Seth. Yesterday, when you came home from school together, I was really worried about how he was talking to you. Maybe I'm wrong or making too much of something, but I felt like he was belittling you. You have the right to have a boyfriend, but you also have the right to have a boyfriend that doesn't tell you things that make you feel bad about yourself or doubt yourself. What do you think about what I just said? Can you see why I'd think these things?"

To which your daughter will say, "Thanks, Mom/Dad, for telling me what you were feeling. I didn't see it before, but now that you've said it, you're right, and I'll break up with him right now." Yeah, right. And then the lotto van will back up to your driveway with your jackpot winnings, you'll fit into your high school jeans, and your gray hairs will disappear.

Or perhaps your daughter will flip out and tell you that you don't understand her relationship. Then you need to respond with "I'm not asking for answers or telling you I want you to stop seeing him. All I'm asking is for you to think about what I've said and talk to me later."

Last year I received a question from a parent whose daughter was dating someone who tweeted sexist jokes and lots of references to drinking and drugs. The daughter said to the mother that it was all a joke. But the mom was still worried . . . of course. I'd say to the daughter: "I know it's up to you to figure out who you want in your life. But as your parent, it's sometimes my responsibility to ask you uncomfortable questions. Twitter is your boyfriend's public face. If he doesn't do any of the things he posts about, why is it so important to him that other people think he does?" Remind her that the guy she chooses to date is a reflection on her, and ask whether she's comfortable with that. Don't expect your daughter to agree with you or to enthusiastically engage in a deep conversation about how she appreciates your good sense. This is a lot to take in. Finish by saying "If you don't want to talk about it now, I'd like you to think about it and then we can talk later." Make a point of checking in with her the next night before you go to bed, so if she has had some epiphanies—and hopefully she has—you can talk them over.

WHAT DO YOU DO IF YOU FIND OUT SHE'S SNEAKING BEHIND YOUR BACK?

The times when I get into trouble are when I'm sneaking around and can't talk to my parents.

—Grace, sixteen

I'm fourteen years old and a freshman in high school. Now, my parents have always been overprotective, but lately things have gotten out of hand. I love my parents, don't get me wrong, but sometimes they are just too much. My mom is more understanding, but my dad just will not listen to anything I have to say. I've gotten into multiple arguments with him before, and every time I try to get my point across he is always interrupting me, telling me that I'm wrong and that I don't make sense. He says that I shouldn't date because he doesn't want me getting distracted from my schoolwork. But the thing is that I'm doing perfectly well in school. I've also had a boyfriend for about two months now. I really want my parents to meet him, because he's such a nice guy and I know for a fact that they will love him once they get to know him. But they (especially my dad) are really quick to judge. But I really want to tell them that I'm actually dating him, so I wouldn't have to sneak around and lie about where I'm going all the time. How can I tell them the truth without having them freak out on me?

—Hayden, sixteen

I'm a fifteen-year-old girl with Hispanic parents, so they're really, like, protective when it comes to guys. I'm OK with them being concerned, just not going overboard. They believe I should just concentrate on school; there is no room for boys. I have a boyfriend that I do really like (no, I'm not going to say love, I don't think I know what that is yet). We have been "dating" for a month but I have known him for a year. It's getting real hard to see him since I always have to be sneaking around. I really don't want to keep lying to my parents, but I feel that if I tell them I will lose a lot of privileges. My mom always tells me that guys are a distraction from school, but I have actually continued getting straight A's. I wish my parents and I could communicate better; they still want to believe I don't know what sex is. Manuel, my boyfriend, doesn't really seem to pressure me into telling my parents, but I can tell he wants me to. He is a genuinely good guy and I

want my parents to know about us without them flipping out like they normally do with me. How do I ease them into the idea about me dating?

—Pilar, fifteen

Like so many girls, Pilar and Hayden understand their parents' concerns. However, they want their parents' approval and for their parents to recognize they can make good choices. This is what I say to girls who come to me for advice:

"Although I totally understand why you are sneaking, you have to stop, because eventually you'll make a mistake and get caught. Then your parents will be so mad about the sneaking that it will be harder for them to see the merits of your argument. Plus, they may also think that the boy is influencing you to sneak, so that doesn't put him in a very good light with them. And it is true that guys can be a major distraction. But if you are handling the distraction by keeping up your grades and your other responsibilities, then I think you go to them like this: 'Mom, Dad, I really respect you and I want you to be proud of me and the decisions I make. I know you don't want me to have a serious boyfriend but I really like a guy and I would like to go out with him. I'd like to go out to the movies with him. How can we work this out so I get a little more freedom and you feel good about how I'm conducting myself?' Now, if you get them to agree, it is *really important* that you abide by the terms. So if you say you will be back by 11 P.M., do yourself a favor and plan to get back home at 10:50—because you will lose all credibility if you don't do what you say."

HELP YOUR DAUGHTER RECOGNIZE AN ABUSIVE RELATIONSHIP

Of course, you want your daughter to have positive experiences with the people she dates, and no parent expects that their daughter will be involved in an abusive relationship. But if you know four girls (your daughter and three of her friends), you know a girl who has been or will be in an abusive relationship. How will you know, and how can you get her the help that she needs?

Girls don't get involved in abusive relationships out of the blue. They're vulnerable when certain ingredients combine. Those ingredients include wanting to be that someone special in another person's life, loving someone and wanting the best for them, being part of a community or family that doesn't admit that family violence could occur within it, seeing verbal and/or physical abuse in the family, and having a peer social system that measures social status based on a boyfriend.

WHAT IS ABUSE?

At its core, an abusive relationship is one in which one person verbally, emotionally, financially, and (oftentimes but not always) physically dominates, intimidates, and controls another. Abuse is at once terrifyingly simple and complex. "Why doesn't she leave?" people ask. Because she loves him and it's impossible to fall out of love overnight, even when the person who loves you treats you like dirt. Because she has been brought down so much that she has lost all confidence that she can make any sort of decision. Because her clique thinks they look good together. And even the most abusive relationships have good moments, especially because abusers can make you feel like the most special person in the world. If you love someone, you want to believe him. You see no other option, so you hope for the best.

Have you ever gone to a party and stayed later than you wanted to because a friend, spouse, boyfriend, or girlfriend wanted to stay? Ever gotten into a car with someone who drank enough wine at dinner that you knew they shouldn't be behind the wheel and you had no business being a passenger? I've done both. If you've stayed at that party or gotten into that car, you did so because you didn't want to offend someone, go against someone else's needs, or openly acknowledge that someone was doing something dangerous and irresponsible. Now imagine that if you did stand your ground, people would ridicule you or talk about you behind your back. If it's so hard to stand up to someone in these situations, imagine how hard it is for someone dealing with abuse.

Girls are particularly vulnerable to abusive relationships simply because of who they are—teens. They think in extremes and in

the short term (next year may as well be the next century), are prone to narcissism and drama, and have little experience with which to compare the relationship.

WHY WOULDN'T SHE TELL YOU?

It's not hard to imagine why your daughter wouldn't want to tell you if she's in an abusive relationship. Look at it from her point of view:

- She wants her privacy: Abusive relationships are maintained by creating a sacrosanct sphere around the couple.
- She thrives on intensity: She could be in love for the first time. An abusive relationship feels like a drug. She needs the fix. The lows are very low, but the highs are amazing. She can feel like the most loved person in the world. The drama reinforces the feeling that she's in a mature, adult relationship and it's them against the world.
- She feels special: She feels as if she's the only one who understands her boyfriend and can take care of him and save him.
- She's afraid of your response: She worries you won't let her see him anymore or date anyone else again for the rest of her life.
- She cherishes her independence: Because of this, she'll resist going to people she sees as authority figures. She could easily feel, rightly or wrongly, that if she seeks help, her newly gained independence will be taken away or her future relationships will be controlled.
- She's afraid of disappointing you: She's ashamed and feels as if she let you down. You may like him, and if she tells you what's happened, you won't like him. Or you tried to warn her, and she didn't listen.
- She's afraid she'll lose her status: Most likely she attends the same school and shares the same friends as her abuser. She could easily perceive her social status as dependent on her relationship with him.

- She's stubborn and feels invincible: She won't admit to anyone (sometimes including herself) that she's in over her head.
- She's inexperienced: She could believe that his jealousy and controlling behavior are expected and normal aspects of relationships, and may have little to compare them to. Perhaps she thinks texting and leaving voicemails every hour is healthy behavior. She could see both as proof of his love—that's why what she sees modeled in her home is so important!
- She feels helpless: She feels the abuser has complete power over her and that nothing will make it better.
- She's afraid he'll hurt others: He could threaten to hurt people, animals, or things she cares for.
- She feels like it's normal: She sees it in her own family and thinks she doesn't deserve better.

WHAT DOES ABUSE LOOK LIKE?

- She apologizes for his behavior (to herself and/or others).
- She's stressed out. She's hypervigilant and overreacts to minor incidents because she's living under extreme tension. Reacting to this kind of constant stress may cause her to explode or become hysterical over things she can give herself "permission" to do—such as lashing out at you.
- She gives up things or people that are important to her, such as after-school activities or friends.
- She has difficulty making decisions on her own, from the clothes she wears to what classes she wants to take. An abuser is very effective at making her feel that any decision she makes is stupid and a mistake, so she becomes paralyzed. She has to check with him for every decision, such as whether she can go somewhere.
- She changes her appearance or behavior because he asks her to.
- She comes home with injuries that she cannot explain, or whose explanation is inconsistent with the nature of the injury.

- She believes jealous, controlling behavior is an expression of love.
- She tries to be the "perfect" girlfriend and seems frightened of her abuser's reaction if she isn't. Or she believes if she can just be better in the ways he wants, he won't treat her badly. That way it becomes all her fault.

HOW SHOULD YOU TALK TO YOUR DAUGHTER IF YOU THINK SHE'S BEING ABUSED?

Do

- Ask about the relationship.
- Maintain open and respectful communication.
- Help her recognize controlling behaviors in the relationship.
- Use all resources at your disposal, including counseling, school, and the legal system.
- Check how often and how long she is spending online and texting with the person. (This would be an example of the importance of needing her passwords. If something goes wrong, you need to be able to see what she's been saying online.)
- Plan for her safety.
- Call your local domestic violence agency for help.
- Assure her confidentiality. If you need to tell someone else, ask her permission first. If you need to tell the police or other authorities, tell her first and then jointly agree about who she wants to talk to. Make a plan with her so she feels safe and in control.
- Appreciate that she believes that sometimes the relationship is good for her and that the two may feel that they're in love with each other. She may feel that she can't survive without her abuser.
- Ask "What can I do to help you?"
- Tell her that you're sorry she feels bad, but you know that you can't understand how she's feeling. (Teens hate it when adults pretend they know what teens are feeling, unless they have their own story to prove they do.)

- Ask questions to help her recognize that her relationship is abusive.
- Support her courage for asking for help and respect her limits. You're helping her establish boundaries with others, including yourself. For example, if she wants to remain in an abusive relationship, don't tell her that her decision is wrong, but do tell her that you're worried for her safety and help her see the danger she's placing herself in. Explain to her how you would intervene if you felt she was in immediate physical danger.
- Help her recognize that the explanations and excuses for his violence don't justify his behavior.
- Help her see that her feelings are valid. The abuser does not have the right to dismiss her feelings or recollection of events.

Don't

- Present her with ultimatums. Don't make her feel that she has to choose between you and her abuser.
- Assume she wants to leave or that you know what's best for her. If you make decisions for her, you reinforce that she can't make decisions for herself.
- Ask what she did to "provoke him." This type of question reinforces her feelings of self-blame.
- Talk to her and the abuser together.
- Take secondhand information. If you want to use information, say what it is and then ask "Is any part of that accurate from your perspective?"
- Pressure her into making decisions.
- Threaten or physically attack the abuser. Not only is this dangerous, but it will likely make her side with the abuser.

HOW TO SPOT A POTENTIAL ABUSER

- Exploits a victim's sympathy and guilt.
- Lashes out, name calling, or demeaning.
- Causes fear through intimidating statements and actions.
- Calls persistently or texts incessantly.

- Shows up without warning at home, at classes, or at an after-school job.
- Follows him/her.
- Tries to enlist family and friends in attempts to maintain the relationship.
- Possessive to the point of controlling behavior.
- Fights with others about the intimate partner.
- Makes public displays of anger or ridicule toward men or women.
- Feels entitled—the community's rules do not apply.
- Has a two-faced personality. Charming in public and mean and degrading in private.
- Abusive toward others, especially small children or animals.

You'll never have a more important opportunity to practice your listening skills. Remind your daughter that she has more courage and resilience than she knows, and that no matter what, you're there for her.

YOU WILL ALL GET THROUGH THIS

In preparing yourself for the worst, it's easy to forget that watching your daughter learn to navigate more adult relationships can be fulfilling for you both. Remember, this can be your time to shine. You can model positive, honest, caring, loving relationships with men. Dad, if she comes up against a guy who is treating her poorly, she'll know by your example that it's not right and that she doesn't have to take it. Mom, you are an important role model, too. Show her by your own actions how to have loving relationships based on mutual respect and equality. All of this can be overwhelming, but as an involved parent you can guide her toward respectful, responsible relationships.

Sex, Drugs, Alcohol, and Partying in Girl World

People say your friends will change in high school and you never believe them and then they do. One of my friends does drugs now; I don't even know who she is. I haven't talked to her in two months.

—Makayla, fourteen

I was eighteen, my sister Morgan was fifteen. The party started out as this well-organized little event, and I was the cool big sister that got us booze from another friend, and all our friends were hanging out and then Morgan totally lost it. She drank almost a full 12-oz. water bottle full of vodka by herself. She couldn't sit up or open her eyes. She was 5'8" and 110 pounds. Then her best friend pulled me into my room and told me that the reason Morgan was so drunk was because she wasn't eating. She was never, ever eating. How at school she would always say she'd already eaten and her friends thought she was throwing up. Before that moment, I had suspicions that she had an eating disorder but after that, all of how she had been acting fell into place. But I remember thinking, "How do I tell my mom what I've seen and heard without getting us both in trouble?" Because part of the proof was in how badly she handled her booze.

—Emma, twenty

WE WILL GET THROUGH THIS CHAPTER!

WORD HAS SPREAD

Gabby is in tenth grade. On a Thursday night, Gabby's mom tells her that her grandmother slipped on black ice in the driveway and broke her ankle. She'll be in the hospital overnight and needs help getting home and through the weekend. Her grandmother lives six hours away, so Gabby's mom plans to leave right after work tomorrow. Then Gabby's dad decides to go because he doesn't want her to make the trip alone. They don't want to leave Gabby behind, but she has a big paper due Monday that she needs to finish over the weekend.

On Friday morning, Gabby tells her friends Anna and Kara what happened to her grandmother and says she wants to have people over Saturday night—but with some ground rules. They have to decide who can come, the parking strategy (because everyone can't park in front of the house or they'll arouse suspicion from the neighbors), no hanging out in the front yard, and all smoking has to be outside. An hour later Gabby texts fifteen of her friends: *Small PARTY Sat. 10 PM My house! Be there!* At Anna's request, Gabby invites Tye, Anna's forever on-again, off-again boyfriend, and Colin, his best friend.

The night begins:

8:30: Pregaming begins. The girls get dressed, put on music, and drink whatever they can find in the liquor cabinet.

9:30: People arrive. Gabby is momentarily anxious about the number of people in her house but then she looks around and tells herself to calm down. It's only fifteen people. They're all following her rules. There's nothing to worry about. No one is trashing anything. It's all good.

WHAT YOU SHOULD KNOW

- When parents go out of town, even the "best" kids have a hard time resisting the temptation to have a party. Teens can be like caged animals. They are acutely aware of opportunities for freedom and usually jump on these opportunities in

case they don't happen again. The risk feels worth the possible consequence.

- There are some girls who don't drink, do drugs, send naked pictures of themselves to boys, or have random sex. But many of them have friends who do and who could drag them into difficult and potentially dangerous situations.
- Teens trust one another. At parties, it's common for a girl to meet someone she doesn't know well but feels she does simply because he goes to the same or a nearby school, and/or has friends in common.
- Girls love having a reputation for having a high tolerance to alcohol, and they'll drink themselves under the table proving it.
- Pregaming (hanging out before a party) is a sacred ritual where girls drink, get dressed, and dance. You don't eat during the pregame because then it's harder to get drunk.
- The postgame analysis is also a sacred ritual where girls usually eat, discuss who got together with whom, who humiliated themselves, and who got totally wasted.
- Teens in any community know which parents will let them party in their house. The worst offenders are the Hip Parents I referred to on page 75. These are the parents who buy alcohol, give it to their kids, lie to other adults, and justify their actions by saying, "I'd rather they drink at my house than somewhere else where they can get into more trouble." These parents are ruthlessly manipulated and ridiculed by their own children and everyone else's children.

When you party at a friend's house and their parents let you do it, you know you're going behind your parents' back but there's something really wrong with other parents doing it. I had one friend whose mom let us drink at her house and then she'd sit next to my mom at swim meets and chat. She was the one who would call my mom and say, "The girls are sleeping over at my house and everything's cool," and then let us drink. I feel really bad about it now and I never had any respect for those parents.

—Emily, twenty

MEANWHILE, ON PARTY NIGHT...

Saturday, 7:00: Tye invited Ally, a ninth grader, to Gabby's party. Ally doesn't know Gabby, and this will be her first high school party. When she asked Tye if she could bring a friend, he said sure, but jokingly (she thinks) said her friend had to be hot. Ally's parents wouldn't approve of her going to the party, so she lied and told them she'd be going to the movies with Bianca and sleeping over at her house. Ally and Bianca are really excited about going to the party. No one else in their grade was invited, and they want to look good, not like pathetic freshmen trying too hard to be cool.

9:00: Ally's dad drives them to "the movie" while Ally sits in the back and texts Tye that they'll be at the mall in ten minutes. As they walk away, Ally's dad wonders if he should have checked in with Bianca's parents but doesn't know their cell numbers. He brushes off his concern while watching the girls walk away and thinks how lucky he is that Ally is steering away from everything he did in high school.

9:30: Tye and Colin pick them up. They drive to Gabby's house while Tye talks to Colin about a lot of people Bianca and Ally don't know but have heard about and who seem very cool.

10:00: They arrive at Gabby's house. Tye and Colin are greeted by a group of guys with affectionate yells and grunts. Ally thinks she hears one of the guys say "Easy" under his breath as she walks by.

10:05: Tye and Colin start drinking. Tye asks Ally if she wants a Watermelon Mimosa Smirnoff Ice. She's conflicted. She wants the drink, but she also doesn't want to be one of those freshman girls who gets really drunk and makes a total fool of herself. As she's deciding what to do, she realizes that a group of girls are standing by the sink and one in particular is looking at her with full-on hatred. Ally grabs the drink. Tye introduces Ally and Bianca to Anna and Kara. Anna responds by refusing to acknowledge Ally's existence. Tye shrugs and pulls Ally out of the room behind him, which prompts the following conversation.

KARA: "Please tell me you aren't going to let him ruin your night. He's just doing it to rub it in your face! It's so obvious! She's a freshman. How much more obvious can you get?"

GABBY: "Who is she? Can you believe what she was wearing?"

KARA: "She can't help herself. She's a pathetic freshman. Seriously, Anna, he so clearly invited her just so he can use her.
Please tell me you're over him. He's such a loser."

ANNA: "Yeah, I can't believe he would bring such a little skank . . ."

10:10: Anna pulls out a bottle of Smirnoff Raspberry vodka
and fumes, "How dare he embarrass me like this and bring that
little slut here? I'll show him he can't do this to me and get away
with it."

10:12: Anna grabs Kara and drags her to the living room, where
they start dancing together.

> I was at a party and watched a girl who weighs a hundred
> pounds and had never drunk before have five shots of vodka
> in fifteen minutes. Her eyes rolled back into her head, she fell
> on the ground, and she was twitching. It was scary and we
> had no idea what to do. Someone eventually took her to the
> hospital.
>
> —Emma, fifteen

> If I see a hot guy and he's drinking beer, I try to avoid going
> up to him because I know it'll be really hard to say no. Half
> the time I'm successful.
>
> —Lynn, sixteen

> When you're at a party, the real girl comes out. A lot of girls
> say, "I don't need drugs. I don't drink beer." Then you see
> someone you like and they're really cute and this is one of
> the few times when you can really talk, so you'll do it [drink
> or do drugs].
>
> —Nia, eighteen

> When a girl gets drunk at a party, guys look at her like it's a
> golden opportunity. She's vulnerable.
>
> —Matt, seventeen

11:00: Gabby is now in full police mode. She stopped drinking
hours ago because she's so busy making sure people don't trash

the house. She looks over at Anna and Kara, who are being encouraged to make out with each other by some guys—and they do. All the boys start clapping and laughing. Anna smiles, takes a swig out of the bottle of vodka, and walks out. Kara follows Anna out to make sure Anna doesn't do anything stupid and then gives up because she's sick of cleaning up after Anna's messes.

> When it's your own party, you can't really drink that much because you have to make sure nothing gets out of hand so people trash things or the cops show up. But even if they [the cops] do shut down the party, you still had the party so it's worth it.
>
> —Maddy, seventeen

> Parents need to realize that Gabby in this situation thinks she's being responsible, even though she knows she's not allowed to have this party.
>
> —Jaden, sixteen

Meanwhile, Ally is at a table in the kitchen having a great time sitting on Tye's lap playing drinking games. Tye keeps telling her how good she is. She's not sure where Bianca is, but the last time she saw her, she was dancing with Colin in the living room. Meanwhile, Bianca is getting a little worried about Ally, but she doesn't know how to bring it up and get her away from Tye.

11:30: Gabby is miserable. She just went into her parents' room and found two random people in their bed. It dawns on her that she's going to have to clean the sheets before her parents get home.

11:30: Ally becomes aware that the girl who had been giving her death stares is now above her, arms crossed.

ANNA: "Tye, we need to talk right now."
TYE: "Can it wait? I'm sort of busy right now."
ANNA: "No, it's really important."

Tye follows Anna out, leaving Ally behind to continue playing drinking games with his friends. As soon as they're outside, Anna

falls apart crying, and Tye tells her that he still cares a lot for her but wants to be able to do his own thing. He suggests doing something next weekend, after his game. When they come back inside, Anna goes back to Kara to dissect the conversation with Tye, and Tye goes back to Ally.

TYE: "Let's go somewhere else, away from my crazy ex."

ALLY: "Sure, but is she OK?"

TYE: "Oh yeah, she's fine. Come on, let's get away from all these people."

They go to a bedroom; he closes the door, locks it ("So no one will bother us"), and sits on the bed with her. He confides in Ally that he used to go out with Anna and he's tried to let her down nicely, but she just won't drop it. But he's really glad Ally is here. Tye kisses her, and Ally can't believe she's hooking up with a guy like Tye. A few minutes later, he pushes her back so she's lying on the bed. Ally laughs nervously and says, "Maybe I should check on Bianca. She seemed pretty drunk." Tye keeps kissing her and now he's putting his hand up her shirt while he says, "Bianca's fine. I've been wanting to get you alone all night." Tye keeps going and Ally laughs nervously again and kisses him back.

Why Is It So Hard for Ally to Hold Her Own in This Situation?

There is a chance that Tye and Ally make out and that's it. But it's far more likely that Ally will do whatever Tye wants her to do, which could run the spectrum of making out to giving him a blow job to having sexual intercourse. Overall, she's not the one in control, he is. Why? The most obvious reason is that she's been drinking. But that's only the beginning.

- She's flattered that he's paying attention to her in the first place, because he's older and has higher social status.
- She feels special because Tye is confiding in her (and, in her mind, someone does that only when you trust the person and are close to them). He knows that telling Ally that another, older girl covets him makes Ally feel special. Now

Ally is part of the drama—with a senior, no less—and it feels good because it feels like she won.

- She doesn't want Tye to get mad at her and stop liking her.
- If she pushes him away, he'll think she's immature or a prude.
- She may want to do something sexual with him, but she hasn't ever thought about her own sexual boundaries, and now is an almost impossible time to start making them.
- She believes that if she gives him what he wants, he'll want to have a relationship with her. And because he confided in her, they're already on their way to couplehood.
- For his part, Tye has grown up conditioned by the "Act Like a Man" box to be unintentionally or intentionally blind and deaf to the subtle, or sometimes very obvious, signs that he has created a situation where it's virtually impossible for Ally to tell him what she wants or doesn't (from trying to distract him with the Bianca question, or other possible statements and body language that communicate her discomfort).

In general, I'm not a big proponent of statistics, because they can be easily manipulated to prove what you want. But sexual assault statistics have consistently shown that the vast majority of sexual assaults, including rape, occur when girls are between the ages of eleven and eighteen; and the perpetrator is someone they know and of the same racial and socioeconomic background. In other words, sexual assault is rarely perpetrated by a crazed stranger who jumps out of the bushes. It is much more likely to happen at parties like the one I just described.

I hear versions of this story constantly. A girl walks up to me before class, eyes down, and whispers that she wants to talk to me after class. Later, she'll tell me, often with tears welling in her eyes, "Last Saturday night, I went to this party . . . and I sort of hooked up with this guy. He seemed so nice and I don't really know what happened . . ."

The older girls' feelings of competition only make the younger ones more vulnerable at the hands of the boys who are proving they belong in the "Act Like a Man" box. Even though they probably had the same experiences when they were her age, many ju-

nior and senior girls believe that a younger girl deserves to make her own mistakes. Like Anna and Kara at the party, older girls justify their behavior by saying "What was she doing all over him like that? What did she expect? She should know better. Freshmen know they're just being used."

They don't. As much as a ninth-grade girl may tell you she knows this, when she's in the situation, most girls will think they're the exception. In the moment, she believes the guy really likes her. Meanwhile, the older girls spread around their version of events, so this fourteen-year-old girl has not only just been coerced into sex but also has been labeled a slut in the process.

> *If you are a guy and you can figure this stuff out, you can play girls off each other. All a guy needs to do is tell her she's pretty.*
>
> —Katy, fifteen

Are All These Girls Really Lesbians?

At the party, Kara and Anna made out with each other in front of the boys. Many parents hear stories about girls making out with each other and want to know what this means. Are the girls lesbians? Are there more lesbians than there used to be? Why? Is it a phase? What's going on here?

Here's the way I see it. Yes, it has become cool to make out with a girl—particularly in front of other boys. But this doesn't necessarily mean that these girls are gay. In fact, girls making out in front of boys can be more about trying to turn the boys on than their sexual attraction to each other. These girls are "crazy," "fun," and "open-minded." That's not about being lesbian; that's about pleasing boys. There's nothing more heterosexist than that. Of course, it can also be a cover for girls who really are sexually attracted to other girls but aren't ready to admit that to themselves.

No matter who your daughter is attracted to, your job is to accept that and love her unconditionally. And, of course, everyone must be treated with dignity—period. What you don't want your daughter doing is expressing her sexuality and being sexually active only to please someone else and be objectified.

I'm gay and I have straight girls who ask me to make out with them at parties. I really don't like it. I feel used. I don't feel respected for who I am because they're only asking me to do this for the guys.

—Simone, sixteen

GETTING ATTENTION: WHATEVER THE COST

I don't care if we're talking about girls making out with each other in front of other guys, wearing T-shirts that say "#1 Porn Star," sending pictures of themselves to guys they want to impress, doing a striptease, or having sex with multiple boys in one night—it is all related to trying to get attention, no matter the cost to your dignity. The girls I know who do this have a couple of things in common. They are slaves to the consumer, celebrity culture—and their parents are usually right along with them. They don't have things in their lives that they feel good about—beyond what they wear and what they have. They don't have adults in their lives who unconditionally love them but also hold them accountable.

At my school if a girl doesn't hook up it's because she's either not attractive, a prude, or a lesbian until proven otherwise (the same thing is for a boy). It's sad but it's true. Thus the girls here crave the attention of the boys. They must be the hottest to win. There are girls that will have sex with boys on the first hookup. When I started at this school, I learned of something called the rule of 3 . . . meaning you should be getting pretty far (if not the furthest) by the third hookup. But at the same time we have girls that as freshmen will have sex with boys even before the foreplay. I guess what I'm trying to get at is that yes there is an expectation for girls here but it seems to me that most of the girls that participate go above and beyond the expectations.

—Nathan, seventeen

I want you to understand that there is a possibility that your daughter could do any or all of the things I listed above. If you

don't give her a strong sense of self and make her feel valued for her character, she can fall prey to needing this kind of attention. And she sees role models all around her in this culture to show her how to do it.

DRUGS AND ALCOHOL

You don't want to be the drama drunk. You want to be the fun drunk. The girl who plays drinking games and drinks just enough that she's fun, social, flirty, but not throwing yourself on anyone, and not so wasted that someone has to take care of you. You are in such a good mood that you'll do anything.
                                                    —Annie, seventeen

Alcohol and drugs are a part of everyone's life—whether you drink or use any kind of drugs is not the point. And if you have cough syrup and an old prescription of Valium or Xanax in your medicine cabinet, you have exactly what a lot of teens are looking for to get high. But, seriously, cough syrup will do. You just add it to a can of Red Bull and you're good to go.

Where are your children getting alcohol and drugs? This is what my students answered:

    Your liquor cabinet—and filling bottles back up with water or
        similar-color liquid
    Fake IDs
    Shoulder tapping (when a teen gives an adult money to buy
        alcohol)
    Older friends
    Older siblings
    Younger siblings (especially if they have a prescription for
        ADHD, depression, anxiety, and so forth)
    Visiting grandparents
    House-sitting/babysitting
    Buying from a dealer at school or in the neighborhood
    Garage hopping (usually takes place in the suburbs where kids
        can take alcohol out of garages of friends)

PRESCRIPTION DRUGS

Maybe you know the smell of pot from five hundred feet away or the telltale red eyes and slurred words when someone is drunk. But in my experience, far fewer people know the signs of prescription drug abuse. In general, they are as follows:

Uppers/Stimulants
    Dilated pupils
    Nervous or "on edge"
    Loss of appetite and weight loss
    Euphoria/enhanced movements
    Preoccupation with constructing and deconstructing objects
    Compulsive grooming
    Profuse perspiration
    Dehydration
    Jaw clenching/teeth grinding
    Muscle twitching/jitteriness

Depressants/Antianxiety Medications/Sedatives
    Extreme sleepiness/fatigue
    Impaired coordinated/slurred speech
    Paranoia/mood swings
    Short attention span
    Slow, shallow breathing
    Desensitization/numbness to pain
    Constricted pupils
    Itching
    Flushing

CHECKING YOUR BAGGAGE

- When you were a teen, did you drink or do drugs? Was it fun? Did you use it as an escape? What were you running away from?
- Are you conflicted about how to talk to your child about alcohol and drugs?
- Have you ever been drunk and/or high and done something

(either as a teen or adult) you wouldn't have if you'd been sober?

- What are the ways you run away and escape from problems? Why?
- What would your child say is your position about their use of alcohol and drugs? Would they think your words are consistent with your actions?
- Do you still use alcohol and/or recreational drugs? Does it impact your relationships?

WHAT YOU CAN DO

When most parents think about what can happen to their daughters at parties, their first instinct is to put their Rapunzels up in the tower and throw away the key. But parties are a part of life. Your best bet is to help your daughter enjoy herself responsibly at the parties she throws and those she attends. That means she has to take certain steps to make sure she's safe, thinks clearly about her boundaries ahead of time, and understands the situations that will compromise those promises to herself.

IF SHE'S GIVING THE PARTY

And you thought the boy-girl invitation issue was a tough one. If your daughter wants to host a party when she's in high school, don't veto the idea out of hand. Certainly there are downsides: It's your house that could get trashed; it's your house the police will visit if the volume on the stereo is up too high; and in some parts of the country, it's you who will be held accountable if guests break the law on your premises or after leaving your premises. On the plus side, letting your daughter host the party gives you a chance to supervise her and model how a party should go, and provides an opportunity to meet her friends and observe them in action.

Sit with your daughter beforehand and write down guidelines for both of you. For example, you can insist that there will be no drinking or drugs, that admission is by invitation only (that is, she can't let in anyone she doesn't know, even if it's a "friend

of a friend"—she can blame you if her friends complain), and that the number of people invited not exceed a predetermined limit. You can insist that you will be on the premises during the party. She can ask that you stay upstairs unless she needs your help and/or you're concerned the party is getting out of hand. You may want to discuss what that means, because your definitions could be different. You think having a hundred people in your home is too much, while she thinks that's a definition of a successful party. Clarify under what circumstances you will interrupt the party (too loud, evidence of alcohol or drugs, too late) and the actions you will take (escorting guests out personally, calling parents). Go over her personal degree of accountability, including rules for reimbursement of costs and cleanup. Remind her once again that you'll act as the "eternal out"—her guests have to stick to the rules "because Mom and Dad said so, and they'd kill me if we broke them."

If you're harboring any notion of becoming a Hip Parent (see chapter 3) and buying beer or other alcohol for the party, remember that teens are ridiculing you behind your back and you're exposing yourself to long-term risk that really just doesn't justify the short-term reward of sucking up to a bunch of adolescents.

> Parents who buy the alcohol and have the parties at their house think they have the control, but they don't. They never do in high school parties. They assume that if their kids have the party at their house instead of going to someone else's, they don't get up to trouble. Why don't parents get how wrong they are?
>
> —Malia, fifteen

> My friend's mom has no control over her kids because she drank and did drugs when she was young so she feels hypocritical about it. So she just lets them drink.
>
> —Faith, sixteen

> Teens and parents drink together. During the summer, my parents and their friends wake up, have coffee, go to the

beach, and then start drinking and they don't stop until late—
like 2 a.m. They're so drunk that they aren't paying attention
when their kids walk by the cooler and pick out whatever
they want.

—Morgan, fourteen

BUSTED: THE UNPLANNED PARTY

It's not fun to contemplate, but your daughter might take advantage of your plans to go out of town to throw a party at your house. The best way to prevent this is not only to have a clear conversation about why you won't allow this (which should focus largely on safety issues), but to have a trusted friend or relative stay at the house with your daughter. Yes, she'll complain that you don't trust her and are treating her like a baby, but your house and child will be safe.

Signs She's Planning a Party
- You have the feeling that your daughter is rushing you out of the house.
- You find a large amount of Doritos or other junk food in her closet.
- She's nervous and superficially nice around you.
- She's a little too helpful around the house or with anything you need to do to get ready for the trip.
- She's superfocused on the details of your trip, such as when you're leaving, getting back, and so forth.
- You look at her texts and see that she's planning a party.

Signs There's Been a Party at Your House
- Fresh carpet stains and scuff marks on the walls.
- Empty food cabinets and/or refrigerator.
- Mysterious items of clothing found about the house.
- The outside of your house is littered with cigarette butts.
- The house is cleaner than when you left it; the carpets are so recently vacuumed that you can see the vacuum marks, and the trash cans in the rooms are all empty.

- Your daughter tells you she had a couple of friends over, then jokes about having a party (to distract you from the fact that she really did have one).
- You ask another parent who is Facebook friends with a friend of your daughter's to scan her profile for recently posted pictures, and she sees kids partying in your house.
- There is not one roll of toilet paper anywhere in the house.
- She's really nice to you.
- When you ask her what she did over the weekend, her answers are very specific.

Usually when our parents ask us how we are or about what we did, we say "Fine" and "Nothing." But if we had a party, we talk to our friends so we all agree about what we did. So if we talk to the parent about the movie we went to and how much we liked it, we had a party.

—Lynn, sixteen

What do you do if you make plans to be out of town and learn your daughter is about to have a party? It depends on when you find out. If you find out twenty-four hours or more before, cancel your plans if possible and stay home. (If you leave, she may have the party anyway because she'll feel she has nothing to lose.) If you can't stay in town, leave her with a relative or family friend, or have an ally who has a strong backbone stay at the house (otherwise, she may have the party anyway).

If you find out on the day of the party, take her cellphone and tell anyone who calls that the party is canceled. Monitor the door so you can assure guests that the party is off. If you can't cancel your plans, have a friend or relative go over to your house and monitor the phone and door. Around eight P.M. turn off all the lights in the house. If it's warm enough, the adult can sit on the front steps and tell the people the party is off. Then ground her and cut off her lines of communication for at least two weeks.

If you find out when you're away, then there's nothing wrong with your children having a healthy dose of fear—the kind of fear that stops your daughter in her tracks from doing something really

stupid, irresponsible, and/or dangerous because she thinks "If my mom finds out I had this party instead of babysitting like I told her, I'm dead."

This is also why you need to have at least one neighbor who will watch over the house and have no problem breaking up the party if he or she sees kids over there. Punish your child when you return. If you've caught her sneaking out to go or come back from a party, waiting in the dark and watching her quietly sneak back into her room is always fun, and you definitely have the surprise factor on your side when you flip on the lights. Listen patiently as she attempts to correctly get out the logistics of the excuse she tried to memorize on her way home.

> *My mom always had her sister drive by and check around 11:30. She didn't trust my older sister at all.*
>
> —Becky, sixteen

IF YOU KNOW SHE'S GOING TO A PARTY

- Speak to the parent who is hosting the party, introduce yourself, and tell them who your daughter is if they don't already know.
- By all means ask if the party is going to be supervised but realize that the Hip Parents are going to lie to you or think they're telling you the truth when their actual plan is to show the kids the liquor cabinet and go upstairs to their room.
- Set a curfew and tell that to the hosting parent.

In general I think the best strategy for letting your child go to a party is to pick them up at the end of the night—meaning at the time you have set their curfew. That means your child knows in the back of her mind that she has to be sober enough to see you at the end of the night. As a peace offering (because your daughter likely will hate this plan), I would extend the curfew by thirty minutes and offer to pick her up around the block so you don't embarrass her. Or you can try to get the ally to be her pickup. I would also give a ride home to any other kid who wants to leave. If that

happens and you think the kid is slightly drunk, I would give them amnesty from calling their parents—but I would tell your child your suspicions. If the child is clearly drugged or incapacitated, I would let the parent know when you drop the child off.

I know there are parents who think that it's safer to let the kids sleep over wherever they end up. I don't think so. If your daughter knows she can sleep out under these circumstances, you are giving her a free pass to get as messed up as possible. And even known and trusted hosts have to go to sleep. Once that happens, all bets are off. Someone could be sober and get really upset, "have to go home now," get their keys, and get into an accident on the way home. Someone could bring out drugs they've been stashing until it was safe for them to come out. Just do everyone a favor and bring your daughter home.

IF SHE'S GONE TO A PARTY
AND YOU DIDN'T KNOW

If you discover she's at a party, you need to drive over and pick her up. Even if she hasn't had a sip of alcohol, just being tired from the night or stressed out because you know what's up can severely impair her ability to drive safely. Once you know where she is, tell her to remain there until you come to get her. Leave immediately, and try to go alone—taking siblings is unnecessarily embarrassing, and taking a spouse along might make it seem like it's two on one and immediately put her on the defensive.

> If you want her home, go get her yourself. That'll embarrass her enough so that she won't ever do it again.
>
> —Alex, eighteen

> Under no circumstances should you yell or call her and say, "You need to get home now." I know a lot of parents who freak out when their child is past curfew or out doing something they shouldn't be. When the parents call up and start yelling, it puts a lot of added stress on the kid and then they drive badly. Have her take a taxi or Uber. You shouldn't add stress to driving.
>
> —Katelyn, eighteen

You might not know that she's been to a party, however, until she stumbles in the back door or her friends pull into the driveway at three A.M. Don't let her put herself to bed to simply "sleep it off" and plan on confronting her the next morning—we've all heard those tragic stories where she never wakes up for that confrontation. If her friends are drunk or high, get them inside. Take their keys and call their parents. It isn't your job to punish them, but you can communicate your anger with putting themselves and your daughter in danger. If they, too, are physically impaired, you should take care of them as best you can until their parents arrive to take over.

Once you have your daughter home or in the car, take the following steps:

- Keep in mind that your primary concern is her health. Rid your mind of all punishment ideas until after she's physically stable. Your letting her know this is key to the next step. Say, "I don't want you worrying about what your punishment will be. Right now, I just want to know what's in your body and how much of it there is so that I can take care of you."
- Establish her physical condition—ideally, she'll respond honestly. If she is either incapacitated or unwilling to share, you might have to do some guesswork.
- Give her lots of food and water.
- If she is vomiting or feels like she might, encourage it—her body needs to get rid of the alcohol.
- When you finally put her to bed, make sure that she's on her side so that if she vomits in her sleep, she doesn't choke. Even if she seems OK when going to bed, her body may still be processing alcohol and not have recognized the true level in her system.
- Check on her throughout the night.
- If she is unconscious, has slow/shallow/irregular breathing, does not withdraw from painful stimuli, is choking on vomit, has blue-tinged or unusually pale skin, or is seizing, seek immediate professional medical help—she may have alcohol poisoning or be under the influence of drugs, and it's beyond your abilities to help her.

The next morning, don't give her a vacation—she made the decision to party, and that doesn't mean she gets to sleep in until three that afternoon. In fact, getting her up early for breakfast with the family and chores might be enough, in combination with a hangover, to deter her from repeating the night before. It also shows her the direct consequences of her actions, and she can better connect what she's done to her punishment. Take her aside to talk one-on-one. Emphasize that last night is exactly why you set rules in place against alcohol and drug use, and then use SEAL to communicate.

> *The worst is when they wake up really early and you have to do all the chores and they're in a good mood but they won't tell you if there's any other punishment. So you do your best all day and think, "OK, if I do a really good job, then maybe I'll get out of this" and then you sit down at the dinner table and bam, your life is over.*
>
> —Sam, eighteen

GOLDEN RULES FOR BEING A GUEST

Parties are fun, and there's nothing horrible about your daughter wanting to go to one. You just need to teach her how to act responsibly while she's there.

If you live in a community where there are reliable taxis, always make sure she has enough money for a ride home. Or allow her to use Uber and charge it to your account. In both cases, I'd prefer if she went home with a friend so she's not riding home alone. Also, teach your daughter that you don't leave a friend behind. You at least hold her hair while she's throwing up, and get her a glass or two of water.

SAFETY IN NUMBERS

Overall, the best strategy for your daughter's safety at a party is to have good friends who will look out for her and vice versa. She needs the buddy system now more than ever. She needs to strat-

egize with one or two close friends before the party about how they will look out for each other. Do they need a signal that says "Bail me out"? If your daughter pairs off with a date to a secluded part of the house, does she have an agreement in place that a friend will come looking for her in five minutes to make sure everything's OK? It needs to be absolutely clear that no matter what, their sacrosanct bond is to watch out for each other.

Let's go back to the moment at the party where Bianca thought she should find Ally. She has a friend who has been drinking and has gone somewhere isolated with a guy. If your daughter were in Bianca's place, what could she do? Here is an effective intervention strategy:

> Go up to her friend (or even knock on the door if the girl is already in a room) and say, "I really need to talk to you privately. It's really important." If she gets any resistance from her friend, or if the guy says, "Hey, everything's cool," she can say, "I'm having my period and I need a tampon. So I need to get one from her bag."

EVERY GIRL'S GOLDEN RULES
FOR GOING TO A PARTY

Go with a friend you trust.

Have a code word between you that means "You need to help me get away from this situation right now."

Have another code word that means "You, my friend, have drunk way too much and you are making really bad decisions, so you need to do what I am telling you without arguing with me."

Don't leave drinks unattended.

Don't accept open containers at parties.

Watch the person pour your drink.

***Never* leave your friend because she's gotten really wasted and is now making a fool of herself and embarrassing you. Take her with you.**

---

*Ninth-grade girls should not go to parties with older kids—period. Nothing good can come of it. If your daughter hates you for imposing this rule, have her read this chapter and blame me.

**High school girls, including seniors, should not go to college parties with their older siblings, cousins, or friends for the same reason.

TALK TO YOUR DAUGHTER ABOUT
ALCOHOL, DRUGS, AND SEX

By now, I hope I've convinced you to see how the issues facing girls are interrelated. The decision-making skills your daughter needs are the same no matter what she's making the decision about, whether it's deciding to smoke cigarettes or pot, drink, or have sex. Your role as a parent is to communicate your values and ethics on the subject, help your daughter clarify her own, and teach her how to communicate her boundaries to others and act on her principles.

Your strategy for talking about alcohol, drugs, and sex should follow the same principles:

1. Recognize that they surround your daughter.
2. Talk *with* (not *to*) her regularly.
3. Be clear about your rules and expectations.
4. Be consistent. Your actions must match what you're telling her.
5. Leave a door open for later conversations.
6. Don't be shocked and take it personally when she doesn't follow your rules.
7. Be clear about consequences and follow through.
8. Don't live in denial!

TALK ABOUT PEER PRESSURE

> Peer pressure—where there are groups of people pressuring you to do something—doesn't happen anymore. It's not like they say, "Everyone's doing it, so come on." People are normally cool with your decision to not drink or do drugs. The only time when you will do it is when you want to fit in with an elite group or you want to impress a guy.
>
> —Sydney, fifteen

What else is peer pressure but people you perceive to be cool or better than you convincing you to do something you don't want to do? Peer pressure today is subtle and internalized. Kids doing drugs or drinking are not going to say to someone "If you want to be our friend or be cool, you have to drink." Or "Come on and do it. All the cool people are." It's much more sophisticated. Drugs and alcohol are so much a part of teen culture that the motivation to drink and do drugs comes from an internal pressure to belong, not from someone standing over you with a joint forcing you to smoke.

"JUST WALK AWAY"

One of the more ineffective things to tell your daughter about sex, drugs, or alcohol is "Just walk away" or "If you respect yourself,

don't do it." I guarantee that your daughter knows plenty of teens who respect themselves and regularly have sex and use alcohol and/or drugs.

Zero-tolerance strategies won't work, either, because they smack of the hypocrisy that teens disdain. Your daughter lives in a world where sexual imagery, drugs, and alcohol are around every corner. Parents tend to focus on drugs, drinking, and sex separately, but your daughter uses the same skills to make decisions about all of them. While refusing may be the decision you want her to make, it's a process that she must go through, not an all-or-nothing proposition, and you don't have ultimate control about the outcome. How you help her make decisions must reflect the world she lives in, where advertising and peer pressure surround her.

Here's an example of what you can say to kids; the first part surprises them and gets them listening more seriously:

> "I'm not going to tell you not to drink or do drugs. I know that alcohol and drugs are easy to get, and I'm pretty sure that many people you know and like are drinking and getting high. There may be parents who allow their kids to abuse alcohol, or are alcoholics or drug abusers themselves. And I know that, ultimately, this is your choice. I *will* tell you that I don't want you to drink or do drugs for the following reason: When you're drunk or high, it's harder for you to be in control of yourself, and other people can and will easily take advantage of that. The facts are that bad things happen to really smart people when they drink and use drugs. I'm also really worried about your getting into a car with someone who's drunk or high but seems sober. But I can't control what you do. When you're away from me, I've got to hope that you'll make choices that will keep you safe and out of trouble."

If you have drug addicts or alcoholics in your family, you might say this:

> "Your grandfather has struggled with alcoholism. It has hurt the relationships that matter most to him, his career, and more. Although you are not destined to share the same problem, you are

more prone to it, so you need to take these issues even more seriously."

WHAT IF YOU DID DRUGS OR DRANK ALCOHOL WHEN YOU WERE HER AGE?

Do you find yourself wondering how you can tell your daughter not to do something you did yourself, and then lived to tell the tale? Maybe you think you have no credibility, or that you'll be a hypocrite. Here's how you can do it:

1. Don't lie, but don't share every detail, either. There is a time to talk about it—and that time is when she's thirteen or older.
2. Give your child some credit. Just because you're standing in front of her in one piece relatively sane doesn't mean she won't understand that you made mistakes and learned from them. Share the struggles you have experienced or observed people have while under the influence.
3. Educate her about how drugs and alcohol abuse affect the brain. There are incredible MRI images of brains of teens who have used compared to those who didn't. It's ultimately up to your daughter to decide what kind of brain she wants. The longer she holds off using, the better off her brain will be.

Your obligation to your daughter is to teach her not to abuse alcohol or drugs, and to let her in on some of the "hindsight is twenty-twenty" vision you've gained. Perhaps you *didn't* do those things as a teenager—you might find that your siblings or friends have good advice for your daughter. I'm not talking about sharing advice on obtaining or consuming drugs or alcohol, but sharing experiences that offer real problem-solving templates for her life. If sharing those stories sounds too awful and you can't be motivated by any other reason to divulge, remember that rehab is heartbreaking and very expensive.

Parents can be subtly involved in helping kids navigate difficult situations with alcohol or drugs. My parents, aunts, and uncles have definitely given me and my friends good

advice and tips from their own experiences. My mom was pretty straight-edged growing up, but her sister and brothers weren't. They were the ones who told me their experiences, and I learned from that. I wouldn't have taken their advice as seriously if they had sat me down and lectured me, but that they talked to me from their own lives really made me listen.

—Krissy, sixteen

One of my mom's best friends is the person who told me never to put your drink down because someone did it to him, and my uncle told me about not mixing alcohol and drugs. I know parents don't want to have their kids hear things like this, but it's really helpful. No one is going to listen to their parents about this stuff, but they will listen to their friends and relatives.

—Mercedes, eighteen

SEX TALK 101

OK. Let's just dive in and talk about sex and your daughter. Scared? Grossed out? Flipping out? Resigned? Whatever your feelings, you need a lot of information so you can handle what your daughter is up against. And like anything else, the less you know, the more frightened you'll be. Get educated; you'll be more likely to make sound decisions.

HAVE ANOTHER TALK ABOUT SEX

She'll respect the values you've taught her only if she's internalized them so they've become her code of ethics—for herself and others. Again, you'll have to clarify your own values about sex so you can share them with your daughter. I'm assuming they'll be based on the assumption that when the time is right, your daughter should know how to act responsibly, respectfully, and consensually—and expect the same from her partner. Please see the books listed in the Resources for a more in-depth discussion of these issues.

There's no excuse for not talking about sex with your daughter

several times throughout her childhood and adolescence. If you don't provide her with accurate information, she'll learn everything about sex from her peers and the media. And don't assume that her school will take care of "the talk." The teacher may not be good, or the class curriculum may be restricted. There are parents who believe that talking to children about sex and reading books with sexual content will encourage them to have sex. In my years of teaching, I've never understood this perspective. I believe that denying girls information greatly increases their vulnerability to having irresponsible sex or making bad decisions that can lead to coerced sex.

Talking to your daughter about sex can be uncomfortable. But your discomfort doesn't outweigh her safety. You're also not off the hook by having one conversation with her that superficially covers the facts. You should first talk to her at the latest when she's eight about the nuts and bolts (if she hasn't asked you before then). Talk to her again in sixth or seventh grade. Review the nuts and bolts, and incorporate what you think is important about how to make dating decisions. If your daughter has two people raising her, both people should talk to her. If it's really too hard for you to have this conversation with her, ask your ally to do it for you. Review with your ally the facts and values you want your daughter to learn. However, if at all possible, try to undertake this task yourself. You are the rule maker and caregiver in your daughter's life, and she needs to discuss important things like this with you.

So, how do you start the conversation about boys in such a way that you both won't freak?

KNOWING HER BOUNDARIES

Go back to the party at the moment when Ally goes upstairs with Tye. She needs to know her personal boundaries way before she's walking into that room with Tye. So your daughter needs to ask herself:

"How well do I have to know someone before I do something sexual with them?"

"How do I define knowing someone well?" (Meeting a friend
of a friend at a party doesn't qualify.)
"What do I feel comfortable doing with someone sexually?"
"What do I not want to do?"
"How can I communicate that to the person I am with?"
"What would make it more difficult for me to say what I want
and don't want?"

Obviously, it'll be really uncomfortable for your daughter to
share her answers to these questions with you, let alone have a
discussion, but you need to give her the starting point to establish her boundaries, and then be the person—or find a person—
she can discuss them with. Again, her ally is really important
here.

A common problem girls have is worrying that if they say something about their limits too early, they are assuming that their date
wants to have sex when, in fact, he may not have thought about
sex at all. Please tell your daughters that they can be safe in making the assumption that their date does want to do something
sexual (not necessarily have intercourse, but they're on that road).
If she thinks through all the possibilities, she can be clearer about
where she wants to draw her boundaries, and she doesn't have to
assume that every boy is a predator to take precautions to protect
herself. She needs to remind herself that drinking or doing drugs
will make it harder to do that.

As I've mentioned, girls don't like admitting it, but most are
really bad at saying no clearly because it feels like they aren't in
control. They can sit in my class and tell me confidently that they
have the right to say no whenever they want. But when they're
actually in the situation, things are different. As a result, a girl
often will say no while she's still kissing a boy, and he may understandably be confused by the mixed message and keep going. She
may say "Can't we wait?" or "Maybe we should check on Rachel.
I think she's throwing up in the bathroom" or "I'm not sure this
is a good idea." None of these statements clearly communicate "I
don't want to have sex" or "I don't want to give you oral sex." She
must learn to say what she means: "No, I don't want to have sex."
"No, you have to stop trying to persuade me to have sex."

If you haven't had any conversations, start now. It's up to you to clarify and communicate your beliefs about sexuality. When your daughter is a young teen, it's especially important to discuss puberty, hormones, changing and conflicting feelings, and the essential need to look for mutual respect in every relationship. As your daughter matures, you'll need to address the nuts and bolts of sexual responsibility. Get over your queasiness. Your girl is growing up with or without you.

BEING LEFT BEHIND

Just as some girls feel left behind when others first become interested in boys, many will find themselves trying to keep up again—but this time the stakes are higher. Your daughter is now trying to keep pace with her sexually active friends, trying to hold on to her boyfriend who wants to have sex, and contending with a society that pushes girls to be mature and sophisticated even as it wags a finger at them for being slutty.

> It's weird when you have a friend who has had sex and you haven't. They have entered a whole new realm of being. They're like light-years away from any sort of sexual experience I might have had.
>
> —Ilana, sixteen

> Girls I know have sex to feel popular. Guys know exactly what to say to the girls to get exactly what they want. At school, they may even deny any kind of association with the girls depending on who they are, their social status, looks, et cetera, and of course, what the boys' friends' opinions/reactions are when they hear the "rumors." Sometimes [she has sex] with a boyfriend because the girl fears that the guy will "move to greener pastures" if he doesn't get what "he deserves" or what "he needs." The girl doesn't realize that especially if she has sex with him, this type of guy will still leave her eventually. She will just be prolonging the detrimental relationship and causing herself more suffering, shock, and pain.
>
> —Jane, sixteen

If there's a clique and one of the girls isn't having sex and the rest are, it's not like the girls are going to tell her she's a loser for not having sex. Older girls are too sophisticated for that, and they know that having sex has a lot of risks. But the girl who isn't having sex may still feel the pressure. Where does that pressure come from?

> There's a lot of kinship between girls who have had sex. It's another thing to bond with each other [about], because you can tell each other what you like and don't like. If there's a girl in the group who isn't sexually experienced, then you wouldn't feel comfortable sharing that kind of stuff with her.
> —Monica, seventeen

> Most girls are more supportive of each other [than to pressure someone to have sex]. Having sex is a really personal thing. It's an internal battle for what she's ready for. You will always want to know what you're getting yourself into. If one person in the group has had sex, then the rest of the group doesn't think it's so scary.
> —Mariel, sixteen

It always comes down to sitting in that life raft I referred to in chapter 1. Getting through adolescence is scary. A girl finds a group to sit with and wants to stay put. Friendships are built on going through these rites of passage with one another. Sex is a pivotal right of passage; it can feel lonely being left out.

ORAL SEX: DO TEENS REALLY NOT CONSIDER IT SEX?

> Girls are doing it so they don't have to have sex. It isn't seen as part of sex but a part of foreplay. A lot of ninth graders do it because the older boys will like them and think they're cool.
> —Kim, sixteen

> One of my friends was battling over a guy with another girl— and my friend was losing. So she went out with this guy and some other people and they were all in a car. She was in the

backseat with him. They stopped and everyone got out but them. She gave him head! And people could look into the car! I think she did it because she felt like she had to do what he wanted or else he would like the other girl more.

—Robin, seventeen

Guys say things like, "You're so pretty and this would really make me feel good."

—Alisha, fifteen

Here's a representative sample of opinions from the girls I work with:

It's gross.

It's demeaning.

Oral sex isn't "sex."

Girls are sometimes willing to give boys oral sex to please them.

Oral sex is a bargain—girls don't think they risk getting an STD [they're wrong about that] and they know it won't get them pregnant.

First, let's get something straight. When people talk about teens engaging in oral sex, they're only talking about girls performing oral sex on boys, not the other way around. Second, when today's parents were growing up, oral sex was perceived by most people to be equal to or more intimate than vaginal intercourse; now it is the other way around. So as hard as it may be for you to believe, many girls see oral sex as safe and emotionally distant, and vaginal intercourse as something you "save" for someone special.

But while it's true that many girls don't think oral sex is the same as sexual intercourse, it doesn't mean all girls are doing it or that it means nothing to them. What is clear to me is that girls believe that the dynamics of oral sex reflect the power difference

between boys and girls, but it has become so normalized that they don't question it.

There isn't much a girl won't do to make a boy like her.
                                                    —Maria, fifteen

But what oral sex is also about is getting out of the room without having sex and admitting your powerlessness. It's what you can offer so you please the boy. Think about Ally at the party with Tye. She wants him to like her, but she doesn't want to have sex and she doesn't want to admit to herself that she has no power in the situation. So . . . she may "choose" the best option in front of her. Give the guy a blow job and it seems like all her problems are solved.

OH, GOD, THEY'RE HAVING SEX

The worst, most ineffective things you can say to her are:

"You can never see him again."
"He's such a bad influence."
"You're a slut/whore/tramp."
"If I catch you doing this again . . ."
"You need to think about your reputation."

WHAT SHOULD YOU DO IF YOU FIND CONDOMS?

If you find condoms, you have to admit to yourself that there's a 99 percent probability that your daughter is having sex. But, as uncomfortable as that may make you, it should at least reassure you that she's practicing safer sex. And, if she's not having sex now, finding condoms is a clear sign that she's definitely thinking about it.

Some parents confront their daughters when they find condoms. If you do, here are some common things you'll hear:

"I was buying/holding them for friends."
"An HIV/AIDS/sex-ed teacher was giving them out as part of the presentation."
"Someone gave them to me as a joke."

Please notice that none of these explanations is a denial that your daughter is having sex. They could all be true. She could be buying them for friends and using some for herself. She could have had a presentation in school, but she could also plan to use them. Whatever the reason, I suggest saying something like the following:

> "Whatever the reason you have them, if you are thinking about being sexually active or if you already are, then it's time to see a gynecologist and get a checkup. If you're responsible enough to be sexually active, then there should be no problem going to the doctor. And I want to be clear that I don't believe someone your age should be having sex, but if you are, then we need to sit down and go over what I feel you need to know about sexual responsibility."

IF YOU CATCH HER HAVING SEX

This has to rank up there with the most horribly uncomfortable experiences you can have as a parent. After you get over your shock and/or embarrassment, leave the room and let them dress in private. Meanwhile, calm down and breathe deeply. And while they're getting dressed, get yourself together and tell them to meet you in the living room.

Go sit down in the most comfortable chair in the living room. When they come in, direct them to the least comfortable chairs. (I think you have to find a little humor where you can get it in this situation.)

An ideally effective response is based on the rules you've already established and communicated to your daughter—if not both of them. If you have forbidden boys to be in her bedroom, they broke a rule and disrespected you as a parent. This is what you say:

> "Bree, Ryan, I'm sure that was completely embarrassing for all of us, but that doesn't obscure the fact that you have broken a rule that is important to me and one that I believed I had your agreement on. Your violation of this rule means that I can't trust you

in my house. In addition [looking at your daughter], now that I know you're having sex, you must get a pelvic exam and get tested for STDs. Ryan, while I am not your parent, I would advise you to get tested as well. I also want you to go home and tell your parents in general what happened. I would advise you to tell them sooner rather than later because I will be calling them later tonight."

Ideally your daughter has already been to a gynecologist for a pelvic exam when she began her period. If not, she needs to go ASAP. This is a great thing the ally can do with her. I went with my sister to her first exam. She was nervous, but I told her what would happen. When she came out of the exam, she walked into the waiting room and announced to me—and the ten women waiting for their appointments—"Well, I guess that makes me a woman!" We both laughed, and then we went out to lunch. Bonding moments happen where and when you make them.

And I really do want you to call the other parents. I know this isn't exactly something every parent dreams of doing, but you do need to tell them what happened and how you handled it.

HAVING THE CONVERSATION

You found out an hour ago that your daughter has lied to you about where she went last night. She told you she was at a friend's house, but she went out with her friend and some boys. You found out when a mother called you, thinking her daughter was sleeping over at your house. You've taken some time to calm down and plan your strategy.

YOU: "I want to talk about what happened last night. Tell me what you think happened."

YOUR DAUGHTER: "How should I know? I don't even care, because I'm just going to be punished anyway."

YOU: "Well, what do you think I think happened?"

YOUR DAUGHTER: "You think I lied to you—which I didn't, by the way, because I was supposed to be sleeping over at Maggie's house and I went out instead. But you didn't tell me that

I couldn't go out with them, and I did sleep over at Maggie's house."

YOU: "You did lie to me because you told me information to mislead me about where you would be. Do you agree or not?"

YOUR DAUGHTER: "I didn't lie!"

YOU: "You're not answering my question: Did you give me information to mislead me because you didn't want me to know what you were doing?"

YOUR DAUGHTER: "Whatever" [which means, in this context, "If you say it that way, I guess you're right"].

YOU: "Well, first I want to know why."

YOUR DAUGHTER: "Because you'd get mad, and I was obviously right because you're freaking out over nothing."

YOU: "I'm freaking out for two reasons. First, you intentionally misled me. Two, because you misled me and Maggie's parents, no adult knew where you were. I know that was the point, but the reality is when you make decisions like that, if you get in a situation you want to get out of, it may get considerably harder if no one knows where you are."

YOUR DAUGHTER: "So what's my punishment?"

YOU: "You lied because you wanted me out of your face. The consequence is that I'm now going to be much more in your face. Your lying forces me to act like a controlling parent and treat you like a child. You can't use the phone or email for two weeks. And you will have to build back the trust you have lost. I'm not sure how long that'll take, but I do know that it'll be a process over time."

IF SHE'S SNEAKING OUT OF THE HOUSE

Don't get bogged down in the details so that you're arguing about whether she sneaked out on Thursday or Friday. The important thing is that if she's sneaking out, you have to address the issues of dishonesty and safety. You could say:

"I know you're sneaking out of the house. I don't want to argue about it, but I want you to know that I know it. I could lock you in

the room every night and treat you like a child and a prisoner in your own home, but I don't think that would be an effective way of dealing with this problem, because I'll become the enemy and you'll sneak out whenever you get the chance. I assume you don't want to be treated like a child, yet you're forcing me to treat you like one. If you continue to sneak out, then I'll worry about you until I know you're safe, and I won't trust you. Then we have a relationship of mutual distrust and you see the house as a prison. So what do you want to do about this?"

If she doesn't back down and have a reasonable conversation with you after you've said this, then take away something concrete or a privilege that you do have control over. Remind her that the reason you are treating her like a child is because her actions leave you no alternative.

PORN . . . IT'S NOT JUST THE BOYS

According to Family Safe Media, the average age at which children are first exposed to pornography is eleven—earlier than most parents think they need to talk to their kids about sexual decision making. Ninety percent of kids between eight and sixteen have seen pornography, usually while doing their homework.

It's not parents' fault. Even if you have SafeSearch on your computers—which blocks most videos and pictures—children and teens have access to devices that allow them to research and share topics they're curious about. Sex has always been and always will be a topic kids are curious about.

Now imagine that you want to talk to your child (you've convinced yourself to get past your discomfort) about how to make healthy sexual decisions, and your child responds with "I'm good. Don't worry about it." There is a really good possibility they've seen up-close sexual intercourse and oral sex. But they don't want to tell you because it's embarrassing and you may react by trying to figure out who's to blame and take away their phones or whatever else you think gave them access to porn.

This is what I say:

"I know that if you want to see those pictures, you're going to figure out how to do it. I could take away every computer in the house and every phone, and it wouldn't make a difference. Here's why I don't want you to watch porn. It brings you into a really complicated world where you're being exposed to sex in ways that I don't think you're ready for. But I do think you have the right to be curious and deserve to get accurate information appropriate for you. If you have questions about sex, I want you to ask me or another adult who we both think is a good person to answer your questions."

IN SUM

I worry a lot about girls. I also have my moments of serious frustration and sadness when they do things that degrade themselves or others. I worry that they will drink too much, use drugs, and not be around people who will or can help them if they need it. I worry that your daughter will meet someone she's really attracted to, who pays attention to her, and tells her she's pretty, and she'll have sex with him when she isn't sure she wants to but doesn't know what to do. I worry about the things she'll see and experience that will make her feel less than and not good enough. I worry about the car she'll get into going home and the person driving that car. I worry that she doesn't have an adult in her life who makes it clear to her that she is valued for the things that matter: her ability to live a life of purpose and integrity. So, in sum, my goals for your daughter are that:

1. She can recognize when she is in over her head and has friends who will take care of her.
2. She understands why other girls may turn on her and doesn't let their interactions with her make her feel insecure.
3. She knows her own boundaries about drinking, doing drugs, and having sex and is able to communicate them clearly to others.
4. She trusts her gut.
5. She knows that if she makes a mistake, she can go to you or another adult you both trust for guidance.

6. If she breaks a family rule, she knows you'll be there to hold her accountable but not make her feel forever ashamed of herself.

As I say to my students: I want you to recognize danger on the horizon, not when it's hitting you in the face. With your help, she will.

13
Getting Help

So far, I've concentrated on how you or your ally can help your daughter. But there may come a time when your daughter will need professional help from a therapist or other mental health professional, so watch for the signs and be prepared to get her the help she needs.

One of the most significant advances we've made in the past several decades is to take away much of the stigma of seeking help from mental health professionals. We also have a language for many mental health issues that we didn't have a generation ago. One of the reasons it was so hard for me to talk about my abusive relationship in high school was that I, along with the rest of my community, wasn't educated about abusive relationships. I had no words to define what was happening. Now many girls in my situation—and many other situations—do.

If your daughter is a victim of any kind of abuse, you both will go through a process of recovery. But you need to remember that as her parent you face unique challenges. Your love for her can make it difficult for you to allow her to make her own decisions as she muddles through her recovery. Honestly, one of the most important things I have learned as a parent is what I mentioned in the beginning of the book. Sometimes the very fact that we are

parents stops us from being the best resource for our children. Our love and anxiety blinds us from seeing the most effective course of action.

Recovery is a messy process for everyone involved. If you find out from someone else, much later and after the fact, that your daughter needed professional help, you may feel hurt that she didn't feel comfortable telling you. Remember, a girl doesn't tell her parents for one of two reasons: It's not safe to tell them because their reaction will make her feel worse, or she doesn't want to disappoint them.

People have asked my parents if they knew about my abusive relationship in high school. No, they didn't. I didn't tell them until I was twenty-four and was about to publish my first book. But my parents were still helpful when I was going through it as a teen, even though none of us knew it at the time. What did they say that helped?

My mother always told me that I, like anyone, could and would make many mistakes throughout the course of my life and that I would survive. If I made bad decisions, I could always fix them. Even though she says she didn't, I think she intuited something was wrong. One day, at the airport, while we waited to pick up my father, she said, "I don't know what's going on with you, but I know something is. Everyone makes mistakes. You're very private, but if you ever want to talk, I'm here." She opened a door, albeit just a crack, and I soon walked through it to get help. I was deeply ashamed that I had "let" the relationship get so out of my control. Her words helped me see that there was a possibility of leaving the relationship behind me, and I didn't have to be so ashamed.

My reasons for not getting help are common. It doesn't matter if the problem is bullying, eating disorders, molestation, drugs, drinking, abuse, rape, depression, anxiety, or any combination. Girls feel ashamed, damaged, and unfixable, and they may not think anyone around them has gone through similar experiences. I often say that abusers' insurance policy is the silence of their victims. People don't speak out, and yet there's hardly a person around any of us who hasn't been touched by painful experiences at our hands or the hands of others.

Like anyone, your daughter could easily have problems that are too big to bear by herself, let alone solve. Likewise, even if you're the world's perfect parent, your daughter could go through experiences where one, if not both, of you needs to look outside for help.

So one of the most important things to teach your daughter is that there is no shame and it's not weak to ask for help. It's courageous to admit when you're in over your head. People kill themselves trying to look like they have it together when they're falling apart inside. Unfortunately, many parents themselves are reluctant to ask for help. Why? There's no easy answer. Sometimes it's because parents see their daughter's successes and failures as a reflection of themselves. Sometimes parents don't want others to know their family business. Sometimes looking at such problems is too painful because our children's pain is a consequence of our own choices or circumstances.

For better or worse, being a parent gives you endless opportunities to admit and get over your own baggage. It's your responsibility, duty, and obligation to face your own demons and put them to rest as best you can so that you can provide the love, guidance, and nurturing your daughter needs.

There are some other reasons why girls don't go to their parents for help. It could be any one or a combination of these:

- By the time she admits to herself that she needs help, she's in way over her head.
- She's afraid you'll deny that she's in trouble.
- She doesn't want to change the image you have of her.
- You've been known to freak out when she's come to you with other problems, meaning you do things without her consent or knowledge.
- In your home, family problems (including your daughter's) are private. The family doesn't need the help of outsiders to take care of its own.

"Allison" is one of my favorite girls. She's funny, intelligent, beautiful, and charismatic. She also suffers from anxiety and depression. Until recently, I had no idea. I knew middle school was

painful for her—it was one of the reasons I got to know her in the first place—but she was so good at keeping up her image that I didn't see her struggling.

Allison is a constant achiever. She was accepted early into a great university, has been on varsity sports teams since ninth grade, and has won endless academic and extracurricular awards. After three years of volunteering with me, she told me she couldn't volunteer anymore. I was dumbfounded and angry. I immediately jumped to the conclusion that she was suffering from "senioritis" and was blowing everything off now that she'd been accepted into college. Where was her commitment? She couldn't just walk away from her responsibilities. Then she told me she had been depressed for years. She had even attempted suicide in eighth grade.

What had been her biggest obstacle in getting help? That her parents didn't want her telling anyone. They wanted her to "keep it in the family." A few days later, we went out to lunch, and she shared with me that for years she had been working as hard as she could to be what everyone else wanted her to be. Her identity was so caught up in her accomplishments that she felt as if she were nothing without them. She kept a notebook under her bed with every award she's received since eighth grade, and when she was depressed, she took it out and looked at all her awards. Allison asked me:

"Why are we so special that we have to pretend that we don't have problems? When my older sister had an eating disorder, the doctors wanted to hospitalize her. My parents refused. They thought they could take care of her at home. I overheard my parents discussing that if they did put her in the hospital, they could always tell people that she had mono. My sister was down to eighty-five pounds and they didn't want to get her help because they were too ashamed. When I was first depressed, they took me to a psychiatrist that I actually liked. He told my parents that they were going to have to do some "reparenting." We never went back. Next I went to a therapist my mom knew. When my mom picked me up, they would talk about things, including their kids. There was no way I trusted her. Now I go to a psychiatrist who just sits there and I don't tell him what's really going on with me. Why should I?"

Maybe you're reading this and thinking, *What's wrong with Allison's parents? Can't they see what they are doing to their daughter?* Watch out. Hubris will make you blind. Allison comes from a "traditional" family—a mom and dad who live together in the suburbs, go to church, and are active members of the community. I know Allison's parents. They're caring, loving people. There's no question in my mind that they love their daughter and want what's best for her. Allison's father commuted hours out of his way to drop her off and pick her up at my office. He is warm, caring, and clearly proud of her. So why in the world are they so scared to let Allison talk about her problems? Is it really more important what their neighbors think than getting help for their daughter?

Parents sometimes make miserably foolish decisions in the "best interest" of their daughter and the family. Because it's so hard for parents to reflect on their own parenting, it's easier to close ranks around the family. I'm asking you to keep the door open. Ask your daughter, "You seem upset. Is there anything I can help you with? If you don't want to talk to me, I'd be happy to have you talk to someone else." Keep asking gently if your gut tells you she's troubled but not ready to open up to you about it.

No matter how much you love your daughter, you won't parent her well if you let your issues interfere with getting her the help she needs. She needs to understand that when she makes a mistake, she'll learn from it and move on. She won't be damaged and unfixable if she makes a bad decision or gets into trouble. This doesn't mean you have to share your most intimate family problems with everyone you see. But don't tell your daughter to lie about her problem, pretend it's not there, and think it'll go away. If she has to leave school early once a week to see a therapist, help her come up with what she feels comfortable telling people, but don't tell her to keep it a secret. If you do any of these things, you're sending the message that she should be ashamed. As long as she feels shame, she can't heal her wounds. Respect that she's her own person and you are her guide.

WHO NEEDS HELP

Every one of the following signs could describe a normal teen, but if you're seeing a big difference over a relatively short time period, they could be coping mechanisms for dealing with whatever is bothering her.

Signs She Needs Professional Help
- Isolation and withdrawing.
- Eating too little and/or too much.
- Intense mood swings.

Additional Signs She May Have Experienced Sexual Violence
- She takes showers all the time.
- She keeps constantly busy.
- She covers her body with huge clothes.
- She's fearful in a way she wasn't before.
- She doesn't want to be left alone.

*Additional Signs She May Suffer from Depression and/or Anxiety**
- Sleeping too much or too little.
- Persistent physical symptoms that don't respond to medical treatment (headaches, digestive problems, chronic pain).
- Difficulty concentrating, remembering, or making decisions.
- Thoughts of death and/or suicide.
- Feelings of guilt, worthlessness, hopelessness, pessimism.

CHOOSING A COUNSELOR

At first, my parents had to drag me to the therapist because I thought it was going to be a total waste of time. But around the third time, I began to see why I was there. It's sort of cool to be able to tell someone what's going on in your head and think through stuff. Seeing her makes me feel a lot less anxious about the problems I'm dealing with.

—Corrine, fifteen

---

*   National Institute of Mental Health. See www.nimh.gov.

My doctor told my parents I should go to a psychiatrist. He just stared at me and asked why I hated my dad. There was no way I was telling that man anything about me.

—Karen, sixteen

If you can find a good therapist, they can be a great resource for your daughter. But sometimes they're not easy to find. You probably don't want to have to shop around, but you must. Think of it this way: It's probably going to cost you a lot of money and you're going to spend a lot of time taking your daughter to the appointments, so it better be worth your while.

Prepare three to five questions to ask the therapist over the phone. Ask your daughter to prepare her own questions. Here are a few I ask:

- How would she describe her style? Does she like to listen and sit back? Will she give her opinion?
- How does she see her role as mediator between parent and child? For example, at what point would she notify you of something about your child? Don't ask this question to hear that the therapist will tell you when and if your daughter's in imminent danger. You're looking for a therapist who won't tell you things about your daughter. The best adolescent therapists have a clear understanding of their boundaries between themselves, the parent, and child.
- What are her areas of specialization? Find someone who specializes in teens and the particular issues your daughter has (for example, bullying, eating disorders, rape, abusive relationships).
- Why does she work with teens? What does she find most rewarding? What does she find most challenging?

Here's an example of a mother and therapist doing an effective job. As a result, the girl, a recent rape survivor, is getting the help she needs.

My mom called three [therapists] and said choose one. She told me I didn't have to talk, but she needed to know she tried

*to do something to help me. When I went to the psychiatrist,
she didn't force me to speak about it. I talked about friends
and other things in my life. All the other adults forced me to
talk about it [the rape], but she waited until I wanted to bring
it up.*

—Alexa, sixteen

If your child needs a therapist, it doesn't mean you've failed as a
parent. If you can get her the help she needs, you're doing the best
you can for her—and that's all anyone can ask of you.

GRACE NOTES: BEFORE YOU GO

Now you know Girl World. I know it can be hard to read about
what goes on there. But I hope you've also been able to see how
you can nurture your daughter's confidence and independence.

As a parting note, I've asked some girls to share the messages
they'd most like to leave with parents:

*Don't try to understand your daughter's every thought; just
show her that her feelings are valid and are not wrong. When
you need to listen, listen. When you need to talk, talk. And
most importantly, treat her with the respect you'd like to be
treated with, even if she doesn't do the same. After all, this is
probably the hardest time in her life and no matter what she
says, she does need you.*

—Julie, seventeen

*Communication is the biggest part to making your relation-
ship with your daughter the best it can be. Teenagers love to
know that their parents are really interested in what is going
on in their lives. The most important thing to remember is
not to pressure your child into talking and being open if they
don't feel comfortable doing so. Keep the lines open and always be on the lookout so you know when something is bothering her. Showing your love and concern can do wonders for
a teen's self-esteem.*

—Nia, eighteen

Just be there for me. Don't judge. Don't tell me how to make it better. Just tell me you love me.

—Dia, fifteen

Know that I love you and want to make you proud of me.

—Michelle, fifteen

Even when I'm fighting with you, sometimes I know you're right, but I don't want to admit it.

—Kia, sixteen

You really do make a difference and I really do listen.

—Sara, sixteen

Resources

SUPPORT FOR EDUCATORS

Behind the Counselor's Door: Teenagers' True Confessions, Trials, and Triumphs, by Kevin Kuczynski. Health Communications, 2015.

Breaking Through to Teens: A New Psychotherapy for New Adolescence, by Ron Taffel. Guilford Press, 2005.

Getting Through to Difficult Kids and Parents: Uncommon Sense for Child Professionals, by Ron Taffel. Guilford Press, 2004.

Girls in Real-Life Situations: Group Counseling for Enhancing Social and Emotional Development: Grades K–5, by Shannon Trice-Black and Julia V. Taylor. (Curriculum.) Research Press, 2007.

Girls in Real-Life Situations: Group Counseling for Enhancing Social and Emotional Development: Grades 6–12, by Julia V. Taylor and Shannon Trice-Black. (Curriculum.) Research Press, 2007.

An Improbable School: Transforming How Teachers Teach and Students Learn, by Paul Tweed and Liz Seubert. Lead the Path, 2015.

The Motivation Breakthrough: 6 Secrets to Turning On the Tuned-Out Child, by Richard Lavoie. Touchstone, 2008.

What Works with Teens: A Professional's Guide to Engaging Authentically with Adolescents to Achieve Lasting Change, by Britt H. Rathbone and Julie Baron. New Harbinger, 2015.

Working with Parents: Building Relationships for Student Success, by Ruby K. Payne. aha! Process, 2005.

Working with Students: Discipline Strategies for the Classroom, by Ruby K. Payne. aha! Process, 2006.

SUPPORT FOR PARENTS

The Blessing of a Skinned Knee: Using Jewish Teachings to Raise Self-Reliant Children, by Wendy Mogel. Scribner, 2008.

Childhood Unbound: Saving Our Kids' Best Selves—Confident Parenting in a World of Change, by Ron Taffel. Free Press, 2009.

The Good Enough Teen: Raising Adolescents with Love and Acceptance, Despite How Impossible They Can Be, by Brad E. Sachs. Harper Paperbacks, 2005.

The Pecking Order: Which Siblings Succeed and Why, by Dalton Conley. Pantheon, 2004.

The Pressured Child: Helping Your Child Find Success in School and Life, by Michael G. Thompson and Teresa Barker. Ballantine Books, 2005.

Queen Bee Moms and Kingpin Dads: Dealing with the Difficult Parents in Your Child's Life, by Rosalind Wiseman and Elizabeth Rapoport. Three Rivers Press, 2007.

Teach Your Children Well: Why Values and Coping Skills Matter More Than Grades, Trophies, or "Fat Envelopes," by Madeline Levine. Harper Perennial, 2013.

When Parents Disagree and What You Can Do About It, by Ron Taffel. Guilford Press, 2002.

Worried All the Time: Overparenting in an Age of Anxiety and How to Stop It, by David Anderegg. Free Press, 2003.

CULTURAL COMMENTARY AND CRITIQUE

Can't Stop Won't Stop: A History of the Hip-Hop Generation, by Jeff Chang. St. Martin's Press, 2005.

Freaks, Geeks, and Cool Kids: American Teenagers, Schools, and the Culture of Consumption, by Murray Milner, Jr. Routledge, 2013.

Goth: Undead Subculture, by Lauren M. E. Goodlad and Michael Bibby, eds. Duke University Press, 2007.

Grassroots: A Field Guide for Feminist Activism, by Jennifer Baumgardner and Amy Richards. Farrar, Straus, and Giroux, 2005.

The Nature of Prejudice, by Gordon W. Allport. Perseus Book Group, 1979.

Nerds: Who They Are and Why We Need More of Them, by David Anderegg. Tarcher, 2007.

Teens Take It to Court: Young People Who Challenged the Law and Changed Your Life, by Tom Jacobs. Free Spirit, 2006.

BULLYING, SOCIAL JUSTICE, AND INTERVENTION STRATEGIES

All Rise: Somebodies, Nobodies, and the Politics of Dignity, by Robert Fuller. Berrett-Koehler, 2006.

Best Friends, Worst Enemies: Understanding the Social Lives of Children, by Michael Thompson, Catherine O'Neill Grace, and Lawrence J. Cohen. Ballantine Books, 2002.

Bullying from Both Sides: Strategic Interventions for Working with Bullies and Victims, by Walter B. Roberts, Jr. Corwin Press, 2005.

Letters to a Bullied Girl: Messages of Healing and Hope, by Olivia Gardner, Emily Buder, and Sarah Buder. Harper Paperbacks, 2008.

Mom, They're Teasing Me: Helping Your Child Solve Social Problems, by Michael G. Thompson, Lawrence J. Cohen, and Catherine O'Neill. Ballantine Books, 2004.

Please Stop Laughing at Me: One Woman's Inspirational Story, by Jodee Blanco. Adams Media, 2003.

Safe School Ambassadors: Harnessing Student Power to Stop Bullying and Violence, by Rick Phillips, John Linney, Chris Pack. (Curriculum.) Jossey-Bass, 2008.

Salvaging Sisterhood, by Julia V. Taylor. (Curriculum.) Youthlight, 2005.

Sticks and Stones: Defeating the Culture of Bullying and Rediscovering the Power of Character and Empathy, by Emily Bazelon. Random House, 2013.

Youth Voice Project: Student Insights into Bullying and Peer Mistreatment, by Stan David and Charisse Nixon. Research Press, 2014.

BRAIN DEVELOPMENT AND PUBERTY

Age of Opportunity: Lessons from the New Science of Adolescence, by Laurence Steinberg. Houghton Mifflin Harcourt, 2014.

Brainstorm: The Power and Purpose of the Teenage Brain, by Daniel Siegal. Tarcher, 2015.

The New Puberty: How to Navigate Early Development in Today's Girls, by Louise Greenspan and Julianna Deardoff. Rodale, 2015.

NurtureShock: New Thinking About Children, by Po Bronson and Ashley Merryman. Twelve, 2011.

The Teenage Brain: A Neuroscientist's Survival Guide to Raising Adolescents and Young Adults, by Frances Jensen. Harper, 2015.

What's Happening to Ellie?: A Book About Puberty for Girls and Young Women with Autism and Related Conditions, by Kate E. Reynolds. Jessica Kingsley, 2015.

The Whole-Brain Child: 12 Revolutionary Strategies to Nurture Your Child's Developing Mind, by Daniel Siegel and Tina Payne Bryson. Delacorte Press, 2011.

LEARNING DIFFERENCES

Delivered from Distraction: Getting the Most Out of Life with Attention Deficit Disorder, by Edward M. Hallowell and John J. Ratey. Ballantine Books, 2005.

Driven to Distraction: Recognizing and Coping with Attention Deficit Disorder from Childhood Through Adulthood, by Edward M. Hallowell and John J. Ratey. Touchstone, 1995.

Girls Guide to AD/HD: Don't Lose This Book! by Beth Walker. Woodbine House, 2004.

It's So Much Work to Be Your Friend: Helping the Child with Learning Disabilities Find Social Success, by Richard Lavoie. Touchstone, 2006.

Key Indicators of Child and Youth Well-Being: Completing the Picture, by Brett Brown, ed. Lawrence Erlbaum, 2007.

The Motivation Breakthrough, by Richard Lavoie and directed by Gerardine Wurzburg. PBS Video, 2007.

Thinking in Pictures and Other Reports from My Life with Autism, by Temple Grandin. Vintage Books, 1996.

Understanding Girls with ADHD: How They Feel and Why They Do What They Do, by Kathleen Nadeau, Ellen Littman, and Patricia O. Quinn. Advantage, 2015.

REFLECTIONS ON GIRL WORLD

The Blueprint for My Girls: How to Build a Life Full of Courage, Determination, and Self-Love, by Yasmin Shiraz. Fireside, 2004.

The Born Frees: Writing with the Girls of Gugulethu, by Kimberly Burge. Norton, 2015.

Cinderella Ate My Daughter: Dispatches from the Front Lines of Girly-Girl Culture, by Peggy Orenstein. Harper, 2012.

The Curse of the Good Girl: Raising Authentic Girls with Courage and Confidence, by Rachel Simmons. Penguin, 2010.

Express Yourself: A Teen Girl's Guide to Speaking Up and Being Who You Are, by Emily Roberts. Instant Help Books, 2015.

Female Chauvinist Pigs: Women and the Rise of Raunch Culture, by Ariel Levy. Free Press, 2006.

Full of Ourselves: A Wellness Program to Advance Girl Power, Health, and Learning, by Catherine Seiner-Adair and Lisa Sjostrom. (Curriculum.) Teachers College Press, 2006.

Girls and Sex: Navigating the Complicated New Landscape, by Peggy Orenstein. Harper, 2016.

Girls on Track: A Parent's Guide to Inspiring Our Daughters to Achieve a Lifetime of Self-Esteem and Respect, by Molly Barker. Random House, 2004.

Manifesta: Young Women, Feminism, and the Future, by Jennifer Baumgardner and Amy Richards. Farrar, Straus, and Giroux, 2000.

Meeting at the Crossroads: Women's Psychology and Girls' Development, by Lyn Mikel Brown and Carol Gilligan. Harvard University Press, 1998.

Odd Girl Out: The Hidden Culture of Aggression in Girls, by Rachel Simmons. Harcourt, 2011.

Odd Girl Speaks Out: Girls Write About Bullies, Cliques, Popularity, and Jealousy, by Rachel Simmons. Harcourt, 2004.

Ophelia's Mom: Women Speak Out About Loving and Letting Go of Their Adolescent Daughters, by Nina Shandler. Crown, 2001.

Ophelia Speaks: Adolescent Girls Write About Their Search for Self, by Sara Shandler. Harper Perennial, 2000.

Redefining Girly: How Parents Can Fight the Stereotyping and Sexualizing of Girlhood from Birth to Tween, by Melissa Atkins Wardy. Chicago Review Press, 2014.

Reviving Ophelia: Saving the Selves of Adolescent Girls, by Mary Pipher. Ballantine Books, 1994.

School Girls: Young Women, Self-Esteem, and the Confidence Gap, by Peggy Orenstein. Doubleday, 1994.

See Jane Hit: Why Girls Are Growing More Violent and What Can Be Done About It, by James Garbarino. Penguin, 2006.

See Jane Win: The Rimm Report on How 1,000 Girls Became Successful Women, by Silvia Rimm. Three Rivers Press, 1999.

A Smart Girl's Guide: Drama, Rumors, and Secrets, by Nancy Holyoke. American Girl, 2015.

Stressed-Out Girls: Helping Them Thrive in the Age of Pressure, by Roni Cohen-Sandler. Penguin, 2005.

Tripping the Prom Queen: The Truth About Women and Rivalry, by Susan Shapiro Barash. St. Martin's Press, 2006.

Untangled: Guiding Teenage Girls Through the Seven Transitions into Adulthood, by Lisa Damour. Ballantine, 2016.

You Can't Say You Can't Play, by Vivian Gussin Paley. Harvard University Press, 1993.

MEDIA AND TECHNOLOGY

Adolescents, Media, and the Law: What Developmental Science Reveals and Free Speech Requires, by Roger J. R. Levesque. Oxford University Press, 2007.

The Big Disconnect: Protecting Childhood and Family Relationships in the Digital Age, by Catherine Steiner-Adair and Teresa Barker. Harper, 2014.

Consuming Kids: The Commercialization of Childhood, directed by Adriana Barbaro and Jeremy Ear. Media Education Foundation (www.mediaed.org), 2008.

The Games Believe in You: How Games Can Make Our Kids Smarter, by Greg Toppo. Palgrave, 2015.

It's Complicated: The Social Lives of Networked Teens, by Danah Boyd. Yale University Press, 2015.

Killing Us Softly: Advertising's Image of Women, by Jean Kilbourne and directed by Sut Jhally. Media Education Foundation (www.mediaed.org), 2006.

Reality Is Broken: Why Games Make Us Better and How They Can Change the World, by Jane McGonigal. Penguin, 2011.

The Second Family: Dealing with Peer Power, Pop Culture, the Wall of Silence, and Other Challenges of Raising Today's Teen, by Ron Taffel. St. Martin's Griffin, 2002.

RACE, ETHNICITY, AND DIVERSITY

All About Love: New Visions, by bell hooks. William Morrow, 2000.

The Art of Critical Pedagogy: Possibilities for Moving Theory to Practice in Urban Schools, by Jeffrey M. Duncan-Andrade and Ernest Morrell. Peter Lang, 2008.

Bridges Out of Poverty, by Philip DeVol, Terie Dreussi Smith, and Ruby K. Payne. aha! Process, 2006.

The Color of Success: Race and High-Achieving Urban Youth, by Gilberto Q. Conchas. Teachers College Press, 2006.

A Framework for Understanding Poverty, by Ruby K. Payne. aha! Process, 2005.

Hidden Rules of Class at Work, by Ruby K. Payne and Don L. Krabill. aha! Process, 2002.

Hip-Hop: Beyond Beats and Rhymes, directed by Byron Hurt. Media Education Foundation.

Hopeful Girls, Troubled Boys: Race and Gender Disparity in Urban Education, by Nancy López. Routledge, 2012.

Race in the Schoolyard: Negotiating the Color Line in Classrooms and Communities, by Amanda E. Lewis. Rutgers University Press, 2003.

School Kids/Street Kids: Identity Development in Latino Students, by Nilda Flores-González. Teachers College Press, 2002.

Under-resourced Learners: 8 Strategies to Boost Student Achievement, by Ruby K. Payne and Dan Shenk. aha! Process, 2008.

Up Against Whiteness: Race, School and Immigrant Youth, by Stacey J. Lee. Teachers College Press, 2005.

Urban Girls Revisited: Building Strengths, by Bonnie Leadbeater and Niobe Way. New York University Press, 2007.

We Can't Teach What We Don't Know: White Teachers, Multiracial Schools, by Gary R. Howard. Teachers College Press, 2006.

"Why Are All the Black Kids Sitting Together in the Cafeteria?": A Psychologist Explains the Development of Racial Identity, by Beverly Daniel Tatum. Basic Books, 2003.

Why White Kids Love Hip-Hop: Wankstas, Wiggers, Wannabes, and the New Reality of Race in America, by Bakari Kitwana. Basic Civitas, 2005.

Women Without Class: Girls, Race, and Identity, by Julie Bettie. University of California Press, 2014.

BODY IMAGE AND EATING DISORDERS

The Body Image Workbook for Teens: Activities to Help Girls Develop a Healthy Body in an Image-Obsessed World, by Julia Taylor. Instant Help, 2014.

Brave Girl Eating: A Family's Struggle with Anorexia, by Harriet Brown. William Morrow, 2011.

The Cult of Thinness, by Sharlene Nagy Hesse-Biber. Oxford University Press, 2007.

Ed Says U Said: Eating Disorder Translator, by June Alexander and Cate Sangster. Jessica Kingsley, 2013.

8 Keys to Recovery from an Eating Disorder, by Carolyn Costin and Gwen Schubert Grabb. W. W. Norton, 2011.

The Geography of Girlhood, by Kirsten Smith. Little, Brown Young Readers, 2009.

Go Figure, by Jo Edwards. Simon Pulse, 2007.

Locker Room Diaries: The Naked Truth About Women, Body Image, and Re-Imagining the "Perfect" Body, by Leslie Goldman. Da Capo Press, 2007.

Packaging Girlhood: Rescuing Our Daughters from Marketers' Schemes, by Sharon Lamb and Lyn Mikel Brown. St. Martin's Griffin, 2007.

The Parent's Guide to Eating Disorders, by Marcia Herrin and Nancy Matsumoto. Gurze Books, 2007.

Throwing Starfish Across the Sea: A Pocket-Sized Care Package for the Parents of Someone with an Eating Disorder, by Laura Collins Lyster-Mensh and Charlotte Bevan. CreateSpace Independent Publishing, 2013.

Treatment Manual for Anorexia Nervosa: A Family-Based Approach, by James Lock and Daniel Le Grange. Guilford Press, 2015.

SEXUALITY

Adolescent Sexuality: A Historical Handbook and Guide, by Carolyn Cocca, ed. Praeger, 2006.

Becoming Nicole: The Transformation of an American Family, by Amy Ellis Nutt. Random House, 2015.

Everything You Never Wanted Your Kids to Know About Sex (But Were Afraid They'd Ask): The Secret to Surviving Your Child's Sexual Development from Birth to the Teens, by Justin Richardson and Mark A. Schuster. Crown, 2003.

From Teasing to Torment: School Climate in America: A Survey of Students and Teachers, by Dana Markow and Jordan Fein. Harris Interactive; Gay, Lesbian & Straight Education Network, 2005.

National School Climate Survey: The Experiences of Lesbian, Gay, Bisexual, and Transgender Youth in Our Nation's Schools, by Joseph G. Kosciw and Elizabeth M. Diaz. Gay, Lesbian & Straight Education Network, 2015.

Some Assembly Required: The Not-So-Secret Life of a Transgender Teen, by Arin Andrews and Joshua Lyon. Simon and Schuster, 2014.

SEXUAL ASSAULT AND ABUSIVE RELATIONSHIPS

But He'll Change: End the Thinking That Keeps You in an Abusive Relationship, by Joanna V. Hunter. Hazelden, 2010.

Giving Yourself Permission: A Guide to Reclaiming Your Life After Sexual Assault, by Shaneequa Cannon. Amazon Digital Services, 2015.

I Will Survive: The African-American Guide to Healing from Sexual Assault and Abuse, by Lori S. Robinson. Seal Press, 2003.

Protecting the Gift: Keeping Children and Teenagers Safe, by Gavin de Becker. Dial Press, 1999.

Sexual Assault: Techniques and Exercises to Help You Heal, by Violet Daniels and Joanna Scribe. Amazon Digital Services, 2013.

The Sexual Trauma Workbook for Teen Girls: A Guide to Recovery from Sexual Assault and Abuse, by Raychelle Cassada Lohman and Sheela Raja. Instant Help, 2016.

Should I Stay or Should I Go?: A Guide to Knowing If Your Relationship Can—and Should—Be Saved, by Lundy Bancroft and JAC Patrissi. Berkley, 2011.

Surviving the Silence: Black Women's Stories of Rape, by Charlotte Pierce-Baker. Norton, 2000.

BOOKS FOR YOUNGER CHILDREN

A Bad Case of Tattle Tongue, by Julia Cook. National Center for Youth Issues, 2006.

Bootsie Barker Bites, by Barbara Bottner. Putnam Juvenile, 1997.

Chrysanthemum, by Kevin Henkes. Greenwillow, 1991.

How to Lose All Your Friends, by Nancy Carlson. Puffin, 1997.

Just Kidding, by Trudy Ludwig. Tricycle Press, 2006.

Loud Emily, by Alexis O'Neill. Aladdin, 2001.

My Mouth Is a Volcano!, by Julia Cook. National Center for Youth Issues, 2008.

My Secret Bully, by Trudy Ludwig. Tricycle Press, 1995.

Odd Velvet, by Mary E. Whitcomb. Chronicle Books, 1998.

A Pig Is Moving In, by Claudia Fries. Scholastic, 2000.

The Recess Queen, by Alexis O'Neill. Scholastic, 2005.

Sorry!, by Trudy Ludwig. Tricycle Press, 2006.

The Sneetches and Other Stories, by Dr. Seuss. Random House, 1961.

Stand Tall, Molly Lou Mellon, by Patty Lovell. Putnam Juvenile, 2006.

Too Perfect, by Trudy Ludwig. Tricycle Press, 2009.

Trouble Talk, by Trudy Ludwig. Tricycle Press, 2008.

The Worst Best Friend, by Alexis O'Neill. Scholastic Press, 2008.

WEBSITES AND VIDEOS

About Face. www.about-face.org.

American Civil Liberties Union LGBT Project. www.aclu.org/lgbt.

Anti-Defamation League. www.adl.org.

Body Positive: Boosting Body Image at Any Weight. www.bodypositive.com.

Eating Disorder Referral and Network Center. www.edreferral.com.

Facing History and Ourselves. www.facinghistory.org.

Finding Balance. www.findingbalance.com.

Gay and Lesbian Alliance Against Defamation. www.glaad.org.

Gay, Lesbian & Straight Education Network. www.glsen.org.

Girls Leadership Institute. www.gli.org.

Men Can Stop Rape. www.mencanstoprape.org.

A Mighty Girl: The World's Largest Collection of Books, Toys and Movies for Smart, Confident, and Courageous Girls. amightygirl.org.

National Coalition Against Domestic Violence. www.ncadv.org.

National Eating Disorders Association. www.nationaleatingdisorders.org.

National Sexual Violence Resource Center. www.nsvrc.org.

New Moon Girls: Girls' online magazine and community. Newmoon.org.

Reflections: The Body Image Program. www.bodyimageprogram.org.

The Safe Schools Coalition. www.safeschoolscoalition.org.

Teaching Tolerance: A Project of the Southern Poverty Law Center. www.tolerance.org.

YouTube Channels

SoulPancake

vlogbrothers

Acknowledgments

Having people put faith in you to help them with their children is a deep responsibility and a high honor. *Queen Bees & Wannabes* is always a combined effort; I can't do any of this without the feedback I get from my students sharing their experiences with me (and telling me when I am completely wrong). This version, just like the last two, benefited from having amazing teen editors. First, thank you to my in-house editors, Alex Edwards, Rachel Steinmetz, Grace Milijasevic, Tessa T. Peterson, and Sydney Quynn. These young women made time during their summers or after-school hours to come to my office. They took their responsibilities seriously, while they laughed, answered my questions, talked to the consulting editors, and bossed me around. And thank you to our other summer interns, Kurk Dietrick, Timmy Dolan, Keo Jamieson, and Rainer Wasinger. We depended on you to keep the girls honest.

Thank you to my consulting editors—people who gave me key insights into specific topics: Emily Sorenson, Vanessa Diana, Jennifer Jun, Arlette Luna, Isabella Martinez, Keila Roberts, Payton Sessions, Sofia Larsen, Heather Pylant, Darrow Adderholt, Abby Elliott, Amber Murray, Alexis Heleniak, Callista DeGraw, Chloe Hsueh, Elsy Segovia, Gabriela Bell, Jordyn Saxe, Julia Wunder,

Lea Jalbert, Mallory Wolff, Marinna Binkowski, Maya Anthony, Mayu Lee, Miranda Sullivan, Natalia Howard, Olivia Jackson, Sarah Gorman, Sarah Walters, Simone Mann, Sophie Guimaraes, Stella Fang, and Tal Saidon. Many of you met me only briefly at your schools and then followed up with me for the rest of the project. I am deeply appreciative of the time you took to help me.

Queen Bees often feels like a community project. Parents and educators tell me their stories and questions. They share the book with friends and family. So if you bought earlier editions of the book and recommended it to other people, thank you so much. I hope this version is just as helpful as the last.

Thank you to my partner in work-crime, Charlie Kuhn, who pushes me to do what I am supposed to do, always asks the best questions, and links the issues we work on in ways I don't see. Thank you to my editor, Donna Loffredo, at Harmony. Thank you to Jim Levine and everyone at LGH agency—this may be the last time I rewrite *Queen Bees*, so maybe I can tackle all those other book projects.

Thank you to my husband, James Edwards, and my sons, Elijah and Roane Edwards. I am pretty sure Elijah and Roane have still not read a word of this book. I respect that. They read other books. And lastly, thank you to my mother, Kathy Wiseman, because she was never a mean girl or a Queen Bee.

Index

"slacker attitude," 278
technology and, 278
10 percenters, 283–285
Brain development, in adolescence,
9, 62–63
Bras, 70
Brazilian bikini wax, 65
Breaking up, 278, 317–321,
353–354
Breast development, 61, 62, 64, 70,
159, 187
Bronson, Po, 112
Bulimia, 192, 193
Bullying, 223, 229, 233
in Boy World, 287–288, 291–292
cyberbullying, 142–144 (see also
Facebook)
defined, 203
drama versus, 203–204, 263
example of, 234–238
schools and, 272–275

Celebrities, as role models, 12
Cell phones (see also Technology)
check-in time, 314
late-night calls, 147–148, 314
need for, 133–134
numbers of friends and parents,
121
responsible use of, 135–137
taking break from, 148
Champion, 30, 31, 81
advantages and disadvantages of,
42–43
characteristics of, 41–42
Checking Your Baggage sections,
17, 48, 114, 116, 190–191,
212, 262, 309, 333, 353,
378–379
Cheerleading, 60
Chores, as power struggles, 104
Cigarette smoking, 120, 313, 368
Cisgender, 163
Clash of Clans, 151

Cliques, 13–15, 21–56 (see also
Power plays)
adult, 78
boy-girl relationships and,
328–329
boys and, 281–282
communication about, 48–51
definition of, 22
exclusivity of, 25–28
Indian, 171
in kindergarten, 23
life raft metaphor, 45–49
markers and, 175
matchmaking and, 329–330
positions in, 29–43
as self-reinforcing, 47
sexual relations and, 396
successful, 55–56
teasing and (see Teasing)
timing of, 23
Clothing, 146, 162, 179–180
dress codes, 184, 185–189
sexy, 159, 160, 177–184, 186,
209, 322, 323
Club Penguin, 151
Commercials, 12, 92–111
Communication, 40, 412 (see also
Cell phones; Parenting
styles)
about alcohol and drugs,
388–392
about cliques, 48–51
about friends, 51–54
about power plays, 271–272
about sex, 392–395
allies, 87–90
embarrassment and, 94–95
get-togethers, 100–102
girls' requests for, 82–84
"Having a Moment," and, 96–97
listening, 98
lying (see Lying)
parental agendas, 97–111
reasons for none, 93–94

Also by *New York Times* bestselling author
ROSALIND WISEMAN

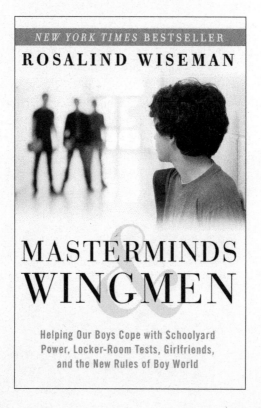

"Rosalind Wiseman, who so insightfully explained the world of girls in *Queen Bees and Wannabes,* has done it again. . . . This is an essential guide—not just for parents but anyone who wants to better understand their own childhood and its impact."

—Anderson Cooper

HARMONY
BOOKS • NEW YORK

AVAILABLE WHEREVER BOOKS ARE SOLD

QUEEN BEES & WANNABES